The 7-Step Reason to be Catholic,
2nd Ed.:

Science, the Bible and History point to Catholicism

An important supplement to
Catholic teaching in:

- Catholic universities
- Home schooling
- Catechesis
- Bible study
- Evangelization

- High schools
- Campus ministry
- RCIA
- Apologetics
- Prison ministry

Subsequent to the writing of the endorsements on the back cover for this second edition a number of topics have been further developed and others added.

Summaries and Wallet Outlines may be reproduced in their entirety only, with attribution.

Scripture taken from the HOLY BIBLE, NEW INTERNATIONAL VERSION®. Copyright © 1973, 1978, 1984 International Bible Society. Used by permission of Zondervan. All rights reserved.

With the passage of time, footnoted Web sites may change or become inoperative. If this occurs, the information can generally be found by entering key words in *Google* or another search engine.

Imprimatur: + Most Reverend Joseph F. Martino, D.D., Hist. E.D.
Bishop of Scranton, October 29, 2007

Nihil Obstat: Father Charles P. Connor, *Censor Librorum*
October 22, 2007

The *Nihil Obstat* and *Imprimatur* are official declarations that a book or pamphlet is free of doctrinal or moral error. No implication is contained therein that those who have granted the *Nihil Obstat* or *Imprimatur* agree with the contents, claims, opinions, or statements expressed. The *Nihil Obstat and Imprimatur* given to this book do not extend to the books noted in the bibliography, Internet Web sites, or non-English text of this book, which have not been reviewed for these purposes.

Publisher: 7 Steps to Catholicism
171 Hickory Ridge Road,
Greenfield Township, PA 18407-3514
To order book, call toll-free: 866 578-4077
Customer service: 570 650-1327
http://7step.catholic.org / jdgilmartin@hotmail.com

ISBN: 978-0-615-21197-8

Library of Congress Control Number: 2008904454

Printed in the United States of America

Cover Consultant: Susan Thye

Dedication / Acknowledgments

This book is dedicated to our daughter Ann, who said:

Dad, you just can't say that Jesus is any more important than any of the other founders of the great religions.

Ann (who again attends Mass and graciously gave her permission for this quotation) was then in a graduate anthropology program at a state university, having had eleven years of education in Catholic schools. The book is also dedicated to our daughter Joan, who, like her sister and most of their generation, came under the influence of many who saw the Gospels as largely myth and legend and doubted the existence of God.

My hope and prayer is that this book will help them, their fine husbands, our grandchildren Shannon and Charlotte, and many others gain a new appreciation of the science-based case for an intelligently designed universe, the historical truth of the Gospels, the uncontested fact that Jesus is unique among all founders of a religion; and that Jesus personally founded one Church that, through the Apostles, he promised to be with always.

Lastly, I dedicate this book to our daughters Johanna and Mary, who went to heaven soon after their premature birth and Baptism.

During the twelve years since I began writing what has become *The 7-Step Reason to be Catholic,* 2nd Ed., I have received encouragement from many people.

First I would like to thank Dr. Scott Hahn for taking the time to read my first book-length effort. Scott, your words of encouragement at that time were invaluable. My thanks also to Fr. Benedict J. Groeschel, C.F.R., who took the time to suggest publishers for the book. A special thanks to you, Fr. Benedict, for taking time out of your busy schedule to write the brief section in the Introduction alluding to Newman, Aquinas, and our need to fall silent before the Lord.

My thanks to you, Jeff Ziegler, for your kind letter indicating that you found the first edition of this book "extraordinarily well reasoned."

To you, Professor Charles E. Rice, Esq. of the University of Notre Dame Law School, a particular word of thanks for your candor in calling one of my earlier literary efforts a *non-starter.* That disapproval made it all the more meaningful when you later said of the first edition of *7-Step Reason,* "You're on the right track with this one" and gave me permission to distribute a summary of it at two conferences at which you were speaking.

My thanks to you, Rev. Msgr. David Bohr, *S.T.D.,* for your constructive comments on the first edition of this book as *Censor Librorum.*

I am especially grateful to you, Fr. Edward B. Connolly, pastor of St. Joseph Parish, Pottsville, and St. Francis de Sales Parish Mt. Carbon, PA, for your continuing encouragement and for your recommendations at several key points in the development of both editions of the book. I am also most grateful to you, Jorge A. Topete, Ph.D., for translating into Spanish the first edition of *7-Step Reason,* as well as the Wallet Outline and Summary. Thanks also to you, Carol Ridenour (Mrs. Jorge) Topete, for assisting in that daunting task. Thanks to Edward J. Capestany, Ph.D., for reviewing this book.

Thanks to you as well, Sr. M. Françoise De Smet, MC, for the initial translation of the Summary into French; your work is much appreciated.

A special word of thanks to you, Marie-Christine Ceruti-Cendrier, author of *Les Evangiles sont des reportages n'en déplaise à certains – The Gospels are the work of Reporters; too bad if that upsets some people* (French; translation into English planned). Although you helped from afar (Minsk, Belarus; Lugano, Switzerland; Rome and Lusaka, Zambia), you provided very important information on the compelling evidence that the Gospels originated with "reporters" and translated the modification of the French Summary and Wallet Outline of *The 7-Step Reason to be Catholic,* 2nd Ed.

And my very special thanks to you, Fr. H. Vernon Sattler, C.S.S.R. You were one of the first to read my work, and your suggestions were invaluable until that day, not so long ago, when God took you from this earthly life.

To you, Most Reverend John M. Dougherty, Auxiliary Bishop of Scranton, my heartfelt thanks. With a true understanding of my primary reason for writing, you encouraged me to seek the *Imprimatur.* For your support and that of Bishop Timlin and Bishop Martino I will be forever grateful.

A special word of thanks to Christopher Wong, who developed *The Catholic Apologist's Scriptural Response Guide* and allowed me to include it as an Appendix to this book. Thanks to your comprehensive *Guide*, Chris, readers can readily appreciate the sound biblical basis for Catholic teaching.

My thanks also to the late Patrick Ferraro, M.D., to Dean Clerico, M.D., and to Kenneth Pondo, fellow members of the Apologetics Committee of the Diocese of Scranton during the years it was active; to Frank Morriss, John W. Blewett and Karen Pautler of The Wanderer Forum; to Joseph and Margaret Dillenburg, who so ably represent Catholics United for the Faith and Lighthouse Catholic Media in

Scranton; to Fr. Luke Anderson, O. Cist.; to Gerry Wargo for his many insights into alternative views of Christian history; to Frank J. Germain, Deacon John Pogash, Alix Fils-Aime, Deacon and Attorney Sam Jennings, Deacon Glenn Biagi, James Scoblick, Joseph Alinoski, Raymond Totten, Attorney Ann Miller, Web consultant Michael D. Austin and the many others whose thoughts and prayers helped to make 7-*Step Reason* a reality. I am also grateful to a number of people of other faiths and of no particular faith, whose critiques of the original 7-*Step Reason* and this second edition have done much to ensure that the book does not misrepresent their beliefs. Though some of my Protestant, Muslim, Wiccan, Atheist and other contacts may prefer to remain anonymous, I am nonetheless in their debt.

A special word of thanks to you, John McGrath, for your critical review of Step 1. As a biology educator/administrator – and one of that select group of contributors to the *New York State Core Curriculum on the Living Environment* – your recommendations were of particular value. Question 1, for example, with its excerpt from that curriculum, is a result of your suggestion.

My thanks to you, Marcus Grodi, Founder and Director of The Coming Home Network International, for listing the first edition of the book in the CHNI online Catalogue and for your support as the second edition was being developed.

My sincere thanks also to you, Raymond de Souza, for translating the Wallet Outline into Portuguese, and to all who so diligently translated the Wallet Outline and Summary into Spanish, French, Russian, Chinese, Indonesian, Arabic, Hindi, Bengali, Tamil and Telugu and, in particular, to all whose endorsements appear on the back cover.

A special word of thanks to you, Msgr. Michael J. Wrenn, and to you, Kenneth D. Whitehead, for your valuable insights into the importance of the work done by scholars studying *Semitisms*; studies that so strongly support early date / eyewitness origins of the Gospels. My thanks to you as well, Fr. Mitch Pacwa, for affirming the importance of *Semitism*-based exegesis, in particular that of Claude Tresmontant.

Re: Quotations from *The Language of God: A Scientist Presents Evidence for Belief,* ISBN: 0-7432-8639-1: Reprinted with the permission of The Free Press, a Division of Simon & Schuster Adult Publishing Group, from THE LANGUAGE OF GOD: A Scientist Presents Evidence for Belief, by Francis S. Collins. Copyright © 2006 by Francis S. Collins. All rights reserved.

Lastly my most sincere thanks to Marie, my dear wife of 41 years, without whose love and support this book would not have been possible.

Jerome D. Gilmartin

iii

Permissions

My thanks to the following publishers and authors for granting permission (including fair use acknowledgment), to quote from their publications in this and / or the first edition:

Augsburg Fortress Publishers; Fr. Kenneth Baker, S.J., *Homiletic and Pastoral Review*; Basilica Press; Beth Mardutho: The Syriac Institute; Michael J. Behe, Lehigh University; Biblical Archaeology Society, *Biblical Archaeology Review*; L. Brent Bozell III, Media Research Center; Christendom Press; Francis S. Collins, author of *The Language of God*; *Crisis Magazine*; *The Daily Star* – Lebanon Wire; *Envoy Magazine*; Joseph Farah, WorldNetDaily.com; *Fikrun wa Fann / Art & Thought;* Franciscan Press; Marcus Grodi, Coming Home Network International; HarperCollins Publishers; Houghton Mifflin Company; Ignatius Press; *Inside the Vatican*; Intervarsity Press; *Journal for Dialogue with the Muslim World*; *The Latin Mass: The Journal of Catholic Culture and Tradition*; The Liturgical Press; Msgr. John F. McCarthy, Roman Theological Forum; The McGraw Hill Companies; Mike McManus, "Ethics and Religion" column, New York Times Syndicate; Moody Publishers; *National Catholic Register*; *Origins: Catholic News Service Documentary Service*; Random House, Inc.; Phyllis Schlafly, Eagle Forum; Fr. Michael Schooyans, writing for *Inside the Vatican*; Simon & Schuster, Inc.; Emily Stimpson, writing for *Our Sunday Visitor*; The United States Conference of Catholic Bishops; The United States Province of Sulpicians, Baltimore, MD; the University of Chicago; George Weigel, Senior Fellow of the Ethics and Public Policy Center in Washington, D.C.; Jonathan Wells, Discovery Institute; John G. West, Discovery Institute; Benjamin D. Wiker, Franciscan University of Steubenville and Christopher Wong, *The Catholic Apologist's Scriptural Response Guide*;

The Seven Ultimate Questions

If, as we shall see, the answer to each of these questions is YES, is Christ's call to embrace Catholicism not clear?

1. **Does strong scientific evidence point to the intelligent design of the universe?**

2. **Is it true that no Non-Christian religious body credibly claims that its founder is comparable to Jesus in fulfilling the Messianic prophecies and manifesting the power of an Intelligent Designer/Creator, including power over death?**

3. **Are the biblical and other historical accounts of Christ's ministry and miracles authentic?**

4. **Did Jesus found only one Church, pray for unity within it, and – through those commissioned with his authority – promise to be with that one Church always?**

5. **Did the risen Jesus personally commission only his eleven Apostles to baptize, teach, and make disciples of all nations, after giving one of them primacy?**

6. **Through the "solemn laying on of hands" by the Apostles and their successors, do Catholic bishops today, as true successors of the Apostles, act with Christ's own authority? ***

7. **Is it true that the Bible includes no "escape clause" to reject the one, holy, catholic and apostolic Church Jesus founded and promised to be with always?**

---

*   Orthodox Christian bishops also have valid orders and thus valid Sacraments. However, beginning in the 11th century, Orthodox Patriarchies rejected the primacy Christ gave to Peter and his successors in the papacy, thus rejecting the unity called for by Christ.

Foreword

Help! I'm attracted to Catholicism!

I have the impression that many non-Catholics who begin to look favorably on Catholicism don't reveal this to family and friends until they are well along the path to conversion. Often the result is loss of friends, and resentment or worse on the part of family members.

The better way, it seems to me, is to alert family, friends and your pastor or other spiritual leader at the first sign of your serious interest in Catholicism (except when conversion may jeopardize your employment or personal safety). Let them walk with you through the steps presented in this book and other Catholic sources. Thoughtfully and prayerfully consider their objections, consulting the *Catechism of the Catholic Church* (2nd ed.), writings of the Early Church Fathers, the apologists at Catholic Answers and the extensive written and audio information available at www.Catholic.com/, http://ewtn.com/ and other sources.

Those closest to you may well join you on the path to conversion. Even if they do not, they will remember that you reached out to them as you sought to discern God's will in this vitally important matter.

Since *The 7-Step Reason to be Catholic* was first published in May, 2001, the United States has been shaken by two great tragedies, the effects of which will long be with us; the horrific series of attacks on 9/11/01 by militant Islamic elements and, beginning about five months later, the news of the sexual molestation scandals that have shaken the Church. This second edition includes added or revised commentary on these topics, as well as the following:

- The section on scientific challenges to evolution by natural selection has been expanded. The Web site of the National Center for Science Education has been added. Web sites of organizations that reject Intelligent Design have been added, as well as Web sites on which Intelligent Design scientists refute a variety of challenges to ID.

- An overview of Pascal's Wager has been added.
- Quotes by Fr. Jean Carmignac, Claude Tresmontant, Jacqueline Genot-Bismuth, Marie-Christine Ceruti-Cendrier, Carsten Thiede and other researchers who challenge the prevailing historical-critical, late-date / no eyewitness view of the origin of the Gospels have been added. These researchers make a compelling case for very early dates of origin of the Gospels based

on Semitisms, philology, papyrology and archaeology. *These important Hebrew / Aramaic-based and other studies strongly support the Gospels, including the miracles, as historically authentic.*

- Further comments have been added exploring the extent to which the commonly held late-date / no-eyewitness view of the Gospels may have weakened the faith of some in the priesthood, thus lessening the moral constraints against scandalous behavior.

- In view of the greatly increased interest in Islam, Part III of the book now includes commentary on Christoph Luxenberg's *Die syro-aramaeische Lesart des Koran (The Syro-Aramaic Reading of the Koran)* as well as a number of additional Bible-based claims of authoritative Islamic apologists and a Catholic response to each.

- More than 200 questions have been added to make the book more useful in classroom settings, from high school through university levels, as well as for home schooling and group discussion.

- The Web site of the *National Catholic Register* has been added. It provides current information on implementation of the *mandatum,* the oath of fidelity, separate male and female dorms and other topics of interest to those evaluating the orthodoxy of Catholic colleges and universities in the United States.

- The etymological meaning of the root of *believe* (to love) further explained, in light of Jn 3:16 and other verses.

- Resolving the difficulties of historical-critical interpretation using the *Neo-Patristic Method* – the work of the Roman Theological Forum.

- *Dominus Iesus* and its applicability in the context of this book.

- The Coming Home Network International; its purpose and rapid growth.

- The five new luminous mysteries added.

- Freely choosing hell further explained.

- Evil of abortion further explained, biblical prohibition added.

- Natural Family Planning; new book and Web sites.

- Added comments on "The Third Way," by Fr. Benedict Groeschel.

- The parallel between the heterodoxy of Arians and that of today (Ven. John Henry Cardinal Newman).

- A debunking of *The Da Vinci Code* based on authentic early Church history.

- The Inquisition; brief thoughts by a Church historian.

- Brief comments on the Crusades.

- The flawed view of Joseph Campbell that the Gospels are largely myth.

- The problematic view of Rev. Rick Warren in the *Purpose-D_ _ _ _ Life* that the Great Commission is the commission of every Christian.

- Comments on the Talmud and its importance in Orthodox Judaism.

- Added thoughts on Hinduism; answers to several additional biblical challenges to Christianity.

- Freemasonry; several new pages of important information.

- Wallet Outlines of the 7 Steps in English, Spanish, French, Russian, Portuguese, Chinese, Indonesian, Arabic, Hindi, Bengali, Tamil and Telugu are included in the Appendix section. The Summary in English (fourteen pages) and in Spanish is also included in the Appendix. The Wallet Outline in all twelve languages and the Summary in seven of the twelve can be downloaded free from **http://7step.catholic.org.** These twelve are the native languages of more than half of the world's 6.6 billion people.

Introduction

In *Story of a Soul* St. Thérèse of Lisieux expresses her deep, God-given desire to ascend the mountain to the summit of sainthood despite her conviction that she could never complete such an arduous climb. Instead, she sought "some means of going to heaven by a little way which is very short and very straight, a little way that is quite new."

The 7-Step Reason to be Catholic, 2nd Ed. is my prayerful effort to provide another "little way," a "very short and very straight" way to Catholicism - the base camp, so to speak, from which St. Therese began her remarkable ascent.

As a pre-Vatican II son of devout Catholic parents, I can't remember a time when my faith wasn't an important part of my life. That faith was developed and reinforced first by some very special Immaculate Heart of Mary nuns, with the help of the *Baltimore Catechism* and, from 1955 to 1961, by Jesuits at the University of Scranton and Fordham Graduate School.

In the late 1960s, however, I began to experience the "liberation" of the "Spirit of Vatican II." I remember being told by a trusted priest to forget what I'd learned about Catholicism at the University of Scranton and Fordham; the Church had changed. It was not uncommon to hear that we (the laity) were now the Church; that the hierarchical pyramid had been turned upside down.

I read the statement of the theologians who dissented openly from *Humanae Vitae*. At the time it seemed to me that, since so many Catholic theologians publicly opposed the Pope in regard to artificial birth control, surely this encyclical could not be truly binding in conscience on Catholics.

On three occasions between 1980 and 1991 our family moved in connection with my employment. We always attended Mass regularly. However, with each move I selected a Catholic parish based on perceived friendliness rather than indications of Catholic orthodoxy.

In the early 1990s another priest whom I knew well told me that scholars concluded that no apostle or other eyewitness to the ministry of Jesus was the author of a Gospel. All four were written late in the first century and probably included substantial embellishment, he said. Among the embellishments by the unknown author of *Matthew* were surely the words of Jesus designating Peter as the Rock on whom he would build his Church and to whom he would give the keys of the kingdom of heaven. The priest explained that this meant that the Pope has no more authority than any other Bishop; his true authority is limited to Rome. This and other discussions with priests and religious opened my eyes to the widespread dissent in the Church. The Church may have been holy, catholic and apostolic, but at that time it seemed no longer "one."

This concern, and indications that our daughters were drifting away from the Church, prompted me to shift my Catholic reading from books, newspapers and magazines that were generally liberal to those that were well-grounded in loyalty to the Pope and Magisterium.

Rumblings of dissent within the Church and some of its lay adjuncts are evident today. A Catholic News Service article dated February 8, 2005 stated that the Vatican forbade a U.S. Jesuit to continue to teach as a Catholic theologian. The Doctrinal Congregation concluded that his book, published in 2000, contained doctrinal errors. The charges included downplaying or denying that Jesus was divine, and that in Jesus the biblical Word became flesh. Rather than bring his book into compliance, he left his teaching position in 2004.

Perhaps the most disturbing aspect of this story is that, when published in 2000, the errant book won an award as the "year's best book on theology" by the Catholic Press Association. It was also a selection of the Catholic Book Club, which is operated by America Press.[1]

Such a report will test the faith of more than a few Catholics and discourage others from becoming Catholic. Why would this learned theologian – a Catholic priest – downplay or deny the very *divinity* of Jesus? And why would the Catholic Press Association and America Press hold that book in such high regard?

Surely this theologian believed in the divinity of Jesus when he entered the priesthood. What may have influenced him to lose his faith in Christ as our divine Savior? The news article did not address this question.

In many cases, however, dissent originates with misuse of the widely used historical-critical method of biblical exegesis. Step 3 of this book addresses the inherent limitations of this method. It also includes an overview of the compelling case for Catholic orthodoxy based on the Early Church Fathers, archaeology, papyrology, and more than four centuries of *Semitism*-based biblical scholarship. Part II of this book provides further information on the various aspects of dissent and how to graciously bring this concern to the attention of a priest,

---

1 "Vatican forbids U.S. Jesuit to teach as Catholic theologian," by John Thavis and Cindy Wooden, Catholic News Service, February 5, 2005. **www.catholicnews.com**

instructor or other person who is under its influence.

In regard to the broad topic of religion it seems natural to ask, "*What* should I believe?" But many highly intelligent people who have spent a lifetime studying religion disagree among themselves about what to believe. The more prudent question, it seems to me, is, "*Whom* should I believe?"

For example, of all the founders of the various religions, so many of which have teachings that are mutually contradictory, *which of these founders manifested the power of the Creator, and thus would have power, in the hereafter, to keep his promises?* Was Jesus unique in manifesting such power? And what about the claims of many scientists that faith in God is pointless and that evolution can account for all human and other life? On what basis do many biblical scholars question the authenticity of the Gospels? Have other biblical scholars refuted that view and established the Gospels as solidly authentic? And what about the Protestant Reformation? Is there biblical support for it?

As the pages of this book indicate, the answers to these and many other questions point surely to the Catholic Church and to the *Catechism of the Catholic Church*, the "sure norm" summarizing its teaching.

Let me note here at the outset that I write not as a biblical scholar or scientist but as one reporting on the work of others in various fields. Many fine books describe what it means to be Catholic and outline, in greater or lesser detail, the essential teachings of the Church, its special call to holiness, its history and much more. This book is only incidentally about what it means to *be* Catholic. Instead it provides a wide-ranging but concise, easily learned, seven-step answer to the question "*Why be Catholic?*"

These steps fall into the categories of science, the Bible and history. For many, faith is like the roadway on a pontoon bridge – easily severed by debris from the storms of life. For the Catholic, however, that roadway of faith can be lifted high above the river on the sturdy piers of science, the Bible and history. Anchored in prayer and sound *Catechism*-based teaching, this faith will endure, no matter what may slam into those supports below.[2]

7-Step Reason originated not as a book but as a wallet-sized leaflet. Realizing that few Catholics can convincingly answer the question "Why be Catholic?," I set out to write a concise, science / Bible / history-based wallet outline, an updated version of which is in the

---

2 *Catechism of the Catholic Church*, 2nd Ed.

Appendix section of this book in English, Spanish, French, Russian, Portuguese, Chinese, Indonesian, Arabic, Hindi, Bengali, Tamil and Telugu. It is also on the Internet in these languages at **http://7step.catholic.org**.

A more complete answer was needed for any serious discussion, of course, resulting eventually in the 7-Step Summary. The Summary is included in the Appendix section in English and Spanish and, at this writing, can be downloaded from the 7step Web site in seven languages.

As noted in the Foreword, the first edition of this book, intended for general use, was published in 2001, before the widespread publication of the sexual abuse scandals within the Church and before the devastating events of September 11, 2001 turned the attention of the world toward militants within Islam. This edition takes these events into account, includes many discussion questions and provides a more in-depth treatment of most topics covered in the first edition.

Among the most important new topics is the philological and other evidence that strongly indicates: (a) early authorship of the *Gospel according to Matthew* in Hebrew or Aramaic; (b) early authorship in Hebrew or Aramaic of the *Gospel according to Mark*, possibly by Peter himself; (c) that the Greek of the *Gospel according to John* is the Greek of translation from a Hebrew or Aramaic original; (d) that the sources of the *Gospel according to Luke* were written in Hebrew or Aramaic [or that the entire *Gospel according to Luke* was translated from a Hebrew or Aramaic original except the introduction].

Fr. Jean Carmignac has shown that these early-date / eyewitness conclusions cannot be refuted by attributing them to the author's attempt to imitate the Septuagint or to the influence of the author's native language.

Late-date conjecture notwithstanding, such findings strongly support the view that the Gospel accounts originated with *eyewitnesses* within a few decades of the Resurrection, and are therefore highly credible history. Most of all, they give very strong support to Jesus Christ as our Divine Savior and risen Redeemer, who said "no one comes to the Father, but by me" (Jn 14:6). The study of *Semitisms*, of course, casts serious doubt on the prevailing late-date / no eyewitness (i.e., post-A.D. 67) view of the origin of the Gospels held by the large majority of biblical scholars today, both Catholic and non-Catholic.

Part II addresses *Revitalizing Faith in the Wake of Scandal and Dissent*. The material is disturbing, but timely, and, I believe, relevant to efforts to understand and begin to resolve these problems.

Part III is, for the most part, an extension of Step 2. It was prompted by the widespread view among Catholics today that, although it is important to have faith, it doesn't really matter very much which Christian or non-Christian faith one practices (or doesn't practice). The focus in this section is not so much on the many and varied beliefs and practices of the other major religions but on the particular aspects of belief that make them incompatible with Catholicism.

Questions at the end of each section are designed to prompt lively discussion. Many Internet-based and other references are included.

To readers who would say that this book is quite out of balance – that Step 3, for example, covers many pages but Steps 5, 6 and 7 few, and that a similar lack of balance is evident in Part III – I can only respond, "Guilty as charged." In my defense I can say only that, for Catholics and others in this first decade of the third millennium, I tried to shed more scientific, biblical and historical light on the topics that seem most in need of illumination.

On June 3, 1963, while on military leave, I was approaching Rome on a bus from the airport when traffic came to a standstill. Our beloved Pope, John XXIII, had died. That afternoon I visited a virtually deserted St. Peter's Basilica. Occupying much of the nave were the multi-tiered seats erected for the Second Vatican Council. The second session opened in September 1963, under the direction of Pope Paul VI, and the Council ended December 8, 1965.

Many changes have since come about in the Church, including new programs of catechesis which began within a decade after Vatican II in virtually every Catholic parish. However, in conversations with a number of Catholics, I find that few today can convincingly answer this question:

Why should anyone be a Catholic rather than an adherent of some other religion or none?

The difficulty may be due in part to a misunderstanding of what our Church means by ecumenism. The opening sentence of the Introduction to the Decree on Ecumenism, *Unitatis Redintegratio; Documents of Vatican II,* reads as follows: "1. **The restoration of unity among all Christians is one of the principal concerns of the Second Vatican Council.**"[3]

Then, in Chapter I, par. 2, the Council Fathers state, **"Christ entrusted to the College of the Twelve the task of teaching, ruling and**

---

3 *Vatican Council II, Vol. 1, The Conciliar and Post Conciliar Documents;* New Revised Edition, 452.

sanctifying," having earlier stated that on Peter Christ would build his Church and that it was Peter to whom he would give the keys of the kingdom of heaven.[4] *"Nevertheless, our separated brethren, whether considered as individuals or as communities and churches, are not blessed with that unity which Jesus Christ wished to bestow on all to whom he has given new birth into one body ...."*[5]

After encouraging dialogue among competent experts from different churches, cooperation in social programs and, where permitted, common prayer, the document states: *"In ecumenical work, Catholics must assuredly be concerned for their separated brethren, praying for them, keeping them informed about the Church, making the first approaches toward them"*[6] (Emphasis added).

As indicated in the *Catechism of the Catholic Church,* 2nd Ed., the Council did not intend that ecumenism be pursued at the expense of the doctrine of our 2,000-year-old Church, nor with any compromise of its unique position as the *only* Church founded by Christ himself: "The sole Church of Christ [is that] which our Savior, after his Resurrection, entrusted to Peter's pastoral care, commissioning him and the other apostles to extend and rule it ...." This Church, constituted and organized as a society in the present world, subsists in (*subsistit in*) the Catholic Church, which is governed by the successor of Peter and by the bishops in communion with him. [CCC par. 816; *Lumen gentium* 8, par. 2]

Some, however, hold that *subsists in* is not an exclusive term and that, by using it, the Council was indicating that the "sole Church of [founded by] Christ" could also *subsist* in other Christian churches.

This "subsists in other Christian churches" view becomes untenable in light of the first part of *L.G.* 8, 2, where "This Church" – the sole Church of Christ – is defined as the one that meets all three of these criteria: (a) the one "which in the Creed we profess to be one, holy, catholic and apostolic"; (b) the one "which Our Savior, after his resurrection, entrusted to Peter's pastoral care, commissioning him and the other apostles to extend and rule it"; (c) the one "which he raised up for all ages as the pillar and mainstay of the truth" (1 Tim 3:15). [*L.G.* 8].

Clearly, only the Catholic Church meets all three of these criteria. Any doubt on this matter is removed by the following: "Basing itself on

4 Ibid., 454.
5 Ibid., 456.
6 Ibid., 457.

Scripture and tradition, it [the Council] teaches that the [Catholic] Church … is necessary for salvation." [L.G. 14]. A fuller explanation of this statement follows in L.G. 14-16 and in *CCC* 846-848.

Nor was ecumenism to diminish in any way the obligation of the Church to evangelize:

> Although in ways known to himself God can lead those who, through no fault of their own, are ignorant of the Gospel, to that faith without which it is impossible to please him, the Church still has the obligation and also the sacred right to evangelize all men. [*Ad gentes divinitus* 7; CCC par. 848].

The following thought is attributed to Saint Francis of Assisi (1182?-1226): "At all times preach the Gospel; when necessary, use words." If St. Francis did express this thought, he did so when, throughout Western Europe, the word "Christian" meant the one Petrine Church founded by Jesus – the Catholic Church. That changed dramatically three centuries later with the Reformation.

If St. Francis were with us today, surely he would encourage every Catholic to "use words" often – both spoken and written – to draw others to the Church, as Mother Teresa did so effectively on the following occasion: After hearing a talk Mother Teresa gave at Harvard, a Protestant made this comment:

> *Oh well, when it's all said and done, I guess the Lord needs some people in the Catholic Church and some people in the other churches.*

Mother Teresa replied, "No, he doesn't." [See *Dominus Iesus* (August 6, 2000) and *Responses to Some Questions Regarding Certain Aspects of the Doctrine on the Church* (June 29, 2007)][7].

This incident at Harvard was related by Tom Howard, a convert to Catholicism, to Sara McLaughlin. "These words pierced my heart," wrote McLaughlin; "I knew that moment, in the summer of 1991, I was called to be Catholic."[8]

Pope John Paul II, in his encyclical *Tertio Millennio Adveniente (As the Third Millennium Draws Near)* called our attention to the encyclical *Redemptoris Missio* and noted:

> The more the West is becoming estranged from its Christian roots the more it is becoming mission territory (*T.M.A.*, par. 57).

---

7 **www.vatican/va**
8 Sara McLaughlin, "Holy Osmosis," *Envoy Magazine*, July/August 1998, 20.

My hope is that this book will be of some value in the formation of the "missionaries" of which our late Pope spoke – and contribute in some small way to their success both within and outside our Church.

Another reason why few Catholics can defend their faith is that apologetics – the study of *why* we believe as we do and of how to give a well-reasoned defense of the faith – has not been taught in most Catholic universities for several decades.

For these reasons and others, many who were raised as Catholics have only a vague understanding of our faith and have never become aware of its inestimable spiritual value in comparison to other faiths. Is it any wonder that, after completing high school, so many leave the Church, some eventually to join other churches and many to give up all association with formal religion?

Further complicating the picture is the idea that the Christian *unity* we see today is the unity that God intended. The number of separate Christian denominations worldwide today exceeds 33,000.[9] This proliferation of non-Catholic denominations since the Reformation has, as its source, individual interpretation of the Bible based on what one believes to be the inspiration of the Holy Spirit.

Many non-Catholic Christians maintain that this diversity of belief within the "one invisible Christian Church" is what Jesus had in mind when, in the presence of the eleven apostles (all but Judas), he prayed to the Father: "I do not pray for these only, but also for those who believe in me through their word, that they may all be one; even as thou, Father, art in me, and I in thee ...." (Jn 17:20-21).

But can anyone maintain that the diversity of Christian belief today has a parallel in the Trinity? For example, before his incarnation, could Jesus have said the following?

> *Father, I go gladly to become Redeemer and Savior. But, though my love for you is infinite, you are mistaken on some important points. In my earthly ministry I will make the necessary corrections.*

No one familiar with the Bible could believe that such discord could exist within the Trinity. Clearly then, the "one, invisible Christian church," a concept that originated with the Reformation, with its many leaders and inherent diversity, cannot represent the true unity that the Father, Jesus and the Holy Spirit intend for their Church.

The Church acknowledges that not all popes of history proved

---

9 *World Christian Encyclopedia,* 2001.

personally worthy of the office. But, as with Judas Iscariot, Jesus did not suppress the free will of Peter, the other apostles, or their successor popes / bishops. But no pope has destroyed the fabric of doctrine of the one 2,000-year-old Church Jesus entrusted to the Holy Spirit and promised to be with always.

Official Papal / Magisterial Church teaching is summarized in the *Catechism of the Catholic Church*, 2nd Ed. Pope John Paul II has also stated:

> *The Catechism was also indispensable in order that all the richness of the teaching of the Church following the Second Vatican Council could be preserved in a new synthesis and be given a new direction. Without the Catechism of the universal Church this would not have been accomplished.*[10]

In 2006, *Compendium; Catechism of the Catholic Church* was published. In the *Motu Proprio* on this important book, Pope Benedict XVI, successor of Pope John Paul II, included the following:

> The *Compendium,* which I now present to the Universal Church, is a faithful and sure synthesis of the *Catechism of the Catholic Church* .... I entrust this *Compendium* above all to the entire Church and, in particular, to every Christian, in order that it may awaken in the Church of the third millennium renewed zeal for evangelization and education in the faith, which ought to characterize every community in the Church and every Christian believer, regardless of age or nationality. [The *Compendium*] is directed to every human being, who, in a world of distractions and multifarious messages, desires to know the Way of Life, the Truth, entrusted by God to his Son's Church.[11]

The case for Catholicism, properly documented, is uniquely compelling and, in fact, without parallel. For many of our separated brethren, doubts about the biblical and extra-biblical basis for the papacy, apostolic succession and papal infallibility are major obstacles to a proper understanding of the Church. One book in particular stands out as having removed those doubts to a remarkable degree. That book is *Jesus, Peter & the Keys*, co-authored by Scott Butler, Norman Dahlgren and David Hess.

Kenneth J. Howell, Ph.D., a Presbyterian Minister from 1978 to 1996, noted that he found *Jesus, Peter & the Keys* the source of a great deal of

---

10 *Crossing the Threshold of Hope,* 164.
11 *Compendium of the Catholic Church*, xii.

important information as he struggled with Catholic dogma. So overwhelming was the information that Dr. Howell realized he could no longer claim invincible ignorance and he entered the Catholic Church.

As the outline suggests, *The 7-Step Reason to Be Catholic, 2ⁿᵈ Ed.,* "casts the net broadly" by: (a) establishing the reasonableness of belief in an Almighty Creator; (b) showing that Jesus was the *only* founder of a religion who lived among us and, being God, spoke and acted with the authority of the Almighty Creator; (c) pointing out that the Bible is historically authentic and provides no "escape clause" – no basis for forming or joining any church other than the one founded by Christ and led by Peter and his successors; (d) contrasting true Catholicism with its modernist counterfeit; (e) identifying key non-Christian and pseudo-Christian teachings that are irreconcilable with the teachings of the Church founded by Jesus.

Reason, of course, is no substitute for faith and the grace of God. For many, however, a lack of knowledge or mistaken information about the Church can be an obstacle to grace. My hope is that this overview of Catholicism in contrast to other Christian and non-Christian faiths will eliminate such obstacles and lead to a Catholic faith that is graciously but firmly held, reverently practiced and ably defended; to the point where the reader will one day hear these words: "*Well done, good and faithful servant … enter into the joy of your Master.*"

As a work of apologetics, *The 7-Step Reason to be Catholic, 2ⁿᵈ Edition* is not intended to take the place of books and other sources that provide specific answers to the many questions asked of Catholics by Protestants and others. It simply suggests a sound, seven-step, Scripture-based answer to the question, *Why should anyone be Catholic?*

It is important to me to retain the friendship of my Protestant, Jewish, Orthodox, Muslim, Hindu, Buddhist, Jehovah's Witness, Mormon and other friends and acquaintances. However, I believe that none of us is well served, ultimately, unless we can all start at the beginning – the very *origins* of the beliefs we hold – and examine closely the reasons why we believe as we do.

In the final analysis, however, true Faith is not something we arrive at by reason alone. In a homily given at a *Defending the Faith* Conference in Steubenville in 2001, Fr. Benedict Groeschel, C.F.R., referred to the writings of Ven. John Henry Newman, drawn from the book *Healing the Wound of Humanity; The Spirituality of John Henry Newman,* by Fr. Ian Ker. Fr. Benedict gave Newman's analysis of belief as follows:

We come to accept belief by reason of a congruence of probabilities, a succession of insights that leads to an intellectual conclusion. However, for many who realized belief in this manner, the condition is not necessarily a supernatural gift of faith.

A person called by rational arguments must prepare to come to the point where they can't go any further, where they must stop in silence before the mystery of God. An example of this is the silent four months of St. Thomas Aquinas before his death. When he offered Mass on the feast of St. Nicholas he fell into silence and later told his secretary, Br. Reginald, "Such things have been revealed to me in prayer that everything I have written seems to me stubble."

Theories, which are insights of intelligence, are helpful. They assist us toward belief and also can be used to help others to come to belief. They guide the interpretation of beliefs and make sure our adherence to scripture and tradition is consistent and sound. But ultimately, faith is a gift ....

My hope is that you, the reader of this book, will consider its many appeals to the intellect and use them as you see fit in the service of our Lord and his Church. My prayer is that, with Thomas and so many other great saints, we too may receive the grace to fall silent – where possible in the presence of the Blessed Sacrament. And let us then remember the words of the psalmist: "Be still, and know that I am God" (Ps 46:10).

The *Card-Carrying Catholic*™ – Instant Apologetics

Becoming a skilled apologist (defender) of Catholicism takes considerable study – prayerful study. We can all learn much from Catholic apologists such as Karl Keating, Jimmy Akin and Tim Staples of Catholic Answers, as well as from Scott Hahn, Fr. Mitch Pacwa, Colin Donovan, Patrick Madrid, Marcus Grodi, Steve Ray, Fr. John Trigilio, Fr. Robert Levis, Rosalind Moss, John Martignoni, Marcellino D'Ambrosio and many others who come to us through EWTN, Catholic Radio and other Catholic sources. Few Catholics are skilled enough to conduct call-in programs and engage in public debates as do these preeminent Catholic apologists.

What we Catholics *can* do, in as little as one minute, is to each become a *Card-Carrying Catholic*™. In effect, we can each become a Catholic "G.P.A." – General Practitioner of Apologetics – consulting specialists such as those noted above for questions we are not yet able to answer.

The "Card" (Wallet Outline) can be downloaded free in twelve languages at **http://7step.catholic.org**, or photocopied from the Appendix section of this book. With this Wallet Outline, whether on card stock or paper, all Catholics – certainly those of high school age and older – can take part in the New Evangelization, even those who know little about Catholicism.

In response to an invitation to consider another religion (or none), the novice Catholic apologist might say:

"I don't know my faith very well, but I have this Bible–based Wallet Outline of The 7-Step Reason to be Catholic. It's science and history–based too. Can we begin with this and see where it takes us?

Next, invite the other person to read the Summary (14 pages in English). Download it free in English, Spanish, French, Russian, Chinese, Indonesian or Arabic at **http://7step.catholic.org**, or photocopy it from the Appendix section of this book in English or Spanish.

You might then invite your non-Catholic friend to refer to this book, beginning with the Contents and Index pages. If he or she is a *sola scriptura* (Bible-only) Christian, Chris Wong's *The Catholic Apologist's Scriptural Response Guide* will be of particular interest (Appendix P).

In talking with former Catholics, you might begin by asking them to share with you: (a) what it was, exactly, that resulted in their leaving the Church and, (b) what they now see as their reasons for not returning. Hopefully, the Contents and Index pages of this book will provide a sound starting point for resolving those difficulties.

If the person is an agnostic or atheist who believes that science will someday explain all "miracles," I suggest that you begin by asking him or her to consider the restoration of normal vision to young Gemma di Giorgi after Padre (now Saint) Pio prayed over her, *although it remained physically impossible for her to see* (pp. 41-42). Step 1 of this book should then deepen the realization that there is no incompatibility between science and Catholicism.

As a Catholic "G.P.A.," you can refer others to the many apologetics "specialists" listed under *Questions?* in the Summary, as well as to others noted above.

www.catholic.com is a remarkable apologetics / evangelization Web site. It offers more than 100 free tracts and more than 2,000 free archived audio programs featuring Catholic Answers founder Karl Keating, his staff apologists and guests. The "Catholic Answers Live" call-in radio program can be heard live on-line each weekday, 3 to 5 p.m. Pacific time. For local radio stations, click on **www.ewtn.com** > **Stations**. Staff apologists at Catholic Answers headquarters in San Diego, CA can be reached at 619 387-7200 from 9 a.m. to 5 p.m. Pacific time.

———

Part I

The 7-Step Reason to be Catholic

The 7-Step Reason to be Catholic

Step 1. Strong scientific evidence points to the intelligent design of the universe.

Introductory Comments

During the seven years since the first edition of this book was published Intelligent Design (ID) has come under intense criticism.

Seeing an oil-soaked bird flapping at the shoreline after a spill, many will walk by, saying, "That bird can't fly." Others, however, will remove the oil and only then observe the bird to see if it can or can't fly.

Before deciding whether or not ID can "fly," it is essential that strict separation of the two primary categories of analysis – scientific (material) and religious (immaterial) – be maintained. Much of the disagreement on the subject seems due to failure to differentiate between the two.

Although *Wikipedia* strives for objectivity, their currently posted Web article "Intelligent design" seems to exemplify the problem. The first paragraph, which would normally set the stage for discussion, notes that the primary proponents of ID are all members of the Discovery Institute and believe that the Abrahamic God is the "designer." This article, including footnotes, uses the word *God* 39 times, *religion* or *religious* 52 times, *Creator* 12 times, *Christian* 21 times, *theistic* 14 times – a total of 138 references to religion, not counting several uses of the words *Catholic*, *Presbyterian*, *Muslim* and *Jew*.

Are scientific arguments against ID so weak that they must be linked to religion? No scientist worthy of the name would answer, "Yes." Scientific conclusions are based on what is observable and measurable. They are what they are. Whether pro or con, they deserve a fair and unbiased hearing.

Challenging Darwinian Theory, more than 600 scientists have now signed this *Scientific Dissent from Darwinism* statement:

> *We are skeptical of claims for the ability of random mutation and natural selection to account for the complexity of life. Careful examination of the evidence for Darwinian Theory should be encouraged.*[12]

---

12 Scientific Dissent from Darwinism. **www.dissentfromdarwin.org.** "Dissent From "Darwinism 'Goes Global' as Over 600 Scientists Around the World Express Their

The Discovery Institute invites those who agree with this statement and hold a Ph.D. in engineering, mathematics, computer science, biology, chemistry, or one of the other natural sciences, to contact them at **cscinfo@discovery.org**. The Discovery Institute further states: "*The list is growing and includes scientists from the U.S. National Academy of Sciences, Russian, Hungarian and Czech National Academies, as well as from universities such as Yale, Princeton, Stanford, MIT, UC Berkeley, UCLA, and others.*"

Medical doctors who are skeptical of Darwinian evolution are invited to visit Physicians and Surgeons for Scientific Integrity at **www.doctorsdoubtingdarwin.com** and sign their list for doctors who dissent.

Suppose six civil engineers declared, "We are skeptical that this well-traveled bridge can continue to safely carry traffic." What responsible official would not immediately close the bridge and deal with the issue?

In the case of the "bridge" of Darwinian Theory, not six but more than *six hundred* scientists have declared themselves skeptical regarding the science supporting it. Why is that skepticism not made known in every science classroom? And why are public educators not free to discuss with students statements such as the following by mathematician and ID proponent William A. Dembski:

> *[T]here are natural systems that cannot be adequately explained in terms of undirected natural forces and that exhibit features which in any other circumstance we would attribute to intelligence.*[13]

The *Scientific Dissent from Darwinism* statement and Dembski's statement suggest several questions: (a) *Are there, in fact, natural systems that cannot be adequately explained in terms of undirected natural forces?* As noted, more than 600 scientists have answered, "Yes." (b) *Would scientists, in any other circumstance, attribute intelligence to those features?* Clearly, yes; scientists readily attribute features of far less complex systems (e.g., a pencil, ball-point pen, ruler) to an intelligent source. (c) *In doubting that "random mutation and natural selection" can account for the complexity of life, are these scientists not suggesting that such mutation and selection may be*

Doubts About Darwinian Evolution." The Discovery Institute, June 21, 2006.
www.discovery.org/scripts/viewDB/index.php?command =view&id=3622
13 *The Design Revolution*. 27. (2004).

purposeful? (d) *If so, can purposeful mutation and selection be attributed to other than an intelligent mutator / selector?* (e) *Since these complex systems range from sub-microscopic to galactic, could such a mutator / selector be other than the supernatural Creator whom people throughout history have called God?*

Questions (a) and (b), since they deal with observable phenomena, are within the realm of science. To this point, the "bird" at the shoreline is in pristine condition. The DNA, amino acids, complex proteins and other features that result in its circulatory, respiratory, muscular, immune, nervous, digestive, reproductive and other systems – as well as the finely tuned *interaction* of all its systems in one superbly integrated flying "system" – can be studied.

As noted, hundreds of scientists doubt that Darwinian Theory can explain such complexity. And yet such doubt - although purely science-based – is banned from discussion in the public science classroom. Why? Could it be because students, aware of that doubt, might raise such questions as (c) through (e) and begin to develop a *science-based* belief in God?

A number of evolution-only proponents defend their anti-ID view with arguments in support of *macroevolution.*[14] In this edition, I note some of these arguments against the teaching of ID in public schools and provide Web sites for others.

I am told that most scientists in academia believe that macroevolution is a sound explanation for the existence of life. However, Jonathan Wells, author of *Icons of Evolution,* expresses the hope that biologists will give a fair hearing to the case for Intelligent Design; he notes that most do not work in the field of evolutionary biology and are influenced by what they read in their professional journals which, as a rule, do not objectively present the case for ID.

For an introduction to both sides of this issue, I recommend a special report reprinted from *Natural History* magazine, published by the American Museum of Natural History.[15] On this Web site pro-ID conclusions by three of the most prominent ID scientists are followed by science-based rebuttals by three well-qualified peers. The article does not include follow-up pro and con arguments. However, it includes links to Web sites chosen by each participant in support of his / her views.

In fairness to scientists who defend macroevolution theory against

---

14 The formation of new taxonomic groups (categories of organisms) over time.
15 **www.actionbioscience.org/evolution/nhmag.html**

ID, many do not deny the possibility of a Creator / Designer.

I do not have the science credentials to evaluate claims for Intelligent Design. Where I express my own views in these pages they are simply those of one whose university and graduate study of the sciences included one to three courses each of math, physics, biology, chemistry, and probability & statistics. However, The ID scientists I quote are well qualified; each holds a Ph.D. in his or her area of specialization.

Taking into account probability, ID scientists conclude that the complexity of certain organic and inorganic entities and / or systems found in nature cannot be explained scientifically.

Undaunted by colleagues who have faith that science will one day explain everything that now seems inexplicable, ID scientists note that science is replete with discoveries that have challenged randomness with ever-more-improbable ordered complexity; e.g., the atom, the universe, DNA, chaos theory, and the biochemical brain as the seat of the mind of man.

ID scientists are not to be confused with *Creationists*, whose views – although they may include scientific references – are primarily Bible-based.

Can science say nothing about the supernatural, but "point" to it?

The prestigious National Academy of Sciences states: *"Science can say nothing about the supernatural. Whether God exists or not is a question about which science is neutral."*[16]

Is this first step therefore unscientific in stating that "Strong scientific evidence *points to* the intelligent design of the universe?" No, it is not. The simple fact is that the purely scientific *material* evidence presented in this step *points to*, or suggests, a reality that is *immaterial* and therefore lies outside the realm of science.

As a parallel, historians would rely on archaeologists, paleontologists and others to verify compelling written evidence pointing to an unknown ancient civilization. Is the written evidence any less historical, or less important, because these historians look outside their discipline for its validation? Obviously, the answer is no. Similarly, scientific evidence suggesting Intelligent Design is no less scientific and no less important because it points outside science for validation.

---

16 *Teaching about Evolution and the Nature of Science.* National Academy Press, Chapter 5, "Frequently Asked Questions About Evolution and Science;" Religious Issues section. **http://search.nap.edu/readingroom/books/evolution98evol5.html**

U.S. and State governments

The U.S. Government does not deny the existence of a Creator. Nor do state governments or other governments of the free world. It is true that the U.S. Supreme Court has ruled that creation of the universe by "God" cannot be taught in public schools, at the expense of taxpayers. But this applies only in public schools, not in private schools and elsewhere. Legal challenges notwithstanding, the traditional view of the U.S. Government has long been reflected in the motto it stamps on our coins: "In God we trust."

And so, *in teaching that God exists, the Church is not in conflict with science or with the U.S. Government.* Regarding evolution, the Catholic Church does not deny the possibility that scientists may some day conclude, beyond reasonable doubt, that evolution (i.e. *macroevolution* as described below) played some part in how we came to be. To do so convincingly, however, they will have to overcome the formidable challenges to random macroevolution presented by scientists of the Intelligent Design Movement and others.

The position of the Church on the origin of life

In any event, as noted in the *Catechism of the Catholic Church,* 2nd Ed., par. 302, the teaching of the Church is clear, "God created the universe in a state of journeying ..." In 1996 Pope John Paul II reaffirmed the statement of Pius XII (*Humani Generis*) to the effect that, even if it is found that the human body takes its origin from pre-existent living matter, "the spiritual soul is immediately created by God."[17] In the *Catechism* the Church affirms that "every spiritual soul is created immediately by God ..." [CCC par. 366], and that "The account of the fall in Genesis 3 uses figurative language, but affirms a primeval event, a deed that took place *at the beginning of the history of man.*" [CCC par. 390].

Although he spoke of new knowledge regarding evolution, in his address to the Pontifical Academy of Sciences in 1996 Pope John Paul II described evolution as a theory. His remarks included the following: "A theory's validity depends on whether or not it can be verified; it is constantly tested against the facts; wherever it can no longer explain the latter, it shows its limitations and unsuitability. It must then be rethought."

In his inaugural Mass April 24, 2005, Pope Benedict XVI said, "We are not some casual and meaningless product of evolution. Each of us is the result of a thought of God. Each of us is willed, each of us

---

17 **www.catholic.net/RCC/Periodicals/Inside**

is loved, each of us is necessary."

Improbable probability

For my part, having read Behe's *Darwin's Black Box,* Wells' *Icons of Evolution* and various articles pro and con about ID, it seems that the central basis of disagreement between pro and anti-ID scientists is *degree of probability.*

ID scientists acknowledge that mere chance can account for "small steps," e.g., *microevolution,* as in a mutation resulting in a change in the outer coat of a virus. They maintain, however, that, beyond those first small steps, the odds against the observed increasing degrees of order and complexity increase *exponentially* – to a level far beyond what can be explained by mere chance, even over a period of tens of billions of years.

ID scientists have searched for solid answers in the writings of their pro-evolution peers in their respective specialties and, in their view, have found *no credible scientific explanation* for the astonishing degree of *order* seen everywhere in nature. Finding no such explanation, and seeking credible, objective truth, ID scientists in effect say, "Science is at a loss to explain how life, with its incredible variety and complexity, came to be. The explanation must therefore lie outside science; thus the positing of an *Intelligent Designer* or, one might say, an *Intelligent Orderer.*

ID scientists have made this suggestion knowing they would incur the enmity of many peers, would lose the opportunity for publication of their work in mainstream peer-reviewed scientific journals, would severely limit their chances to obtain research grants, and would limit their employability.

I wonder if Aryabhata, a fifth century scientist in India, faced similar difficulties when he rocked the Ptolemaic boat of astronomy – and probably those of philosophy and theology as well. He concluded that the earth was a rotating sphere in orbit around the sun and calculated the length of the solar year. In western history, at least, this heliocentric view was successfully resisted for eleven centuries until Copernicus published his studies in support of a sun-centered solar system. Let's hope it won't take that long to resolve the Intelligent Design versus designerless evolution question.[18]

---

18 *The Last Two Million Years*, 163.

A double standard of probability?

Suppose I arrive home one evening and am greeted with a resounding "Surprise!" by ten friends who, on that particular day, at that time and place, and with all the varied food, gifts and other ingredients necessary for a great party, came together to celebrate my birthday. Suppose I say to the group *"What a wonderful coincidence; that all this could happen without any planning or coordination!"* Would my friends, wide-eyed, share in my amazement? Or would they say, "Yeah, right!" and joke about my sanity?

And yet if, in the halls of academia, I make precisely the same remark about *the entire universe including every living thing in it,* am I not likely to receive nods of approval? Should we not ask, "What's wrong with this picture?"

Could it be that we have developed a double standard for the bar of probability? Do we set it impossibly high when we fear that our *Creator* might be trying to get our attention ("When I look at thy heavens, the work of thy fingers ..." comes to mind; Ps 8:3), but realistically low for all else? In light of *Probability 101*, does this double standard reflect intellectual honesty on our part? Does it give evidence of what we might call intellectual integrity, i.e., a "oneness;" an ordered, unbiased process of thought?

Surely this question of skewed probability – this "bias of the bar" – must be addressed not only in physics but in every field of knowledge. It would seem particularly relevant today in biology, where the concept of Irreducible Complexity is generating much heated debate.

The Intelligent Design movement

An important Web page of the Intelligent Design Movement is that of the Access Research Network.[19] At this writing this web page includes an article by Stephen Goode titled "Scientists Find Evidence of God."[20] In his article Goode introduces us to a number of ID scientists and gives an overview of the basis on which they believe it is probable that we owe our existence to an Intelligent Designer rather than to blind chance.

Conclusions based on physics

Until the latter part of the twentieth century, there were many scientific questions regarding the origin of the universe that could not be answered with any degree of certainty due to the limitations of

---

19 **www.arn.org**
20 **www.arn.org/docs/insight499.htm**

technology. Now, thanks to a mountain of evidence that has been accumulated using highly sophisticated measuring equipment and specialized techniques, *there is compelling scientific evidence that seems to rule out all explanations but the one that is beyond the realm of science: That an all-powerful "Intelligent Designer" created the universe.*

That is the clear, well-documented conclusion of astrophysicist Hugh Ross, Ph.D. Ross, author of *Fingerprint of God* and four other books to date, and founder of the "Reasons to Believe" Christian ministry:[21]

In *The Fingerprint of God*, Ross refers to the large number of "coincidences" (93 at this writing), which indicate that the universe seems to have been precisely designed to support life. In *Fingerprint of God* Ross examines such careful design in regard to various parameters (e.g., the strong nuclear force coupling constant, the ratio of electron to proton mass, the velocity of light, essential "coincidences" in regard to beryllium-8, carbon-12 and oxygen-16 nuclear energy levels,). If these relationships / characteristics were even slightly different, life would not be possible. See Ross' "coincidences" in his on-line article updated in August, 2006, "Fine-Tuning for Life in the Universe."[22]

Not long ago, I related to a physicist my belief that the astonishing degree of order in the universe (e.g., Ross' "coincidences") constitutes a high probability that we owe our existence to an Intelligent Designer. He politely disagreed, saying that if there were not such order life could not exist.

It later occurred to me that, by the same reasoning, I could argue that the 747 carrying me over the Atlantic just came together as a result of a great tornado that hit the parts warehouse at Boeing. Obviously, such an argument sidesteps the essential step of considering the im-probability of so many precisely ordered parts, each randomly but precisely crafted to fit only into its proper place, all by sheer happen-stance brought together in the same warehouse at the same time and all slammed together by that fierce but fortuitous wind, which somehow must assess which variant of jet fuel the engines require, make that fuel

---

21 **www.reasons.org/about/index.shtml?main.** Unlike most ID scientists, Ross has made use of the many indications of Intelligent Design in founding a Christian ministry: "Reasons to Believe."
22 **www.reasons.org/resources/apologetics/design_evidences/200608_fine_tuning_for_life_in_the_universe.shtml**

and fill all tanks without spilling much.

The "Primeval Atom" – a matter of faith?

In 1927 Catholic priest, physicist and astronomer Georges Lemaitre proposed that the universe began as a *primeval atom*. Various branches of science have since confirmed that our vast and astonishingly *ordered* universe - and ultimately all life – began with such an infinitesimal *atom* of unknown origin.

No scientist has explained to the satisfaction of peers the precise nature of this unique *atom,* (now called *gravitational singularity*), and how it came into existence. Although virtually all scientists and the general public believe that it existed and was the point of origin of the universe and our physical existence, it remains ultimately incomprehensible.

Believing without comprehending means, simply, having faith. If by faith we believe in that *atom* as the source of the Big Bang, is it not consistent with that faith to believe that both *atom* and Big Bang were generated by a *Creator-Orderer* with power and intelligence at least up to those awesome tasks?

Quantum physicists and other scientists have proposed a number of many-universe or *multiverse* theories ranging from the Many-Worlds interpretation of Hugh Everett to the 11-dimension String Theory of Michio Kaku. However, given the constraints of randomness and probability, can one posit the existence of multiple, unseen, exquisitely *ordered* material universes without acknowledging an equivalent strengthening of the case for an *Intelligent Orderer*?

No such theory credibly suggests that we can avoid physical death by stepping from this universe into another. Is it prudent, then, to reject the existence of an *Orderer,* especially since, according to Catholic doctrine, that *Orderer* will be, for each of us, our ultimate *Judge?*

Chaos theory – exquisite order within disorder

Until the 1960s, the evident disorder in such things as atmospheric and ocean currents, fluctuations in wildlife populations and, at times, in bodily organs such as the brain and heart, was seen by some as an argument against Intelligent Design.

In 1961, however, research meteorologist Edward Lorenz noticed an aberration in a simple weather forecasting model. Further investigation led to the discovery of astonishing *order* behind the chaos, not just in weather patterns but in many other fields. Many examples of that long-hidden order have since been discovered and graphically depicted: (a) The Koch Snowflake - an infinitely long line surrounding a finite area; (b) The Cantor Dust - an infinite number of points with a total length of zero; (c) The Menger Sponge - a latticed cube solid in appearance, but of infinite surface area and zero volume; (d) Strange Attractors; (e) Fractal Time; (f) The stunning beauty of Mandelbrot Sets, and much more. In his endorsement of James Gleick's best selling book, "*Chaos - Making a New Science,*" Douglas Hofstadter wrote:

> It turns out that an eerie type of chaos can lurk just behind a fa-çade of order - and yet, deep inside the chaos lurks an even eerier type of order.

Gleick's book, published in 1987, includes breathtaking photographs and drawings of this order behind apparent disorder. Examples can also be seen on a number of Web sites.

In discovering such exquisite order deep within apparent chaos, has science not found still another phenomenon that points to the intelligent design of the universe?

Quantum mechanics as the "Designer?" Don't bet on it

I had a conversation with a geologist who attributed his agnosticism in part to *quantum tunneling*. This is the phenomenon by which a subatomic particle can sometimes pass through an energy barrier intact, without disturbing the barrier, even though the particle has insufficient energy to do so. He referred to this as the *ball through the wall* phenomenon.

If mere chance can result in such "tunneling" of a particle through a barrier, he reasoned, then the universe as we know it just might be the result of a series of highly unlikely occurrences. As in the above case, it seems to me, this view ignores all we know about *probability* – and order of magnitude.

In fact, physicists acknowledge that it is rare for something even as big as an atom to "tunnel," as explained by researcher James P Sethna.[23]

For a concise refutation of Quantum Mechanics processes as alternatives to Intelligent Design, I suggest "*Quantum Mechanics, a Modern Goliath,*" by Hugh Ross:[24]

Ross' arguments are presented under these five headings: 1. "Quantum Tunneling." 2. "Infinite Chances." 3. "No Singularity." 4. "Man as Creator." 5. "Universe becoming God."

---

23 **www.lassp.cornell.edu/sethna/KinkTunneling/KinkTunneling.html**
24 **www.origins.org/articles/ross_modgoliath.html**

In keeping with Ross' conclusions, I think we can safely make this statement: On the day we see a home run ball pass through the wall without disturbing it at Yankee Stadium we should look skyward – that improbable 747 just might be flying over.

Conclusions based on biochemistry

Michael J. Behe, Ph.D., is an Associate Professor of Biochemistry at Lehigh University in Bethlehem, Pennsylvania. In his book *Darwin's Black Box"* published in 1996, he explains that in the last four decades biochemists have uncovered the secrets of the cell, something about which Darwin [1809-1882] had no knowledge.

Behe acknowledges that on a small scale – microevolution – Darwin's theory "has triumphed." He gives as an example the micro-evolution evident in the mutation of the coat of a virus such as AIDS.

[Note: Five years after publication of Behe's book, author Brad Harrub reported that research casts doubt on the long-accepted *mutation* of RNA viruses in response to drugs. In the year 2000, in a study of 85 sets of proteins at the Pasteur Institute in France, researchers concluded that – *instead of mutating ("evolving"), drug-susceptible viruses die. Other preexisting drug-resistant viruses then emerge* due to *a random, non-evolutionary, genetic drift process.*[25]]

Behe insists, however, that Darwin's theory is inadequate to explain "large jumps" – macroevolution – and that such "unbridgeable chasms occur even at the tiniest level of life."[26]

In his concluding comments Behe notes that, instead of the relative simplicity that was expected within the cell, biochemists have found systems of *irreducible complexity* which Darwinian Theory cannot account for. He adds: "we are left with no substantive defense against what feels to be a strange conclusion: that life was designed by an intelligent agent."[27]

Behe, a Catholic, does not take issue with the "common ancestor" claim of the evolutionists nor the support it may derive from what may be considered transitional forms. Nor does he deny the Catholic teaching that "the universe is in a state of journeying." He points out, however, that *fossils cannot serve as a basis for belief in Darwinian evolution.* Why? *Because we cannot tell by looking at fossilized animals what it was that changed the shape of their bones or reposi-*

---

25 "Are Viruses Really 'Evolving'"?
www.creationequation.com/archives/AreVirusesReallyEvolving.htm
26 *Darwin's Black Box,* 15.
27 Ibid., 252.

tioned their organs.[28]

In proposing the existence of an "intelligent designer," Behe places himself at odds with the NAS and its view that science can say nothing about the supernatural.

His "irreducible complexity" view has drawn criticism from colleagues and others. He continues to maintain, however, *that no one has been able to explain at the molecular level how the many irreducibly complex systems essential to life can be explained other than by Intelligent Design.*

The Irreducibly complex blood coagulation cascade

In "Rube Goldberg in the Blood," Chapter 4 of *Darwin's Black Box*, Behe focuses on just one of the many bodily systems of irreducible complexity – the astonishingly complex blood coagulation cascade system. Behe quotes at length from an article by Russell Doolittle, Ph.D., a professor of biochemistry and recognized authority on the subject, "The Evolution of Vertebrate Blood Coagulation; A case of Yin and Yang" that appeared in *Thrombosis and Haemostasis*, 70, 24-28 (1993). Behe begins his critique of Doolittle's article as follows,

> The first thing to notice is that no causative factors are cited. Thus tissue factor "appears," fibrinogen "is born," antiplasmin "arises," TPA "springs forth," a cross-linking protein "is unleashed," and so forth. What exactly, we might ask, is causing all this springing and unleashing?

Behe brings this 23-page chapter to a close with the statement, "The fact is, no one on earth has the vaguest idea how the coagulation cascade came to be."

Behe refutes arguments that evolution can explain the blood coagulation cascade

Professor Doolittle responded to Behe's challenge in 1997. What is surprising, however, is the apparent ease with which Behe was able to refute Doolittle's challenge and others. He did so in July, 2000 in "In Defense of the Irreducibility of the Blood Clotting Cascade: Response to Russell Doolittle, Ken Miller and Keith Robison." This 9-page article, including Behe's equally direct refutation of challenges by Miller and Robison, can be read at the Web site of the Access Research Network.[29] Behe summarized his response to professor Doolittle as

---

28 *National Review,* October 14, 1996, v. 48, n. 19, 83.
29 **www.arn.org/docs/behe/mb_indefenseofbloodclottingcascade.htm**

follows:

> Professor Doolittle argued that new laboratory work showed two components of the blood clotting cascade [plasminogen and fibrinogen] could be eliminated ("knocked-out") from mice and the mice got along fine without them. ***However, Doolittle misread the laboratory work: the double knock-out mice have severe problems and have no functioning blood clotting system. They are not models of evolutionary intermediates.*** Although anyone can misread a paper, in my opinion the fact that an expert cited a recent and contradictory journal article, instead of a publication directly addressing the evolution of blood clotting, shows that ***there are indeed no detailed explanations for the evolution of blood clotting in the literature and that, despite Darwinian protestations, the irreducible complexity of the system is a significant problem for Darwinism*** (emphasis added).

Behe's opponents continue to challenge him, of course, and he continues to hold his ground. In a strongly worded Discovery Institute posting dated February 18, 2004 Behe offers another refutation. The article he posted was "Irreducible Complexity is an Obstacle to Darwinism Even if Parts of a System Have Other Functions: A response to Sharon Begley's *Wall Street Journal Column* [of February 13, 2004]." Since WSJ Science writer Begley relied heavily on the views of Kenneth Miller, Professor of Biology at Brown University, it is Miller whom Behe directly refutes. In Chapter 2 of *Darwin's Black Box*, Behe used a mousetrap to introduce the concept of an irreducibly complex system. In Chapter 3 he describes the bacterial flagellum, an acid-driven rotary motor of staggering complexity; an irreducibly complex system for which "Darwinian Theory has given no explanation," according to Behe. The *e-coli flagellum*, for example, has a reversible engine with rotors, bearings, stators, a drive shaft, U-joint and a long whip-like filament (propeller) that rotates at up to 100,000 rpm. Microbiologist Scott Minnich notes that it is enormously complex, with about 50 genes each as complex as a sentence with hundreds of letters. Minnich noted that *all* these genes are required for this organism to swim. Intermediate steps are non-existent, observed Minich, and therefore this system cannot be explained by Darwinian Theory.

Behe's central concern seems to be the "poison pill" with which Darwinists attempt to discredit any system of irreducible complexity; i.e., if the system can be put to any other use then it is, *ipso facto*, not irreducibly complex. And so Behe writes, "So, for example, Kenneth

Miller has seriously argued that a part of a mousetrap could be used as a paperweight, so not even a mousetrap is IC [Irreducibly Complex]." Of even greater concern to Behe is that Miller applies this specious reasoning to the flagellum:

> Miller's argument is that since a subset of the proteins of the flagellum can have a function of their own, then the flagellum is not IC and Darwinian evolution could produce it. That's it! He doesn't show how natural selection could do so; he doesn't cite experiments showing that such a thing is possible; he doesn't give a theoretical model. He just points to the greater-than-expected complexity of the flagellum (which Darwinists did not predict or expect) and declares that Darwinian processes could produce it. This is clearly not a fellow who wants to look into the topic too closely.

Is resistance to Intelligent Design by the evolutionist establishment likely to end anytime soon? Apparently not, according to Behe: "I have pointed all this out to Ken Miller on several occasions, most recently at a debate in 2002 at the American Museum of Natural History. But he has not modified his story at all."

Miller may not accept Behe's arguments for irreducible complexity. However, according to Catholic writer Steve Weatherbe, Miller – a Catholic – *does* believe in the existence of God:

> What worries Miller about intelligent design and creationism is that they are playing into the hands of those who contend that evolution invalidates the case for God. Miller has argued to the contrary in his book *Finding Darwin's God.* After its publication he received many e-mails from people who 'thanked me for helping restore their faith.' They had been taught as children that Christianity and evolution were inconsistent, so when they became convinced of the truth of evolution, they had reluctantly abandoned their faith.[30]

Author of "The Language of God" (DNA) *attempts to cast doubt on Intelligent Design*

Francis S. Collins, medical geneticist and longtime head of the Human Genome Project, is the author of *The Language of God; A Scientist Presents Evidence for Belief.* Describing the 3 billion base-pair human genome "book," Collins writes: "This book was written in the DNA language by which God spoke life into being" (p. 123).

---

30 "Creationists Hijack Intelligent Design," *Steve Weatherbe, National Catholic Register,* October 6, 2006. **http://ncregister.com/articulo.php?artkod=MTk1**

To the chagrin of many non-Catholic Christians who interpret literally the creation account in Genesis, Collins presents strong evidence challenging that position. For example, based on recent genome data, he writes, "[T]he conclusion of a common ancestor for humans and mice is virtually inescapable" and "humans and chimps are 96% identical at the DNA level" (pp. 136-137).[31]

Collins, a Christian, attempts to resolve the creation v. evolution debate by proposing instead a "Bios through Logos" or "BioLogos" view; i.e., "Life through the Word." He relates this to John 1:1: "In the beginning was the Word, and the Word was with God, and the Word was God." Collins summarizes his belief as follows:

> God, who is not limited in space or time, created the universe and established natural laws that govern it. Seeking to populate the otherwise sterile universe with living creatures, God chose the elegant mechanism of evolution to create microbes, plants and animals of all sorts. Most remarkably, God intentionally chose the same mechanism to give rise to special creatures who would have intelligence, a knowledge of right and wrong, free will and a desire to seek fellowship with Him (pp. 200-201).

These words of Collins are consistent with those of Cardinal Christoph Schönborn:

> [I]t is his Word, Christ, the Logos, through whom and toward whom everything has been created; and that his Spirit ... who is love, is moving in all created things and gives them meaning and purpose. Logos and agape, reason and love, are the material from which the world was made, of which it consists, and with which it is being perfected. It is well worth living in this conviction — and dying in it. For what kind of an evolution would it be if resurrection and eternal life were not its ultimate goal? [32]

---

31 If the great superiority of human cognition seems difficult to account for based on *comparative genomics*, perhaps *comparative proteomics* will one day provide answers. *Wikipedia* indicates that the *proteome* is, in a sense, the protein equivalent of the genome. However, because a single gene can encode a variety of proteins, *Science Magazine* estimated that a proteome is more complex than the genome by an order of magnitude. (Science, Vol. 291, Issue 5507, 1221-1224, 16 February 2001). The great complexity of the human genome prompted Francis S. Collins to see in it the *Language of God*, rather than a marvelous series of accidents. When the vastly more complex *human proteome* is one day mapped, should it not draw scientists in great numbers to the same conclusion?

32 *Chance or Purpose?: Creation, Evolution and a Rational Faith*, p. 175

To the surprise of proponents of Intelligent Design, however, Collins writes that "it now seems likely that many examples of irreducible complexity are not irreducible after all" and that "ID proponents have made the mistake of confusing the unknown with the unknowable" (p. 188). Collins then offers his thoughts of how the human blood clotting cascade, the eye and the bacterial flagellum – all presented by Michael Behe in *Darwin's Black Box* as irreducibly complex – could have evolved according to Darwinian Theory:

Blood Clotting: The human blood clotting cascade may someday be explained based on duplication of ancient genes which "gradually evolved to take on a new function driven by the force of natural selection." Collins admits that science cannot outline those evolutionary steps and "may never be able to do so" (p. 189).

The Eye: Flatworms have a rudimentary pigmented pit. The chambered nautilus has a pigmented spot within a cavity with a light-admitting pinhole. In higher organisms a jelly-like substance is added, enabling focusing. Such a progression could well have "evolved into the modern mammalian eye ..." (p. 190-191).

Bacterial Flagellum: Several components of this acid-driven "outboard motor" have been found to be related to a mechanism by which particular bacteria inject toxins into their bacterial prey. Darwinian Theory holds that this survival advantage would promote the continued existence of these components. Collins suggests that such elements were duplicated hundreds of millions of years ago and then recruited for a new use. By combining them with other proteins that had previously been carrying out simpler functions, the entire motor was ultimately generated. Collins adds, "[W]e are far from filling in the whole picture (if we ever can)" [parenthesis in the original] (p. 192).

In addressing Collins' objections to I.D., as a non-scientist I cannot speak for Michael Behe and other ID. scientists who will surely respond to these challenges.

It seems to me, however, that Collins' challenges to ID fall far short of Behe's standard for *causality,* as noted above in his refutation of Russell Doolittle's claim that the blood coagulation cascade evolved. Reading Collins' critique of the three ID examples above, Behe might well write:

What exactly, we might ask, is *causing,* (a) this 'evolving to take on a new function,' (b) this 'pinhole to admit light,' (c) this 'subtle change in the geometry of the surrounding tissue,' (d) this 'addition of a jellylike substance,' (e) this evolving of a 'light-sensing retina and light-focusing lens,' (f) this 'recruiting [of elements] for a new use,' and (g) this 'generation' of 'the entire motor'?

In fairness to Collins, he may have more specific arguments than those he provides in *The Language of God,* a book he clearly intended for general readership rather than only for those skilled in the biological sciences.

Curiously, under the section on the "blood clotting cascade" (pp. 189-190), Collins cites only one reference; a book in support of his argument against Behe's blood coagulation example of ID: *Finding Darwin's God,* by Kenneth Miller, published in 1999.

Apparently Collins was unaware of two subsequent articles by Behe refuting the anti-ID opinions of Kenneth Miller (and others) noted above under the heading *"Behe refutes arguments that evolution can explain the blood coagulation cascade"*:

- "In Defense of the Irreducibility of the Blood Clotting Cascade: Response to Russell Doolittle, Ken Miller and Keith Robison." July, 2000 (a 9-page refutation); and
- "Irreducible Complexity is an Obstacle to Darwinism Even if Parts of a System Have Other Functions: A response to Sharon Begley's *Wall Street Journal Column* [of February 13, 2004]." Since WSJ Science writer Begley relied heavily on the views of Kenneth Miller, it is Miller whom Behe directly refutes.

It is unfortunate that *The Language of God* – which promotes belief in God based on the human genome and the "big bang" – presents negative views about Intelligent Design with no mention of detailed scientific rebuttals that support ID. Hopefully the above references will help readers evaluate the matter objectively.

Other challenges to Behe's "Irreducible Complexity"

It is no surprise that since publication of *Darwin's Black Box* in 1996 Behe's views on Intelligent Design have been challenged by a number of other scientists, including those considered experts in their specialized fields of biology.

Readers with some understanding of biology may wish to view the Web site "Behe's Empty Box,"[33] a listing of linked articles that, in most cases, attempt to refute Behe's claim that evolution cannot explain systems of irreducible complexity.

It appears, however, that Behe refutes most if not all of his critics in

---

33 www.world-of-dawkins.com/Catalano/box/behe.htm#reviews

articles found on the Intelligent Design Web site.[34]

Here we find, at this writing, eleven of Behe's answers to critics on such topics as "Self-organization and irreducibly complex systems," Philosophical objections, a [flawed] attempt to show an example of a naturally occurring irreducibly complex system, and a defense of the irreducibility of the blood-clotting cascade as noted above. Additional articles by Behe are found on the Web site of the Discovery Institute.[35]

For example, in the article "Michael Ruse is just confused," dated July 1, 2002, Behe appears to soundly refute Ruse's claim that the blood clotting cascade is *not* irreducibly complex and, in this article at least, Behe does so in language the average high school graduate can understand.

As this book is prepared for publication, increased assertiveness by Intelligent Design scientists is evident on the Internet despite intense opposition from their anti-ID counterparts, especially in the field of biochemistry. In an interview by Mark Ryland of the Discovery Institute published in the September 29, 2004 issue of *Our Sunday Visitor,* Behe had this to say:

> But we can readily imagine, say, transitional forms between species, and literally draw a series of paintings in which one form morphs into another. At the micro level, however, we not only find deep discontinuity, but in addition our imaginations run up against hard facts …. To get from one useful protein fold to another requires crossing a huge distance of amino acid sequence space, and in between there are no known folds that can be fixed by natural selection.

The theory of *punctuated equilibrium* attempts to explain the phenomenon that, after many millions of years without significant genetic change, new species appeared over a very short span of geologic time, as observed in the "Cambrian Explosion." Niles Eldredge and Stephen Jay Gould introduced the theory in 1972.[36]

The Cambrian period has long confounded scientists who promote evolution. Even the late paleontologist Stephen Jay Gould, an ardent proponent of evolution, is quoted as describing that period as, "the enigma of paleontological enigmas."[37] Increasingly compelling argu-

---

34 **www.arn.org/behe/mb_response.htm**
35 **www.discovery.org/crsc/fellows/MichaelBehe** > Articles by M. J. Behe.
36 "Punctuated equilibria: an alternative to phyletic gradualism." in *Models in Paleobiology,* 1972. T.J.M. Schopf (ed.). San Francisco: Freeman, Cooper, 82-115.
37 *What Darwin Didn't Know*, Geoffrey Simmons, M.D.

ments for Intelligent Design from various fields of science – in particular, systems of irreducible complexity – further erode any argument for pure evolution.

In a peer-reviewed article published August 4, 2004 Dr. Stephen C. Myer concluded that *"no current materialistic theory of evolution can account for the origin of the information necessary to build novel animal forms* [e.g., the Cambrian explosion]*. He proposes Intelligent Design as an alternative explanation for the origin of biological information and the higher taxa."* The article, "The Origin of Biological Information and the Higher Taxonomic Categories," appeared in the *Proceedings of the Biological Society of Washington* (volume 117, no. 2, pp. 213-239). The *Proceedings* is a peer-reviewed biology journal published at the National Museum of Natural History at the Smithsonian Institution in Washington, D.C. The article is posted on The Discovery Institute Website, from which the above quotation is taken.[38]

Calvin & Hobbes; Calvin "flies" – in a cardboard box

In his book *Icons of Evolution,* published in 2000, molecular / cell biologist Jonathan Wells, Ph.D., shakes the foundations of macroevolution theory.[39]

Wells holds a Ph.D. in cell and developmental biology from the University of California, Berkley. He also holds a doctorate in theology from Yale, where he wrote his Ph.D. dissertation on the nineteenth century Darwinian controversies. Wells notes that it was then that he learned that "the historical conflict between Christian theology and Darwinian evolution had almost nothing to do with biblical chronology, but turned primarily on the issue of design."

In explaining his views to the Evolutionary Biology Virtual Discussion Group in 1994, Wells took issue with the conclusions of an article published by two colleagues which suggested a model by which the eye may have evolved.

In refuting their conclusions, Wells noted that their model "not only ignores known mechanisms of morphogenesis, but also takes an overly simplistic view of the inheritance of morphological features."

Wells added that the above article reminded him of the comic strip *Calvin and Hobbes* in which Calvin "flies" using only a cardboard box: Holding the box, suppose Calvin begins by hopping at five second intervals. His first hop takes him an inch high. Then, "If every increase in altitude has adaptive value (say, by protecting Calvin from ants, then

---

38 **www.discovery.org**
39 **www.iconsofevolution.com**

dogs, then wild elephants, and eventually predatory birds), we need only to assume a mechanism for keeping him in the air, and in less than two days Calvin will be flying higher than Mount Everest! Of course, this is absurd. But [the model in question for evolution of the eye] is less absurd only because it does not violate something as obvious to us as the law of gravity. It does, however, wave aside our knowledge of vertebrate eye development and our ignorance of morphological inheritance, and replaces them with imagination."[40]

Wells summarizes Icons *of Evolution* convincingly in his ten "Warning Labels" for textbook owners (regarding flawed teaching about four-winged fruit flies, *archaeopteryx*, the Miller-Urey experiment, etc.). Wells also refutes *exaptation,* the adapting of something for a use other than that for which it apparently evolved.

As with other Intelligent Design scientists, Wells has his critics. Readers with some understanding of biology may wish to read and evaluate a collection of articles refuting Wells' criticism of the ten "Icons of Evolution."[41] Readers may then view Wells' "Responses to Critics" on the Intelligent Design Web site.[42]

Scientists who still dismiss challenges to macroevolution as non-science (or *non-sense)* may wish to test their mettle against the wide-ranging arguments for Intelligent Design by these and other *scientists* (not theologians) at the *Creation-Evolution News* Web site.[43]

Can the hand of a marble statue wave?

"It [The Intelligent Design Movement] may well be the most important intellectual movement to occur in the last 200 years, if not the last half-millennium." So wrote Benjamin D. Wiker in his informative two-part article "Does Science Point to God?" (*Crisis*, April 7, 2003; July 9, 2003).

Richard Dawkins, author of *The Blind Watchmaker: Why the Evidence of Evolution Reveals a Universe Without Design* (1986), is one of the foremost opponents of Intelligent Design. In "Does Science Point to God?" Wiker has this to say about Dawkins' understanding of probability: "Dawkins believes that anything can be explained by chance, even a miracle."

Wiker then quotes from *The Blind Watchmaker* (pp. 159-160)

---

40 **http://ist-socrates.berkeley.edu:7521/projects/IB160/VDG/Fall94 Wells/Wells.html**
41 **www.nmsr.org/text.htm#preface**
42 **www.arn.org/wells/jwhome.htm**
43 **www.creationsafaris.com/crevnews.htm**

Dawkins' claim that ***the hand of a marble statue could actually wave,*** if all the molecules of the marble hand were to simultaneously move in one direction and then in the opposite direction. Dawkins acknowledges that the odds against this far exceed what we can imagine, but insists on the *possibility* that in this way a marble statue could "wave."

Dawkins may be on to something. Perhaps in a back issue of *Le Monde* we will find the headline, "Venus de Milo loses arms waving to tourists." Or maybe not. Wiker's two-part article may be read on the *Crisis* Web site.[44, 45]

Benjamin D. Wiker is a senior fellow at the Discovery Institute and the author of *Moral Darwinism: How We Became Hedonists*. He is a lecturer in theology and science at Franciscan University of Steubenville.

In a recent debate on the Ryan Tubridy Show, *Irish Independent* columnist David Quinn challenged Dawkins, whose most recent book is *The God Delusion*, to refute Aquinas' argument that without an uncaused first cause [God], matter could not exist. Dawkins' answer is thought-provoking on several levels: "But if science can't answer that question, then it's sure as hell theology can't either."[46]

Time magazine's designation of Dawkins as an "atheist" in its November 13, 2006 issue seems inaccurate in light of his closing comment in a *Time*-sponsored debate with Francis Collins, author of *The Language of God* [DNA]. *Time* correspondent David Van Biema quotes Dawkins as follows: "*If there is a God, its going to be a whole lot bigger and a whole lot more incomprehensible than anything that any theologian of any religion has ever proposed.*" In that thought, how far is Dawkins from "*Eye has not seen, nor ear heard, nor has it entered into the heart of man, what things God has prepared for those who love him*"?[47]

Lee M. Spetner, author of *Not by Chance; Shattering the Modern Theory of Evolution* (© 1998), earned a Ph.D. in physics from M.I.T. in 1950 and from 1951 to 1970 was a member of the staff of the Applied Physics Laboratory of Johns Hopkins University.

In "The Watchmaker's Blindness," Chapter 6 of his book, Spetner notes that Dawkins is not alone in failing to make a convincing case for

---

44 www.crisismagazine.com/april2003/feature1.htm
45 www.crisismagazine.com/julaug2003/feature1.htm
46 http://catholiceducation.org/articles/science/sc0086.htm
47 1 Cor 2: 9, *The Holy Bible*, New American Catholic Edition, © 1950, Benziger Brothers.

the spontaneous origin of life – many research scientists failed as well, he observed, though they have worked on the problem for the past generation (p. 166).

Unprecedented rapid development of genes of the human brain

In 2004 scientists made a discovery that may well rival the Cambrian explosion for the title of "enigma of enigmas." Bruce T. Lahn, Ph.D., is an assistant professor of human genetics at the University of Chicago and an investigator at the Howard Hughes Medical Institute. On December 28, 2004, a University of Chicago news release included the following statements made by Lahn:

> For brain-related genes, the amount of evolution in the lineage leading to humans is far greater than the other species we have examined [macaque monkeys, rats and mice] …. Humans evolved their cognitive abilities not due to a few accidental mutations, but rather, from an enormous number of mutations acquired though exceptionally intense selection favoring more complex cognitive abilities …. To accomplish so much in so little evolutionary time – a few tens of millions of years – requires a selective process that is perhaps categorically different from the typical processes of acquiring new biological traits …. The making of the large human brain is not just the neurological equivalent of making a large antler. Rather, it required a level of selection that's unprecedented …. Our study offers the first genetic evidence that humans occupy a unique position in the tree of life. Simply put, evolution has been working very hard to produce us humans.[48]

Such a report would seem to prompt even the most adamant opponents of Intelligent Design to "think outside the box," i.e., to consider explanations that may lie beyond the limits of evolution theory.

Normally mutations are *detrimental*, often severely so. How then could "an enormous number of mutations" result in phenomenal *improvement* in human cognition? And why only humans and not macaques, rats and mice? And how can evolution theory credibly explain Lahn's observation that human cognitive abilities are "not due to a few accidental mutations [but the result of] an enormous number of

---

48 Press release: **www.uchospitals.edu/news/2004/20041229-brain-evolution.html**
Article: "Accelerated Evolution of Nervous System Genes in the Origin of Homo Sapiens" by Bruce T. Lahn, Ph.D., et. al., published in the Journal *Cell*, December 29, 2004, 1027-1040; **www.cell.com/content/issue?volume=119&issue=7**

mutations acquired though exceptionally intense selection ...."? And what are the implications of Lahn's conclusion that this phenomenon "requires a selective process that is perhaps categorically different from the typical processes of acquiring new biological traits ...."? Could such extraordinary *selection* – surely inexplicable in terms of blind chance – be the work of an extraordinary *selector*?

This last question, obvious though it may be, cannot be safely addressed in a public school classroom in the U.S.A. today. To do so would place the teacher at risk for violating the rule of "separation of church and state." Elsewhere, however, Lahn's report will prompt many further questions, such as: "Is this extraordinary selection not a strong indication of extraordinary design, and therefore of an extraordinary *designer*? The widely used college textbook *Biology*, states, "Vertebrates seem to have evolved largely by the addition of new instructions to the developmental program."[49] Can we have "instructions" and a "program" without an Instructor and Programmer? What capabilities or attributes would such an Instructor / Programmer need to bring about such awesome order as opposed to the chaotic disorder of blind chance? Does history yield evidence of such an Instructor / Programmer? What other disciplines might be explored for such information?"

In *Darwin's Black Box*, Behe does not attempt to link Christ to the "Intelligent Designer" of the universe. However, biblical and later well-attested miracles present a problem for those who reject the idea of the Intelligent Designer. Why? Consider, for example, Christ's raising of Lazarus *four days* after his death (Jn 11:1-54).

Every scientist knows that about *four minutes* after the heart stops brain cells begin to die. And one does not have to be a scientist to know that after four days of decomposition in a tomb the cells of the body are dead beyond any human ability to bring them back to life. As the Gospel says "There will be a stench!" For those who witnessed it, the raising of Lazarus was an astonishing event.

But biochemists today realize that, to raise Lazarus, Jesus had to bring about the reestablishment of every rotted cell of every bodily system and organ, including the brain. To do so required the *precise recomposition and reorientation* of all four types of nucleotide that make up DNA, the RNA polynucleotide chains, all cellular components

---

49 *Biology*, 7th ed., Peter H. Raven, George B. Johnson, Johnathan B. Losos, Susan R. Singer, 1095, © 1996 ... 2005, McGraw-Hill. Reproduced with permission of the McGraw Hill Companies.

such as plasma membrane, nuclei, mitochondria, endosomes, perox-isomes, lysomes, golgi apparatus and far, far more. If ever there was a manifestation of an *Intelligent Designer*, this was certainly it. And soon afterward the people of that day would see an even greater manifesta-tion – the resurrected, glorified Body of Christ himself which was capable not only of eating as we do (Lk 24:42-43), but of materializing and dematerializing at will (Jn 20:19).

Writing in about A.D. 56, less than 30 years after the Resurrection, St. Paul tells us the risen Jesus appeared to about 500 people "most of whom are still alive ..." (1 Cor 15:6). We know that such prodigies are far beyond the power of any mere man. How was it possible for Jesus to accomplish them?

At this point I know that some readers will roll their eyes saying "Here he goes, assuming he can impose his faith in Jesus on me." Not at all. I only ask that you bear with me, at least to the end of Step 3, and consider also the *history-based* case for Christ.

The answer to how Christ accomplished those prodigies is found in the many verses of Scripture in which Jesus identifies himself as *The Word*, in light of the following:

> In the beginning was the Word, and the Word was with God and the Word was God. He was in the beginning with God; *all things were made through him* ... (Jn 1:1-3).

Lazarus, then, can be seen as the *remaking* of just one of the "things made through him."

For many scientists and others, the rational mind prompts the rejection of such biblical miracles; how can they be more than myth or fable? Later in this book we will see that – even for those who have no Christian faith – the many thousands of pages of non-biblical *historical* affirmation of the Gospels, by many different authors, is compelling.

"But wait!" many raised Catholic will object. "Since Vatican II, we have been hearing in homilies and reading in many Catholic publica-tions that almost surely no eyewitness to Jesus was the author of any Gospel. Much that appears "miraculous" in the Gospels – e.g., the feeding of the multitudes, the walking on the water, maybe even the Resurrection of Jesus – may have simply been "loving embellishment" added decades later by unknown authors based on hearsay accounts of those who themselves never heard Jesus.

Unfortunately, such hedged homilies which blur the Gospels are not uncommon today. They can be attributed largely to the influence of modern historical-critical biblical scholarship which maintains that no eyewitness to Jesus authored a Gospel and all probably originated between about A.D. 67 and 100, thus allowing time for all four of them to be "lovingly embellished" with myth, legend and folklore.

However, before relegating the Gospels to the classic fiction shelf, consider the well-researched conclusions of Fr. Jean Carmignac, Claude Tresmontant and others noted in Step 3 who conclude that the Gospels originated quite soon after the Resurrection and are based on eyewitness accounts. In *The Birth of the Synoptic Gospels*, Fr. Carmignac lists more than forty other early date / eyewitness (about A.D. 45 to 67) Bible scholars.

Unlike most of their far more numerous late-date / no eyewitness peers, *these "early-date / eyewitness" scholars have "looked behind" the canonical Greek and,* as earlier noted, their studies strongly support: (a) early authorship of the Gospel of Matthew in Hebrew or Aramaic; (b) early authorship in Hebrew or Aramaic of the Gospel of Mark; (c) that the Greek of the Gospel of John is the Greek of translation from a Hebrew or Aramaic original and; (d) that the sources of the Gospel of Luke were written in Hebrew or Aramaic, or that the entire Gospel of Luke was translated from a Hebrew or Aramaic original except the introduction.

Papyrologist Carsten Thiede's study of an ancient papyrus fragment of the Gospel of Mark, found in Qumrân among the Dead Sea Scrolls, also proves challenging to any late-dating of the Gospels. He draws a similar conclusion from papyrus fragments of Matthew's Gospel. As we will see in Step 3, the thoroughness and historical importance of these studies prompted several important books, including *The Birth of the Synoptic Gospels*, by Fr. Jean Carmignac, *The Hebrew Christ*, by Claude Tresmontant; *Eyewitness to Jesus* by Carsten Thiede and *"The Gospels Were Written by Reporters,"* by Marie-Christine Ceruti-Cendrier. All but the last have been published in English.

Immediate, medically inexplicable cures

We should not be surprised to learn, then, that miracles – flashes of the power of the "Intelligent Designer" – did not end with the Resurrection of Christ. Many thousands have been associated with the saints through the ages and are so today. Of special interest is the bureau of physicians of various faiths that was established at Lourdes, France, some years after miracles began occurring there in 1858. These physicians examined all reported "miraculous" cures (At one point this commission included several thousand physician-members). To be deemed miraculous by this bureau, the healing had to be immediate, permanent and medically inexplicable. The physicians closely examined previous medical records, as well as the subsequent medical history. The criteria were so strict that only a few cases per year were categorized as miraculous.

And what scientific explanation can be given for more recent reports such as the following in which normal vision was suddenly experienced by a girl born bind, who, based on all medical evidence, *remained blind*? Fr. Armondo Dasseville, O.F.M. Cap, describes the event, which occurred in 1947:

> A little girl named Gemma di Giorgi lived in Sicily. She was born without pupils in her eyes on Christmas night in 1939. Competent doctors and specialists declared that nothing could be done about her blindness. But little Gemma's grandmother, a woman of great faith, took her to Padre Pio for help. Gemma went to Confession to this renowned friar and received from him her first Holy Communion. He touched and blessed each eye. From that day Gemma has been able to see clearly although she still had no pupils. ***Many eye specialists have since examined her eyes, but the fact remains that she is able to see perfectly without any pupils in her eyes***. I met her at the funeral of Padre Pio, more than 20 years after her cure [Bold italics added].⁵⁰

Then and now, intellectual integrity requires that such physician-authenticated miracles of healing must be dealt with by anyone who doubts the existence of an Intelligent Designer. Science makes no credible attempt to explain such events.

Note, however, that Gemma di Georgi's miracle was essentially different from most in that – *instead of a one-time miraculous correction of an abnormality – it was ongoing*. For her, it seemed that light somehow *continued* to penetrate the opaque scleral (white) tissue *only* where the pupils of varying diameter (as controlled by a normal iris) would be found, resulting in normal vision. (Whether or not miraculous restoration of sub-scleral corneas, lenses, retinas and other parts of both eyes occurred, I do not know).

Breathes there a "Someday science ..." atheist anywhere who will claim that, eventually, science will provide a credible natural explanation for the fact that Gemma di Giorgi, at age eight in 1947, began to

---

50 "St. Pio of Pietrelcina, 1887-1968," *The Wanderer*, June 6, 2002. **http://thewandererpress.com/b6-6-02.htm.** Popular atheists such as Richard Dawkins, Christopher Hitchens and Sam Harris make no serious attempt to explain such contemporary miracles which, of course, make atheism untenable.

see normally without pupils? As a parallel, we might imagine the absurdly improbable wave of the hand of Dawkins' statue occurring not just once, but continuously for 20 years.

It would seem that even proponents of the punctuated equilibrium theory of evolution might begin to ask themselves: "Is it possible that an all-powerful God could be the *Divine Punctuator?*

Will litigation and political correctness prohibit classroom discussion of scientific challenges to evolution?

As implied above, for many in academia today the mere mention of Intelligent Design causes a rise in blood pressure. The belief that evolutionary processes can fully explain the existence of human and other *life forms* (the word *creature* has fallen into disfavor; it implies a *Creator*) might as well be carved in stone.

To the dismay of many, however, new standards of science education that allowed *teaching the controversy* (i.e., science-based alternatives to evolution) were given final approval by the Ohio Board of Education on December 10, 2002. John G. West Jr. included the following remarks as guest columnist in the *National Review Online*, December 17, 2002:

> In Ohio critics of Darwinism were compared to the Taliban, and Ohioans were warned that the effort to allow students to learn about scientific criticisms of Darwin was part of a vast conspiracy to impose nothing less than a theocracy. Happily ... the Ohio Board of Education saw through such overheated rhetoric. So did 52 Ohio scientists (many on the faculties of Ohio universities) who publicly urged the Ohio Board to require students to learn about scientific criticisms of Darwin's theory.[51]

Dr. West is a Senior Fellow and Associate Director, Center for Science and Culture of the Seattle-based Discovery Institute and formerly the chair of the department of political science at Seattle Pacific University.

The new Ohio standards were prompted by a conference report submitted in connection with the Federal "No Child Left Behind Act of 2001." The Act was signed into law January 8, 2002

The new standards allowed, but did not require, scientific alternatives to evolution to be taught. Under the standards, however, students were required to "describe how scientists continue to investigate and critically analyze aspects of evolutionary theory." State tests were to be

---

51 **www.nationalreview.com/comment/comment-est121702.asp**

given to ensure students gain such knowledge.

In her story in the *National Review*, October 18, 2002, Pamela R. Winnick noted that the standard did not mention Intelligent Design. However, she quoted board member Mike Cochran who said that the language does "allow students to understand that there are dissenting views within the scientific community" regarding evolution.[52]

However, in February, 2006, the Ohio Board of Education voted to delete language in the science curriculum that encouraged students to investigate and critically analyze evolution theory.

It appears, however, that rather than being debated strictly on its scientific merits, the vote was influenced by the threat of litigation. As noted by reporter Ignazio Messina of the *Toledo Blade*, "In January, the board voted 9-8 to keep the language. The vote in February was a reversal of that – partially prompted by threats of litigation."[53]

And consider the plight of a science teacher in a public high school in Kansas in recent years. Suppose a student asked for instruction as follows:

> Teacher, this article quotes several scientists who claim that, in addition to evolution, students should be made aware of *purely scientific* challenges to evolution such as, (a) irreducibly complex organic systems, (b) the top-down pattern of the Cambrian explosion, (c) The sudden "explosion" in complexity of the human brain compared to other mammals and, (d) how mere chance could have produced our astonishingly complex DNA. Would you explain these challenges and how they might conflict with the claims made for evolution by natural selection in our textbook?

If such a question were asked in 1999, the science teacher could have presented all scientific viewpoints objectively, explaining that in 1999 Kansas mandated that *"no evidence or analysis of evidence that contradicts a current science theory should be censored."*

In 2001 however, if that teacher were to risk complete honesty with the class, he or she would explain that the 1999 mandate had been rescinded and reply along these lines: "The new requirement is that, rather than addressing scientific challenges to evolution, I *'should explain why the question is outside the domain of natural science.'"*

---

52 **www.nationalreview.com/comment/comment-winnick101802.asp**
53 "Intelligent design may resurface in Ohio talks - Group criticizes teaching plan under board's review." **www.toledoblade.com/apps/pbcs.dll/article?AID=/20060907/NEWS04/609070349/-1/NEWS**

In 2005, after 2004 elections again placed "evolution-only" members in the minority, the teacher could again answer with complete scientific objectivity. This was because of a new regulation that stated: *"To promote good science, good pedagogy and a curriculum that is secular, neutral and non-ideological, school districts are urged to follow the advice provided by the House and Senate Conferees in enacting the 'No Child Left Behind Act' of 2001."*

In August, 2006 however, elections again placed "evolution only" board members in the majority in Kansas. Anticipating that the teacher would again be placed under the censorship from which he / she was released in 1999 and 2005, Phyllis Schlafly wrote in August, 2006: *"The newly elected school board members immediately pledged to work swiftly to restore a science curriculum that does not subject evolution to criticism. They don't want students to learn 'the full range of scientific views' or that there is a 'controversy' about evolution."*[54]

This change was, in fact, made by the Kansas Board February 13, 2007, the day after Darwin Day, prompting the following statement from John G. West of the Discovery Institute: *"As was expected, earlier today the Kansas State Board of Education voted 6-4 to adopt dumbed-down science standards that delete any mention of scientific data that might be perceived as critical of Darwinian evolution."*[55]

Now that this censorship has again been imposed, the Kansas teacher might answer the above question as follows: *"In the public school classroom, our state has again banned all discussion of challenges to evolution, even those that are purely scientific. However, you all use the Internet. Need I say more?"*

On December 20, 2005, in *Tammy Kitzmiller, et al., v. Dover Area School District, et al.,* the United States District Court for the Middle District of Pennsylvania ruled that,

> In making this determination [that the Board's ID Policy violates the Establishment Clause and Lemon tests], we have addressed the seminal question of whether ID is science. We have concluded that it is not, and moreover that ID cannot uncouple itself from its creationist, and thus religious, antecedents …. [ID] is an untestable alternative hypothesis

---

54 "Criticism of Evolution Can't be Silenced."
www.eagleforum.org/column/2006/aug06/06-08-16.html
55 "Kansas Board of Education adopts dumbed-down curriculum standards on evolution and the history of science," John G. West, February 13, 2007,
www.evolutionnews.org/2007/02/kansas_board_of_education_adop.html

grounded in religion ...." Nor do we controvert that ID should continue to be studied, debated, and discussed .... [However] our conclusion today is that it is unconstitutional to teach ID as an alternative to evolution in a public school science classroom.[56]

This ruling is problematic for several reasons. Proponents of Intelligent Design do not claim that it is *science* as such (no more than the laws of thermodynamics are *science*), but insist that their claims are purely *scientific.* In *Darwin's Black Box,* for example, Behe's arguments for ID are purely scientific; there is no trace of any Creationist argumentation. Is it reasonable, then, to dismiss Behe's exclusively scientific arguments simply because Creationist authors have previously reached similar conclusions? If so, it would seem that all U.S. laws against murder could be challenged due to the religious antecedent prominently depicted on the south wall of the Courtroom of the U.S. Supreme Court – the Commandments, given to Moses by the Creator.

And suppose a pastor were to say to a chemist-parishioner, "John, I think it would be especially meaningful if you would combine hydrogen and oxygen to produce the water I will use to baptize your son." The chemist does so. The pastor blesses the water and baptizes the baby with it. Does the religious antecedent (and use) render the production of that water unscientific? Certainly, it does not.

In *How the Catholic Church Built Western Civilization,* author Thomas E. Woods, Jr., provides compelling evidence that it was in the Catholic Church that modern science was born; that Catholic priests developed the idea of free-market economics five hundred years before Adam Smith; that the university originated with the Catholic Church and that it was out of Church canon law that Western law grew. Obviously, these religious antecedents could never convince a court to prohibit public schools from teaching economics and the other sciences, to close all public universities, or to void all Western law. Clearly then, any objection to ID as pure science based on some religious antecedent is without merit.

Unfortunately, the *Kitzmiller / Dover* ruling is unlikely to be appealed because evolution-only school board members have replaced those who promoted suggesting that students be introduced to Intelligent Design concepts in addition to evolution.

At this writing, there is much activity nationwide in regard to the

56 **http://en.wikisource.org/wiki/Kitzmiller_v._Dover_Area_School_District/6: Curriculum%2C_Conclusion**

teaching of scientific alternatives to evolution. Perhaps the most comprehensive and up-to-date coverage of the topic can be found on the Web site of the National Center for Science Education.[57]

Most articles now posted on the NCSE Web site indicate a reluctance to allow classroom discussion of scientific challenges to evolution. I leave it to you, the reader, to discern in each instance if the decision seems based on rigorous, unbiased evaluation of scientific merit, or if it seems predominantly a concession to political correctness and fear of costly litigation.

Fingerprint evidence inconclusive? Don't ignore DNA

I have the impression that many who give no credence to scientific alternatives to evolution (Step 1) and hold fast to macroevolution consider themselves "off the hook"; i.e., free to ignore the arguments from history and archaeology in Steps 2 through 7 and the rest of this book. They are not. Why not? Let me suggest a courtroom parallel.

Suppose, on the witness stand in a criminal trial, the head of a forensics laboratory said: "*Our experts disagreed as to whether the fingerprint evidence was conclusive, so we didn't bother examining the DNA evidence.*"

Such an answer would astonish everyone in the courtroom. Obviously, DNA evidence is unrelated to fingerprint evidence. Each, independently of the other, can establish with high probability the presence of a suspect at the crime scene.

Similarly history, independently of science, can establish with high probability the existence of an *Intelligent Designer* to which we owe our existence.

Steps 2 through 7 suggest a history-based common-sense means of identifying that *Designer* and learning what he asks of us whom he has, directly or indirectly, "designed."

Somewhere along the way, we should not be surprised if the logic of the mind gives way to love in the heart for the one who is the object of our search.

The IDEA and ISCID organizations

The fierce suppression of scientific arguments for Intelligent Design in the classroom is leading students to seek this knowledge outside the classroom. One organization meeting this need is IDEA, the Intelligent Design and Evolution Awareness Center. Formed in 2001 in San Diego, IDEA chapters host discussions promoting Intelligent

---

57 **www.natcenscied.org/default.asp**

Design theory, friendly dialogue, and understanding of creation-evolution issues.

The majority of the approximately twenty-five IDEA chapters are on university campuses in the United States. Others are in Kenya, Canada, Ukraine, and The Philippines. A few are associated with high schools and with communities. The IDEA Web site is: **www.ideacenter.org**

The International Society for Complexity, Information, and Design, ISCID, is a professional research society that investigates the purely empirical scientific methods for detecting intelligent design. It was founded by William A. Dembski in 2001. ISCID fellows hold a wide variety of religious and metaphysical beliefs, but see scientific merit in Intelligent Design theory. The ISCID Web site is: **www.iscid.org**

Lee Strobel's, "The Case for a Creator"

In his book published in 2004, *The Case for a Creator: A Journalist Investigates Scientific Evidence That Points Toward God*, best-selling author Lee Strobel quotes a number of scientists who make a compelling case for Intelligent Design.

They cast doubt on evolutionary theory by bringing scientific, non-religious arguments to bear against such concepts as: (a) "prebiotic soup"; (b) Stephen Hawking's imaginary numbers argument; (c) the many universes hypothesis; (d) The oscillating universe hypothesis; (e) disteleology; (f) cladistics; (g) the Gaia hypothesis and; (h) quantum theory-based explanations.

Their arguments for Intelligent Design include: (a) irreducible complexity, (b) the top-down pattern of the Cambrian explosion; (c) the *kalam* cosmological argument; (d) the "Big Bang;" (e) the astonishing information content of DNA; (f) the cosmological constant; and (g) the circumstellar habitable zone.

In the concluding chapter of *The Case for a Creator*, Strobel notes the comment of nanoscientist James Tour of Rice University to the effect that only one who knows little about science could say that science diminishes his faith; those who really study science are drawn closer to God.[58]

Pascal's Wager

The pilgrims were in their third year in the new world in 1623, after the *Mayflower* brought them to the place they would call Plymouth, when Blaisé Pascal was born in France.

---

58 *The Case for a Creator*, 286.

Pascal proved to be a brilliant mathematician and physicist. He is well known for his contribution to hydraulics – Pascal's law of pressure. But Pascal was also a philosopher and a Christian. Not satisfied with applying pressure to fluids, he decided to apply a little pressure of a different kind to his friends who rejected the idea of an almighty God. He did so through what has come to be known as "Pascal's wager."

Pascal acknowledged that we mortals cannot know for certain whether there is a God. However – if I may simplify a bit – Pascal noted that either God exists or doesn't exist. And, he added, we can either live as we please (i.e., at times willfully and deliberately committing gravely sinful acts without repentance), or live to please God. If God exists and we live to please God we can anticipate a reward of eternal joy in heaven with God. Otherwise we can lose that reward. In tabular form it looks like this:

	God exists	**God does not exist**
I live as I please.	I will not go to heaven.	I will not go to heaven.
I live to please God.	I may well go to heaven for all eternity.	I will not go to heaven.

Pascal noted that there is far more at stake here than in a simple game of chance. He acknowledged that if I live to please God – but there is no God – I will die without having engaged in some forbidden pleasures or self-serving activities I might otherwise have enjoyed.

However, if I live to please God and God exists, I can expect indescribable happiness *for all eternity:* "But, as it is written, 'What no eye has seen, nor ear heard, nor the heart of man conceived, what God has prepared for those who love him,' God has revealed to us through the Spirit" (1 Cor 2:9-10).

As indicated thus far in Step 1, the order in the universe alone indicates an *extremely high probability* that we owe our existence to a Creator. In the context of history and comparative religion, subsequent steps will indicate which of the many founders of a religion best manifested the power and authority of the Creator and what the Creator requires of each of us to attain heaven.

Pascal points out that, even if we attribute a low probability to the existence of a Creator, how foolish we are if we do not make the small sacrifices involved in living to please God, in order to have the chance to enjoy *forever* a reward that far surpasses our wildest dreams.

It doesn't take a mind as brilliant as Pascal's to grasp the truth of what he said. For some it may help to see his reasoning in terms of money. Forego a few hundred dollars worth of sinful pleasure in this life on the chance that your sacrifice will be rewarded in the next with wealth untold in the form of joy and happiness *for all eternity*. Who wouldn't make such a bet?

With this in mind, and based on the many references to hell found in the New Testament (and here, for the moment, I beg the indulgence of our non-Christian readers), most readers will agree with the following refinement of the above table:

	God exists
I live as I please.	I may well go to hell for all eternity.
I live to please God.	I may well go to heaven for all eternity.

By eliminating the possibilities that God does not exist and that we may cease to exist (the Bible indicates that once created, we will never cease to exist) – *and adding the biblically-based possibility that we may suffer forever in hell*, do we not multiply many times the importance of living to please God?

"god is not Great" - The flawed reasoning of Christopher Hitchens

Applying a decision tree template to an author's writing can be quite revealing. Successive claims that reflect serious research into just one side of an issue do not serve an author well. In his best-selling book, *god is not Great: How Religion Poisons Everything,* author, literary critic and journalist Christopher Hitchens seems to exemplify this problem. His opinion of God is consistent with the lower-case *g* in *god* in the title of his book, while an upper-case *G* is used in *Great*.

Hitchens begins by declaring religion man-made (p. 10). He calls Augustine an "ignoramus" (p. 64), states that religion teaches people to be self-centered and conceited (p. 74), wrongly conflates purely science-based Intelligent Design with largely faith-based Creationism (p. 86), considers a rebuttal to any of the three monotheistic religions (Christianity, Judaism and Islam) a rebuttal to all three (p. 98) and claims that the authors of the Gospels agree on nothing of importance (p. 111). By mid-book Hitchens reaches a conclusion that, speculation aside, no responsible biblical scholar would even try to defend: The Gospels are certainly not literally true (p. 120). Even Pascal's wager is not spared criticism by Mr. Hitchens (p. 211).

As if Hitchens had not given his readers enough reason to question his reasoning and motivation, after stressing that Moses Maimonides (1135-1204) – esteemed by much of Judaism as a brilliant physician, scholar and codifier of the Talmud – vilified Jesus as a detestable Jewish heretic (p. 111), Hitchens questions the very *existence* of Jesus (p. 114).

Hitchens was rightly disturbed upon seeing the following sign as he entered an ashram in India: "Shoes and minds must be left at the gate" (p. 196). Let me assure Mr. Hitchens and all atheists and agnostics that – as I hope this book with its *Imprimatur* will attest – in Catholicism, minds (and shoes) are welcome.

Fundamentals of the Faith

Readers interested in the classical arguments for the existence of God will find the five set forth by St. Thomas Aquinas in his *Summa Theologica.* For a concise review of these arguments I recommend *Fundamentals of the Faith* by Peter Kreeft, Professor of Philosophy at Boston College. Kreeft offers a concise restatement of the argument from design (p. 24); the first-cause argument (p. 29); the argument from conscience (p. 36); the argument from history (p. 42); and Pascal's wager (p. 48). He also addresses the problem of evil, the four last things (death, judgment, heaven and hell; pp. 153-162), and much more.[59]

The Prayer of the Skeptic

It is one thing to use our minds to consider intellectually the reasons for belief in an Almighty Creator, but at some point we must move beyond the realm of the intellect to the realm of faith. Perhaps I should have placed the following prayer-related thoughts at the end of this book, but somehow they seem to belong here.

In 1864, in *Apologia Pro Vita Sua,* Ven. John Henry Newman refers to the following statement as classic: "O God, if there be a God, save my soul, if I have a soul." It is attributed to the American agnostic Robert Ingersoll (1833-1899) in an expanded form: "O God, if there be a God, save my soul, if I have a soul, from hell, if there be a hell."

Certainly a non-believer would be well advised to utter such a prayer, especially if near death and – one would hope – repentant. In essence, however, with such a prayer we ask God to do a very great thing for us, but offer nothing in return.

In his "Prayer of the Skeptic" Peter Kreeft transforms this passive prayer into one that is active and full of hope: "Go out into your back

---

59 *Fundamentals of the Faith; Essays in Christian Apologetics*; 24-54; 153-162.

yard alone some night, look up into the vastness of the star-filled universe and say:

> God, I don't know whether you exist or not. Maybe I'm praying to nobody, but maybe I'm praying to you. So if you are really there, please let me know somehow, because I do want to know. I want only the Truth, whatever it is. If you are the Truth, here I am, ready and willing to follow you wherever you lead.[60]

A Catholic friend of mine who works with troubled youth recommended such a prayer to a young agnostic who was dabbling in Satanism. After much reluctance, the young man prayed in that manner. His answer came quickly and he underwent a remarkable transformation. Things began to happen in his life that he could attribute only to God's intervention. No longer self-centered and interested in the occult, he became kind, forgiving, and very much interested in responding to God's influence in his life. He said to my friend: "Now I know why I was sent to this place. It was to meet you."

Choosing a religion? First evaluate the founder / first promulgator

Believing in an almighty Creator is an essential first step, of course. But, if we believe the Creator has made himself known to us (a reasonable supposition), through which of the many founders of a religion has the Creator done so? Many use a "leaves on the trees" approach to choosing a religion. They look for a religion with beliefs that do not conflict with one's lifestyle; one that has a convenient location; suitable social / recreational programs, a pleasant leader of worship, one that is politically correct, etc. Often, the most compelling "leaf" is the family or society into which one was born, or the faith of close friends.

Instead of making our choice based on the "leaves," it seems to me far more prudent to look at the "root" of each religion. By this I mean the founder. *Which of the many founders (or first promulgators, or first or most recent reformers) by his life and works, clearly indicated that he spoke and acted with the authority of the Creator, and is thereby in a position to keep, in the hereafter, the promises he made to us?*

---

60 Ibid. 47.

Discussion Questions

1. As a member of the Board of Education of your State, you are presented with a measure requiring that all science textbooks carry the statement signed by more than 600 scientists indicating that they remain unconvinced by the evidence for evolution by natural selection. Would you vote for or against the measure? Why?

2. The "New York State Core Curriculum on the Living Environment" can be found on the Web *at* **www.nysed.gov**. In Key Idea 3 it states, in part: *"Evolution is the change of species over time. This theory is the central unifying theme of biology. This change over time is well documented by extensive evidence from a wide variety of sources .... The diversity of life on Earth today is the result of natural selection occurring over a vast amount of geologic time for most organisms, but over a short amount of time for organisms with short reproductive cycles such as pathogens in an antibiotic environment and insects in a pesticide environment."* Is this statement in accord with the conclusions of: M. J. Behe? S. C. Meyer? S. Minnich? B. Lahn? J. Wells? B. Harrub (Pasteur Institute)? Why? For each researcher whose conclusions seem incompatible with the NYS statement, which do you see as more credible? Why?

3. The universe was created in a state of journeying (CCC par. 302). What does this mean?

4. On Intelligent Design Web sites such as **www.arn.org**, which of the articles do you find most informative, and why?

5. In his book *Icons of Evolution*, biologist Jonathan Wells includes "10 warning labels for biology textbooks" that together cast doubt on evolutionary theory. Some school districts in the United States reportedly prohibit the use of any such "warning labels" in their textbooks. Should such labels be prohibited, or should they be allowed or encouraged? Why?

6. Science has a number of laws; Kepler's laws of planetary motion and the laws of thermodynamics come to mind. Why is *evolution* still classed as a theory?

7. Astrophysicist Hugh Ross has listed 93 "coincidences" in nature that together he sees as strong evidence for an intelligently

designed universe. Discuss the likelihood of these cumulative occurrences from the standpoint of mere coincidence vs. Intelligent Design.

8. What do you think of the strength of Ross' arguments against *quantum tunneling* as an explanation of how the universe came into being and developed over the approximately 13.5 billion years of its existence?

9. Do you agree with the author that belief in a Creator / Orderer requires no more faith than that needed to believe in an incomprehensible *primeval atom* as the source of the universe? If not,

10. Why does Behe, an Intelligent Design scientist, state that *microevolution* has triumphed? Isn't this contradictory to the ID view? Should the subsequent article "Are Viruses Really Evolving" cast doubt on the view that microevolution has triumphed?

11. In his book *Darwin's Black Box,* biochemist Michael Behe concludes that the great complexity of the cell cannot be credibly explained by anything other than Intelligent Design. Those who believe in macroevolution by natural selection disagree. What do you think?

12. In stating "We cannot tell by looking at fossilized animals what it was that changed the shape of their bones or repositioned their organs," Behe challenged a central principle of evolutionary thought. How might one who supports evolutionary theory respond to this challenge? What do you think about Behe's statement?

13. Using the Internet, read "Behe's Empty Box," The *Wikipedia* articles on Intelligent Design and other articles challenging claims of ID scientists. Then read articles by ID scientists in defense of their views. Religious, political and other non-science driven commentary aside, and focusing on what is purely scientific, which arguments seem more convincing?

14. Esteemed evolutionist Stephen J. Gould, a paleontologist, acknowledged that the "Cambrian Explosion" is "the enigma of paleontological enigmas." How then should scientists regard the recent brain-related studies of Bruce Lahn who concluded that human cognitive abilities are "not due to a few accidental

mutations [but the result of] an enormous number of mutations acquired through exceptionally intense selection …."?

15. Is an argument based on history, to be presented in Step 3, relevant to a discussion of evolution?

16. Are reported miracles, such as those documented at Lourdes and that of Gemma di Giorgi, relevant to a discussion of how we human beings and the rest of the universe came into being?

17. Wells' compared a presentation on the evolution of the eye to comic strip character Calvin being able to "fly" in a cardboard box. Do you think Wells' use of this metaphor was appropriate?

18. If, as a member of a state board of education, you were asked to cast a vote for or against "teaching the controversy," i.e., also teaching purely scientific alternatives to evolution, how would you vote and why?

19. Explain Pascal's Wager. Do you agree with Pascal that the only sensible choice is to live to please God? How would you attempt to convince someone who disagreed with you?

20. Of the five classical arguments for the existence of God, which do you think is most compelling? Why?
www.newadvent.org/summa/100203.htm

21. What are "The four last things"? From what standpoint could one argue that there is only one last thing?

22. What do you think of Peter Kreeft's "Prayer of the Skeptic"? Is it a prayer you might recommend to a friend who does not believe in God?

23. In choosing a religion, we can give priority to: (a) the degree to which we find appealing the teachings of the founder / reformer, or; (b) the manifestations of the power and authority of the Creator manifested by the founder indicating that, in the hereafter, he can keep his promises to his faithful followers. Which is the more prudent choice? Why? What problems might the other choice present?

Step 2. No other founder of a religion is comparable to Jesus

Of *all* founders of a religion, *only* Jesus Christ manifested the authority of the Creator – *Only* Jesus did <u>all</u> of the following:

(a) *Fulfilled the many Messianic prophecies of the Old Testament;*

(b) *Proved by his works that he had the authority of the Creator;*

(c) *Acknowledged that he was God;*

(d) *Died on the cross to redeem us and make possible our salvation;*

(e) *Rose from death on the third day, appeared to many, and ascended into heaven;*

(f) *Said he would personally be our judge after death and;*

(g) *Said that no one comes to the Father except through him.*

These matters have all been historically verified. [See Step 3, following]. No authoritative apologist for any non-Christian faith makes these seven definitive claims – or equivalent claims – for his or her founder [See Part III, Other Religions].[61]

(a) Jesus Christ fulfilled the many Messianic prophecies of the Old Testament.

Jesus stands alone in clearly fulfilling the Messianic prophecies of the Old Testament – more than 100 in number. In his book *Y'shua: The Jewish Way to Say Jesus,* Moishe Rosen provides a concise summary of these important prophesies. [Some Islamic apologists claim that Muhammad fulfilled certain prophecies. See the section on Islam in Part III for the problems inherent in these claims].

In rejecting Jesus as the Messiah, some maintain that not Christ but the *Nation of Israel* fulfills such prophecies. Surely Israel has experienced much persecution. But can we hold that Israel was born in Bethlehem Ephrathah (Micah 5:1); was born of a virgin (Isaiah 7:14); was triumphant, riding upon an ass (Zechariah 9:9); that it gave sight to the blind, hearing to the deaf and to the lame the ability to leap (Isaiah 35:5-6); that its hands and feet were pierced, its bones numbered, and lots cast for its garment (Psalm 22:17-19); led like a lamb to slaughter but opened not his mouth (Isaiah 53:7)? These verses are based on the

---

61 In Kersey Graves' *The World's Sixteen Crucified Saviors,* we read that "Mithra the Mediator" of Persia did rise from death after three days, one of several pagan deities to do so. However, according to *The Da Vinci Hoax,* 151, Graves offers no documentation for this, and this "work of pseudo-scholarship and anti-Christian polemics ... is so shoddy that many atheists and agnostics disavow it."

Septuagint – "The Seventy" – a Greek translation of the Old Testament by about seventy Jewish scholars in the third century B.C. The Septuagint was widely used in the time of Jesus. But it was seen as problematic by those of the Sanhedrin and others who survived the destruction of Jerusalem in A.D. 70. Christianity was growing at a rapid pace in those apostolic and post-apostolic times, largely because – using the Septuagint – it was so easy to see how Jesus had fulfilled the many Messianic prophecies. However, in about A.D. 100, a new Greek translation of the Old Testament known as the Palestinian Canon was prepared at Jamnia, not far from Jerusalem, by the Pharisee-dominated remnant of the Sanhedrin. Soon afterward, these Pharisaic scholars condemned the Septuagint as inaccurate.[62]

Were the Jamnia-based scholars truly objective in rejecting the Greek translation so painstakingly prepared by "The Seventy" – their Jewish Scripture-scholar counterparts – some two to three centuries earlier? Or, as some claim, did their interest in stopping the rapid growth of Christianity play a part in the way they developed their new translation? [See Judaism in Part III of this book for further thoughts on this subject].

(b) Only Jesus proved by his works that he had the authority of the Creator.

The Gospels are replete with proof that Jesus spoke and acted with the authority of the Creator. Through the ages, apparent miracles of healing have been experienced by some not associated with Jesus; God loves all his children. But the miracles performed by Jesus, by a simple act of his will and often by not even touching the person – including raising the dead and himself arising from death – are of an order of magnitude never seen in history before or since. *No authoritative apologist for any non-Christian religion claims that the founder or first promulgator of his religion is even remotely comparable to Jesus in the supernatural power he displayed.*

Some Christian biblical scholars, in an apparent attempt to make the miracles of Jesus appear unremarkable, have written that Jesus was "just one of many wonder workers" of that age. Are they correct?

Using the Internet, we can readily find that ancient Jewish literature lists such persons as, ᶜHoni the Circle-drawer (60-50 B.C.), Hilkiah (20-10 B.C.) and Hanan ha Neᶜhba (20-10 B.C.) as "wonder workers."

At this writing the three above are listed on the Internet, with a note

---

62 *R.S.V. Catholic Edition*, vii, Ignatius Press.

that dates are approximate.[63]

Of the "miracles" attributed to these three figures of Jesus' era, the greatest is an account of a Rabbi who, from a distance, prayed for the recovery of someone who had an illness. It was later reported that, at that moment of prayer, the person recovered. The other two "wonders" were accomplished during droughts. On separate occasions each Rabbi prayed for rain and, before long, it rained.

"Workers of wonders" such as these were certainly known to those who saw Jesus, particularly to the Pharisees who made so many attempts to discredit Jesus. If their "wonders" were comparable to those of Jesus, why is there no record of the Pharisees pointing this out publicly? When the man born blind said, "Never since the world began has it been heard that anyone opened the eyes of one born blind" (Jn 9:32), why did they not correct him? Why did they not say, for example, "You are wrong. Hilkiah also gave sight to one born blind."?

And many Jews saw Jesus raise Lazarus after four days in the tomb. But where is it written that anyone in the crowd said, for example, "Ho hum, what's the big deal? ᶜHoni also raised a decaying corpse after four days in the tomb." No. *The authentic literature of that time includes nothing to indicate that anyone other than Jesus worked wonders of such magnitude.* As proof that the Pharisees could not discredit Jesus in that manner, Scripture notes their concern: "If we let him go on thus, every one will believe in him and the Romans will come and destroy both our holy place and our nation" (Jn 11:48). Unable to discredit him, they began plotting to kill him.

Perhaps the account of Simon Magus provides the strongest indication that – other than those acting in the name of Jesus – no one else manifested anything like the supernatural power of Jesus. Simon Magus amazed the people of Samaria with his wonders. St. Cyril of Jerusalem wrote that his fame prompted the Emperor Claudius to erect a statue to him labeled "To the Holy God Simon."[64]

But the limitations of Simon Magus became evident when he tried to buy the power of Jesus he saw manifested in Peter. (Acts 8:9-25). Every generation has its workers of wonders. In our generation David Copperfield and the late Doug Henning would surely be seen as such. Clearly, to be a wonder worker cannot be equated with being comparable to Jesus.

---

63 **http://religion.rutgers.edu/iho/rabbis.html**
64 Catechetical Lectures; 6, 14; *The Faith of the Early Fathers*, V. 1, par. 822c, 354.

(c) Jesus acknowledged that he was God.

Jesus led the apostles, disciples and others gently toward the realization that he was more than just an extraordinary messenger sent by God. Early on he is seen as: a prophet, e.g., by the woman at the well (Jn 4:19); as the Son of God (e.g., by Nathaniel; Jn 1:49, Jn 5:19-30); as a worker of miracles (e.g., at Cana, Jn 2:1-12); as the Son of Man (e.g., Jn 8:28); and as the Messiah (e.g., Jn 1:42).

When Jesus began to speak not just as one sent by God but *as God,* e.g., "Before Abraham was, I am" (Jn 8:58); the words by which God identified himself to Moses (Exodus 3:13-15) and elsewhere in the Old Testament; and "I and the Father are one" (Jn 10:30); Jesus was met by accusations of blasphemy by his detractors and, quite probably, by raised eyebrows among the apostles.

Even then some of his closest followers may have thought that Jesus meant that Yahweh sent him as a kind of special angelic spokesperson who was created by Yahweh before Abraham, who lived about 1,800 years earlier.

After his death and Resurrection Jesus acknowledged that he was truly God in language that is crystal-clear. The risen Jesus did so when he asked Thomas to touch his pierced hands and to put his hand into the wound in his side. Thomas then said *"My Lord and my God!"* (Jn 20:28). Did Jesus respond along these lines:

> "In your astonishment, Thomas, you have spoken in haste. But in calling me God you have blasphemed. I am your Lord. But, although sent by God to redeem mankind, I am not God."?

Of course Jesus never made such a statement. But if he were God's "Chief Steward," so to speak, but not truly God, Jesus would have been *obligated* to correct that egregious error of Thomas immediately. Otherwise Jesus would have been guilty of grave sin, particularly because Thomas spoke in the presence of the other ten apostles. But, instead of correcting Thomas, Jesus *unequivocally affirmed* what Thomas said by responding:

> Have you believed because you have seen me? Blessed are those who have not seen and yet believe [Jn 20:29].

(d) Jesus died on the cross to redeem us and make possible our salvation.

Many biblical verses affirm this truth; e.g., Mt 26:26-28; Romans 5:10-11; Ephesians 1:7; many more. It is also affirmed extensively in the Early Church Fathers as well as in other extra-biblical history.

(e) Jesus rose from death on the third day, appeared to many, and ascended into heaven.

Mt 28:1-10; Mk 16:1-18; Lk 24:1-49; in the letters of Paul and, as above, extensively in the Early Church Fathers as well as in other extra-biblical history.

(f) Jesus said he would personally be our judge after death.

In John's Gospel, Jesus makes this statement after defending himself against breaking the law by curing on the Sabbath. Jesus explains that *the Father has given all judgment to the Son*, that all men may honor the Son as they honor the Father (Jn 5:22-23).

(g) Jesus said that no one comes to the Father except through him.

As if to underscore the above passage, Jesus speaks of the reward in store for those he judges worthy of heaven. Here Jesus says "I am the way, and the truth, and the life; no one comes to the Father but by me" (Jn 14:6).

Discussion Questions

1. Of what importance is it that Jesus fulfilled many Messianic prophecies? What are some of those prophecies?

2. The Bible indicates that, before his Resurrection, Jesus did not clearly acknowledge that he was God. Instead, he led us to conclude that for ourselves by his miracles and by saying such things as, "Before Abraham was, I Am" and "I and the Father are one." Suppose, instead, Jesus began his public ministry saying something like: "Listen up, everybody; *I am God*. Watch, I'm going to prove it to you by bringing this dead man back to life." Given that we human beings have free will and a tendency toward pride and the other capital sins, which method seems most in keeping with the wish of Jesus to draw us to him as our Savior and Redeemer and to show how much he loves us?

3. Jesus said he would personally judge each of us after we die. What does this mean in light of the assurance of Jesus that we have a God of justice (e.g., Lk 18:7) and of mercy (e.g., Lk 1:50)?

4. No apologist for any non-Christian religion claims that the founder or first promulgator of his religion is even remotely comparable to Christ in the supernatural power Jesus so often

displayed. Given our desire for eternal salvation, is this important in the choice of one's religion? Why?

5. "Wonder worker" Simon the magician amazed the people of
    Samaria. St. Cyril of Jerusalem wrote that his fame was such
    that the Emperor Claudius erected a state to him inscribed: "To
    the holy god Simon." [W. A. Jergens, *The Faith of the Early
    Fathers*, par. 822c]. And yet Simon the magician, upon seeing
    the power of God as manifested by Peter, John and Philip, tried
    to buy this power from Peter (Acts 8:9-24). What conclusions
    might we draw about Simon the magician and the "wonders" he
    worked?

6. How do the "wonders" attributed to ᶜHoni the Circle-drawer,
    Hilkiah, and Hanan ha Neᶜhba compare to those of Jesus? Does
    this comparison help us understand the statement of Thomas
    upon seeing the risen Jesus: "My Lord and my God"? Why?

7. Do the Crucifixion and Resurrection of Jesus set him apart from
    all other founders of a religion in all of history? Explain your
    answer.

Step 3. History affirms the biblical Jesus

Introductory Comments

For the first 1,700 years of its existence, despite storms of heresy great and small, the Church rested secure in her history. Not Muhammad, not Luther, not Calvin – not even ex-Catholic and anti-Catholic Voltaire (1694-1768) attempted to "late-date" the Gospels. However, in the early 1830s Ferdinand Christian Baur of the Tübingen School successfully promoted the idea that *Matthew*, seen as the earliest Gospel, was not written until about A.D. 130; *John*, the latest, as late as 180.

Baur and his associate David Friedrich Strauss admitted that it was their [Hegelian[65]] ideology, not any careful study of early writings, that resulted in their late-dating of the Gospels.[66]

Such late dates of origin allowed Baur, Strauss and their followers to remove the Gospels from the History shelf, so to speak, and consider key aspects of the Gospels non-historical; in particular the supernatural manifestations attributed to Jesus.

By the end of the nineteenth century, however, virtually every biblical scholar held that each of the four Gospels was written before the year 100.[67]

Today most biblical scholars hold a "late-date / no eyewitness," view, i.e., that all four Gospels originated between about A.D. 68 and 100. "Early-date / eyewitness" scholars generally hold that they originated between about 40 and 70.[68]

As we shall see, the late Fr. Raymond E. Brown, one of the most influential Catholic biblical scholars following the Second Vatican Council, believed that no apostle or other eyewitness was the author of a Gospel.

For Fr. Brown, it appears that formal study of the Gospels must be-

---

65 Philosopher Georg Hegel (1770-1831) believed that maturity of the spirit is attained in stages through successive resolution of conflicting ideas; *thesis–antithesis–synthesis*. Each *synthesis* becomes the *thesis* for the next cycle. Karl Marx (1818-1883), however, applied to politics what Hegel had applied only intellectually. The result was *synthesis* as a result of class struggle as promoted by Marx and Friederich Engels in their *Communist Manifesto*.

66 G. H. Duggan, S.M.; "The Origin of the Gospels"; *Christian Order*; May 2002, 333.

67 Ibid. 333.

68 i.e., based on testimony of one or more eyewitness to Jesus, to one or more of the twelve apostles, to Paul, or to Mary the Mother of Jesus.

gin by accepting as fact that *"no one of the evangelists was an eyewitness to the ministry of Jesus. Rather the evangelists were 'second generation' Christians...."*[69]

Depending on motivation, such a late-date / no eyewitness view can offer a biblical scholar much latitude in influencing how believers perceive the Gospels. For example, label as late-date / no eyewitness Mt 16:18-19 (Peter named the "Rock" and promised the "keys" by Jesus) and you cast doubt on the primary biblical basis for the Papacy. By doing the same with the miracles of Jesus and certain other passages one casts doubt on his divinity. To late-date Mt 28:16-20 (the Great Commission) is to cast doubt on the authority of the apostles and all bishops of history.

Fr. Brown seemed to believe, however, that such casting of doubt on the historicity of the Gospels need not diminish the faith of Catholics:

> If everything in the Bible is not necessarily historical, Catholics are *not* left without the guidance of the church as to what they must believe. [Italics in original].[70]

To some extent, Fr. Brown was certainly correct; doubt about a literal star over the birthplace of our Lord, for example, is unlikely to result in one's leaving the Church. Doubt about such matters as the institution of the Eucharist by Jesus, and Jesus as our Divine Savior, risen Redeemer and ultimate Judge, is a very different matter.

In 1897 Francis P. Church published in the *New York Sun* his memorable "Yes, Virginia, there is a Santa Claus ..." and, no doubt, eight-year-old Virginia believed. But did this faith survive for long as a maturing Virginia subjected it to historical reality checks? I think not.

Surely it is important that the Church guides us in what we must believe as Catholics. But, does our Catholic faith fare much better than that of Virginia when we read in Catholic publications and hear in homilies that the Jesus of the Gospels fails to pass key historical reality checks? We know in our hearts, and through Church statistics, that it does not. As we shall see, however, there is compelling Semitic and other evidence that the Jesus of the Gospels *does pass* all truly objective historical reality checks.

In the following pages, after a general historical overview, we will focus on Catholic late-date / no eyewitness scholarship and its best

---

69 *Biblical Exegesis and Church Doctrine*, 14.
70 Ibid., 16.

known proponent, the late Fr. Raymond E. Brown, and the strong influence of Fr. Brown and others who "late-date" the Gospels and who typically promote the idea that no Gospel originated with an eyewitness to the ministry of Jesus.

Few late-date / no eyewitness biblical scholars "look behind" the canonical Greek, i.e., few give evidence in their writings of any serious study of the influence of ancient Hebrew and Aramaic on the canonical Greek of the New Testament.

During the past five centuries, however, many biblical scholars skilled not only in Greek but in ancient Hebrew and Aramaic have studied the canonical Greek Gospels. As we shall see, these scholars collectively make a compelling case for *early* dates of origin of the Gospels, i.e., all four having their origin between about A.D. 45 and 70.

Of particular interest is the compelling evidence for earlydate / eyewitness historicity offered by scholars such as the late Fr. Jean Carmignac, philologist and recognized authority on biblical Hebrew; and the late Claude Tresmontant, Hebraist and professor of philosophy at the Sorbonne, University of Paris.

In his Conclusion section of *The Birth of the Synoptic Gospels,* Fr. Jean Carmignac stated: **"It is *certain* that Mark, Matthew, and the documents used by Luke were redacted in a Semitic Language"** and **"It is *probable* that this Semitic language is Hebrew rather than Aramaic"** (Italics in original).

In the Epilogue of his book *The Hebrew Christ* Claude Tresmontant draws a similar conclusion in regard to all four Gospels: **"[A]ll four of the Gospels, as well as some of the other New Testament books, were evidently translations into Greek from earlier texts originally composed in Hebrew."**

The implications of these early-date / eyewitness findings are profound, especially in view of the predominant belief among Catholic and other biblical scholars today that none of the four Gospels originated with an eyewitness and that all are of doubtful historicity.

Fr. Brown based his studies primarily on the Canonical Greek and, as far as I have been able to determine, cast doubt on, but did not refute *specific statements* of Early Church Fathers affirming that the Gospels were written by hearers of Jesus (Matthew and John) or of other apostles (Mark and Luke). In 1985, he did acknowledge the value of "Church Fathers" in the developing thought of the Church. However, he then stated: *"[B]ut unless those writers [Church Fathers] had historical information they cannot answer historical questions.*"[71]

It would seem that, in 1985, Fr. Brown was of the opinion that, almost 2,000 years later, we have a clearer historical understanding of Christ and his teachings than, for example, Irenaeus, who was a disciple of Polycarp, who was a disciple of John the apostle / Evangelist, who was a disciple of Christ.

Throughout most of the 2,000-year history of Christianity believers accepted the Gospels as sound history and heard them preached in all their fullness. In large numbers they practiced their faith; more than a few to the point of sainthood.

In contrast, since the 1960s the late-date origin of the Gospels has been taught to the virtual exclusion of all other views in most Catholic seminaries, religious formation centers, Catholic universities, colleges and high schools in the United States and, with the exception of some third world countries, in most of the free world. The same applies to Catholic adult education and other catechesis. This is well documented.

Isn't it time for those in leadership positions at all levels within the Church and in Catholic academia to begin teaching the reasons for believing the early-date / eyewitness view of the Gospels? Isn't it time to make this information known in every Catholic home?

With this in mind, let us now proceed with an overview of key aspects of the predominant late-date / no eyewitness view of the Gospels, and a similar look at elements that characterize the early-date / eyewitness view.

As noted above, since the mid-1960s the prevailing view of Gospels – as taught in many Catholic seminaries, religious formation centers, Catholic universities and Catholic catechetical programs – is that the Gospels are of doubtful historicity. In particular, doubt is cast on accounts of Christ's manifestations of his divinity – his miracles. Why? Because of the prevailing belief that the Gospels originated long after the time of Christ and, almost certainly, that no Gospel originated with an apostle or other eyewitness to Jesus.

The casting of doubt on aspects of the ministry of Jesus is by no means a recent phenomenon. As we know, it occurred even during his life on earth (e.g., the claim that he expelled demons by power of Satan). Paul warned believers about letters falsely attributed to him (2 Thes 2:1-2).

---

71 *Biblical Exegesis and Church Doctrine*, 20.

In regard to the establishment of the Canon of Scripture, the *Catholic Encyclopedia* notes that, at the request of Pope Damasus, St. Jerome attended the Synod of Rome in the year 382:

> The result of its deliberations, presided over, no doubt, by the energetic Damasus himself, has been preserved in the document called '*Decretum Gelasii de recipiendis et non recipiendis libris,*' a compilation partly of the sixth century, but containing much material dating from the two preceding ones. The Damasan catalogue presents the complete and perfect Canon which has been that of the Church Universal ever since.[72]

It was not until about twelve centuries later that Protestant reformers revised this Canon of the Bible to accommodate *sola scriptura, sola fide* and other new interpretations of Scripture. But, in general, even these revisions were limited to rejecting entire Old Testament books (and, briefly, the rejection of the letter of James by Luther), rather than calling into question the historical authenticity of the New Testament.

The Council of Trent addressed the matter in 1546, in response to the claims made by the reformers. The Council declared that all books customarily read in the Catholic Church and included in Jerome's *Latin Vulgate* Bible are accepted as sacred and canonical, and, as the standard Latin Bible for purposes of common reference, the Council accepted the Vulgate.

As noted in the *Catholic Encyclopedia*: "The most explicit definition of the Catholic Canon is that given by the Council of Trent, Session IV, 1546."[73]

However, during the century after the rise of Protestantism, the "Age of Enlightenment" dawned and with it the seeds of a serious challenge to the *historical truth* of the New Testament.

The birth of Modernism

Humanism, which began in Italy near the end of the fifteenth century, turned the interest of many away from reverence for God and an interest in an afterlife. As the first of the Rationalist philosophers, Rene' Descartes (1596-1650) convinced many that everything must be doubted until one arrives at first principles which are beyond doubt. For him the first principle was thought: "I think, therefore I am."

Baruch Spinoza (1632-1677), a Dutch philosopher, developed a method of historical criticism of the Bible intended to eliminate any

---

72 *Catholic Encyclopedia*: **www.newadvent.org/cathen/03274a.htm** > C. 2.
73 *Catholic Encyclopedia:* **www.newadvent.org/cathen/03267a.htm** > Section II.

apparent anti-Semitism; a method that many later scholars would make use of, often unaware of its origin, to de-emphasize the historical authenticity of the Gospels. D. L. Dungan notes that "like a sugar-coated poison pill," Spinoza's *Theological-Political Treatise* "systematically destroyed the entire medieval religious worldview, repeatedly putting one thing in its place: the commandment to *love God* [understood simply as 'nature'] and *love your neighbor.*" [Italics in original][74]

For Scottish philosopher David Hume (1711-1776), however, even thought was not convincing. Contrary to Descartes, Hume believed there could be no certain truth about *anything* (One may wonder if Hume pondered how it was that he could arrive on the continent *dry* after crossing the English Channel).

And so it comes as no surprise that this extreme skepticism was soon applied to the Bible. In 1775 Hermann Samuel Reimarus wrote his *"Apologia" or Defense for the Reasonable Worshipers of God*, in which he denied what is supernatural in religion, and the rationalist school of historical criticism was born. In 1835, in a similar vein, David Friedrich Strauss wrote *Life of Jesus Critically Examined*. These authors and others went to great lengths to question how various events in the Gospels could have occurred, particularly the miracles of Jesus, leaving readers with the impression that such events probably never happened. Strauss gives the impression that in his study of the life of Jesus, if an event appeared to be miraculous, then, *ipso facto*, the event was not historical – it never happened[75] (See Strauss and *The Jesus Seminar*, below).

In an *article in Homiletic and Pastoral Review*, Fr. George H. Duggan, S.M., quoted Giuseppe Ricciotti: *"But Strauss honestly confessed that his theory would collapse if the Gospels were composed during the first century. If they were so early, there would not be enough time for the myths to develop."*[76] As we will see, that early-date evidence Strauss discounted is now formidable.

Strauss lived in Germany and died February 11, 1858. About fifteen years before his death the first of eighteen apparitions of the Blessed Virgin Mary to Bernadette Soubirous took place in Lourdes, France. As earlier noted, physicians using rigorous standards, including thorough pre- and post-miracle medical records, have documented

---

74 *A History of the Synoptic Problem,* 209-210, 346.
75 *The Life of Jesus Critically Examined,* Introduction, Section 16; "Criteria by which to Distinguish the Unhistorical in the Gospel Narrative."
76 *Homiletic & Pastoral Review*, 1997; From *The Life of Christ*; Giuseppe Ricciotti, (E.T. Alba I. Zizzamia), Bruce, Milwaukee, 1944, 186.

numerous miracles there. But I found nothing to indicate Strauss showed the good grace – and simple objectivity – to investigate those inexplicable events and address them in his published writings.

Strauss was surely familiar with the stigmata, the phenomenon in which the wounds of Christ have appeared on the bodies of many saintly persons. Such cases had been reported for six centuries before Strauss lived. I wonder what Strauss would have thought of Padre Pio, the extraordinary Italian priest and stigmatist of the twentieth century. A skeptic one day dismissed the stigmatic wounds of Padre Pio (now Saint Pio) as a psychological phenomenon brought on by his gazing excessively at the Crucifix. Padre Pio responded by suggesting that the skeptic find a cow, stare at it, and see how long it took before he grew horns.

The influence of Reimarus and Strauss can be seen in the works of later Protestant "modernists" such as Rudolf Bultmann. One must wonder if Bultmann really saw himself as a Christian; his writing indicates that he considered resurrection after death simply not conceivable.

By the late nineteenth century some Catholic priests had begun to promote modernism; Alfred Loisy and George Tyrell refused to retract their modernist views and were excommunicated. From 1881 to 1893 Loisy was a professor at the *Institut Catholique de Paris.*

In 1893 Pope Leo XIII found it necessary to issue the encyclical *Providentissimus Deus*, which affirmed the inerrancy of Scripture. In July 1907, Pope Pius X issued *Lamentabili Sane*, a broad condemnation of sixty-five positions of modernism. On September 8, 1907, Pope Pius X issued *Pascendi Dominici Gregis, On the Doctrines of the Modernists*, an encyclical in which he characterized modernism as a "synthesis of all heresies." The Pope required that all priests, superiors of religious orders and seminary professors of theology and philosophy take an oath disavowing modernism (September 1, 1907).[77]

Was it coincidence that just a decade later, in Fatima, Portugal, three children became the object of worldwide attention when they reported that the Blessed Virgin Mary was appearing to them? Lucia, Jacinta and Francisco reported that the Blessed Mother said that many souls were going to hell and asked that the following prayer be said:

Oh my Jesus, forgive us our sins; save us from the fires of hell; lead all souls to heaven, especially those most in need of thy mercy.

---

77 This oath was abrogated in July, 1967 by Pope Paul VI.

The steps taken by Pope Pius X brought to a halt the promulgation of modernist views within the Church. For about five decades, during what has been called the golden age of Catholicism, Catholic schools proliferated; the *Baltimore Catechism* in the U.S.A.[78] and the "Penny Catechism" (*A Catechism of Christian Doctrine*) in England and Wales ensured that young Catholics properly understood their faith, including its basis in the Bible and Church Tradition. Catholics read about the lives of saints and many, in greater or lesser measure, attempted to imitate them. Catholics attended Mass with reverence every Sunday and holy day, and few would even think of receiving Holy Communion without first having gone to Confession, repenting, and being forgiven for any mortal sin. Congregations turned out in large numbers for novenas and other special services. There was an abundance of vocations for the priesthood and for orders of nuns, and the breakup of a marriage followed by remarriage, with the resulting shuttling of shared children, was almost unheard of.

Pope Pius XII encourages scriptural scholarship

In 1943, Pope Pius XII issued the encyclical *Divino Afflante Spiritu* which included the following:

> In like manner therefore ought we to explain the original text which, having been written by the inspired author himself, has more authority and greater weight than any even the very best translation, whether ancient or modern; this can be done all the more easily and fruitfully, if to the knowledge of languages be joined a real skill in literary criticism of the same text. [par. 16.][79]

Elsewhere in *Divino Afflante Spiritu* Pope Pius XII affirms the historicity of the Bible with such statements as: "With all our energy we ought to lead back all men to our most *merciful Redeemer*. He is the *divine Consolor* of the afflicted."

Within about four decades of the issuance of *Pascendi Dominici Gregis in 1907,* however, the modernist influence so effectively checked by Pope Pius X began to reemerge.

Catholics may have Pope Paul VI to thank for ensuring the unity of our Church. As a condition for approving the Council Document *Constitution on the Church,* the Pope attached a note (November 21, 1964) to the effect that, acting collegially, the bishops (as successors of

---

78 **www.catholic.net/RCC/Catechism/Doit.html**
79 *Divino Afflante Spiritu*, September 30, 1943.

the apostles) had supreme authority in the Church *only when acting in concert with and not independently of, the Pope.*[80] Thus the Pope retained the clear intention of Jesus when, in the presence of the apostles, he gave primacy to Peter alone (Mt 16:18-19; Jn 21:15-18).

The resistance to Church teaching initially fostered by modernism would gain much momentum soon after the close of Vatican II in 1965.

On July 25, 1968 an event occurred that George Weigel described as *"perhaps the crucial moment in the formation of a culture of dissent that would influence the Catholic Church in the United States for the rest of the twentieth century."*[81] The event was the release by Pope Paul VI of *Humanae Vitae.* This encyclical reaffirmed the teaching of the Church that, "for just reasons" a married couple may space the births of their children, but may use *only* "methods of birth regulation based on self-observation and the use of infertile periods ...." Using other means to render procreation impossible [e.g., a contraceptive pill or condom] "is intrinsically evil."[82]

Weigel notes that *"Public dissent from Humanae Vitae ... was led, not by disappointed laity, but by priests, religious, and theologians, some of them men and women of considerable influence."*[83] Further thoughts on this topic will be found in Part II.

In addition to public dissent along the lines described above, an increased assertiveness on the part of many Catholic biblical scholars became evident – an assertiveness not always in accord with the direction and guidance given to the faithful by the Pope.

Modernist biblical scholarship – The Jesus Seminar

As an extreme example of modernist biblical scholarship today, consider "The Jesus Seminar." The following conclusions are noted in their book, *The Five Gospels*: (a) Of all the words ascribed to Jesus in the Gospels, eighty-two percent were not spoken by him (p. 5); (b) A majority of the Fellows doubted that Jesus was celibate; they believe that he probably had a "special" relationship with Mary of Magdala (pp. 220-221); (c) Based on the color-coding system used throughout *The Five Gospels* to judge authenticity of Bible verses, the Fellows believe it is highly doubtful that Jesus ever performed *any* miracle.

In short, *The Five Gospels* implies that Jesus was a sinner, appears to reject everything about Jesus that would affirm his divinity, and

---

80 *The Oxford Dictionary of Popes,* 313-314.
81 *The Courage to be Catholic,* 68.
82 *Catechism of the Catholic Church,* paragraphs 2366-2379.
83 *The Courage to be Catholic,* 68.

credits him with saying only what any wandering holy man might have said.

How could this group of Bible scholars ostensibly representing Catholicism and various other Christian denominations differ so sharply with the innumerable Bible scholars who affirm the divinity of Jesus today and have done so for almost twenty centuries? The answer appears to lie in the "Seven Pillars of Scholarly Wisdom," also called the "Seven Pillars of Modern Biblical Scholarship," on which the Seminar Fellows based their conclusions.[84]

Miracles can't happen

The first "pillar" is most revealing: Pillar one is the *distinction* between the historical Jesus and the Christ of faith described in the first creeds. In fact, one of those to whom the Seminar Fellows dedicated *The Five Gospels* is David Friedrich Strauss who, in 1835, wrote *Life of Jesus Critically Examined,* as noted above.

The Five Gospels points out that Strauss *distinguished* what he considered *myth* in the Gospels (apparent legend and occurrences that seemed beyond natural explanation) from what he accepted as *history* (p. 3).

In other words, *any supernatural occurrences in the Gospels,* such as Jesus' raising of Lazarus, his own Resurrection, and his many other miracles *are by Strauss' definition mere myths or legends, and not historically true.*

And so, with Strauss's unsubstantiated *assumption,* actually a *false dichotomy,* as their first "pillar" of scholarly wisdom, their rejection of Jesus as Son of God and miracle-worker was a foregone conclusion for The Jesus Seminar fellows as it was for Reimarus, Bultmann and other modernists.

With such reliance on assumption at the expense of objectivity, it would seem that no one would pay any attention to such groups as The Jesus Seminar. If a scientist attempted to publish a paper using the same assumption-based method to *prove* his hypothesis, what peer-reviewed journal would risk its reputation by publishing it? But denigrating Jesus and his Church sells books, magazines, CDs, rock concert tickets, MP3 downloads, films and TV programming, and the modernists have been riding a wave of popularity. With their self-admitted speculation and hypothesizing, they have caused many to doubt the

---

84 At least nine of the seventy-four participants on the "Roster of the Fellows of the Jesus Seminar" in *The Five Gospels,* including the co-chair, are listed as representing a Catholic college or university.

biblical accounts of the ministry of Jesus.

Myth and legend; Joseph Campbell's concept of Christ

In *The Five Gospels*, Joseph Campbell (1904-1987) is not listed as a Fellow of *The Jesus Seminar,* which was founded in 1985. But, in considering the Gospels as largely myth and legend, and quoting from the *Gospel of Thomas* despite its rejection by Eusebius of Caesarea, Campbell seemed to share at least some of their views. Campbell claimed, for example, that – other than the *legends* which, he claims, tell us the meaning of Christ's life – we know *nothing* about Christ.[85] The Crucifixion was simply a model for us to *release ourselves* from sin. [86]

For Campbell, who was raised as a Catholic, Christ seemed swept up in a mythical whirl of pan-religious symbolism. Campbell saw the wound in the side of Christ, and the bleeding caused by his crown of thorns, in light of the Celtic Maimed Fisher King and Tristan's poisoned wound. In Christ's crown of thorns Campbell saw the turning wheel of Bodhisattva and, in the cross of Christ, Ixion's wheel.[87]

If the late-date / no eyewitness speculation about the origin of the four Gospels were credible, one might reasonably consider Campbell's conjecture about Christ, which was popularized in 1988 by Bill Moyers in the six-part PBS special, "Joseph Campbell and the Power of Myth."

As we shall see, however, the compelling evidence for the early dates of origin of all four canonical Gospels lifts Christ out of the realm of Campbell's religio-mythical musing and affirms him *historically* as our divine Lord and Savior.

As we will later see, the Achilles' heel of modernists – and of all proponents of Christ as merely myth and legend – is the Internet. Through it the public at large now has ready access to the writings of the Early Church Fathers and other non-biblical history, as well as information about the findings of Fr. Carmignac, Tresmontant, Robinson and others whose studies affirm early-date / eyewitness Gospel origins. Now, pointed questions can be asked, such as:

> Why do many late-date / no eyewitness proponents virtually ignore the Early Church Fathers and other extra-biblical history and fail to take into account the Hebrew and Aramaic "behind" the Greek?

---

85 *The Hero's Journey: The World of Joseph Campbell,* 173.
86 Ibid., 179.
87 *The Masks of God: Creative Mythology*, 425.

Why do *The Jesus Seminar* fellows place such credence in the *Gospel of Thomas* in their book *The Five Gospels,* when Eusebius, Bishop of Caesarea, reported that this "Gospel" is *not authentic?*

In about A.D. 324, Eusebius stated that the *Gospel of Thomas* was one of several *"works cited by the heretics under the name of the apostles* [which] *no one belonging to the succession of ecclesiastical writers has deemed worthy of mention in his writings."* [Eusebius: *The History of the Church; 3.25;*][88]

Speaking now about modernists and myth proponents in general, the central question for Catholics and others today is this: Whom should we believe:

(a) Modern scholars and others who, as Fr. Carmignac said, "operate from the Greek" and arbitrarily apply late dates to Gospel authorship. Many of these scholars cast doubt on the teachings and miracles of Jesus through self-admitted speculation and have been criticized by Joseph Cardinal Ratzinger for virtually ignoring much well-attested extra-biblical history [which would include the Early Church Fathers], or;

(b) Scholars proficient in a*ncient Hebrew and Aramaic, as well as Greek,* whose studies indicate that the Synoptic Gospels originated largely in Hebrew, thus indicating early-date, eyewitness author-ship. The findings of these Greek / Hebrew-Aramaic scholars are in accord with the statements of the Early Church Fathers regarding Gospel authorship.

Clearly, as we shall see, the more compelling scholarship has been done by the Greek / Hebrew-Aramaic Scholars, who affirm, as noted in Step 4, that Jesus gave primacy, in the one Church he founded, to Peter and his successors and gave "The Great Commission" to the apostles, the spiritual and historical predecessors of our bishops.

Many of the key statements of the Early Church Fathers, organized by topic, are quoted in *The Faith of the Early Fathers,* a three-volume set edited by Fr. William A. Jurgens. Also, many are quoted in the *Catechism of the Catholic Church,* 2nd Ed.

Dead Sea Scrolls – hypothesis-based views

Let me add a word of caution in regard to some studies of the Dead Sea Scrolls. The book *Jesus and the Riddle of the Dead Sea Scrolls* was

---

88 **www.ccel.org/fathers2**

published in 1992. In it author Barbara Thiering, Ph.D., is referred to as a biblical scholar, theologian, and Dead Sea Scrolls expert. The publisher of her book summarized along these lines some of the author's opinions: (a) Jesus was not born in Bethlehem. (b) Mary was not really a virgin. (c) Jesus performed no miracles. (d) Jesus married twice and was the father of three children. (e)Jesus was drugged when crucified; he survived. (f) No death on the cross means there was no Resurrection.

And so it would seem that we should set aside belief that Jesus was the Messiah, the Son of God.

Before rejecting Jesus as true Messiah and Son of God, however, let me relate the opinion of Hershel Shanks, editor of the prestigious *Biblical Archaeology Review:*

"Few, if any, scholars have been convinced by the arguments adduced by Eisenman, Thiering, or Teicher, but the popular press has sometimes given their sensational views widespread coverage."[89]

And so, before relying on the conclusions of Thiering and others who promote conjecture, it would be well to consider the *assumptions* made by such authors. In particular, please note that what is in Thiering's book she herself considers hypothetical. (p. 2).

In contrast, objective study of ancient papyrus fragments, including some found at Qumrân, as well as other archaeological studies, can yield important results, as noted below.

Papyrology plus stichometry: Papyrus fragments confirm early dates for Matthew and Mark[90]

In *Eyewitness to Jesus*, a book co-authored by Carsten P. Thiede and Matthew d'Ancona, Thiede, a German papyrologist, documents his study of "The Magdalen Fragments." These three thumbnail-sized bits of papyrus were found in Luxor, Egypt in 1901, donated to Magdalen College in Oxford, England, and initially dated to about A.D. 180-200. On these fragments an ancient hand had written part of the *Gospel according to Matthew*, Chapter 26 in ancient Greek; this was not in dispute.

However, an international controversy erupted on Christmas Eve, 1994, when the *Times* of London carried the news that Thiede had

---

89 "Understanding the Dead Sea Scrolls," a reader from the *Biblical Archaeology Review,* 1992, 185.

90 *Papyrology*: The study of ancient documents written on a paper-like substance made from the papyrus plant. *Stichometry*: A *stich* is a line of text. Stichometry is used in the reconstruction of ancient documents from fragments by such means as discerning the pattern of number of letters per line and the comparability of the beginning, middle and end of adjacent lines of visible text.

dated these fragments to about A.D. 60. The impact of this conclusion is indicated by a comment by Richard N. Osning of *Time* magazine to the effect that these three ancient bits of papyrus could revolutionize the scholarship of the New Testament.

Carsten Thiede answers a challenge to his dating of the Magdalen Fragments of Matthew which was cited by Fr. Raymond E. Brown

In *An Introduction to the New Testament* (1997) Fr. Raymond E. Brown cast doubt on Thiede's dating of the Magdalen fragments of the *Gospel according to Matthew* to about A.D. 60, citing 1995 reports by K. Wachtel and S. Pickering – specialists in epigraphy (the study and interpretation of inscriptions) – which called Thiede's dating flawed. Instead, Wachtel and Pickering dated the fragments more than one hundred years later.[91]

Apparently Fr. Brown was not aware of Thiede's strong rebuttal of such studies a year earlier in *Eyewitness to Jesus* (1996). Thiede noted that Klaus Wachtel "may not have been aware of all the relevant information." In any case, Thiede wrote:

> [Wachtel's] conclusions as to the dating ... are thus marred by factual errors. As for St. Matthew 26:22, [Wachtel's] misjudgment may be attributed to his ignorance of the microscopal analysis of the line.

Resistance on this matter cannot last, Thiede observed, "The facts are now beyond dispute."[92]

Fr. Brown's reference to Stuart Pickering may have been based on Pickering's Internet-listed comments dated March 2, 1995 in which he and others cast doubt on Thiede's early-dating of the Magdalen Fragments and called for further study.[93]

Subsequently, however, in *Eyewitness to Jesus*, Thiede wrote as follows, "The final, clear answer came in June, 1995, when the Magdalen Papyrus was ... analyzed [under an] epifluorescent confocal laser scanning microscope." The controversial unresolved issues of the 'high point' and the 'obligatory *nu* after the *omega*' were thus resolved in support of Thiede. Thiede adds:

> The result of this analysis was presented at the Twenty-first Con-

---

91 *An Introduction to the New Testament*, 216, Footnote 102.
92 *Eyewitness to Jesus*, 62; Footnote 50, 176.
93 **www.ibiblio.org/bgreek/test-archives/html4/1995-08/10158.html**

gress of the International Papyrologists' Association in Berlin on August 15, 1995, *and met with unanimous approval.*[94] [Italics added]

Regarding fragment of Matthew, Thiede's critics fall silent

On the Internet, I found several scholarly articles strongly critical of Thiede's conclusions about the Magdalen Fragments of the *Gospel according to Matthew*. In fact I was about to delete my references to Thiede's work for this reason.

But then, using *Google*, I did several searches for scholarly criticism of the analysis Thiede presented at the IPA Congress in August, 1995; the analysis which received the unanimous approval of that Congress. *I found no such criticism.*

I did find an e-mail message dated in 1999 and posted by the author, a German scholar who, prior to August 1995, had been one of Thiede's strongest critics. In that e-mail the scholar noted, with apparent satisfaction, that T. C. Skeat, another scholar formerly critical of Thiede, had written a related article in 1997 which was published in *New Testament Studies.*

According to the first critic, this 1997 article – written about two years *after* the IPA Conference at which Thiede said he received unanimous approval – *did not even mention Thiede's claims.*

The title of Skeat's article was "The Oldest Manuscript of the Four Gospels?" (I could not find it on the Internet to verify this point).

As I have noted, I write as an author / reporter; I have no expertise in papyrology. However, this apparent sudden silence – this absence of scholarly criticism after Thiede's presentation to the IPA Congress in August, 1995 – adds a strong measure of credibility to Thiede's claim that the Magdalen fragments of *Matthew* originated not later than about A.D. 60 – which fits nicely into the time frames given by Fr. Carmignac and C. Tresmontant.

Thiede's critics include some who claim that later occupants of the Qumrân caves may have deposited the fragment in question. Thiede presents several arguments against this, including, "the results of all serious archaeological investigations rule out any rehabilitation or reuse of the Qumrân caves after A.D. 68."[95]

These findings by Thiede are consistent with the findings of Fr. Carmignac, Tresmontant and others who also concluded that the

---

94 *Eyewitness to Jesus,* 60-61.
95 *Eyewitness to Jesus,* 30-31.

Gospel according to Matthew is of very early origin.[96]

Archaeology: Enclosed stern in Peter's boat?

In *Mark* 4:35-41 we read that Jesus, before calming the storm, was *in* or *inside* the stern, sleeping on a cushion while the wind sent high waves into the boat. It would be one thing to sleep in a small boat tossed by wind and wave. But who could sleep while being soaked with large waves? It is not surprising that the credibility of *Mark* was challenged in view of this Gospel passage. But Ceruti-Cendrier calls our attention to the work of Bonnet-Eymard, who notes that *the wreck of a boat of Jesus' time was discovered in Lake Gennesaret in 1986; it had a rear deck with a cover that would shelter a man.*[97]

Archaeology and Scripture

Although archaeologists have found many artifacts from biblical times, few have been directly associated with key people, places and events described in Scripture and none with Patriarchs Abraham, Isaac, Jacob and Joseph. Nor, to my knowledge, is there yet any conclusive archaeological evidence for the exodus of the Jews from ancient Egypt. In a few cases artifacts have revealed apparent anachronisms, affirming the existence of a people at the expected location, but not quite in the time period indicated in the Old Testament.

On the other hand, artifacts and non-biblical records of the era of the Patriarchs (about 2000-1550 B.C.) provide a historical context largely consistent with the Old Testament Scriptures in regard that era.

In some cases, the Bible can actually guide archaeologists. For example, for archaeologist Yigael Yadin, the Bible was an important resource in his successfully finding and excavating the great Gate of Solomon.[98]

Given the obstacles faced by biblical archaeologists, however, their limited success should not be surprising. Political unrest, extensive overbuilding on sites, funding limitations and other difficulties often hinder them. Perhaps the best explanation, however, is simply that few of the important sites have been studied. It is estimated that about 5,000 sites in Palestine have been determined to be of archaeological significance. However, *only about seven percent of these have been excavated and only about two percent of the total number have been excavated extensively.* For an informative summary of archeological arguments

---

96 See "N. T. Ancient manuscripts": **www.biblefacts.org/history/oldtext.html**
97 "The Gospels – Direct testimony or later writings?" Marie-Christine Ceruti-Cendrier; *Homiletic and Pastoral Review*, January, 2005.
98 Ibid., 120.

for and against the historical authenticity of the Bible I recommend the book, *Is the Bible True?: How Modern Debates and Discoveries Affirm the Essence of the Scriptures,* by Jeffery L. Sheler. When his book was published in 1999, this award-winning journalist had been a religion writer at *U.S. News and World Report* for ten years.

Sheler quotes Egyptologist Kenneth Kitchen as using the adage: *"Absence of evidence is not evidence of absence."* Ignoring this truth can prove to be professionally embarrassing. Sheler notes that as recently as 1993 certain archaeologists and biblical scholars were claiming that David, for example, was not a historical figure. In July, 1993, however, Gila Cook, a member of a team led by Avraham Biran, found a fragment of a monument at Dan in Galilee on which was written, *"of the House of David ...."* Although initially disputed, its authenticity has since been widely accepted by archaeologists as well as biblical scholars.[99] In his concluding chapter Sheler notes:

> The impact [of archaeology] overall has been to affirm the histori-
> cal essence of the Scriptures, to disclose its solid roots [and] to
> confute the bedrock skeptics who dismiss the Bible as nothing
> more than a collection of myths and legends.[100]

Modernist speculation on "mindset" of Gospel writers

Modernists seem inclined to view the writers of the Gospels and Early Fathers of the Church as having a "different mindset," implying that their love for Jesus induced them to fabricate miraculous tales of healing, raising others and himself from death, and so on – even though to do so would be to perpetrate an egregious lie; to "bear false witness," which was forbidden by Jesus.

Paul, the poor fellow, was a highly educated Pharisee, nobody's fool, and a feared persecutor of Christians. If only he had not had that sudden change of mindset on the way to Damascus that day. How else can one explain his extraordinary zeal as an apostle that led to his martyrdom? To save his life all he had to do was give up his nonsensi-cal proclaiming of the myths and fables of Christianity and deny Christ. Peter and the other apostles who persisted in proclaiming the glorious fabrication to the point of martyrdom were equally foolish. And the countless martyrs through the centuries; what a waste of lives.

Modernists tend to dismiss the early Christian martyrs, saying: "all

---

99 "The Bible and Archaeology;" United Church of God Web site:
www.ucgstp.org/lit/booklets/true/archaeol.html
100 *Is the Bible True?: How Modern Debates and Discoveries Affirm the Essence of the Scriptures.* 255

religions have their martyrs." It seems that they fail to recognize the difference between the early Christian martyrs and others whom the world may call martyrs. Many through the ages have died, often heroically, for a variety of religious and non-religious causes. Of these, many have been innocent victims of persecution. Some commit murder / suicide publicly to call attention to their cause and in the belief that they thus receive an eternal reward. Others do so privately believing they are following the will of their deity.

But there is a qualitative difference between these and the martyrs of the early Church who *were killed primarily because they refused to deny the divinity of Christ and worship false gods, and who died while living the Commandments, loving God and neighbor to the fullest, and forgiving those who were killing them* (e.g., Stephen: Acts 7:54-60).

And, of course, there have been many martyrs in the tradition of the Holy Innocents – the earliest Christian martyrs – who died through no fault of their own at the hands of those who opposed Christ.

Anyone who fails to appreciate the qualitative difference between Christian and non-Christian martyrs has not read Alban Butler's *The Lives of the Saints,* historical accounts of the era of the catacombs, or other related books.

In her pre-publication review of this book, Marie-Christine Ceruti-Cendrier commented on the bias against Christian martyrs commonly seen today: "Anyone can die for a wrong cause. But the Christians, the first Christians, are supposed (by our new theologians) to have *invented* the Gospels and *then to have gone to martyrdom for them.*" She further observes that this insult to one's intelligence and discernment is hurled only at Christian martyrs, "Non-Christian martyrs are never presumed to have written or invented the books, events or the leader they were dying for."

Flavius Josephus

There are several historical references to Jesus by non-Christian near-contemporaries. The most compelling, perhaps, is that of Flavius Josephus. According to Eusebius, Josephus was born Joseph – his father was Mathias – in Palestine. He became a priest in Jerusalem – a Pharisee – and was captured in the Jewish War. He gained the attention of Vespasian when he predicted that Vespasian would become Emperor. When this occurred in 69 Josephus was set free and took Flavius as his name.[101]

Josephus was born just a few years after Christ's death and Resur-

---

101 *Eusebius; The History of the Church,* 381 (Penguin).

rection (A.D. 37-100?). The following is an excerpt from *The Jewish Antiquities*, from *The Complete works of Flavius Josephus*:

> *Now, there was about this time Jesus, a wise man, [if it be lawful to call him a man], for he was a doer of wonderful works, a teacher of such men as receive the truth with pleasure. He drew over to him both many of the Jews and many of the Gentiles. [He was (the) Christ]. And when Pilate, at the suggestion of the principal men amongst us, had condemned him to the cross, those that loved him at the first did not forsake him, [for he appeared to them alive again the third day, as the divine prophets had foretold these and ten thousand other wonderful things concerning him]. And the tribe of Christians, so named from him, are not extinct at this day.*[102]

In addition to Pontius Pilate, Josephus describes Herod Agrippa I, Tiberius, Herod Antipas, Herodias, the beheading of John the Baptist and the stoning of James. But he has little else to say about Jesus and his followers; he is not a Christian and his focus is on the Jews. Brackets (other than for the word *the,* before *Christ)* do not appear in Whiston's translation. I inserted them to identify phrases that some, not surprisingly, have questioned. They claim that the bracketed comments did not appear in another translation and therefore were *added* later by others. It should be pointed out, however, that no one claims to have the original document written by Josephus. And so it is equally possible that the bracketed comments were later *omitted* by some scribes for whom such an affirmation of the divine nature of Jesus and his fulfillment of Messianic prophecy would have been totally unacceptable. Adding strongly to the credibility of the full text is that Eusebius included a similar translation of the above words of Josephus in his own *History of the Church* in about A.D. 328. In this *History,* Eusebius includes "*doer of wonderful works …. He was the Christ* and, *For he appeared to them again alive on the third day.*" And, Eusebius adds: "*Since an historian, who is one of the Hebrews themselves, has recorded in his work these things concerning John the Baptist and our Savior, what excuse is there left for not convicting them of being destitute of all shame, who have forged the acts against them?*" [Here Eusebius is referring to the *forged memoranda;* documents forged by

---

102 "The Jewish Antiquities,"18.3.3; from *The Complete Works of Flavius Josephus*; trans. W. Whiston; The Flavius Josephus Home Page, **http://members.aol.com/FLJOSEPHUS/home.htm#testimonium** (Christian Classics Ethereal Library).

the enemies of Christ in the third century with the approval of the despot emperor Maximinus.][103]

Surely, with the bracketed comments, the above passage would have caused great turmoil among the very people who had not seen fit to accept Jesus as divine and as Messiah.

In any case, when Josephus wrote his moving tribute to Jesus and the apostles several decades had passed since the Crucifixion; plenty of time for the Sanhedrin to uncover evidence of any Resurrection hoax. It is said that Josephus was allowed to use official government records and surely he also spoke with many people in compiling his multi-volume works. Any who spoke sympathetically about Christians during much of that period risked being accused of being one. That could well have meant a martyr's death in such places as Nero's Circus or, after A.D. 80, in the Colosseum.

If there had been any hint of evidence that, instead of the Resurrection, the dead body of Jesus had been stolen – or that Jesus had somehow survived crucifixion, surely many of those interviewed would have told Josephus. In that event, would that prestigious historian have jeopardized his reputation by writing the above words about Jesus? Even if we delete the bracketed comments in question, Josephus described Jesus as:

[A] *wise man ... a doer of wonderful works ... a teacher of such men as receive the truth with pleasure.*

Is it not inconceivable that Josephus could have learned enough about Jesus to write even these uncontested complimentary remarks without also learning that Jesus claimed to be the Messiah and foretold his Crucifixion and Resurrection from death?

If Josephus' inquiries had led him to conclude that Jesus was not the Messiah and did not arise from death would he not have described Jesus very differently? Instead of the above words of praise, would he not have written along these lines:

"He appeared wise, but misled many. He claimed to be the Messiah, but his claim died with him on the cross."?

And if those who opposed Jesus had found evidence to refute the Resurrection, would word of the hoax not have been announced throughout the land and appear in other documents of that and later eras? But, although many authors through the ages have attempted to

---

103 *Eusebius: The History of the Church*; 1.11; **www.ccel.org/fathers2**

undermine Christianity through books based on speculation and conjecture – *no credible evidence has ever been found to discredit Jesus as he is described in the Bible, including the Resurrection.* For further information on this topic see the Flavius Josephus Home Page referred to above.

The Historical-Critical Method

Ann Roche Muggeridge, in her book *The Desolate City; the Revolution in the Catholic Church*, outlines the means by which radical late-date / no eyewitness scholars (not necessarily all such scholars) attempt to strip Jesus of his divinity. Simply put, they interpret the Bible using (actually misusing) the *historical-critical method*:

These radical scholars, Muggeridge points out, tell us that the intention of the writers of the Gospels – none of whom, in their view, an eyewitness to Jesus – was not to lie, but *to tell a story.* Each story would be understood in the context of the mythical (not prophetic) writings about the coming Messiah. Only in this way, we are told, could the disciples make sense of the life of Christ, in particular his passion and crucifixion. The "Resurrection," in the view of these scholars, is something less than the literal rising from the dead described in the Gospels.

Muggeridge notes that by subtle misuse of the historical-critical method, particularly critique of form and genera, the reader can be led to believe that particular biblical occurrences are to be understood as **folklore**, or in a **mythical, poetic, allegorical** or other sense, rather than as actual historical events.

As earlier noted, in order to interpret as historically doubtful what the Gospels describe as the miracles of Jesus, *considerable time must pass before it is recorded and the author cannot have been an eyewitness to the event.* As we will see, the assumption of **late-date redaction** (later compiling or writing) is essential in promoting the idea that key events such as miracles never actually happened.

For example, if the Gospels *Matthew* and *John* originated after the probable death of those apostle / evangelists, those Gospels would be less credible as historical documents since they would not have been based on *eyewitness* reports.[104]

Two important factors in the successful promotion of the modernist view have been, (a) the fact that most virtually ignore the voluminous writings of the Early Church Fathers and, (b) they dismiss the scholarly works of colleagues who – skilled not only in ancient Greek but in

---

104 *The Desolate City,* 27.

ancient Hebrew and Aramaic – conclude that it is highly probable that the Gospels in the canonical Greek were based on Semitic writings (Hebrew or Aramaic) that originated with eyewitness.

There is nothing intrinsically wrong with the historical-critical method. Its proper use has been encouraged by the Church.[105] By its nature, however, its potential for misuse is great. In recent decades a number of late-date scholars – through their use of dubious assumptions and their virtual disregard of the Early Church Fathers and the findings of early-date scholars who disagree with them – have led Catholics and other Christians in great numbers to doubt or abandon their faith. As noted by Muggeridge, the historical-critical method obviously presents the opportunity to make many such dubious assumptions.

Seeds of dissent – and of scandal

In his devastating book *Goodbye, Good Men; How Liberals brought Corruption into the Catholic Church,* Michael S. Rose writes:

> All too often seminary faculty members use textbooks [parroting] Catholic dissent: that the Bible is not to be taken seriously …; one religion is as good as the next; the pope is not infallible; the Magisterium is authoritatively abusive; the Real Presence of Christ in the Eucharist is just an old pre-Vatican II myth; Christ was not really divine; God is feminine; Mass is simply a meal in which we should eat bread that 'looks like real bread'; women should be ordained priests …; homosexuality [i.e., homosexual acts] is normal; and contraception is morally acceptable.[106]

Rose has his critics. However, in several subsequent issues of the *New Oxford Review* both he and NOR have been forthright in defending this book and the research on which it is based. In any case, all the conditions noted above by Rose have been well documented for decades in many Catholic books, articles and in non-print Catholic media.

And so as Catholics, we must ask: *"Why, since the late 60s have so many in Catholic education at all levels – particularly in our seminaries, universities, colleges and high schools – been teaching such dissent?"* Can the answer be other than that *they lost their faith in Jesus*

---

105 Pontifical Biblical Commission: "The Historicity of the Gospels," April 21, 1964; "The Interpretation of the Bible in the Church," March 18, 1994.
106 *Goodbye, Good Men,* 90. © 2002 by Michael S. Rose, Published by Regnery Publishing, Inc. All rights reserved.

as he is described in the Gospels, and in the Catholic Church as authoritative interpreter of the Bible?

"But WHY did so many of what appeared to be Catholicism's finest lose their faith in the biblical Jesus?"

As indicated at the outset of Step 3, in addition to the dissent following *Humanae Vitae*, I submit that it was due largely to the influence of books and articles by some of our most prestigious Catholic biblical scholars; those who popularized the "late-date / no eyewitness – lovingly embellished" view of the origin of the Gospels.

As earlier noted, one of the most prominent of these late-date scholars, until his death August 4, 1998, was Fr. Raymond E. Brown, S.S.

Once this late-date blurring of the Gospels is accepted by the seminary faculty member (as well as others in Catholic education) he / she may begin thinking along these lines:

> Surely the prestige of Fr. Brown and his late-date colleagues must be based on exemplary *objective* biblical scholarship.

> As shattering as this will be to the Catholic faith of so many young men in this seminary, if the Gospels really *are* of doubtful historicity – originating with unknown authors who never met Jesus but who lovingly embellished the Gospel stories – I *must* teach accordingly.

> I must make known to my students that prestigious Catholic biblical scholars have cast doubt on the historicity of the Gospels and, in the extreme, even on the divinity of Jesus.

> Admittedly, after being taught these views some seminarians and others may throw off all spiritual and moral constraints. But, ultimately, will any resultant gravely aberrant behavior (what we used to call mortal sin) keep them out of heaven forever? That is by no means certain, according to many who speak on behalf of the Church today.

> In any case, even though some many may leave this seminary upon hearing it, I must teach that the Gospels are of late origin, as discerned by authoritative Catholic exegetes and affirmed by many Catholic theologians. After ordination as priests, these seminarians may prefer to reveal only gradually to their congregations the doubtful historicity of much of the Gospels. Otherwise too many parishioners might leave the Church. But reveal it they must. Catholics should not continue to maintain the rigid, pre-Vatican II notion that the Gospels originated with eyewitnesses to Jesus

(apostles Matthew and John) or with Peter (Mark) or Paul (Luke).

More about dissent in the Church in Part II. At this point, however, let us cut through all of this to the central question: *Who has the stronger case, objectively, in regard to the Gospels; Fr. Brown and his late-date colleagues, or other scholars who conclude that the Gospels were of quite early origin?* Let the evidence, outlined in these pages, speak for itself.

The many assumptions on which late-date / no eyewitness biblical scholars base their theories.

As earlier noted, without doubt, until his death in 1998, one of the most influential Catholic biblical scholars of the last quarter-century in the English-speaking world was Fr. Raymond E. Brown. With conviction, Fr. Brown set forth his belief that no eyewitness wrote a Gospel, that all Gospels were written late (roughly between A.D. 68 and 100) and, quite probably, were lovingly embellished by later followers who never knew Jesus.

Fr. Brown's popularity was such that, in the mid-1990s, I was told *"If you write critically about Father Brown, you will not be read."* This well-intended advice came from a priest who now appears regularly on EWTN Catholic Global Television and whose loyalty to the Pope and Magisterium is unquestioned. This priest knew that Fr. Brown's twenty-five or so books were extremely popular in most seminaries and Catholic universities in the U.S. and elsewhere and that scholarly works challenging his views, regardless of the merit of the challenge, are summarily ignored, or dismissed and their authors denigrated. At this writing I am told that Fr. Brown's popularity among priests remains high.

Fr. Brown was also co-editor of the *Jerome Biblical Commentary* and of the substantially revised successor, the *New Jerome Biblical Commentary*, which carries his *Nihil Obstat.* At the time of his death he was a member of the Pontifical Biblical Commission; he had been reappointed in 1996. He had previously served on the Commission from 1972 to 1978. Although he had been strongly criticized by some as a modernist, Fr. Brown described himself as a centrist. One indication of this is his disapproval of the methods of the Jesus Seminar.[107] His exegesis on the *Gospel according to John* was held in particularly high regard by many biblical scholars.

Fr. Brown was esteemed by many Catholic and Protestant biblical

---

107 e.g., *An Introduction to New Testament Christology,* 24-25.

exegetes and indicated a general acceptance *on faith* of what the Catholic Church teaches. However, because he cast doubt on the historical authenticity of a number of biblical passages, he was seen by many as undermining the faith of Catholics and other Christians.

As we shall see, much of Fr. Brown disagreement with Catholic teaching in regard to the historical authenticity of the Gospels can be attributed to his belief that, after the death of Christ, several decades passed before any of the four canonical Gospels was written and that none of the four was written by an eyewitness to Christ's ministry. For example, in *The Birth of the Messiah* Fr. Brown wrote:

> Since *no one of the four evangelists was himself an eyewitness to the ministry of Jesus* the arrangement of ministry material in the Gospels was logical rather than chronological.[108]

On what basis does Fr. Brown make this claim, as a result of which, surely, so many have lost their faith? In his book *Biblical Exegesis and Church Doctrine*, published in 1985, Fr. Brown provided an answer. There he noted that the Vatican II document on Divine Revelation (*Dei Verbum*) respects the "ancient terminology of 'apostles and apostolic men'" in referring to those who wrote the Gospels. However, Fr. Brown then made the following problematic statement:

> [The Biblical] Commission made a clear distinction between the apostles who preached and those who wrote the Gospels in dependency on that preaching. *Implicitly, then, the Commission allowed for the view of most scholars today that no one of the evangelists was an eyewitness of the ministry of Jesus"* (Emphasis added).[109]

It appears, however, that what the Biblical Commission implicitly allowed is quite contrary to what *Dei Verbum* explicitly stated:

> *The Church has always and everywhere maintained, and continues to maintain, the apostolic origin of the four Gospels. The apostles preached, as Christ had charged them to do, and then, under the inspiration of the Holy Spirit, they and others of the apostolic age handed on to us in writing the same message they had preached, the foundation of our faith: the fourfold Gospel, according to Matthew, Mark, Luke and John"* (Cf. St. Irenaeus, *Adv. Haer*, III,11, 8: *Petrologia Graeca* 7, 885; Ed. Sagnard, p. 194.).[110]

---

108 *The Birth of the Messiah*, 1993 edition, 27.
109 *Biblical Exegesis and Church Doctrine*, 14.
110 *Vatican Council II Documents;* New Revised Edition; *Dei Verbum, Chapter* V,

The apostles who had been charged by Christ to preach were the eleven, including Matthew and John (Lk 6:12-16, Mt 28:18-20). *They and others of the apostolic age* (Mark and Luke meet this criterion) *handed on to us in writing the same message they had preached ....* Do these words of the Council Fathers somehow imply that no apostle "handed on to us in writing" a Gospel? I think not.

Here, from another source, are the words of Irenaeus to which the bishops of the Council referred:

> *Matthew issued a written Gospel among the Hebrews in their own dialect, while Peter and Paul were preaching at Rome and laying the foundations of the church. After their departure, Mark, the disciple and interpreter of Peter, did also hand down to us in writing what had been preached by Peter. Luke also, the companion of Paul, recorded in a book the Gospel preached by him. Afterwards, John, the disciple of the Lord, who also had leaned upon His breast, did himself publish a Gospel during his residence at Ephesus in Asia.*[111]

Irenaeus wrote, "*Matthew issued a written Gospel among the Hebrews in their own dialect.*" Irenaeus, pupil of Polycarp, became the second Bishop of Lyons at about age 37. He succeeded martyred bishop St. Pothinus in A.D. 177 or 178.[112] Surely Irenaeus would either have seen *Matthew* in Hebrew or otherwise have been certain of its origin and its content. In particular, he would certainly have been aware of what was later designated Mt 16:18-19 (Peter named the Rock, and promised the keys, by Jesus himself).

Is it conceivable that Irenaeus could have written so forthrightly of these Gospels if any of them were not in full accord with what Irenaeus had learned as a disciple of Polycarp, who was a disciple of John, who was an apostle of Jesus?

But the literal truth of *Matthew* (or any of the four Gospels) is nowhere questioned by Irenaeus or any of the other Early Church Fathers. And so – in regard to the authenticity of "Thou art Peter and upon this Rock I will build my Church ... I will give you the keys of the kingdom of heaven ..." and the rest of *Matthew* 16:13-19 – whose opinion is more likely to be the correct one: (a) Irenaeus, who wrote little more than one century later, or; (b) The modernist biblical scholar,

---

par. 18, 760-761.
111 CCEL; Irenaeus, III. 1, 1, **www.ccel.org/ccel/schaff/hcc1.i.XII.79.html**
112 *The Faith of the Early Fathers*, Vol. 1, 84.

writing after almost twenty centuries?

But, for reasons he does not make clear, Fr. Brown seems to imply that the unknown writer who produced what became the canonical Greek version of *Matthew* made up the words of Jesus at Caesarea Philippi. This view, if substantiated, would cast doubt on the historical basis for the papacy.

As noted above, other than mere speculation, there is no basis on which to doubt the historicity of the Gospels, including the primacy of Peter. Nonetheless, this doubt in regard to Petrine primacy has been promulgated not only within the Church but also as part of our ecumenical outreach to our separated brethren.

Consider the following words of Fr. Brown, made as a member of the Lutheran-Catholic Dialogue, which imply that Petrine primacy did not have its origin with Christ – and with God the Father – near Caesarea Philippi but probably originated sometime after the Resurrection. Of course, no Gospel records any such post-Resurrectional statement by Christ or anyone else:

> I have reported that we [members of the Lutheran-Catholic Dialogue] did not concentrate on Matt 16:17-19 in any isolated way, but we did come to significant agreement that much of what is peculiar to Matthew in that Caesarea Philippi scene is probably post-resurrectional in origin.[113]

Now Mt 16:17-19 ("Thou art Peter and upon this Rock I will build my Church ... I will give you the keys of the kingdom of heaven ....") is, as noted, the primary scriptural passage in support of the primacy of Peter and, thus, of the papacy for the past 2,000 years. Denial of its meaning, after fifteen centuries, was central to the cause of the Reformation and all the upheaval and bloodshed that has followed.

What explanation can be given for the fact that Fr. Brown, in this public ecumenical forum, could so casually cast serious doubt on what the Church has taught for almost 2,000 years and affirmed at the Second Vatican Council and in the *Catechism of the Catholic Church*, by saying "much of what is peculiar to Matthew in that Caesarea Philippi scene is probably post-resurrectional in origin."?

It is commonly (and superficially, as indicated below) argued that, because Mark (Mk 8:27-30) and Luke (Lk 9:18-22), in describing that event are silent in regard to Jesus designating Peter as the "Rock" and stating that he would give Peter the "keys," that Jesus never called

---

113 *Biblical Reflections on Crises Facing the Church.* 72.

Peter the "Rock" or promised him the keys.

Why did Mark and Luke omit "Thou art Peter and upon this rock ..." from their Gospels?

Suppose, after hearing Peter preach on many occasions, Mark said to him:

> "Peter, I have learned [whether from the *Gospel according to Matthew* or another source] that Jesus appointed you the 'Rock' on which he would build his Church, that he would give you the keys of the kingdom of heaven and the power to 'bind and loose.' And yet I have not heard you speak of these matters to the crowds here in Rome. In my account of your preaching, may I add these important points?"

> Peter replies: "Mark, whom do we wish to convert here in this city?" "Why Romans, of course." answers Mark. "And do you think these Romans – knowing little about our faith, having no clear concept of heaven and quick to oppose any perceived threat to their Empire – would be receptive to a Gospel that speaks of me as holding the keys of a kingdom, with the power to bind and loose, exalted as the Rock, etc.? How do you think the Emperor [Claudius, 41-54; Nero, 54-68] would respond upon hearing these words about me from his informers?"

> "I see your point, Peter." says Mark. "Write your Gospel," says Peter, "but omit those details. Your Gospel will help us introduce the Romans to the teachings of our Lord and Savior. It is of no importance, for now, that they learn what Jesus said to me near Caesarea Philippi. When the time is right – when they understand who Jesus was and what he taught – they will know that the kingdom of which we speak is no threat to them or to Rome. Then, when the facts you mention will present no obstacle to them, we can make them known here."

This scenario is plausible whether or not Mark was then in possession of the apostle Matthew's account of the life of Jesus. It is also plausible if the *Gospel according to Mark* was "composed in a Semitic language by St. Peter the apostle," which Fr. Carmignac stated was "sufficiently probable."[114]

Although Luke gives no location, his account of Peter's *confession* (Lk 9:18-22) is similar to Mark's, ending with, "But he charged and commanded them to tell this to no one ..." and not including, "Thou art

---

114 *The Birth of the Synoptic Gospels,* 87.

Peter and upon this rock ... I will give you the keys ..." (Mt 16:18-19).
[115]

One explanation for Luke's omission may be the following from the Introduction to *The Gospel according to Luke* in the NAB: *"Most scholars agree that Luke made use of Mark's gospel as one of his sources; some even consider it to be Luke's principal source ...."*[116]

Through Paul and other sources, Luke would almost certainly have known that, after Peter's confession, Matthew had written, "Thou art Peter and upon this rock ... I will give you the keys ...." (Mt 16:18-19).

Luke's Gospel almost certainly preceded *Acts*, and the last chapter of *Acts* refers to Paul as still living. It is well attested that Peter and Paul were martyred in Rome, under Nero, about A.D. 67. Therefore it is virtually certain that Luke composed his Gospel before 67, while Peter and Paul were still living.[117]

Did Luke see Mark's omission of "Thou art Peter and upon this rock ... I will give you the keys ..." as prudent, given the very real risk to Peter's life, particularly in Rome during the reign of Nero (A.D. 54 to 68)? Was this the reason that Luke, possibly at Paul's direction, also omitted that passage from his Gospel? This seems to me a reasonable explanation for Luke's omission.

Given the great risk to Peter at that time, the omission of the Matthean "Thou art Peter and upon this rock ... I will give you the keys ... " by Mark and Luke lends no weight to the claim of some that Jesus never said these words to Peter. Even those who disagree must acknowledge that, (a) there is sound biblical evidence that it was Christ's intention that Peter lead the apostles (e.g., Lk 22:32 and Jn 21:15-17) and (b) based on the "Great Commission" of the apostles (Mt

---

115 In all three synoptic Gospels Jesus strictly charges the disciples to tell no one that he is the Christ: Mt 16:20, Mk 8:30, Lk 9:21.

116 *The New American Bible, The New Catholic Translation,* © 1983 by Thomas Nelson, Inc., 1107.

117 In several verses of *Luke* – (13:34-35, 19:43-44, 21:20-24, 23:28-31) – Christ clearly foretells the destruction of Jerusalem. That event occurred in A.D. 70, more than 30 years later. However, during the latter half of the 20ᵗʰ century many biblical scholars inexplicably claimed that those verses indicated that Luke wrote his Gospel *after* the year 70; possibly as late as 90. The difficulty with this view is twofold: (a) In each of these verses Luke clearly quotes Christ describing an event that *will* occur, not one that *has occurred.* (b) Luke addressed his Gospel to *Theophilus* so he would "know the truth ...." If he composed his Gospel after the year 70, *how could Luke fail to write that those prophecies of Christ came true*? The fact that Luke is silent about the fulfillment of those prophecies strongly indicates that Luke composed his Gospel *before* the destruction of Jerusalem in A.D. 70.

28:16-20), *it is with Christ's own authority that those apostles and their successors have elected successor pontiffs.*

In answer to a question in *101 Questions and Answers on the Bible,* Fr. Raymond E. Brown indicated that none of the four evangelists identified himself and that, although the fourth Gospel refers to the "disciple whom Jesus loved" (e.g., Jn 21:20), the Gospel does not name that disciple (p. 60).

Inexplicably, Fr. Brown does not inform the reader of *101 Questions* of the following words of Irenaeus, Bishop of Lyons, who was linked historically to Christ through the apostle John and martyred Bishop Polycarp, as earlier noted. After affirming that Matthew, Mark and Luke wrote Gospels, Irenaeus, writing between A.D. 180 and 199, states:

> Afterwards, John, the disciple of the Lord, who also had leaned upon His breast, [Jn 21:20] did himself publish a Gospel during his residence at Ephesus in Asia.[118]

And how can one explain Fr. Brown's silence in *101 Questions* in regard to Origen, who, in Book V of his *Commentary on John's Gospel,* ca. A.D. 230-250, wrote:

> Why need we speak of him who reclined upon the bosom of Jesus, John, who has left us one Gospel, though he confessed that he might write so many that the world could not contain them? And he wrote also the Apocalypse ....[119]

Nor does Fr. Brown note that Eusebius of Caesarea, ca. A.D. 290-340, wrote similarly of the "apostle ... whom Jesus loved," and that his Gospel was "genuine" and "known to all the churches under heaven ...":

> At that time the apostle and evangelist John, the one whom Jesus loved, was still living in Asia, and governing the churches of that region ....[120]

> And in the first place his [John's] Gospel, which is known to all the churches under heaven, must be acknowledged as genuine. That it has with good reason been put by the ancients in the fourth place, after the other three Gospels, may be made evident in the

---

118 Irenaeus; *Against Heresies,* III.1.2, **www.ccel.org/fathers2**
119 *Eusebius; The History of the Church,* VI.25. **www.ccel.org/fathers2**
120 Ibid., III.23.1, **www.ccel.org/fathers2**

following way ...."[121]

In addition to John, Matthew the apostle is also affirmed in a number of documents of the Early Church Fathers as the author of the Gospel that bears his name. For example, Origen (244 A.D.) wrote twenty-five books of commentaries on *Matthew*. He is quoted by Eusebius, in *History of the Church:*

> Among the four Gospels, which are the only indisputable ones in the Church of God under heaven, I have learned by tradition that the first was written by Matthew, who was once a publican, but afterwards an apostle of Jesus Christ, and it was prepared for the converts from Judaism, and published in the Hebrew language.[122]

In *The History of the Church,* by Eusebius of Caesarea (*ca.* A.D. 325), we read:

> For Matthew, who had at first preached to the Hebrews, when he was about to go to other peoples, committed his Gospel to writing in his native tongue ....[123] and;

> Pantænus was one of these [early evangelists] and is said to have gone to India. It is reported that among persons there who knew of Christ, he found the Gospel according to Matthew, which had anticipated his own arrival. For Bartholomew, one of the apostles, had preached to them, and left with them the writing of Matthew in the Hebrew language.[124]

In addition, similar affirmations in regard to Matthew and his Gospel are found in *Jesus, Peter and the Keys* by St. Athanasius, ca. A.D. 350; Epiphanius, A.D. 376; C. Lapide in regard to Jerome, A.D. 390; and Augustine, ca. A.D. 400. The C. Lapide reference is of particular interest, as noted in *Jesus, Peter and the Keys*, p. 368:

> S. Jerome declares that he had seen S. Matthew's Gospel, written in Hebrew, in the Library of Pamphilus the Martyr, at Caesarea, and from it had transcribed his own copy. This Hebrew text is now, however, lost.[125]

---

121 Ibid., III.24.2, **www.ccel.org/fathers2**
122 Ibid., VI.25, **www.ccel.org/fathers2**
123 Ibid., VI.25.6, **www.ccel.org/fathers2**
124 *Eusebius; The History of the Church,* **www.ccel.org/ccel/schaff/npnf201.iii.x.xi. html**
125 Cornelius A. Lapide, *The Great Commentary upon the Holy Scriptures,* trans. Thomas W. Mossman, (London: John Hodges, 1893), xxxvii.

We can almost see Jerome at his table writing "Thou art Peter and upon this Rock .... I will give you the keys ...." the Great Commission given exclusively to the eleven remaining apostles by the risen Jesus, etc., as Jerome translated into Latin, referring to his own transcribed copy of Matthew's Gospel written in Hebrew. And, of course, Jerome placed the *Gospel according to Matthew* first in his Latin Vulgate translation.

But, in the 1993 revision of *The Birth of the Messiah,* we again find Fr. Brown presenting the idea that evangelist "Matthew" was not an eyewitness to Jesus' ministry.[126] However, as we have seen and will see below, there is very strong historical evidence that the *Gospel according to Matthew* and the *Gospel according to John* originated with those apostles.

In *The Birth of the Messiah* Fr. Brown makes the following supposition:

> Most scholars today maintain that the Gospel [according to Matthew] was written in Syria by an unknown Greek-speaking Jewish Christian, living in the 80s in a mixed community with converts of both Jewish and Gentile descent. This is the theory presupposed in my discussion of the Matthean infancy narrative.[127]

In the preceding pages of this work of Fr. Brown's I found no sound basis for this self-described *theory*; actually several assumptions.

But unless he labels his assumptions, theories, etc., as such and gives a solid factual-historical basis for each for the scrutiny of the average reader, how are we to evaluate his views in light of the wealth of material written by scholars who study Semitisms, the Neo-Patristic Scholars (described below), the Fathers of the early Church and other non-biblical historical sources?

As earlier noted, Fr. Brown expressed doubt about the historical value of the writings of the Early Church Fathers as follows: "*but unless those writers [Church Fathers] had historical information they cannot answer historical questions.*"[128]

Eighteen hundred years ago, Marcion, an otherwise unknown Christian, wrote about the martyrdom of St. Polycarp as follows in a letter from the Church of Smyrna to the Christian Community of Philomelium in Greater Phrygia. Polycarp was martyred – stabbed after

---

126 *The Birth of the Messiah*, 1993 ed., 45-46.
127 Ibid., 45.
128 *Biblical Exegesis and Church Doctrine*, 20.

an unsuccessful attempt to burn him alive – in about A.D. 155. Let us ask ourselves if we can doubt St. Polycarp's grasp of history, or that of the many other martyrs of the early Church:

> *[T]he Proconsul urged him and said, 'Take the oath and I will re lease you; revile Christ.' Polycarp answered: 'Eighty-six years I have served Him,* [i.e., since about the year 69] *and he has never done me wrong. How then, should I be able to blaspheme my King who has saved me?* '[129]

In *Faith of the Early Fathers*, Fr. W. A. Jurgens was moved to write as follows about this passage: "It is a singularly implacable person who can read it without tears."

Fr. Manuel Miguens affirms early-date Gospels

In his book *The Battle for the American Church* the late Msgr. George A. Kelly documents the criticism of Fr. Brown's scholarship by Fr. Manuel Miguens, O.F.M., S.T.D., S.S.D.; a priest who held doctorate degrees in theology and scripture, and whose language skills included four biblical languages (Greek, Hebrew, Aramaic and Syriac), Latin, Spanish, English and four other languages. In a review in *Triumph* magazine Fr. Miguens had this to say about what Fr. Brown had written about apostolic succession:

> Brown's argument is affected (and infected) by constructions like likelihood, probability, almost certainly, plausibly, it would seem, seemingly, etc. This precaution and uncertainty in argumentation is in sharp contrast to the certainty with which he states his conclusions. Brown appears to be not nearly so certain of his arguments as he is about what he wants them to prove.[130]

Msgr. Kelly also notes that Fr. Raymond Brown and Fr. Joseph Fitzmyer had evaluated the historical basis for Jesus' virginal conception and "concluded that the scriptural basis for the belief is dubious if not negative." In Fr. Miguens' subsequent scholarly work, *The Virgin Birth*:

> [Fr. Miguens reexamines] the same evidence [and] concludes quite

---

129 "The Martyrdom of St. Polycarp," *The Faith of the Early Fathers*, Vol. 1, par. 79a, 31.

130 Quoted in *The Battle for the American Church*, 123. It originally appeared in the April, 1972 edition of *Triumph*, a conservative Catholic magazine published from 1965 to 1975 by L. Brent Bozell, former Senior Editor of *National Review* and author of *Conscience of a Conservative*.

oppositely that the scriptural evidence as to the historicity of the virgin birth is affirmative.

Msgr. Kelly noted that Fr. Miguens' book received decidedly negative reviews in two Catholic publications,[131] but was welcomed in many quarters. As examples of favorable reviews, Msgr. Kelly noted that a Lutheran review described it as a defeat of the methodology of Fr. Brown and Fr. Fitzmyer and an excellent defense of divine revelation. A Greek Orthodox priest also praised Fr. Miguens' book, noting that it strongly affirmed the virgin birth of Jesus in regard to its historical credibility.

For his skilled effort in defending the orthodox teaching of the Catholic Church, and at that time having completed five probationary years at Catholic University of America in Washington, D.C., one would think the University would have been quick to grant him tenure. But, despite unanimous endorsement from the Theology Department, as well as from many students and others, C.U.A. refused to grant tenure to Fr. Miguens and he was forced to leave. Msgr. Kelly noted that C.U.A. gave no reason for denying Fr. Miguens' tenure.[132]

We might expect a better outcome at C.U.A. today. When elected as president of Catholic University in 1998, Vincentian Fr. David M. O'Connell took the Oath of Fidelity to the Pope, reportedly the first president of C.U.A. to take this oath. Under the 1983 Code of Canon Law, college and university presidents are required to take this oath, which requires that they "hold fast to the deposit of faith in its entirety and "avoid any teachings opposed to the faith." However, most presidents of Catholic colleges and universities in the United States have not taken this oath.

For further insight into the extent to which hypothesis and conjecture has been used by biblical scholars, consider *The New Biblical Theorists: Raymond E. Brown and Beyond,* also by Msgr. George Kelly. Again we find Fr. Miguens in the forefront in pointing out serious flaws in Fr. Brown's reasoning. For example, in regard to the infancy narratives:

> Miguens replies that Brown goes beyond the evidence. *He simply declares the infancy narratives unreliable without proving it.* This, Miguens says, is not a sound starting point for historical research .... Brown unduly limits the kind of witness he accepts as provid-

---

131 *The Catholic Biblical Quarterly* (Vol. 38, 1976) and *Theological Studies* (Vol. 37, No. 1, 1977).
132 *The Battle for the American Church,* 121-124.

ing suitable testimony to Christ's conception and birth. *Sometimes he does this by making a new translation which distorts the meaning of the evangelist* (Emphasis added).

Miguens acknowledges that Fr. Brown indicates in a footnote that infancy narrative coverage is provided by Mary. (page 431, footnote 76 of *The Birth of the Messiah).* However, according to Miguens, Fr. Brown states that there is *a priori unlikelihood* that Mary is the source for the material in the Matthean infancy narrative, which centers on Joseph.

Miguens counters that Mary was close enough to the apostles and disciples to give any information she wanted (Mk 3:31, Jn 2:1-11, Jn 12:19:26), and that Fr. Brown has no evidence to offer that before or after the Resurrection she did not talk to the disciples or to anyone else.[133]

As an argument against the historicity of the infancy narratives, Fr. Brown's view of a sequestered Mary is completely without biblical / historical foundation. Any evangelist writing about the birth and infancy of Jesus surely could have found Mary or someone to whom Mary gave detailed information.

To make up an infancy narrative would have been foolish; surely any evangelist would have anticipated that – sooner or later – someone would show his infancy narrative to Mary – or one to whom Mary had told the true story. Then, if his version were not substantially true, he would have been quickly exposed as a fraud. Once labeled as such, he might as well make a bonfire of the rest of the material he may have written about Jesus; no one would accept any of it as true. And so it seems highly probable that the evangelist's accounts of the infancy came from Mary herself, perhaps indirectly, which would account for the differences in those accounts. Fr. Miguens presents a formidable case to the effect that Fr. Brown has not proved otherwise.

Historical authenticity of Gospels – a necessary starting point for historical criticism

In his article "Scriptural Duurchinander" [German, meaning *tangle*], the late Fr. William G. Most commented on the confusion among Scripture scholars. He noted that Reginald Fuller had been in the forefront of Form Criticism before abandoning it as "bankrupt." Fr. Most quotes as follows from Fuller's review of Fr. Brown's book *The Birth of the Messiah:* "It is ironic that just at the time when the limita-

---

133 *The New Biblical Theorists,* 58-60.

tions of the historical-critical method are being discovered in Protestantism, Roman Catholic scholars should be bent on pursuing it so relentlessly."[134]

Fr. Most, acknowledging that abuses have occurred, suggests corrective measures. Although in this article he does not include among them the study of *Semitisms*, he argues for the same end result by listing a number of historical reasons to believe that the Gospels are historically authentic. When viewed as such, he indicates that historical criticism as an exegetical tool can be useful.[135]

Semitisms and their importance as a basis for Historical-Critical study

Introductory Comments

Having seen the extent to which the late-date / no eyewitness view relies on hypotheses, let us now consider the findings of Fr. Jean Carmignac, Claude Tresmontant and other early-date / eyewitness scholars. Most of the late-date / no eyewitness scholars base their biblical studies on the Greek, with little attention if any given to the *Semitisms* of the Gospels. In contrast, these early-date scholars have studied the Gospels not only in Greek but also in Semitic languages (i.e., ancient Hebrew and Aramaic) and present evidence that, in large part, the Gospels were first written in a Semitic language. *These findings indicate very early Gospel authorship, almost certainly by hearers of Jesus or one or more of the apostles.*

In his book, *The Birth of the Synoptic Gospels*, Fr. Jean Carmignac outlines the history of the study of Semitisms – evidence that the canonical Greek *Gospel according to Matthew* and the *Gospel according to Mark* were translations from a Semitic language (Hebrew and to some extent Aramaic) and that the same is true for the sources used by Luke.

Fr. Carmignac notes that the scholarly practice of "looking behind the Greek" is by no means new; in 1518, Erasmus "had sorted out the earliest Semitisms" and by 1750 more than one hundred philologists in Germany and the Lowlands had conducted such research.[136]

Unfortunately, in 1555, Jonathan Albrecht von Widmanstadt began

---

134 *Catholic Biblical Quarterly*, 1978, Vol. 40, 120.
135 The Catholic Resource Network; Trinity Communications, Manassas, VA
www.ewtn.com/library/SCRIPTUR/TANGLE.TXT
136 *The Birth of the Synoptic Gospels*, 17.

successfully promoting the error that, by the time in which Christ lived, the Hebrew language had fallen into disuse. Instead, when the Fathers referred to "Hebrew," scholars should understand that they were referring to Aramaic. This error was not corrected until about 1950; following the discovery of the Dead Sea Scrolls, almost all of which were written in Hebrew.[137]

Toward the latter part of the eighteenth century, Semitisms were a source of embarrassment to F. C. Baur and other late-date proponents of the Tübingen School. These scholars glossed over these studies or dismissed them by vaguely attributing them to the native language of the Evangelists or their wish to imitate the *Septuagint*.[138]

Interest in Semitisms increased in the decades preceding the twentieth century. Soon, large quantities of papyrus from the early Christian era were unearthed in Egypt on which were found phrasing similar to that found in the New Testament. Rather than making use of this resource to sort out false parallels of language and better identify true Semitisms in the Gospels, scholars became divided, as noted by Fr. Carmignac:

> One [group of scholars] especially widespread in Germany, refuses to study Semitisms seriously, under the old pretext that they are not sufficiently numerous or that they are due to the mother tongue of the authors, or that they result from a more or less conscious imita-tion of the Septuagint.
>
> The other tendency, represented in England and the United States, sorts out the many Semitisms, especially from the poor translations of the supposed original; but it often forgets to prove the existence of them and to be specific about their exact probative value ....
> Certainly a more balanced position is represented by Lagrange, Millar Burrows and R. Martin; but they never succeed in posing the problem in such a way that they can elicit the assent either of the opponents or the proponents of Semitisms.[139]

Fr. Carmignac set out to "take up the problem at its roots and remain on a strictly scientific plane." To do so he specified nine distinct categories of Semitisms, which he used to screen out all but valid

---

137 Ibid., 65.
138 The *Septuagint* is a Greek translation of the ancient Jewish scriptures. It was translated in Alexandria sometime between 150 and 300 B.C. by about seventy Hebrew scholars. It was widely used in the Holy Land at the time of Christ. The New Testament includes numerous references to the Septuagint.
139 *The Birth of the Synoptic Gospels*, 20.

Semitisms.[140] Fr. Carmignac confronts critics with a two-stage argument for the early-date historicity of the synoptic Gospels:

(a) *Only the Semitisms of the final three categories (composition, transmission, translation) have been retained in order that no objection could be made regarding either the mother tongue of the authors or their desire to imitate the Septuagint.* (b) *But even in the first five categories (borrowing, imitation, thought, vocabulary, syntax) and especially in the sixth (style), the abundance of evidence presented goes far beyond any possibility that the author was influenced by his mother tongue or by the prestige of a venerable text.*[141]

Fr. Carmignac noted that the technical study of the above, which specialists will require, was "on the drawing boards." He anticipated it would be "even more convincing and, let us hope, irrefutable."

Unfortunately, Fr. Carmignac died before he was able to prepare and publish, in detailed written form, the findings he outlined in *The Birth of the Synoptic Gospels.* Surely his completed study would have been formidable.

Although unable to complete his detailed study, Fr. Carmignac has given us his key conclusions:

In short, the latest dates that can be admitted are around 50 for *Mark* (and the *Collection of Discourses*), around 55 for *Completed Mark*, around 55-60 for *Matthew*, between 58 and 60 for Luke.

But the earliest are clearly more probable: *Mark* around 42, *Completed Mark* around 45, (Hebrew) *Matthew* around 50, (Greek) *Luke* a little after 50.

These conclusions, insofar as they refer to *Matthew,* are in full agreement with all the indications furnished by the Fathers. They easily harmonize with the precision furnished by Eusebius that Matthew would have wanted, before departing from Palestine, to leave a continuation of his preaching. They easily justify the reflection of Papias on the mediocre Greek translations which were attempted before a complete and official translation was produced.[142]

Note that, in contrast to Claude Tresmontant, Fr. Carmignac

---

140 Ibid., 21-41.
141 *The Birth of the Synoptic Gospels,* 40.
142 Ibid., 61.

believed that *Competed Mark* preceded *Hebrew Matthew*. In his chapter "The Synoptic Problem," Fr. Carmignac writes: "I admit that *Mark* seems to be the first and the earliest of our three Synoptics."[143]

Fr. Carmignac also wrote in support of a *Collection of Discourses*, a collection of the words of Jesus, which, although never found, probably originated at about the same time as the *Gospel according to Mark*.

> "By and large, it corresponds to the passages which are not found in *Mark* and which figure in identical or very similar terms in *Matthew* and *Luke*. German scholars of the last [nineteenth] century have given this source ... the name *Quelle* (meaning source, in German; commonly called "Q") and they have made it one of the pillars of their interpretation. I find myself in agreement with their opinion. This source was certainly in Hebrew...."[144]

Fr. Raymond E. Brown and Fr. Carmignac seem to agree that *Competed Mark* may have preceded *Hebrew Matthew* and that there is reason to believe that something like "Q" probably existed.

There the similarity ends, however. Contrary to Fr. Brown's views, Fr. Carmignac: (a) suggests that Peter was the author of the *Gospel according to Mark*; and (b) that all three synoptic Gospels were written not later than A.D. 60, and probably "a little after 50."[145]

Fr. Carmignac thus dates the origin of the Gospels according to Matthew, Mark and Luke within only about 17 to 27 years after the Resurrection. *Since, in about A.D. 56, Paul wrote that most of the five hundred who had seen the risen Christ were still living, these early dates given by Fr. Carmignac strongly support the historical authenticity of these Gospels.*

———

With the above as background, let us consider further information on Fr. Carmignac, Claude Tresmontant and several other biblical scholars and others who conclude that *all four Gospels originated before the year 70*.

Fr. Jean Carmignac spent six years in Qumrân translating the texts of the Dead Sea Scrolls. During this time he noted on index cards the many connections he found between the Scrolls and the New Testa-

———

143 Ibid., 43.
144 Ibid., 45.
145 Ibid., 61-63.

ment. His collection of such index cards became very large.

Fr. Carmignac then decided to see what the result would be if *Mark* [in the Canonical Greek] were translated into the Hebrew of Qumrân [i.e., the Hebrew of the earliest days of the Church.]:

> *I had imagined that this translation would be difficult because of the considerable differences between Semitic thought and Greek thought, but I was absolutely dumbfounded to discover that this translation was on the contrary, extremely easy. Around the middle of April, 1963, after only one day of work, I was convinced that the Greek text of Mark could not have been redacted directly into Greek and that it was in reality only the Greek translation of an original Hebrew.*[146]

After spending twenty years studying the Synoptic Gospels (and developing his nine categories of Semitisms), Fr. Carmignac wrote *La naissance des Evangiles Synoptiques,* O.E.I.L., Paris, a brief outline of his extensive studies, which was published in 1984. *The Birth of the Synoptic Gospels,* the English translation by Msgr. Michael J. Wrenn, was published in 1987. In this 109-page book Fr. Carmignac gives an overview of his own studies and outlines the work of more than forty other scholars – Catholics, Protestants and Jews – who, since the late nineteenth century, "*have recognized that the original language of the Gospel of Matthew [29 exegetes]; or of Mark [29 exegetes], or of the sources of Luke [31 exegetes] was indeed a Semitic language, either Hebrew or Aramaic.*" *In fact, among these sources noted by Fr. Carmignac, seven exegetes also claim an Aramaic or Hebrew source for significant parts of the Gospel according to John and of Acts.*[147]

The book, *Aramaic Sources of Mark's Gospel,* written by Maurice Casey was published in 1998, eleven years after the death of Fr. Carmignac. Beginning with certain verses of the *Gospel according to Mark*, Casey reconstructs the Aramaic from which he concludes they originated.

Although Casey used only thirty-nine verses of *Mark* in this study, his book is significant because; (a) *it is reported to be the first book to make use for this purpose of ALL the Aramaic scrolls found at Qumrân, and; (b) Although on several points Casey argues for Aramaic origin versus the Hebrew origin considered probable by Fr. Carmignac, Casey reportedly concluded that Mark's Gospel originated about A.D.*

---

146 *The Birth of the Synoptic Gospels,* 1.
147 Ibid., 66.

40, very close to Fr. Carmignac's estimate of 42 to 45.[148]

The late Claude Tresmontant was a distinguished Hebrew Scholar who produced his first work dedicated to Hebrew thought in 1953. He was a member of the faculty of the Sorbonne, University of Paris, where he taught medieval philosophy. He was the author of *The Hebrew Christ* and other studies of the history of Hebrew and Christian thought, including an Old Testament Hebrew-to-Greek (Septuagint) dictionary.

Tresmontant's critics may question whether, as he stated in *The Hebrew Christ*, he actually *proved* that "the four Gospels are, from one end to the other, translations from Hebrew writings set down earlier" (p. 22). [Fr. Carmignac affirmed this claim of Tresmontant in *The Birth of the Synoptic Gospels* (p. 81)]. We can understand the claim of some of Tresmontant's critics that in such matters, after two millennia, the best anyone can claim is a very high level of *probability.*

Another critic noted that Tresmontant might have gained greater recognition if he had quoted specific arguments set forth by individual late-date exegetes and, in each case, explained why his Semitism-based early-date conclusions were more compelling.

He could have been more gracious in defending his early-date conclusions. Labeling as *"simply absurd"* a conflicting opinion, as noted below, surely did not endear him to late-date scholars.

However, skilled as he was in ancient Hebrew, there can be no doubt that Tresmontant challenged the basis for the late-date / no eyewitness view of the Gospels in a way that no serious biblical scholar can ignore.

After an extensive study, Tresmontant became convinced that all four of the Gospels originated in Hebrew because of the many Semitisms so obviously transferred over into the original Greek translations of the Gospels.

In regard to the three synoptic Gospels he had studied, Fr. Carmignac concluded that he was equally convinced of the Semitic origin of the *Gospels according to Matthew* and *Mark* and of sources of the *Gospel according to Luke*, making allowance for Aramaic as the language of probable origin for some passages.

Tresmontant is unequivocal in his view in regard to note-taking by

---

148 "Aramaic Sources of Mark's Gospel," Maurice Casey, 1998, #102 in the *Monograph Series* of the Society for New Testament Studies, 58-60 and introductory editorial comments.

eyewitnesses:

> The hypothesis that no one actually hearing Jesus could or would ever have taken down any notes is simply absurd – psychologically as well as historically …. It would have been therefore the most natural thing in the world for the disciples of Jesus, educated according to the fashion of the time and place, to have noted down words, acts and gestures of Jesus in Hebrew …. It is very likely that a number of such collections of written notes in Hebrew existed.[149]

Tresmontant acknowledges the certainty that Aramaic was the *spoken* language of the people of that time, but is convinced that notes were taken down in Hebrew, not in Aramaic:

> The notes that were made were taken down in Hebrew, not in Aramaic. How do we know this? Quite simply because Hebrew was the written language, the language of the scribes and scholars. There were *oral* translations in Aramaic of the sacred books written in Hebrew; they were called *targumin* …. But in the era before the destruction of the Temple, putting these translations into writing was formally prohibited.

Tresmontant explains that, in particular, when we read *Matthew, Mark* and *Luke* in the original Greek,

> [W]e are constantly struck by the number of typically Hebrew expressions we find that have simply been lifted out of a Hebrew idiom and transferred over into a discourse that is Greek. These typically Hebrew expressions … would in many cases have been unintelligible for a [Greek] pagan reader living at the end of the first century, just as the same expressions would be unintelligible in a French translation, if they were simply rendered literally as they actually occur in the Hebrew and as they were in fact rendered in the Greek translations of the underlying Hebrew originals which constitute the finished Gospels.[150]

In regard to such difficult expressions, however, Tresmontant explains that later translations of the original Greek have been "diligently scraped, planed and honed until they were made intelligible, or else they were changed or simply dropped. The modern French reader

---

149 *The Hebrew Christ*, 4-5.
150 *The Hebrew Christ*, 10.

does not see any of this happening."[151] Based on his many examples, it would seem that the same applies in English and other modern languages.

Tresmontant tells us that, in contrast to the translators of the Gospels, Flavius Josephus had his works translated into "authentic and natural" Greek that would be welcomed by educated pagans.[152] Why then, we might ask, did those ancient Hebrew-into-Greek translators not also "scrape, plane and hone" those difficult Hebrew expressions? Why would they have simply lifted so many expressions from the Hebrew idiom directly into Greek? Surely the best explanation is the reverence they would have had for the very words written by those who were eyewitness to the ministry of Jesus or by indirect witnesses to Jesus through Peter and Paul.

Tresmontant explains that both the *word order* and *structure* of phrases in Hebrew are distinctive – not at all like Greek. He notes that In Hebrew the verb is typically placed before the subject, as in "Then went on his journey, Jacob, and came to the land of the people of the east" (Gen 29:1).[153]

An example of a difficult Hebrew *expression* is Luke 9:51. The Greek text reads: "He set his face to go to Jerusalem," which, Tresmontant explains, makes no sense either in Greek or in English. However, it proves to be a Hebrew expression frequently used in the Old Testament meaning he made a firm decision to go to Jerusalem..

Taking "set their faces ..." as an example from Jeremiah 44:12, Tresmontant states *"Interestingly enough, the Septuagint translators did not dare to translate it literally; they may have considered it too much for an ear accustomed to Greek. The translator of Luke, however, did dare to translate it literally* [from Hebrew into Greek]."[154] This is just one example of many pointed out by Tresmontant and others of the respect the evangelists showed for the original text from which they were translating, even though in some cases it produced what Tresmontant called "ear-grating" Greek.

Fr. Carmignac described the Greek of the Gospels more poetically: "It is the good Greek of a translator who has respect for a Semitic original, who conserves the flavor and scent of the original."[155]

---

151 Ibid., 10.
152 Ibid., 63.
153 *The Hebrew Christ*, 12.
154 Ibid. 113.
155 *The Birth of the Synoptic Gospels*, 3-4.

Tresmontant and a number of others also noted the following passage in John (5:2): "There *is* in Jerusalem by the Sheep Gate a pool...."
He points out, however, that this gate would have been destroyed in
A.D. 70. Why would the author use the present tense if the gate had
been razed?[156] Even if that gate had been spared, an author writing after
A.D. 70 surely would have said something like, "Jerusalem has been
destroyed, but the Sheep Gate and pool remain." But of course, other
than Jesus' predicting it (Mt 24:1-2, Mk 13:1-2 and Lk 19:41-44), the
entire New Testament is silent in regard to the destruction of Jerusalem.
Strong evidence, it would seem, that even this Gospel of John – long
regarded as the last of the Gospels – was written by A.D. 70; not more
than about four decades after the death and Resurrection of Jesus, i.e.,
during the lifetime of many who would have been witnesses to Jesus
himself and who would surely have challenged anything erroneous in
it.[157]

It was this difficulty that convinced John A. T. Robinson of the
early dates of origin of the Gospels. Until 1976 Robinson, a recognized
New Testament scholar and, for some years Anglican Bishop of
Woolrich, England, spoke and wrote in strong support of *late* dates of
the Gospels. However, to the astonishment of all biblical scholars, in
1976 he published a book in which he forthrightly affirmed pre-A.D. 70
dates for all four Gospels.[158] *He did so primarily because nowhere in
the New Testament is there any mention of the actual cataclysmic
destruction of Jerusalem in A.D. 70.*[159]

As earlier noted, Paul, in about A.D. 56 (about 23 years after the
death and Resurrection of Jesus), wrote that ***most of the more than five
hundred brethren who saw the risen Jesus were still alive*** (1 Cor
15:6).

In his book *The Gospel of Matthew; Translation and Notes,* Claude
Tresmontant concludes:

> The Gospel of Matthew is a translation into the Greek language of
> a collection or collections of notes or documents written in He-
> brew. These notes were taken down 'live,' on the spot, from one
> day to the next.[160]

---

156 *The Hebrew Christ,* 254-255.
157 Ibid., 255.
158 *Redating the New Testament.*
159 *The Jesus Papyrus*, 45.
160 *The Gospel of Matthew, Translation and Notes*, 597.

"The Synoptic Problem" is minimized if the Gospel of Matthew was the first written

In *The Hebrew Christ,* Claude Tresmontant devotes an entire chapter ("The Synoptic Problem;" 86 pages) to pointing out the many difficulties in accepting the popular late-date time frame for origination of the Gospels (A.D. 65-70 for the first, to A.D. 90-120 for the last), as well as the sequence now accepted by most biblical scholars: (Mark, Luke, Matthew, John). At the outset of this chapter Tresmontant writes:

> *If we agree that the Gospel according to Matthew is the earliest of the three synoptic Gospels – the hypothesis that appears to be by far the most plausible one, if it is not in fact a virtual certainty – many of the difficulties that have arisen out of an acceptance of the contrary hypothesis to the effect that Mark is the earliest of the synoptic Gospels and Matthew the latest disappear.*[161]

In May 1997, in his article *The Dates of the Gospels,* Fr. George H. Duggan, S.M., writes, "*the nearer a document is to the facts it narrates, the more likely it is that it will be factually accurate, just as an entry in a diary is more likely to be accurate than memoirs written forty or fifty years afterwards.*"[162]

Fr. Duggan cites C. C. Torrey, professor of Semitic Languages at Yale from 1900 to 1932. *Torrey challenged his New Testament exegete peers to point out a single passage in any of the four canonical Gospels which clearly indicates that it was written after A.D. 50. None could do so.*[163]

Pinchas E. Lapide, an Israeli scholar, produced several publications indicating the "Hebraicity" of the Gospels, including *Hidden Hebrew in the Gospels, Insights from Qumrân into the Languages of Jesus and Hebrew in the Gospels.*[164, 165]

Samuel Tobias Lachs, another Israeli Scholar, wrote articles showing that it was not by Aramaic but by Hebrew that some passages of Mathew, Luke and Acts are to be explained, His articles were published in 1977 and 1980 in the *Jewish Quarterly Review.*

---

161 *The Hebrew Christ,* 128.
162 See article in Appendix R. **www.catholic.net/rcc/Periodicals/Homiletic/May97/gospels.html**
163 J. Wenham; *Redating Matthew, Mark, and Luke,* 299, note 2.
164 *Judaica*; March, 1977 (in German); noted in *The Birth of the Synoptic Gospels,* 80.
165 *The Birth of the Synoptic Gospels,* 80.

Codices and Synod of Jerusalem of 836 affirm pre-A.D. 70 dates of Gospel origin

Marie-Christine Ceruti-Cendrier notes that several codexes from the 9th, 10th and 11th centuries also affirm early dates for all four Gospels: *Matthew* was written only eight years after the Ascension; *Mark,* eleven years after that event; *Luke,* fifteen years afterward and *John*, thirty-two years afterward. These time periods were also stated by the Synod of Jerusalem of 836. This indicates that all four Gospels were written before the fall of Jerusalem (A.D. 70) when eyewitnesses to the ministry of Jesus would have ensured the historical accuracy of those Gospels. This synod was presided over by the Melkite Patriarchs of Antioch, Alexandria and Jerusalem.[166]

Opposition to findings of early date / eyewitness scholars

As documented by Fr. Carmignac, writing in 1983, opposition to the conclusions of the early-date scholars was strong. For example:

(a) "Such audacity provoked an outcry of indignation and censure" (Against A. Resch, 1835-1912); (b) "[Julius] Wellhausen (1844-1918) was fiercely and bitterly criticized." (c) Protestant pastor Paul Vulliaud, in 1936 "presented ... the controversies which have succeeded, up to now [1984], in stifling scientific study of the Semitic substratum of the Synoptic Gospels .... The mere name of P. Vulliaud is never mentioned in present day biblical circles."[167]

On the back cover of his paperback book, under the heading "Why did I write this book?," Fr. Carmignac notes that it was inspired by the Dead Sea Scrolls; specifically, by the detailed knowledge of Ancient Hebrew he gained in his study of those scrolls. As earlier noted, he then spent more than twenty years studying the origins of the Gospels. His comments, on the back cover of his book, are therefore most authoritative:

- *The Gospels therefore have been redacted earlier than is customarily claimed*

- *They are much closer to the events.*

- *They have a historical value of prime importance.*

---

166 *Les Evangiles sont des reportages n'en déplaise à certains* (*The Gospels are the work of reporters, too bad if that upsets some people*).
167 *The Birth of the Synoptic Gospels*, 67-74.

- *They contain the witnesses of disciples who followed and listened to Jesus.*

- *These scientific arguments should prove reassuring to Christians and attract the attention and interest of nonbelievers.*

- *But they overturn theories presently in vogue and therefore they will be fiercely criticized.*

Fr. Brown's response to the study of Semitisms.

Fr. Raymond E. Brown was well aware that scholars studying Semitisms set pre-A.D. 70 dates for the original writings on which all four Gospels are largely based. As noted, these scholars dated some of those original writings to within a decade or two of the Resurrection, which means that they give the canonical Gospels high historical credibility.

In an article published in 1985, soon after publication of books on this subject in French by Fr. Carmignac and Tresmontant, Fr. Brown wrote unfavorably of the conclusions of both authors, but offered no refutation.[168]

Instead, in this 1985 article Fr. Brown simply dismissed such studies as reflecting the view of only a small minority of biblical scholars and referred readers to a critique written by Fr. Pierre Grelot in French, which very few Americans can read, and which apparently has not been translated into English. But, of course, such responses are no substitute for a point-by-point refutation by Fr. Brown.

In *An Introduction to the New Testament* (1997) Fr. Brown did address many issues in regard to the origins of the Gospels. In the section on the authorship of *Matthew*, Fr. Brown mentioned Fr. Carmignac by name as one of the scholars who believed that *Matthew* originated in a Semitic language.

Surely here Fr. Brown would have make known any substantive arguments he had against Semitism-based scholarship. But I found no such argument. Surely here, if he had a sound scholarly basis for doing so, Fr. Brown would have challenged Fr. Carmignac's nine categories of Semitisms by which he was able to show that a great many Semitisms cannot be dismissed, for example, as simply patterned after the Septuagint, or due to the influence of the mother tongue of the translator. But I found no such challenge on the part of Fr. Brown.

---

168 "All Gaul is Divided: A Review Essay," *Union Seminary Quarterly Review,* v. 40, 1985.

Surely here, if he were able, Fr. Brown would have pointed out what he considered to be the flaws in the reasoning of Claude Tresmontant, who wrote in the Introduction to his book *The Hebrew Christ:*

> *I am going to undertake to present compelling evidence for the fact that the four Gospels we possess in Greek are actually translations of anterior Hebrew writings.*[169]

In the Epilogue of the same book Tresmontant described his reaction after closely examining the historical-critical views he himself had accepted:

> *the entire superstructure collapsed like the proverbial house of cards.*[170]

But again, I found no attempt by Fr. Brown to point out any flaws in what Tresmontant had written. As noted above, in *An Introduction to the New Testament* Fr. Brown covered many issues regarding the origin of the Gospels – but I found no argument against Semitism-based scholarship.

Surely in *An Introduction to the New Testament,* it would seem that Fr. Brown would at least have referred his readers to the latest work by Fr. Pierre Grelot, who adamantly opposed Fr. Carmignac's Semitism-based, early date conclusions: *L' Origine des Evangiles: Controverse avec J. Carmignac* (Paris, 1986). But that might have called for acknowledging a preemptive point-by-point refutation of Fr. Grelot's views on the subject by Fr. Carmignac, the year before he died, in the March, 1985 issue of the Italian magazine *Jesus.*

And all of that might have called attention to the investigative reporting done by the European periodicals *Il Sabato* and *30 Days.* These reports were the subject of an article in the March 19, 1992 issue of *The Wanderer,* an American Catholic weekly newspaper.

In particular, *The Wanderer* called attention to *Il Sabato*'s discovery that Fr. Carmignac's entire archive was being held by the *Institut Catholique* in Paris, where Fr. Grelot was a professor (later Professor Emeritus) and that:

> *In all these years, the Institut Catholique has taken care not to tend to the publication of those pre-announced works, and, above all, it*

---

169 *The Hebrew Christ*, 24.
170 i.e., the collapse of the arguments of modern scholars to the effect that "[T]he Gospels written in Greek are relatively late documents, dating at the earliest to the period toward the end of the first century A.D." *The Hebrew Christ*, 24, 319.

has prohibited people from seeing the material when they ask to see it. [171]

In 2006, twenty years after Fr. Carmignac's death, a French biblical researcher – a member of *L'Association Jean Carmignac* – told me that, to her knowledge, the *Institut Catholique* had still not published Fr. Carmignac's extensive research.

More than one year prior to the date on which I write this, I mailed a letter to a well-known colleague of Fr. Brown who has also written in support of the late-date / no eyewitness view of the Gospels. I told this exegete of the pending publication of this book and asked for his help in locating any writings I may have missed in which he or Fr. Brown had specifically refuted the Semitism-based scholars in regard to early dates of Gospel origin. I received no response.

Divino Afflante Spiritu

With the encyclical *Divino Afflante Spiritu,* issued in 1943 by Pope Pius XII, The Church formally recognized the importance of explaining the Bible in light of a knowledge of Greek, Hebrew, other oriental languages, philology, literary criticism, textual criticism, archaeology, ancient history and more.

However, when we search this encyclical looking for a basis for the special importance generally attributed to historical criticism in comparison to the other disciplines, none is evident.

Instead, as indicated in the excerpt below, it appears that Pope Pius XII *first* called exegetes to become proficient in biblical Greek and Hebrew and other oriental languages and to use that knowledge to explain the original text (This is the sequence that has been followed by Fr. Carmignac, Tresmontant and other scholars who study Semitisms):

> *Wherefore let him diligently apply himself so as to acquire daily a greater facility in biblical [Greek, Hebrew] as well as in other oriental languages and to support his interpretation by the aids which all branches of philology supply ….* In like manner therefore ought we to explain the original text which, having been written by the inspired author himself, has more authority and greater weight than

---

171 Asked for a response to this *Il Sabato* report for publication in this book, Rector Pierre Cahné sent a gracious e-mail reply in French which included the following, concisely translated: *After consulting our archive service, I can answer that, with particular exceptions ... access to the various archived writings of Father Carmignac will not be granted before the year 2016.*

any even the very best translation, whether ancient or modern; *this can be done all the more easily and fruitfully, if to the knowledge of languages be joined a real skill in literary criticism of the same text.* [From par. 16; Italics added].[172]

Only secondarily, it seems, does the encyclical describe the role of literary criticism, to accomplish the task "more easily and fruitfully." This additional excerpt from the same encyclical appears to affirm the secondary role of criticism:

> Being thoroughly prepared by the knowledge of the ancient languages and by the *aids* afforded by the art of criticism, let the Catholic exegete undertake the task, of all those imposed on him the greatest, that namely of discovering and expounding the genuine meaning of the Sacred Books. [From par. 23, Italics added].

Can we not conclude, then, that literary criticism is intended to *improve* an explanation of the original text rather than to *produce* an explanation, especially one not solidly based on Greek, Hebrew and oriental languages?

There can be no doubt that, in writing this encyclical in 1943, the pope was well aware of what Fr. Carmignac would note, decades later; that *by 1518 Erasmus "sorted out the earliest Semitisms" and that by the year 1750 excellent philologists had completed more than 100 treatises on Semitisms.*[173] Surely the Pope intended that exegetes would take these and later studies of Semitisms as a starting point for literary criticism.

Of course, prior to the rise to prominence of the historical-critical method in the latter half of the twentieth century, Semitism-based scholarship was fully consistent with the prevailing early-date / eyewitness view of the Gospels and would not have drawn the critical attention it now merits.

Pontifical Biblical Commission acknowledges Importance of study of Semitic composition

In 1993, the Pontifical Biblical Commission acknowledged as follows the importance of the study of Semitic composition:

> The study of the multiple forms of parallelism and other procedures characteristic of the Semitic mode of composition allows for

---

172 From the Vatican Web Site; See full text at: **www.vatican.va/holyfather/pius_ xii/encyclicals/documents/hf_p-xii_enc_30091943_divino-afflante-spiritu_en.html**
173 *The Birth of the Synoptic Gospels*, 17.

a better discernment of the literary structure of texts, which can only lead to a more adequate understanding of their message.[174]

In 1998 Msgr. Michael J. Wrenn wrote that Fr. Carmignac *"once observed to me his conviction that by the year 2000 scriptural scholarship will start with the Hebrew or Aramaic rather than the Greek. Sooner or later, specialists will be hit right between the eyes and see themselves like me staring directly at the very backdrop of the Gospels"* (Appendix Q).[175]

This has not yet happened, of course, but when it does, what changes in biblical interpretation might we expect? This is a question best answered by our biblical scholars.

It can be expected, however, that renewed confidence in the Gospels as accurate history would soon be reflected in the written and spoken word throughout the Church. Doubt would give way to a renewal of faith that, before long, would be felt in every seminary, throughout Catholic academia, in every Church ministry and apostolate and – most important of all – in the spirituality of the faithful. Such renewed awareness could substantially accelerate the New Evangelization called for by our late Pope John Paul II.

Cardinal Ratzinger criticizes biblical scholarship that ignores historical context

On January 27, 1988, Joseph Cardinal Ratzinger, Prefect of the Congregation for the Doctrine of the Faith – now Pope Benedict XVI – delivered the annual Erasmus Lecture in New York.[176] The program was sponsored by the Rockford Institute's Center on Religion and Society, an independent, ecumenical agency. In his address, then-Cardinal Ratzinger said: "In the last 100 years, exegesis has had many great achievements, but it has brought forth great errors as well. These latter, moreover, have grown to the stature of academic dogmas. To criticize them at all would be taken by many as tantamount to sacrilege, especially if it were to be done by a non-exegete" (3.4).

Cardinal Ratzinger was not critical of the historical-critical method as such:

---

174 "The Interpretation of the Bible in the Church," presented by the Pontifical Biblical Commission to Pope John Paul II on April 23, 1993; I., B., 1., Par, 6. (Published in *Origins*, January 6, 1994), **http://www.c-b-f.org/start.php?CONTID= 03_01_02_00&LANG=en**
175 **www.ewtn.com/library/SCRIPTUR/CERTHYPO.TXT**
176 "Biblical Interpretations in Crisis: Foundations and Approaches to Biblical Exegesis," *Origins* NC Documentary Service, 2/11/88, V.17, No 35, 593-602.

Certainly, texts must first of all be traced back to their historical origins and interpreted in their proper historical context. But then, in a second exegetical operation, one must look at them also in light of the total movement of history and in light of history's central event, Jesus Christ. Only the combination of both these methods will yield understanding of the Bible (3.3,b).

The Cardinal concluded his talk with some thoughts on how the tools of the historical method might be joined "with a better philosophy which would entail fewer drawbacks foreign to the text, which would be less arbitrary and, would offer greater possibilities for a true listening to the text itself" (3).

In a sidebar commentary on the two-day conference and the press conference held January 28, *Origins* noted that then-Cardinal Ratzinger "agreed with Fr. Raymond Brown's paper" presented at the conference and added, "I would be very happy if we had many exegetes like Fr. Brown," but that "he and Brown might have a marginal difference' because of their different experiences in their homelands, Germany and the United States" (p. 595).

My purpose in presenting this commentary on late-date / no eyewitness scholarship based on the historical-critical method is not to call into question the high regard in which the late Fr. Brown and many of his colleagues are held by many in the Catholic Church today. Again, I regret that Fr. Brown is no longer among us and able to respond to these concerns.

But it is ironic that today so many Catholics, unfamiliar with the Early Church Fathers, early-date Hebrew / Aramaic-based biblical scholarship and Qumrân-related papyrology, and instead accepting modernist influence, are moving away from the Catholic Church, while so many Protestants, discovering these sources – in particular the Early Church Fathers – and rejecting modernist influence, are becoming Catholics.

Clearly the writings of the Early Church Fathers, the conclusions of the early-date / Semitism-based biblical scholars, as well as the conclusions of papyrologists such as Carsten Thiede, are essential to a thorough understanding of biblical history. The conclusions of skilled researchers in all three of these separate areas of research are in substantial agreement and strongly affirm history's central event – Jesus – as described in the Bible. So, too, do the lives of so many saints who, in light of that early history, were able to follow the biblical teachings of Jesus in such an exemplary and often heroic manner.

Neo-Patristic biblical scholarship – The Roman Theological Forum

Noteworthy in the effort to gain insight into the meaning of the Gospels in the spirit of *Divino Afflante Spiritu* is the *Roman Theological Forum*, founded by Msgr. John F. McCarthy. RTF is "an association of scholars working with other interested persons for the advancement of theology and philosophy within the tradition of the Roman Catholic Church. It addresses contemporary questions of theology and philosophy, beginning from a Thomist point of view, and it is promoting with special attention a neo-Patristic approach to the interpretation of Sacred Scripture."

On the RTF Web site,[177] Msgr. McCarthy gives the following answer to the question "Why promote the neo-Patristic approach?":

> Meditation upon things said in Sacred Scripture is important for every Christian. The Fathers of the Church have laid out a basic Christian approach to the study and meditation of the inspired word.
>
> This approach of the Fathers was followed by all Catholic exegetes, especially as regards the literal sense, but in recent centuries with lessening emphasis upon the spiritual senses except for certain texts relating to the dogmas of the Church.
>
> However, towards the end of the nineteenth century some Catholic exegetes (interpreters) began to follow what is now known as the historical-critical approach, developed by rationalist and liberal Protestant exegetes, and this new approach has now with some exceptions virtually supplanted the Patristic approach among Catholic biblical scholars.
>
> But many problems and logical contradictions have arisen from the results of historical-critical interpretation, even when used by Catholic exegetes.
>
> The neo-Patristic approach aims to address and solve these problems and contradictions and to reinstate the Patristic approach by the use of an updated framework based upon the largely implicit framework of the Fathers of the Church in the hope of enabling insights old and new and of making it easier to pray the Scriptures.

"To be deep in history is to cease to be a Protestant"

The Church acknowledges inconsistencies in the writings of the Early Church Fathers. Nowhere have these been addressed more

---

177 **www.rtforum.org/index.html**

thoroughly than by Ven. John Henry Newman in *An Essay on the Development of Christian Doctrine*. Newman wrote his essay as a Protestant; an Anglican minister. Before its publication in 1845, however, he became a Catholic and was later ordained a priest. Raised to the cardinalate in 1879, he became one of the most esteemed Cardinals in the history of the Catholic Church (A revised edition of Newman's *An Essay on the Development of Christian Doctrine* was published in 1878). In Part I of this *Essay*, under the heading "Doctrinal developments viewed in themselves"; Introduction; #4; Newman quotes Chillingworth:

> There are popes against popes, councils against councils, some fathers against others, the same fathers against themselves, a consent of fathers of one age against a consent of fathers of another age, the Church of one age against the Church of another age.

After referring to Chillingworth as a "smart but superficial writer," Newman acknowledges that there are variations that call for clarification. However, in #5, in the paragraphs immediately following the above, Newman summarily refutes Chillingworth as follows:

> History is not a creed or a catechism. It gives lessons rather than rules; still no one can mistake its general teaching in this matter, whether he accept it or stumble at it. Bold outlines and broad masses of colour rise out of the records of the past. They may be dim, they may be incomplete, but they are definite. And this one thing at least is certain; whatever history teaches, whatever it omits, whatever it exaggerates or extenuates, whatever it says or unsays, at least the Christianity of history is not Protestantism … and Protestantism has ever felt it so …. To be deep in history is to cease to be a Protestant.[178]

Before publication of his *Essay* in 1845, and after an agonizing ten-year period of intense study and soul-searching, Newman became a Catholic. He was ordained a priest and became a highly esteemed Cardinal. In 1864 Newman wrote:

> From the time that I became a Catholic … I have had no anxiety of heart whatever. I have been in perfect peace and contentment; I never have had one doubt …. It was like coming into port after a

---

178 *An Essay in the Development of Christian Doctrine*, Ven. John H. Newman; Reprinted, with Foreword by Ian Ker, by University of Notre Dame Press, Notre Dame, Indiana, 1989.

rough sea; and my happiness on that score remains to this day without interruption.[179]

Objective historical-critical scholarship supports Catholicism, including Petrine primacy

This book will have its critics, of course. Among them will surely be scholars skilled in the historical-critical method of biblical exegesis – scholars that, as Fr. Carmignac wrote, operate primarily from the Greek and, in their writings at least, rarely "look behind the canonical Greek" to the ancient Hebrew and Aramaic *Semitisms* that so strongly indicate early origin and sound historicity of the Gospels. These historical-critical scholars might well say:

> Why even consider the views of this author, admittedly not an exegete, who bases his criticism of the historical-critical method essentially on just one of its proponents – the late Fr. Raymond E. Brown? Is this author unaware of the fact that, although we may arrive at somewhat different conclusions, today most biblical scholars worldwide embrace the historical-critical method and are in general agreement that no Gospel was written before the late 60s CE?

Surely this book would be more complete – and of considerably greater length – if the varied conclusions of numerous other historical-critical scholars were cited. I invite interested readers to read some of the many works by historical-critical scholars and by others through the ages who attempted to solve the synoptic problem using other methods.

To serious seekers of biblical truth, however, I suggest that you include in your reading two important books. The first is *A History of the Synoptic Problem: The Canon, the Text, the Composition, and the Interpretation of the Gospels,* by David Laird Dungan (1999). This graduate of Harvard Divinity School and acknowledged authority on the historical-critical method is Distinguished Professor of the Humanities at the University of Tennessee, Knoxville. In particular, note that Professor Dungan concludes that *Markan priority is untenable*:

> One might think that in the wake of this kind of crippling criticism [of Markan priority], proponents of Markan priority would finally admit that it is an untenable hypothesis. Not at all. It continues to be used far and wide as if nothing had happened, resembling the headless horseman who rides across the countryside every Hallow-

---

179 *Apologia Pro Vita Sua*; Ven. John H. Newman; **www.fordham.edu/halsall/ mod/newman/apologia1.html** > Chapter 5, par. 1.

een in the light of the full moon. [180]

[A]fter forty-five years of steady criticism, knowledgeable defenders of the hypothesis have been forced to abandon one argument after another to the point where there are, at present, no formal arguments left that will justify it and the compositional arguments are just as questionable. It has rightly earned the sobriquet "the Teflon hypothesis."[181]

The other important book is *The Gospel of Jesus: The Pastoral Relevance of the Synoptic Problem*, by William R. Farmer (1994). In this book Farmer makes the case for the priority of *Matthew* rather than *Mark,* in effect restoring to *Matthew* the priority it was given by such early Church fathers as Irenaeus, Clement of Alexandria, Eusebius, and Augustine.[182] Jerome, of course, placed *Matthew* first in his *Latin Vulgate* and it retains this position in virtually all Bibles published since then.

In *The History of the Church,* Bishop Eusebius of Caesarea (*c.* A.D. 260 – 339) quoted Clement of Alexandria (A.D. 150 – 211/216) as follows regarding the order of the Gospels:

"The Gospels containing the genealogies [*Matthew* and *Luke*]," he says, "were written first. The circumstances which occasioned that of Mark were these: When Peter preached the Word publicly at Rome, and declared the Gospel by the Spirit, many who were present requested that Mark, who had been for a long time his follower and who remembered his sayings, should write down what had been proclaimed. Having composed the Gospel, he gave it to those who had requested it. When Peter learned of this, he did not positively forbid it, but neither did he encourage it. John, last of all, seeing that the plain facts had been clearly set forth in the Gospels, and being urged by his acquaintances, composed a spiritual Gospel under the divine inspiration of the Spirit."[183]

William R. Farmer wrote as follows about the above words of Clement, which clearly indicate that *Matthew* preceded *Mark*: "*This one direct statement by Clement, the most highly respected Christian scholar of his day, is of more historical value than all the theories that have ever been propounded about the sequence in which the Gospels*

---

180 Proponents of Markan priority theorize that *Mark* was the first Gospel written.
181 *A History of the Synoptic Problem,* 389-390.
182 *The Gospel of Jesus: The Pastoral Relevance of the Synoptic Problem,* 15.
183 *Faith of the Early Fathers,* Vol. 1, 188.

were written, including the theories of Augustine."[184]

Why then, we may ask, would historical-critical scholars in great numbers today prop up the "headless" Markan priority and have that horse continue to gallop across the pages of their books and articles?

Could this headless Markan priority still ride because <u>*Matthean*</u> *priority – given its rightful place in the saddle – brings down the entire Protestant Reformation and its multi-denominational aftermath and calls every believer to recognize that Jesus actually named Peter the "rock" on whom he would build his Church (i.e., the Catholic Church) and promised, to Peter alone, the keys of the kingdom of heaven (Mt 16:18-19)?*

Why would most of these same late-date historical-critical scholars also continue to turn a blind eye toward the 400-year-old body of *Semitism*-based scholarship – scholarship consistent with *Divino Afflante Spiritu,* endorsed by the Papal Biblical Commission and championed in the last century by Fr. Jean Carmignac, Claude Tresmontant and so many others who conclude that *Matthew* originated as early as seven (Tresmontant) to seventeen (Carmignac) years after the Crucifixion and Resurrection of Jesus?

Could it be because Semitism-based scholarship strongly supports the view that Matthew actually originated in Hebrew with Matthew, the Levite/apostle who heard every word Jesus said to Peter at Caesarea Philippi – a view that affirms that Jesus actually named Peter the "rock" on whom he would build his Church (i.e., the Catholic Church) and promised, to Peter alone, the keys of the kingdom of heaven (Mt 16:18-19) as noted above?

For the reasons noted under the heading, "Why did Mark and Luke omit 'Thou art Peter and upon this rock …' from their Gospels?" the Caesarea Philippi passages in *Mark* and *Luke* do not render *Matthew* 16:18-19 doubtful or erroneous. Clearly we can accept the passage in *Matthew* as the *full* account of what Jesus said at Caesarea Philippi and the passages in *Mark* and Luke as *abbreviated* accounts of the same event. But what about the speculation that the writer of *Matthew* falsely attributed primacy to Peter?

The flawed speculation that "Matthew" falsely attributed primacy to Peter

Let us suppose, for the moment, what some proponents of Markan

---

184 "The Statement of the Hypothesis," *The Interrelations of the Gospels: A Symposium* (ed. David L. Dungan, BETL 95, Leuven: Leuven University & Peeters, 1990) 145. Cambridge Journals Online: **http://journals.cambridge.org/abstract_ S0028688501000091**

priority imply – that Matthew lied. No doubt this lie would have troubled Matthew's conscience a bit – after all he was an apostle. But Matthew would have realized something that Jesus had apparently overlooked. The apostles, and surely their successors, would not always agree on essential matters of Church doctrine. For example, what if one of them declared that Jesus was merely speaking *symbolically* when he said "This is my body"? Unless one apostle, and each of his successors, had primacy that originated with Jesus, the one Church founded by Christ was doomed to splinter into many, each claiming that, through the great commission, its leader acted with Christ's own authority. And so – no doubt saying to himself, "Jesus forgive me, I'm telling this lie for you and your Church," – Matthew would have written, "Thou art Peter and upon this rock .... I will give you the keys ...."

But, good intentions notwithstanding, every lie – if it *is* a lie – has repercussions. Let's look at some of the inevitable consequences of this one. Imagine the shock of each surviving apostle (with the exception of Matthew – and Peter if we assume his complicity) when each learned of the lie in the *Gospel according to Matthew* by which he attempted to make them subordinate to Peter! The indignation of each such apostle – and of the disciples and other Christians as well – would surely have been recorded by some if not all of the early Church writers. How could Matthew <u>dare</u> to do what Jesus himself did not do!

Can any reputable scholar doubt that at least the apostle John, who lived until about the end of the first century, would have rebuked Matthew for that outrageous "lie" and, through a letter, assured all of Christendom that Christ has given <u>no</u> apostle primacy; that each reported to God alone?

But – as Sherlock Holmes might have said of the apostles who heard Jesus give Peter primacy at Caesarea Philippi and who later read the *Gospel according to Matthew* – "*The watch dog(s) did not bark.*" In other words, there is no authentic historical record that any apostle objected to anything he later read in *Matthew*, including the verses in which Jesus gives Peter primacy.

Let us further suppose, in the extreme, that *Matthew* was written after the death of <u>all</u> the apostles. In the "Matthew lied" scenario, all successor bishops would have been consecrated understanding that, since Christ had given no apostle primacy, no bishop had any divinely authorized primacy.

Imagine the consternation of these bishops upon reading, in the newly written *Gospel according to Matthew,* that one bishop now had primacy over all the others. Regardless of when *Matthew* was written and promulgated, such a bold-faced "lie," falsely instituting papal primacy, would surely have disqualified this Gospel for later canonical approval. In addition, the absence of any priority of authority among the apostles and all their successors would have been well documented in early and later Church writings and in proceedings of Church councils.

Instead, not a word affirming such full apostolic collegiality with no primacy appears in any authentic document of Church history. *On the contrary, in the first three centuries after the Resurrection, early Church writers referred directly or indirectly to the primacy of juris-diction of Peter and / or his successors more than thirty times.*[185]

And, as we know, *Matthew* – including what we now refer to as Mt 16:18-19 – did receive canonical approval in the late fourth century and later at the Council of Trent and books such as *Faith of the Early Fathers* and *Jesus, Peter and the Keys* are replete with solid historical affirmation of papal primacy.

Clearly, from its earliest days, the Church recognized that Matthew, an eyewitness, had written a complete account of what Jesus said to Peter at Caesarea Philippi. The omission of *Matthew* 16:18-19 in *Mark* and *Luke* would be expected if Peter never preached on those points in Rome and Luke had used *Mark* as a primary source. As earlier noted, there is good reason to believe that in Rome Peter did not preach about his primacy.

Media bias against the biblical Christ

Given this weight of evidence for the early origin of the Gospels based on eyewitness testimony – evidence that supports the Bible as sound history – what are we to make of the prime-time programs on respected TV channels that cast doubt on the divinity and miracles of Jesus?

These TV programs seem concentrated around Easter and Christmas, the most important Christian holy days, and are often coincident with feature articles in the same vein in respected news magazines. Typically featured are religious educators, Protestant ministers and former Catholic priests.

Often a Catholic priest in full clerical garb will also speak or be quoted briefly, seldom directly contradicting Church teaching, but planting seeds of doubt. Asked by a TV commentator whether Jesus may have had an affair with Mary Magdalene, one such priest said not a word about the compelling evidence debunking that notion. Instead

---

185 *The Faith of the Early Fathers*, Vol. 1, Doctrinal Index, 421.

he said, in effect, that if Jesus did have a love affair it surely would have been with Mary Magdalene.

In March, 2007 a TV documentary aired strongly suggesting that an ossuary (bone box) containing the bones of Jesus had been found in a Jerusalem suburb. However, according to the *Jerusalem Post*, the archaeologist who supervised the uncovering of the ossuary in 1980, Prof. Amos Kloner, later said the documentary's claims were "nonsense." A number of archaeologists, biblical scholars and others are quoted on the Web site of the Catholic League also debunking the claim. One of them, William Dever, archaeologist and professor emeritus, University of Arizona, was quoted as follows: "I don't know a single archeologist in this country or Israel who agrees with their findings." (CNN's "Anderson Cooper 360°," February 28, 2007).

I suggest that, after such biased programs or articles, readers contact the TV network or publisher, as well as advertisers, and request better-balanced coverage of such topics. Fair-minded media representatives will ensure that Catholicism is represented by qualified spokespersons recommend by solid Catholic sources, such as EWTN, Catholic Answers and the Catholic League.

All the points made in Step 3 above lead to this conclusion and no other: Late-date / no-eyewitness conjecture notwithstanding, compelling evidence indicates that all four Gospels originated with eyewitnesses before the destruction of Jerusalem in A.D. 70 and that the earliest originated within seven to twelve years after the Resurrection. This evidence provides a rock-solid historical foundation for the faith in the biblical Jesus held by Christians for the past 2,000 years.[186]

Discussion Questions

1. Baur and Strauss attributed dates of A.D. 130 to 180 to the origin of the Gospels. On what objective basis did they do so? Should such late-dating affect the credibility of the Gospels? Why?

2. In the opinion of the late Fr. Raymond E. Brown and most

---

186 For further analysis in support of the early date / eyewitness origin of the Gospels read **"Contemporary Catholic Biblical Scholarship: Certitudes or Hypotheses?"** by Msgr. Michael J. Wrenn (Appendix Q) and **"The Dates of the Gospels"** by Rev. George H. Duggan, S.M. (Appendix R). For an concise overview of the "Two Source," Two Gospel" and other hypotheses regarding the origin of the Gospels, see **"The Synoptic Problem FAQ**," www.mindspring.com/~scarlson/synopt/faq.htm

Catholic biblical scholars today, during what time frame did the Gospels originate? On what do they base this conclusion?

3.   Fr. Brown wrote: "If everything in the Bible is not necessarily historical, Catholics are *not* left without the guidance of the church as to what they must believe." Late-dating the Gospels, of course, conceivably allows the reader to doubt the historicity of *everything* in the Gospels, including the basis for belief in the divinity of Jesus, his founding of one Church, the Great Commission of the eleven by Jesus and his giving primacy to Peter. With this in mind, to what extent are late-date proponents likely to accept the guidance of the Church "as to what they must believe"?

4.   In 2 Thes 2:1-2, Paul warns his followers about letters falsely attributed to him. In his *History of the Church,* Eusebius of Caesarea gave a similar warning about three centuries later in regard to the *Gospel of Thomas.* What ramifications do such warnings have for us today?

5.   The Canon of Scripture was established by Catholic Bishops in Church Councils in the latter part of the fourth century. In view of later developments such as the Reformation, why is this important?

6.   Why is the Council of Trent (1545-1563) important to the Church and to those who left it in the wake of the Protestant Reformation?

7.   Why was Jerome's Latin Vulgate important? Why, near the end of the fourth century, do you think he chose the order of the Gospels as *Matthew, Mark, Luke* and *John*?

8.   Scottish philosopher David Hume (1711-76) believed there could be no certain truth about anything, including its very existence. A contemporary responded to a similar claim by kicking a rock; "I refute it thus," he said. [*The Last Two Million Years*; © 1973; The Reader's Digest Assn. Ltd., London, p. 293] What do you think about Hume's view?

9.   Consider the view of David Friedrich Strauss and others that anything in the Gospels that appears miraculous could not have really happened. Is this an objective conclusion? How do you think stigmatist St. Pio (Padre Pio) might have responded to

Strauss' denial of the possibility of miracles?

10. Why were priests Alfred Loisy and George Tyrell excommunicated?

11. Why did Pope Leo XIII find it necessary to issue the encyclical *Providentissimus Deus*?

12. Discuss the stipulation in the encyclical *Pascendi Dominici Gregis* of Pope Pius X that required all priests, superiors of religious orders and seminary professors to take an oath disavowing modernism. Why was it necessary? What effect do you think these measures had on the faith of Catholics of that and succeeding generations?

13. Why was the *Baltimore Catechism* important?

14. What activity did the encyclical *Divino Afflante Spiritu* issued by Pope Pius XII encourage? Do you think Catholic late-date / no eyewitness biblical scholars have been faithful to the letter and spirit of this encyclical? Why? Do you think the early-date / eyewitness bible scholars have been faithful to it? On what do you base your opinion?

15. Do you think that the Second Vatican Council was convened in order to bring the Church more in line with modernist views? What evidence is there of that intention on the part of Pope John XXIII? What evidence is there that the Church intended to make pastoral improvements but leave doctrine unchanged?

16. What is the meaning of "collegiality" among the bishops? If the primacy of the Pope among the bishops were to cease, with each of the world's bishops becoming a fully independent successor of the apostles, what effect might this have upon the Church, its doctrine and its continuing unity?

17. Discuss some of the conclusions of "The Jesus Seminar" that are in conflict with Church teaching. Do the "Seven Pillars of Modern Biblical Scholarship" provide a sound basis for the conclusions of the Jesus Seminar fellows?

18. Some today dismiss all Christian martyrs by saying "All religions have their martyrs." In making that statement, what do such critics fail to take into account?

19. Why is the testimony of the non-Christian Flavius Josephus

important in affirming the divinity of Jesus? Some have criticized much of what Josephus wrote about Jesus and proposed deleting, among other things, affirmations of his Resurrection. Do you think Josephus, a Jew, believed Jesus rose from the dead?

20. Why did the news that The Magdalen Fragments had been dated to about A.D. 60 prompt Richard N. Osning of *Time* magazine to write that those small bits of papyrus could revolutionize New Testament scholarship?

21. Do you think forensic studies of the kind done by papyrologists should be part of any serious attempts to determine dates of origin of the Gospels?

22. Discuss the historical-critical method of Bible interpretation and give examples of how it can be used and misused. Discuss the merits of this method of biblical scholarship in comparison to the Semitism-based approach taken by the early-date / eye-witness scholars.

23. The traditional view of the Church is that Matthew and John, apostles and eyewitnesses to Jesus, were the authors of the Gospels that bear their names. Using the historical-critical method, many Catholic and Protestant Bible scholars claim that it is highly improbable that any apostle was the author of a Gospel. However, these late-date scholars largely ignore, rather than attempt to refute, the Early Church Fathers who affirm apostolic authorship of *Matthew* and *John*. Do you think this affects the credibility of the late-date claim? Why?

24. As an alternative to the traditional *Matthew-Mark-Luke-John* order of the writing of the Gospels, on what historical foundation does *Markan priority* (e.g., the two-source hypothesis) rest?

25. There are sound historical indications that *The Gospel according to Matthew* originated with this apostle / eyewitness, writing in Hebrew. It is in this Gospel that Jesus gives primacy to Peter among the apostles: "Thou are Peter and upon this Rock I will build my Church ... and I will give you the keys to the kingdom of heaven" (Mt 16:18-19). Of what importance is it that these words originated with an apostle-eyewitness rather than added later by some unknown writer?

26. Of what historical importance is the statement of Origin (ca. 244) affirming that the apostle Matthew wrote his Gospel in Hebrew for Jewish converts?

27. Jerome (ca. 400) visited the extensive library of Pamphilus (which later burned) and transcribed the Gospel Matthew had written in Hebrew. Of what historical importance was Jerome's transcription of this Semitic *Matthew*?

28. In Mark's account of the meeting of Jesus with the apostles near Caesarea Philippi (*Mark* 8:27-30), he does not include "Thou art Peter and upon this Rock I will build my Church ... and I will give you the keys of the kingdom of heaven," which Matthew, an eyewitness, included in his Gospel (Mt 16:18-19). Why might Mark have been silent on these two important statements of Jesus?

29. In his Erasmus Lecture in 1988, why did Cardinal Ratzinger say that modern exegesis "has brought forth great errors ...."? What two steps did he say must be taken to correct those errors?

30. In *Birth of the Messiah* Fr. Raymond E. Brown states, "Since *no one of the four evangelists was himself an eyewitness to the ministry of Jesus* ...." On what objective basis do you think Fr. Brown make this statement? In regard to the apostles Matthew and John in particular, how should Fr. Brown's statement be evaluated in view of the Vatican II document *Dei Verbum*, which states: "*The Church has always and everywhere maintained, and continues to maintain, the apostolic origin of the four Gospels* ...."

31. How might an early-date / eyewitness biblical scholar respond to Fr. Brown's statement in the previous question?

32. Fr. Manuel Miguens wrote quite critically in regard to Fr. Raymond E. Brown's conclusion that the Infancy Narratives were not based on any eyewitness account (i.e., an account given by Mary, Mother of Jesus). Was Fr. Miguens' criticism substantive? Explain your opinion.

33. The Lutheran-Catholic Dialogue "did not concentrate on Mt 16:17-19 in any isolated way [but they came to] significant agreement that much of what is peculiar to *Matthew* in that

Caesarea Philippi scene is probably post-resurrectional in origin." How do you think this statement was understood by non-Catholic members of this group in regard to the primacy of Peter and his successors in the papacy?

34. Based on study of the Dead Sea Scrolls, some scholars hypothesize that Jesus performed no miracles, did not die on the cross and did not arise from death. What is your opinion of this view? What value should be placed on the contrary opinions of other authorities such as Hershel Shanks of the *Biblical Archaeology Review,* who, having studied the same scrolls, see no conflict with the Bible??

35. In *Goodbye, Good Men*, Michael S. Rose expressed strong concern about the use in seminaries of textbooks that promote dissent and can lead to scandalous behavior. To what extent do you agree or disagree with Rose's views on these matters?

36. To the extent that Rose's claims regarding dissent taught in our seminaries may be true, what effect do you think this may have had on the faith of the average Catholic during the past several decades? Explain your answer.

37. Fr. Jean Carmignac commented that "One [group of scholars] especially widespread in Germany, refuses to study Semitisms seriously [because] they are not sufficiently numerous or that they are due to the mother tongue of the authors, or that they result from a more or less conscious imitation of the Septuagint." Do you think these are substantive reasons for refusing to take seriously the work of scholars such as Fr. Carmignac and Tresmontant?

38. On what basis does Fr. Carmignac fault many scholars in England and in the United States? In your opinion, what grounds, if any, exist for this concern raised by Fr. Carmignac?

39. Why did Fr. Carmignac separate Semitisms into nine categories? Do you think these categories helped him achieve his purpose?

40. Fr. Carmignac wrote that, after only one day of translating into Hebrew the Canonical Greek Gospel according to Mark, he became convinced that "it was in reality only the Greek translation of an original Hebrew." Is this conclusion compatible with

the view that Mark, as Peter's amanuensis in *Rome,* was the originator of this Gospel? Is it compatible with the view that Peter may have been the author of much of the Gospel of Mark? Explain your answers.

41. Challenging the popular late-date / no eyewitness view, Claude Tresmontant wrote: "The hypothesis that no one actually hearing Jesus could or would ever have taken down any notes is simply absurd – psychologically as well as historically ...." Do you agree or disagree? Why?

42. Tresmontant is convinced that notes used as a basis for the Gospels were taken down in Hebrew, although the common spoken language of the people was Aramaic. And yet *"E'li, E'li, la'ma sabach'-tha'ni?"* "My God, my God, why hast thou forsaken me?" spoken by our crucified Jesus, is Aramaic. What explanation can be given for this apparent inconsistency?

43. Why would those translating the Gospels simply lift many Hebrew expressions into Greek, thereby producing some very awkward translations?

44. Tresmontant and others quote John 5:2: – "There *is* in Jerusalem, next to the Ewes Gate ...." – as proof that the Gospel was written before the destruction of Jerusalem in A.D. 70. Do you agree? On what basis, if any, might a late-date scholar disagree?

45. C. C. Torrey challenged his colleagues to "designate one passage from any of the four Gospels giving clear evidence of a date later than 50 A.D." None could do so. Can you?

46. Pinchas E. Lapide wrote several publications pointing out the "Hebraicity" of the Gospels. Why were his conclusions of special significance?

47. As we have seen, Fr. Carmignac's extensive studies make a strong case for early, eyewitness authorship of the documents that became the Gospels – too early for anything erroneous to have gotten past the many who witnessed the events of the Gospels. Why, then, on the back cover of *The Birth of the Synoptic Gospels*, did Fr. Carmignac write that his conclusions "overturn theories presently in vogue [1987] and therefore they will be fiercely criticized."?

48. Does the encyclical *Divino Afflante Spiritu* appear to give priority to making use of a knowledge of ancient languages, *aided* by literary criticism? This question is best answered after reading the entire encyclical. See full text at:
www.vatican.va/holy_father/pius_xii/encyclicals/documents/ hf_p-xii_enc_30091943_divino-afflante-spiritu en.html

49. Why, in 1988, did then-Cardinal Ratzinger state: "In the last 100 years, exegesis [biblical scholarship] has had many great achievements, but it has brought forth great errors as well."? What did he call upon exegetes to do to correct the errors?

50. Discuss the merits of the historical-critical method versus the neo-Patristic method of biblical interpretation. Which is likely to result in a more objective rendering of biblical history?

51. Ven. John Henry Newman wrote, "To be deep in history is to cease to be a Protestant" Why do you think he made this statement? Do you agree or disagree with him?

52. What is your view of the quoted opinion of David Laird Dungan regarding the priority of *Matthew* versus *Mark*?

53. Do you agree or disagree with William R. Farmer's conclusion regarding the priority of *Matthew* over *Mark*? Why?

54. Do you believe there is bias against the biblical Christ in the major media? If so, what examples can you cite? What would you suggest to correct this problem?

Step 4. Jesus founded, and protects from error, one Petrine Church

God loves all his children, including our separated brethren (CCC par. 822), many of whom pray and practice their Christian faith with great fervor. But did Jesus not pray *"that they may all be one"* (Jn 17:17-23)? Speaking as the Good Shepherd, did Jesus not say *"[T]here shall be one flock, one shepherd"* (Jn 10:16)?

Jesus founded only ONE Church, not the tens of thousands that carry his name today, and Jesus (a) at the direction of the Father, founded his ONE Church on Peter alone (Mt 16:18); (b) gave the keys of the kingdom to Peter alone, (Mt 16:19); (c) said "Feed my lambs .... Tend my sheep .... Feed my sheep" to Peter alone (Jn 21:15-17); (d) provided for papal and apostolic succession in Mt 28:20 and, in Mt 16:19, using the metaphor of the key, which, in Is 22:22, indicates authority transferable to a successor, and; (e) protects the Church he founded from doctrinal error [Paragraphs 888 through 892 of the *Catechism of the Catholic Church*, 2nd Ed.]. Also see a related article by Scott Hahn.[187] At this writing the reader may also view a detailed, wide-ranging biblical / historical defense of the Catholic teaching on Papal primacy by Phil Porvaznik: "Refutation of James G. McCarthy's *The Gospel According to Rome;* Section IV: Authority."[188]

More than any other passages of Scripture, since the sixteenth century the reinterpretation by reformers of the verses in (a) through (d) above has led Christians in great numbers to reject the Church Christ himself founded upon Peter.

Once the early reformers had shown that one could reject the authority of Peter and his successors and fashion one's own Church and call it Christian – with no foundation other than one's own interpretation of the Bible – the splintering of non-Catholic Christianity became inevitable.

The Protestant Reformation can be dated from 1521, the year of Luther's excommunication. Calvin, after initially following Luther, soon disagreed with him on the nature of the Eucharist and other doctrinal issues. England moved toward schism after 1533, when Pope Clement VII declared the divorce and remarriage of Henry VIII void. By the eighteenth century (aside from the Orthodox) the non-Catholic Christian world could be divided into four groups: Lutheranism,

187 www.ewtn.com/library/scriptur/POPE.TXT
188 www.bringyou.to/apologetics/a64.htm

Calvinism, Anglicanism and the Independent or Radical.[189]   Of these, only the Anglican Church (predecessor of the Episcopal Church in the United States) claimed to have valid *orders* (validly consecrated bishops who could in turn consecrate new bishops and ordain priests). However, Pope Leo XIII formally denied this claim.

In the centuries after the Reformation the process of reforming the reformers continued, slowly at first, but then with increasing rapidity. Today the fragmentation of non-Catholic Christianity is proceeding at a pace that would have astonished the early reformers. As earlier noted, the number of separate Christian denominations worldwide today is growing rapidly and in 2001 exceeded 33,000.[190]

By following one or another of these reformers, millions of non-Catholics today are rejecting the Church their ancestors embraced for more than 1,000 years.

Luther acknowledged that Jesus gave the keys to Peter – but denied that his successors received them

Probably the best known figure of the Protestant Reformation was Martin Luther, an Augustinian monk. On October 31, 1517 Luther nailed his *Ninety-five Theses Against Indulgences* to the door of the Chapel at the University of Wittenberg, Germany. This was the common method of inviting disputation at the University; it didn't necessarily mean that those posting such notices adamantly held the views thus advocated. There was merit to Luther's concern about *indulgences* and some other matters, which were later addressed by the Council of Trent (1545-1563). Later, however, Luther contradicted Church doctrine by stating that salvation is by faith alone (*sola fide*); and that the Bible is to be interpreted by each individual for himself, disassociated from Peter, his successors and the Tradition of the Church (*sola scriptura*). After refusing to accept approved Church doctrine in accordance with his vows of ordination to the Catholic priesthood, Luther was threatened with excommunicated in 1520. After Luther did not, within sixty days, formally withdraw 41 of his propositions and destroy the books in which they were written, Luther was finally excommunicated by Pope Leo X on January 3, 1521.[191]   It is well known that Luther denied that the Pope had the keys (e.g., in his *Thesis #26*). However, in *Jesus, Peter and the Keys* [p. 60] we find that Luther, in *The Keys* – a tract he wrote in 1530, nine years after his excommunication – emphatically

---

189 *Separated Brethren,* 10.
190 *World Christian Encyclopedia.* © 2001.
191 **www.newadvent.org/cathen/09438b.htm**

affirmed Peter's true authority as holder of the keys, stating:

> So we stand there and with open mouth stare heavenward and in-
> vent still other keys. Yet Christ says very clearly in Mt 16:19 that
> he will give the keys to Peter. He does not say he has two kinds of
> keys, but he gives to Peter the keys he himself has and no others. It
> is as if he were saying: Why are you staring heavenward in search
> of the keys: Do you not understand I gave them to Peter? They are
> indeed the keys of heaven, but they are not found in heaven. I left
> them on earth. Don't look for them in heaven or anywhere else ex-
> cept in Peter's mouth where I have placed them. Peter's mouth is
> my mouth, and his tongue is my key case. His office is my office,
> his binding and loosing are my binding and loosing.[192]

And Luther heard confessions for some time after his excommunication in 1521. And so it is not surprising that in 1967 a convention of
the Lutheran Student Association of America called for an organic
reunion of the Lutheran and Catholic Churches. The student resolution
declared:

> The Lutheran tradition is not one of a separate church so much as
> an emergency movement within the pale of Roman Catholicism.[193]

Luther readily admitted the Jesus gave the keys of primacy to Peter.
However, Luther did not acknowledge that Jesus intended that primacy
to pass to Peter's successors (See comments below on Isaiah 22:22
under "Apostolic / Papal Succession").

Difficulties with "Sola Scriptura" – justification by Scripture alone

Many who have rejected the authority of Peter and his successors
are adamant that Christians must rely on Scripture alone (*sola scriptura*) and not on Church Tradition.

The difficulty is that **nowhere in the Bible is there a verse that
indicates that Jesus wanted the apostles and their successors to rely
on the Bible alone.** The one verse generally quoted in support of *sola
scriptura* and as an argument against the *Tradition* of the Catholic
Church is:

> All scripture is inspired by God and profitable for teaching, for
> reproof, for correction, and for training in righteousness, that the

---

192 Luther, Martin. *The Keys*; in Conrad Bergendoff, ed, trans., *Luther's Works,* vol.
40, 365-366.
193 *Separated Brethren,* 38.

man of God may be complete, equipped for every good work (2 Timothy 3:16-17).

If I write "*All* food is given by God and is important for life and health"; I have not excluded water. If I then write, "Water is given by God and is important for life and health"; the second sentence does not contradict the first.

In the same way, Paul's statement regarding "all scripture ..." is not incompatible with the teaching of the Catholic Church in regard to Tradition. And when the risen Jesus commissioned the apostles did he say:

> Go therefore and make disciples of all the nations. Write down what I have told you and what you have seen. Then recruit scribes in great numbers to copy the *Good News* and distribute it to everyone you meet. In this way make disciples of all nations ....

We know that Jesus never said such a thing. Instead, he said:

> Go therefore and make disciples of all nations, baptizing them in the name of the Father, and of the Son, and of the Holy Spirit, teaching them to observe all that I have commanded you ... (Mt 28:19-20).

In the early days of the Church the apostles had to rely on Tradition. Most of the books and letters of what we know as the New Testament were not written and copied until decades after the Resurrection.

And it was not until the Council of Hippo in 393 and the Council of Carthage in 397 that Catholic bishops agreed on what books and letters should be included in the New Testament. This of course, was subsequent to the earlier noted Damasan catalogue (Synod of Rome, in 382) which, as noted in the *Catholic Encyclopedia*, "presents the complete and perfect Canon which has been that of the Church Universal ever since."

For more than three and one-half centuries after Christ's Resurrection, then, the compilation of books and letters known as the New Testament did not have the official approval of the Church. *And so the "Scripture" to which Paul referred in 2 Timothy 3:16 would have been the Old Testament.*

In contrast, In 2 Thes 2:15 Paul tells his readers to *hold fast to the **spoken and written traditions*** he has given them. And in 2 Tim 2:1 Paul tells Timothy that the things he has **heard** from Paul he must hand on to trustworthy men who will teach others.

And, as we know, the risen Jesus himself sent forth the apostles to proclaim the spoken "Tradition" long before the written New Testament existed (Mt 28:19-20).

Since the Reformation, Protestants have considered the following books non-canonical, referring to them as the Apocrypha: 1 and 2 Esdras (3 and 4 Esdras), Tobit, Judith, Wisdom, Sirach (Ecclesiasticus), Baruch with the letter of Jeremiah, 1 and 2 Maccabees, additions to Daniel and to Esther, and the Prayer of Manasseh. With these exceptions, most Protestant denominations accept the Canon of books of the Bible compiled by Athanasius and affirmed by the Church Councils of Hippo and Carthage near the end of the fourth century - the Canon which was declared complete and closed at the Council of Trent (1545-1563).

Perhaps the most important point of the above discussion for us today is that, although a great many writings about Jesus existed during the time of the early Church – *for about one-sixth of the entire existence of the Church there was no "Bible." From its very first day, however, the Church had "Tradition."*

Difficulties with "Sola Fide" – justification by faith alone

To assure our salvation, is it enough to simply have faith in Jesus and say from the heart "*I accept you, Jesus, as my personal Lord and Savior*"? Many of our Protestant separated brethren hold this view. For them, such an act of true faith results in God "covering" our past and *future* sins, no matter how grave, and is sufficient to guarantee our entry into heaven when we die. But even in the early days of the Reformation Calvin disagreed with Luther on the precise meaning of *sola fide*. It is not surprising, then, that a number of different interpretations are held today among the many Protestant religious bodies, each relying of its own interpretation of certain verses of Scripture.

Three biblical verses that appear to support *sola fide* are: "For God so loved the world that he gave his only Son, that whoever **believes** in him should not perish but have eternal life" (Jn 3:16); "For this is the will of my Father, that every one who sees the Son and **believes** in him should have eternal life; and I will raise him up at the last day" (Jn 6:40) and; "Truly, truly, I say to you, he who **believes** has eternal life" (Jn 6:47; Emphasis added).

However, in his answer to the rich young man in Mt 19:16-17, Jesus appears to contradict what he said in the three verses from St. John's Gospel above: "Teacher, what good deed must I do, to have eternal life? And he [Jesus] said to him "***If you would enter life, keep*** *the commandments."* Not a word about believing in Jesus. And can we simply accept John 3:16, for example, but ignore Jn 3:36: "He who *believes* in the Son has eternal life; *he who does not obey the Son shall not see life*, but the wrath of God rests upon him"? And is it possible to *obey* without engaging in *works*; that is, doing what we ought to do and refraining from doing what we ought not to do?

Is it enough to simply "believe" Jesus, or must we also "keep the commandments"?[194] (We know that "believing" that Jesus was the Son of God did not save Satan).

If salvation is assured simply by belief in Jesus, even though one may live a life of unrepentant grave sin, why did James strongly deny this? (James 2:14-26). Luther, in an apparent attempt to create biblical support for his *sola fide* view, changed the meaning of Paul's letter to the Romans by adding the word *alone*: "For we hold that a man is justified by faith *alone* apart from observance of the law" (Rom 3:28). Luther's colleagues later prevailed and Paul's original text was reinstated.

It is interesting to note that a primary meaning of the Indo-European root of the word *believe* is *leubh*, meaning "To care, desire; love." In Old English *leof*, "dear, beloved." Germanic *galaubjan* "to hold dear." Latin *libēre* "to be dear" (Emphasis added).[195]

When *believe* in Jn 3:16 and in the other passages noted above includes the aspect of *love*, all four passages above are seen as fully compatible, consistent with Catholic teaching, and in accord with other "love" passages such as, *"If you love me you will keep my commandments"* (Jn 14:15) and, *"If a man loves me, he will keep my word, and my Father will love him, and we will come to him and make our home with him. He who does not love me does not keep my words; and the word which you hear is not mine but the Father's who sent me"* (Jn 14:23).

Jesus spoke of two Great Commandments: "You shall love the Lord your God with all your heart, and with all your soul, and with all your mind (Deut 6:5). This is the great and first commandment. And a second is like it: You shall love your neighbor as yourself" (Lev 19:18, Lev 19:33, Mt 22:37-39). (Similarly, "The stranger who sojourns with you shall be to you as the native among you, and you shall love him as

---

194 "Believing," in some Christian denominations, means sincerely "accepting Jesus as my personal Lord and Savior," without any requirement for works.
195 Copyright © 2006 by Houghton Mifflin Company. Adapted and reproduced by permission from *The American Heritage Dictionary of the English Language, Fourth Edition.*

yourself").

As an example of how we are to love our neighbor, Jesus gives us the parable of the Good Samaritan (Lk 10:30-37). In describing the Last Judgment, Jesus makes clear the eternal consequence we can expect depending not on our mere sentiment toward our neighbor but on what we *do* or *fail to do* for them. To those entering into eternal life, Jesus will say "I was hungry and you gave me food ..., thirsty ..., a stranger ..., naked ..., sick and in prison ...." But to those going away into eternal punishment, Jesus will say "I was hungry and you gave me *no* food ..., thirsty ..., a stranger ..., naked ..., sick and in prison ..." (Mt 25:31-46).

For the definitive meaning of *believe* in Jn 3:16, 6:40 and 6:47, of course, we must look to the Canonical Greek. There, in all three verses, we find *(ho) pisteuon,* the *active* voice, present tense participle, which means "the believing one" or "the one who believes" or "the believer." Note that this indicated *continuing, persevering belief*, not a "once and done" occurrence.[196]

St. Paul makes clear the dire consequence of our failure to *love* this truth: *"They refused to **love** the truth and so be saved. Therefore God sends upon them a strong delusion to make them believe what is false, so that all may be condemned who did not believe the truth"* (2 Thes 2:10-11).

Claude Tresmontant notes that Luther, Pascal, Descartes, Kant, Kierkegaard, and many others have sadly distorted the original biblical meaning of the words "faith" and "belief." Tresmontant then writes that because of this distortion "To believe" [no longer includes] the idea of a certitude about one's knowledge of the truth which the Hebrew *aman* conveyed. *Amen,* which is derived from the same root word [*emunah*], thus means "truly."[197]

Is the concept of "truth" far removed from that of "love"? As noted above, Jesus said, "If you love me you will keep my commandments." If our love for Jesus is superficial are we likely to be resolute in keeping them? I think not. If our love for Jesus is deeply rooted in "truth" can we expect a far better outcome? Of this there can be no doubt.

"Let your sins be strong"

Over the centuries, of course, *sola fide* has become central to

---

196 Translation provided by Fr. Edward B. Connolly, St. Joseph / St. Francis deSales parishes, Pottsville / Mt. Carbon, PA; Diocese of Allentown.
197 *The Hebrew Christ,* 151.

Protestant belief. For those who firmly hold this idea it is important, I believe, to consider its logical conclusion as seen by Luther. On August 1, 1521 – three years and nine months after posting his 95 theses on the door of Wittenberg Chapel and seven months after his excommunication – Luther included the following in a letter to Philipp Melanchthon, his theologian / associate:

> If you are a preacher of mercy, do not preach an imaginary but the true mercy. If the mercy is true, you must therefore bear the true, not an imaginary sin. God does not save those who are only imaginary sinners. Be a sinner and let your sins be strong, but let your trust in Christ be stronger, and rejoice in Christ who is the victor over sin, death, and the world. We will commit sins while we are here, for this life is not a place where justice resides. We, however, says Peter (2, Peter 3:13) are looking forward to a new heaven and a new earth where justice will reign. It suffices that through God's glory we have recognized the Lamb who takes away the sin of the world. No sin can separate us from Him, even if we were to kill or commit adultery thousands of times each day. Do you think such an exalted Lamb paid merely a small price with a meager sacrifice for our sins? Pray hard for you are quite a sinner.
>
> On the day of the Feast of St. Peter the apostle, 1521.[198]

Suppose your daughter, a college student, says, "Mom, my boyfriend has been pressuring me to 'prove my love' to him. But I want to keep God's Commandment and not 'prove my love' until I am married." Should you reply: "You know I love you with all my heart. You know that Jesus loves you too, and that Jesus won for us the victory over sin and death. If you truly love each other, but you feel you will lose him if you do not accommodate him then by all means do so. Take the necessary precautions, of course, and *let your sins be strong* – but let your trust in Christ be stronger."

And suppose your son, a high school student, says: "Dad, my dislike for many of my classmates grows stronger each day. They ignore me except to make fun of me in front of others. I try to just shrug it off, but lately I've been thinking of ways to get back at them." Should you respond: "I don't know what you mean by 'getting back at them,' son; surely it would be best to continue to shrug it off, as you say. But if you find yourself reacting in some unchristian manner, just

---

198 "A Letter From Luther to Melanchthon," par. 13, Letter no. 99. Translated for Project Wittenberg by Erika Bullman Flores. **www.ctsfw.edu/etext/luther/letters**

remember this: For those like us who have recognized and accepted Jesus as the Lamb who takes away the sin of the world, no sin can separate us from Him, even if we were to kill ... thousands of times each day."

Imagine, if you will, that you are on a business trip in a large city far from home. After a few drinks with a very attractive person of the opposite sex, she / he invites you to her / his room. Words and body language tell you that what awaits there has nothing at all to do with business. But you are convinced that your wife / husband would never find out. Is this a good time to remember the words of Luther: "No sin can separate us from Him; even if we were to ... commit adultery thousands of times each day"?

Clearly, to act in any such manner would be to egregiously violate the letter and spirit of the Bible. No true Christian believer would ever suggest that Luther's words be applied as in the above scenarios. Surely no true Protestant minister would ever give such advice from the pulpit or in private. I am sure that our separated brethren wish that Luther had never written this letter. Any defense of Luther as its author must begin by insisting that he was using hyperbole when he wrote "let your sins be strong ...." Surely it was just his way of stressing the infinite spiritual value of the sacrificial death of Jesus on the cross. And the above represents less than a page of Luther's more than fifty volumes.

But, to the extent the above reflects Luther's understanding of *sola fide* – justification by faith alone – how can any Christian accept it? Following Luther, should we *go and sin boldly*? Or, following Christ, should we strive to *go and sin no more*? (Jn 8:11)

Since the Reformation, Protestants have been divided among themselves on what is required for *salvation*. Some believe that *justification* alone is sufficient. Most, however, believe that *sanctification* (becoming holy) is also required. For an in-depth study of these and related matters (*works, merit,* etc.), I suggest reading *Fundamentals of Catholic Dogma,* by Ludwig Ott, pp. 250-269.

The "solemn laying on of hands" through the ages

Through the solemn laying on of hands through the ages, Catholic priests receive their authority to forgive sin from Jesus himself, through the apostles. The risen Jesus appeared to the apostles, "*breathed* on them, and said to them, 'Receive the Holy Spirit. If you forgive the sins of any, they are forgiven; if you retain the sins of any, they are retained.'" (Jn 20:22-23).

In contrast to Luther's capitulation to the inevitability of sin, if a

Catholic went to Confession with the unspoken intention to continue committing mortal sin, he would not be forgiven. Even though the priest spoke the words of absolution, the sin would remain because the person lacked a "firm purpose of amendment."

When, as part of a properly made confession, a Catholic makes a firm purpose of amendment, it means that he / she truly resolves to resist the temptation to sin and to avoid what for him / her are the occasions of sin. Many Catholics can attest to the efficacy of the sacrament of *Penance* (*Confession / Reconciliation*) in helping them grow spiritually to the point where they hardly ever commit a mortal sin and when they do they go to Confession without delay. Through this sacrament instituted by Christ himself they again become pleasing to him and may again receive him in the Eucharist.

When celebrating the sacrament of Penance, "The priest is the sign and instrument of God's merciful love for the sinner ... he must love the truth, be faithful to the Magisterium of the Church and lead the penitent with patience toward healing and full maturity. He must pray and do penance for his penitent, entrusting him to the Lord's mercy."[199]

The Eucharist – eliminated in the name of reform

No one makes any substantive claim that in the Bible Jesus authorizes believers to follow a shepherd whose pastures are stripped of vital elements of spiritual nourishment that are freely given to those who follow the successors of Peter, in particular pastures that – in the name of "reform" – have been stripped of the Eucharist.

It is important to be aware that Jesus said: *"I am the living bread which came down from heaven; if any one eats of this bread, he will live for ever; and the bread which I shall give for the life of the world is my flesh"* (Jn 6:51) and; *"Truly, truly I say to you, unless you eat the flesh of the Son of man and drink his blood, you have no life in you; he who eats my flesh and drinks my blood has eternal life and I will raise him up at the last day"* (Jn 6:53-54). And, of course, the words Jesus spoke to the apostles at the Last Supper: "And as they were eating, *he took bread, and blessed, and broke it, and gave it to them, and said, 'Take; this is my body.' And he took a cup, and when he had given thanks he gave it to them, and they all drank of it. And he said to them, 'This is my blood of the covenant, which is poured out for many.'"* (Mk 14:22-24; Also see Mt 26:26-28 and Lk 22:19-20).

If Jesus intended the Eucharist simply as a symbol, he committed a grave injustice by not calling back the departing disciples to clarify the

---

199 *Catechism of the Catholic Church*, par. 1465-66.

matter; disciples who were stunned by Jesus' statement (Jn 6:53-54). Bread, *as a mere symbol, is available at many Christian services. The Eucharist is available only on apostolic altars.*

A common Protestant objection to the above is Jn 6:63, in which Jesus says: "It is the spirit that gives life, the flesh is of no avail ...." This is a perfect example of the danger of *sola scriptura*. Why? Because someone with a narrow, superficial understanding of the Bible and of Christ, may then say, "I'm outta here! As a Christian, I believed that it was only through Christ's own flesh-and-blood Crucifixion that I could be saved. But now I read that Jesus himself said that the 'flesh is of no avail.' Therefore the Crucifixion was of no avail and we will all die in our sins. And so I say 'good-bye, Christianity!'"

The answer, of course, lies in a deeper understanding of scripture in its full context. How but through our "flesh," i.e., the use of our minds and bodies, can we keep the commandments, feed the hungry and meet all the other biblical requirements for salvation? And so the flesh *is* of avail in enabling us to do what the Bible calls us to do to attain salvation. Our flesh is of no avail only in the sense that, no matter what good we do as "flesh," unless the spirit *gives* us that *life* – that is, eternal life and what Catholics call the Grace in this life that leads to eternal life – we cannot be saved.

John Calvin – the force behind the Reformation

It is commonly believed that Martin Luther (1483-1546) was primarily responsible for the Protestant Reformation. But, we are told by Church historian Hilaire Belloc, if it had not been for John Calvin (1509-1564), that reform movement might well have failed.[200]

As a model to precisely imitate, Calvinism is of little importance to Protestantism today. If Calvin were to return in our time he would be hard pressed to find a denomination anywhere in which all of his key teachings are presented as he intended.

The real importance of Calvin to Protestants today is that Calvin laid what was seen as an alternate track of Christian belief – *The Institutes of the Christian Religion* and *The Commentaries.*

The biblical "lever" that Calvin used to switch believers off the main track of the 1,500-year-old Church founded by Christ and onto his new track was his *flawed commentary* on Mt 16:18 (Peter named the "Rock"); Mt 16:19 (Peter given the keys)*; and* Jn 21:15-17 ("Feed my lambs .... Tend my sheep .... Feed my sheep"). These are the three biblical verses in which Jesus *personally* confers on Peter primacy in

---

200 *The Great Heresies*; 114-115.

the Church Jesus was then founding.

The following is an analysis of what Calvin wrote about these three verses. If Calvin's statements were biblically sound, then it might seem to our Protestant separated brethren that they might remain in their own particular alternate-track Christian church in good conscience.

However, as we will see, there are *serious biblical (and logical) errors* in Calvin's "lever." As this becomes evident in the following pages, it will become clear that *Calvin had no biblical basis* for rerouting so many millions of Christian believers away from the main track – the One Church founded by Christ himself. The question in the minds of those who belong to other Christian denominations will then be:

> *On what biblical basis can I remain in my particular Christian denomination and fail to come home to the one Church founded by Jesus himself?*

As noted above, it was Calvin's comprehensive *Institutes of the Christian Religion* that was seen as a framework on which a religion could be built. Protestantism has seen a myriad of reformations since then, as schematic drawings of the history of the various Protestant denominations attest. But it was Calvin's *The Institutes*, and his explanatory *Commentaries*, that made him the driving force of the Reformation.

Luther, Calvin and other reform-minded Catholics in the early to mid-sixteenth century may well have been influenced by the recent memory of Alexander VI (1492-1503), arguably the most humanly corrupt pope ever to hold the office. Girolamo Savonarola, a Dominican monk, became widely known for his continuing denunciation of papal corruption and his call for a council to reform the Church and to remove the pope from office. When Savonarola refused to remain silent, Alexander excommunicated him and in 1498 had him burned at the stake as a heretic (At this writing the Catholic Church is evaluating Savonarola for beatification, which could be followed by recognition as a saint).

The Church remained in need of important reforms after Pope Alexander VI but, due to a number of difficulties, reform was not addressed until 1545 when the Council of Trent began. Christopher Dawson, first occupant of the Charles Chauncey Stillman Chair of Roman Catholic Studies at Harvard, has written an excellent summary of these and other aspects of the Reformation.[201]

---

201 *The Dividing of Christendom.*

We know today that, of all the Popes who held the office from Peter to the present, half of them held it for only about five years or less. That figure would have been similar in Calvin's day [There were nine popes in Calvin's lifetime, including Paul III (1534-1549) who convened the Council of Trent, which initiated the needed reforms].

How Calvin erred in denying that Jesus gave primacy to Peter alone

In any case, for Calvin to draw Catholics in large numbers away from the Church they and their ancestors had belonged to for many centuries, he had to successfully argue that Jesus did not give primacy to Peter alone. Was Calvin's reasoning valid? In *The Institutes*, Calvin notes the biblical basis for papal primacy, stating: "In the New Testament there is nothing which they [Catholics] can produce in confirmation of their opinion, but it having been said of one, 'Thou art Peter, and upon this rock I will build my Church' (Mt 16:18). Again, 'Simon, son of Jonas, lovest thou me? ... Feed my lambs.'" (John 21:15).[202]

Calvin seems to overlook the fact that Mt 16:18 was the fulfillment of what could be called a prophecy by Jesus in the first words he spoke to Peter: "So you are Simon the son of John? You shall be called Cephas (which means Peter)" (Jn 1:42).

Although Calvin will go on to try unsuccessfully to give new meaning to these clear words of Jesus, it is important to note that in Mt 16:18 he first quotes the Bible accurately. In this time before Modernism, he does not claim that the Bible is historically unreliable.

In any case, however, Calvin goes to great lengths to make it appear that these passages – and Mt 16:19 in which Jesus tells Peter he will give him the keys of the kingdom of heaven – do not mean that Jesus gave Peter primacy over the entire Church. Calvin draws analogies with secular government, noting that all the nations of the world could never be led by one head. He adds that colonies of bees worldwide are autonomous; that no bee has primacy. He notes that the letters of Paul do not affirm the primacy of Peter and that some passages of Paul's letters appear to present Paul as the equal to Peter (Gal 1:18, 2:8, 2:11-14).

Upon analysis, however, we find that none of Calvin's arguments against Peter's primacy are substantive. For example, we can as easily interpret Gal 1:18 as meaning that it was because *Paul knew that Jesus had given primacy to Peter* that Paul went to Jerusalem to spend fifteen

---

202 *Institutes of the Christian Religion,* Book IV, Ch. VI, Section 3, trans. Henry Beveridge, Esq., Christian Classics Ethereal Library, **www.ccel.org**

days with Peter rather than with another apostle. Gal 2:8 simply alludes to the parallel of Paul spreading the faith among the Gentiles as Peter did among the Jews. Gal 2:11-14 seems a more formidable argument, with Paul saying, "But when Cephas came to Antioch I opposed him to his face ...." But how did Paul do this? Did he order Peter to cease and desist as one in authority might do? No, Paul did not. Instead he *presented his concern to Peter as a question as one might do with a superior:* "If you, though a Jew, live like a Gentile and not like a Jew, how can you compel the Gentiles to live like Jews?" [By one early account, it seems that the "Cephas" Paul then confronted may not have been Peter. Eusebius, Bishop of Caesarea, *c.* 313-39, notes that Clement of Alexandria (*Outlines*, Book V), wrote that this Cephas was a disciple, one of the seventy, who had the same name as the apostle Peter.][203]

Several other occurrences indicate that God did not intend that Paul "report to God alone," independently of the Church in which Jesus had given Peter primacy. With no intermediary, Jesus struck down and blinded Paul on the road to Damascus (Acts 9:3). Jesus could as easily have restored Paul's sight with no intermediary. Instead Jesus sent not an apostle, but Ananias, a disciple in the Church led by Peter, as the instrument through whom Paul would regain his sight, receive the Holy Spirit and be baptized (Acts 9:17). It was only after several days with the disciples in Damascus that Paul began to proclaim Jesus. Later he attempted to join the disciples in Jerusalem and one of them, Barnabas, brought him to the apostles (Acts 9:26). And if Paul saw himself as preaching independently of the Church in which Jesus had given Peter primacy, why – *after fourteen years* – would Paul write:

> *I went up [to Jerusalem] by revelation; and I laid before them (but privately before those of repute) the gospel which I preach among the Gentiles, lest somehow I should be running or had run in vain* (Gal 2:2).

Note that Paul did not write "lest somehow *they* [Peter and the other apostles] should be running in vain," as one who thought his "primacy" exceeded that given to Peter by Jesus. Nor did Paul try to negotiate new scriptural interpretations, as if he saw his authority as equal to that of Peter.

Clearly, Paul subjected his teaching to the Church in which Jesus had given Peter primacy, and Peter and the other apostles held Paul in

---

203 Eusebius; *The History of the Church*, Book 1, par. 12.

the highest regard. When Paul and Barnabas came to Jerusalem they were "welcomed by the church and the apostles and the elders ..." (Acts 15:40). The apostles chose men to return to Antioch with "our beloved Barnabas and Paul" (Acts 15:25). And Peter sees Paul as "our beloved brother" (2 Peter 3:15).

Calvin also refers to the following verse in his argument against papal primacy:

"For no other foundation can any one lay than that which is laid, which is Jesus Christ" (1 Cor. 3:11).[204]

Obviously, Jesus is the foundation of the Church he founded. Since the Church can have no other foundation, how can Catholics claim that Jesus built his Church on Peter? Clearly, Catholics misinterpret Mt 16:18, right?

Well, not exactly. It is Jesus himself who provides the basis for understanding that 1 Cor 3:11 is fully compatible with his appointment of Peter as the "Rock" in Mt 16:18. Jesus points out that there is an important *difference* between a foundation and the rock on which it is laid. He does so in his parable about a man who, building a house, "*dug deep and laid the foundation upon rock*," and Jesus also tells us about the ruin of the house of the man who did not do so (Lk 6:46-49). The same warning is found in the *Gospel according to Matthew* (7:24-27).

It is always important to read Gospel verses in context. At this point in history, with tens of thousands of separate religious bodies carrying the Christian banner, the verses that precede Mt 7:24-27 may well be seen as ominous: "Enter by the narrow gate ..." (7:13). "Beware of false prophets ..." (7:15). "Not every one who says to me 'Lord, Lord,' shall enter the kingdom of heaven, but he who does the will of my Father ..." (7:21). "[We] did many mighty works in your name ... [But Jesus says] I never knew you; depart from me, you evildoers" (7:22-23). Why would Jesus relate such dire events as a preface to his call to "lay the foundation on rock" if this were of no importance?

Calvin gives to all apostles the keys Jesus gave to Peter alone

There are a number of other difficulties with Calvin's arguments against papal primacy in *The Institutes*, as well as in his *Commentaries*.

---

204 *Institutes of the Christian Religion,* Book IV, Ch. VI, Section 4, trans. Henry Beveridge, Esq., Christian Classics Ethereal Library, **www.ccel.org**

For example, Calvin falls into the following logical errors in rejecting Peter as holder of the keys of the kingdom of heaven. Here, from *The Institutes*, is what Calvin had to say on the matter of "the keys":

> Christ, (they say), constituted Peter prince of the whole Church when he promised to give him the keys. *But what he then promised to one he elsewhere delivers, as it were hands over, to all the rest.* If the same right, which was promised to one, is bestowed on all, in what respect is that one superior to his colleagues? (Italics added).[205]

The problem here for Calvin is that, *according to The Bible, Jesus never gave, or promised to give, the keys of the kingdom of heaven to anyone other than Peter.* Other translations insert verses Calvin may have had in mind – Mt 18:18, Jn 20:23. *But a careful reading of Mt 18:18 reveals that Jesus says not a word about the keys of primacy or "Chief Stewardship"* [Isaiah 22:22] *that Jesus gave to Peter alone in Mt 16:19* [See "Apostolic Succession," below]. In Jn 20:23 the risen Jesus gives the apostles the power to forgive or retain sins, but *again, in Jn 20:23, Jesus does not give to any other apostle the keys of authority he gave to Peter alone in Mt 16:19.* Calvin thus attempts to make for the apostles (including Judas Iscariot) eleven extra sets of the keys of primacy / chief stewardship that Jesus gave to Peter *alone.*

Calvin begins his Commentary on Mt 16:19 as follows:

> *And I will give thee the keys* …. Here Christ begins now to speak of the public office, that is, of the apostleship, which he dignifies with a twofold title. First, he says the ministers of the Gospel are porters, so to speak, of the kingdom of heaven, because they carry its keys; and, secondly, he adds, that they are invested with a power of binding and loosing which is ratified in heaven.[206]

Here Calvin is correct in regard to the apostolic power to bind and loose (Mt 18:18). But again, where in the Bible do we read that, in addition to Peter, the *other apostles* were given the *keys of the kingdom of heaven*? The answer, of course, is nowhere. And further, where in the Bible do we read that *ministers of the Gospel* … carry the keys of the kingdom of heaven? Again, the answer is nowhere.

In his *Commentaries,* in regard to Mt 16:19, Calvin makes the same

---

205 *Institutes of the Christian Religion,* Book IV, Ch. VI, Section 4, trans. Henry Beveridge, Esq., Christian Classics Ethereal Library; **www.ccel.org**
206 Ibid.

logical error – *applying to many what Jesus applied to only one.* But here ***Calvin compounds the error by misquoting the words of Jesus in regard to Mt 16:19***:

> The comparison of *the keys* is very properly applied to the office of teaching; *as when Christ says (Luke 11:52) that the scribes and Pharisees, in like manner, have the key of the kingdom of heaven,* because they are expounders of the law.[207]

Here Calvin tells us that in Lk 11:52 Christ says that the scribes and Pharisees likewise have the key to the kingdom of heaven. ***But in Lk 11:52 Jesus says not a word about the keys of the kingdom of heaven*** – Jesus is speaking about the ***key of knowledge*** – a very different matter. Even if one holds that such knowledge can lead one to heaven, Jesus has made it very clear that many who *know* what *is required* to gain heaven *act in a way quite contrary* to that knowledge and do not attain it. How many with great knowledge, like Lucifer, have been forever barred from heaven?

In defense of Calvin, some may quote Mt 23:13: "But woe to you, scribes and Pharisees, hypocrites! Because you *shut* the kingdom of heaven against men ..." (emphasis added). Thus begins Jesus' scathing denunciation of the scribes and Pharisees that continues for twenty-six verses. Central to this denunciation is that when they make a proselyte they make him "twice as much a child of hell as yourselves" (Mt 23:15). It is in this sense that they "shut" (block?) the door of heaven to those who otherwise might enter; a door which has been unlocked not by them but by one with the authority to do so. In this sense, of course, there are many who "block" the door of heaven by causing others to become unworthy of entering.

Calvin thus becomes the great key-duplicator of the Reformation. I wonder if in the midst of all of this anyone tapped him on the shoulder and said "Monsieur Calvin, didn't you notice what Jesus, in effect, stamped on the keys of the kingdom of heaven when he gave them to Peter alone? It says, 'Do Not Duplicate.'"

"Feed my Lambs" – Calvin gives to others the authority Jesus gave to Peter alone

In *The Institutes* Calvin acknowledges that Jesus said to Peter *and no one else* "Feed my lambs .... Tend my lambs .... Feed my sheep"

---

207 *Calvin's Commentaries; A Harmony of the Gospels; Matthew, Mark, and Luke,* Table 52, (19); trans. Rev. William Pringle, Christian Classics Ethereal Library; **www.ccel.org/ccel/calvin/calcom32.ii.lii.html#ii.lii-p40.2**

(Jn 21:15-17). However, Calvin again outdoes Jesus by *applying to others* the authority Jesus gave *only* to Peter:

> *But as Peter had received a command from the Lord, so he exhorts all other presbyters to feed the Church (1 Peter 5:2). Hence we are entitled to infer, that, by that expression of Christ, nothing more was given to Peter than to the others, or that the right which Peter had received he communicated equally to others.*[208]

In his inference that Christ had given "nothing more ... to Peter than to the others" Calvin, in effect, attempts to either delete those words of Jesus (Jn 21:15-17) from the Bible or apply them to "others" in addition to Peter. Either way, Calvin is rewriting the words and context of what Jesus at that moment said to Peter *alone*. Calvin offers no reason for doing so and he does not pretend that he has such a reason.

Also, in 1 Peter 5:2, Peter *does not exhort "all other presbyters"* to *feed the Church, but only those who have been duly "consecrated by the Spirit to a life of obedience to Jesus Christ ...,"* in particular, those *disciples (those we would today call priests) in Pontus, Galatia ... who preached under Peter's direction* (1 Peter 1:1-2).

In 1 Peter 5:2 he wrote to his disciples "Tend the flock of God that is your charge, not by constraint but willingly, not for shameful gain but eagerly...." If by these words Peter "equally shared with others the *right* he had received" from Jesus, then the general who exhorts his officers in battle makes every lieutenant a general; every chief executive who encourages his managers to excellence makes every manager a chief executive; every parent who gives guidance to a child gives the child authority equal to that of the parent.

In regard to these claims, the key points are these: (a) Calvin offers no biblical basis for denying that Jesus authorized *only Peter* to "Feed my lambs ...." (b) In Peter 5:2 and elsewhere Peter in turn authorizes *only disciples under his direction* to feed Christ's lambs with a "shepherd's care." (c) Peter would have rebuked Calvin or anyone else who even suggested that his authorization to his disciples also applied to reformers who rejected Peter's authority and preached a very different message.

In summary then, the objective reader of the relevant sections of *The Institutes* and *Commentaries* will see that Calvin's biblical interpre-

---

208 *Institutes of the Christian Religion*; Book IV, Ch. VI, Section 3, trans. Henry Beveridge, Esq., Christian Classics Ethereal Library; **www.ccel.org**

tations regarding the Church and the papacy were seriously flawed.

Calvin swung his sledgehammer mightily and with repeated blows tried to smash the Rock on which Christ built his One Church; the Church of which Calvin himself had been a member until 1533. But, when the dust settled, the Petrine base of the Church was unscathed, and Mt 16:18-19 and Jn 21:15 – as well as Mt 28:20 – had lost none of their Scriptural force.

The thirty-two theologians, followers of Luther, who signed Melanchthon's document *Of the Power and Primacy of the Pope* at Smalcald in 1537 made errors similar to those made by Calvin. They wrongly equated the authority to "bind and loose" given to all the apostles in Mt: 18-18 with the keys of the kingdom of heaven Jesus promised to Peter alone in Mt 16:19, as if the authority of law enforce-ment officials of a city were equal to that of the mayor to whom they ultimately report (p. 5).

They also failed to acknowledge that Jesus would have been speaking in *Aramaic* – not in the canonical Greek – when he said to Peter "upon this Rock I will build my Church" and that in Aramaic these words of Jesus can mean *only* that Jesus applied the promise to Peter as a *person*. ["Thou art *Kepha* and upon this *kepha* ..."].

Augustine calls all to Catholicism

Consider the words of Augustine, Bishop of Hippo, regarding those who sever their relationship with the Catholic Church:

> The Holy Spirit is to the Body of Christ which is His Church what the soul is to the body of man; the Holy Spirit acts in the entire Church as the soul acts in all the members of the body. See what you should avoid, what you should pay attention to; what you should fear. It happens that in the human body some member – hand, finger, foot – is cut off from the body. Does the soul follow the severed member? While it was in the body it lived; cut off, it loses life. So the Christian man is a Catholic while he lives in the Body; cut off, he becomes a heretic; The Holy Spirit does not fol-low the amputated member.[209]

This excerpt must be interpreted in light of the *Catechism* (e.g., par. 2089, 819, 846 and, more broadly, 813-822). As a historical document, however, it makes very clear Augustine's view of the importance of becoming and remaining *Catholic*.

---

209 St. Augustine; Sermon 267. Quoted in *The Early Years of the Church*, 29, Catholic Information Service; Knights of Columbus.

And so it would seem that one is hard-pressed today to look to either Luther or Calvin, or to any other reformer, for a reason for continuing to "protest" against the primacy of Peter or trying to prevail against the One Church Christ himself founded on Peter.

I offer these thoughts not with any uncharitable intent, but in the hope that they will encourage our separated brethren to reexamine the reasons that keep them from coming *home* – as Marcus Grodi and so many others have done – to the One Church Jesus founded and, through the apostles, promised to be with always.

Apostolic / Papal succession – Isaiah 22:22

That the risen Jesus intended the authority of primacy he gave to Peter as "Rock," as well the authority he gave to the apostles, to be held by their successors through time should be clear based on Mt 28:20: "and lo, I am with you always ...."

The biblical basis for the transference of the Petrine keys to successors is indicated by Isaiah 22:22, in which the king takes the key of authority from Shebna and gives it to Eliakim: "*And I will place on his shoulder the key of the house of David; he shall open and none shall shut; and he shall shut and none shall open.*" In view of Isaiah 22:22 and the context in which it is written it is quite clear, in the interest of order, that one steward at a time – and *only* one at a time – must hold the key of full authority (i.e., chief steward, vizier, etc.,) under the king. Note that the king did not eliminate the office and destroy the key – a chief steward was essential to the orderly running of the kingdom. Nor did the king make duplicate keys and make every steward a "chief steward" – giving everyone "full authority," which surely would have been equally disruptive. No. The one key of full authority was to be held by one chief steward while he served in the office and then passed on to his successor.

Let us test this view by imagining that Jesus had acted differently: Suppose, at that moment in the district of Caesarea Philippi, Jesus said to each of the original twelve apostles:

> I call each of you "Rock" (remember that Judas Iscariot was present). And after I am raised up another most extraordinary "Rock" will join you. His name will be Paul. On each of you I will build my Church. And I will give each of you (again including Judas Iscariot), the keys of the kingdom of heaven. This means that each of you, and your successors through the ages, will have full authority, as my co-equal chief stewards, to lead my Church.

Given the diversity of strongly held views among bishops through the ages, how long could the Church have remained ONE if Jesus had established a "Full authority is vested in every apostle (bishop)" Church?

Let us suppose that, when he spoke to the twelve that day, Jesus had gone even further:

In addition to the keys I gave to each of you, I hereby give full authority to anyone and everyone down through the ages who, in good faith, forms a Church and calls it Christian. The authority of each such person shall be equal to that of yours and your successor bishops. Such a person will have full authority as Chief Steward over his or her flock just as you and your successor bishops will have over yours. They shall have the authority to interpret the Bible, when it is written, in any way they wish. If they declare acceptable anything forbidden by the Commandments – adultery and other sexual activity outside of a marriage between one man and one woman, killing of the unborn or the elderly, etc. – that shall be their right and you shall not object. When they and their followers stand before me in judgment I will not fault them for such acts. Whatever they do as a Christian church I, looking down from heaven, shall approve.

When I pray to the Father that all may be ONE I will not be praying for uniformity of teaching and belief under Peter and his successor pontiffs through the ages. I desire only that, whatever beliefs people fashion for themselves in the religions of the future, they remember me with love and include the word Christian in the name of each religion. It is primarily to immortalize the name Christian that I will die on the cross.

Of course there is nothing in the Bible to support the idea that Jesus authorizes any person or group to separate from the One Church he founded, reinterpret Scripture and devise their own code of morality.

In the Bible, Jesus appoints *only Peter* as the Rock on which he will build his Church and it is *Peter alone* – with papal succession addressed as indicated – to whom Jesus gives the keys of the kingdom of heaven. Having done so, Jesus can later pray to the Father:

I do not pray for these [the apostles] only, but also for those who believe in me through their word, that they may all be one; even as thou, Father, art in me, and I in thee ... (Jn 17:20-21).

This is not the first time a prayer or blessing of Jesus was given through the apostles. As earlier indicated, *the Eucharist is found only on apostolic altars* (Mt 26:26-28). But Jesus said "unless you eat the flesh of the Son of man and drink his blood, you have no life in you" (Jn 6:53-54).

As spiritual sons and daughters of the reformers, our Protestant separated brethren reject the true Eucharist which Catholic bishops and priests consecrate in accordance with the words of Jesus at the Last Supper. Obviously, Jesus was not speaking of physical life – billions are alive today who are not Catholic.

Clearly, however, Jesus was speaking of spiritual life that is somehow lacking in those who do not receive the true Eucharist and receive it worthily. Nor could Jesus have been speaking metaphorically. If he were, as earlier noted, the case could be made that Jesus per-formed a gross injustice by allowing so many formerly loyal disciples to reject him based on a misunderstanding *for which Jesus would have been at fault.*

And Jesus did not qualify his statement by saying, alternatively, that that life could be gained by intensive prayer, fasting, or good works. No. Jesus gave no alternative. To forego the Eucharist is to forego the life of which he spoke.

In any case, having said the above prayer, Jesus suffered and died on the Cross to redeem us and bring about that holy unity. What must Jesus think of us and "Christian unity" in the world today?

"The pillar and bulwark of the truth" – the Church in which Jesus had given Peter primacy

Paul wrote, "*the household of God, which is the church of the living God, the pillar and bulwark of the truth*" (1 Tim 3:15). Clearly, Paul was writing about the One Church led by Peter the "Rock" to whom Jesus himself had given the keys and the authority to "feed my sheep." As earlier noted, Paul warned against the false teachings that were even then being promulgated in his name (2 Thes 2:1-2), and declared "accursed" anyone who preaches a different message (Gal 1:8-9). If Paul could speak to us from heaven today, what would he be likely to say to those who reject the primacy of Peter (something Paul never did) and, as spiritual descendants of the reformers, preach a very different message?

Salvation outside the Catholic Church?

Is salvation possible outside the Catholic Church? The Second Vatican Council addressed this matter as follows, as quoted in the *Catechism of the Catholic Church,* 2nd Ed. (par. 846, 847):

150

Basing itself on Scripture and Tradition, the Council teaches that the Church, a pilgrim now on earth, is necessary for salvation: the one Christ is the mediator and the way of salvation; he is present to us in his body which is the Church. He himself explicitly asserted the necessity of faith and Baptism, and thereby affirmed at the same time the necessity of the Church which men enter through Baptism as through a door. Hence they could not be saved who, knowing that the Catholic Church was founded as necessary by God through Christ, would refuse to enter it or remain in it.[210]

Those who, through no fault of their own, do not know the Gospel of Christ or his Church, but who nevertheless seek God with a sincere heart, and, moved by grace, try in their actions to do his will as they know it through the dictates of their conscience – those too may achieve eternal salvation.[211]

Dominus Iesus was written by Joseph Cardinal Ratzinger, Prefect of the Congregation for the Doctrine of the Faith (now Pope Benedict XVI), ratified by Pope John Paul II, and issued August 6, 2000. It clarifies the position of the Church regarding several aspects of its view of other Christian denominations and salvation outside the Church. Although the following excerpts give some insights into its intent, to avoid misunderstanding, *Dominus Iesus* should be read in its entirety.

Just as there is one Christ, so there exists a single body of Christ, a single Bride of Christ: "a single Catholic and apostolic Church" (IV 16; Vatican II, *Lumen Gentium*, 8).

Regarding the separated Christian Churches:

The spirit of Christ has not refrained from using them as a means of salvation which derive their efficacy from the very fullness of grace and truth entrusted to the Catholic Church" (IV 17; Vatican II; *Unitatis Redintegratio*, 3) Jesus himself explicitly asserted the necessity of faith and baptism (cf. Mk 16:16, Jn 3:5) and thereby affirmed at the same time the necessity of the Church which men enter through baptism as through a door (Vatican II: *Lumen Gentium*, 14; *Ad Gentes* 7; *Unitatis Redintegratio*, 3).

But the Cardinal noted that "This doctrine must not be set against the universal salvific will of God (cf. 1 Tim 2:4). It is necessary to

---

210 *Lumen Gentium* 14; cf. Mk 16:16, Jn 3:5.
211 *Lumen Gentium* 16; cf. Denzinger-Schonmetzer. In *The Companion to the Catechism of the Catholic Church,* page 360, see explanatory letter issued by the Holy Office (now the Congregation for the Doctrine of the Faith).

keep the two truths together, namely, the real possibility of salvation in Christ for all mankind and the necessity of the Church for this salvation."

Dominus Iesus can be viewed on the Vatican Web site.[212]

Jesus protects the Church he founded from doctrinal error.

The Church explains this protection from doctrinal error in paragraphs 888 through 892 of the *Catechism of the Catholic Church,* 2nd Ed. Here are a few excerpts:

> In order to preserve the Church in the purity of the faith handed on by the apostles, Christ who is the Truth willed to confer on her a share in his own infallibility.[213]

> The Roman Pontiff, head of the college of bishops, enjoys this infallibility in virtue of his office, when, as supreme pastor and teacher of all the faithful – who confirms his brethren in the faith – he proclaims by a definitive act a doctrine pertaining to faith or morals. The infallibility promised to the Church is also present in the body of bishops when, together with Peter's successor, they exercise the supreme Magisterium, above all in an Ecumenical Council.[214]

In his presentation *A Closer look at Christ's Church; Answering Common Objections*[215], Scott Hahn, convert from Protestantism to Catholicism, notes that non-Catholic Christians hold that the Bible is infallible. Why? Because, with respect to the books of the Bible, God ensured that Matthew, Mark, Luke, John, Peter, Paul, James and Jude wrote without error; i.e., they wrote the truth and did so infallibly.

But an infallibly written Bible, *without God's own continuing infallible interpretation* through the ages, could lead only to spiritual chaos. As a parallel, Hahn asks us to imagine that, after writing the U.S. Constitution, our founding fathers did not provide for its *continuing authoritative interpretation.* Instead, suppose they just mailed a copy to every citizen and invited each one to interpret each of its provisions as he chose to, guided by the spirit of Washington! That single, vital omission would have doomed the bright promise of what

---

212 **www.vatican.va/roman_curia/congregations/cfaith/documents/rc_con_cfaith _doc_20000806_dominus-iesus_en.html**
213 *Lumen Gentium* 12; cf. *Dei Verbum* 10 (CCC par. 889).
214 *Lumen Gentium* 25 (CCC par. 891).
215 **www.ewtn.com/library/scriptur/POPE.TXT**; Program 14 Transcripts, The Catholic Resources Network.

was to have been "one nation indivisible ...."

But, if I may add a comment to Hahn's concerns, has the Reformation not done such a disservice to the vast number of its adherents since that time?

As noted, at this writing there are tens of thousands of separate Protestant denominations worldwide. They remain separate and distinct largely because of their somewhat different interpretations of the Bible. For example, it is said that there are more than one hundred different interpretations of "This is my Body."

Hahn goes on to ask if we believe that the founding fathers of our Country had greater wisdom than Jesus. If they clearly saw the need for just this one nation to have *one court of last appeal,* can we really believe that Jesus failed to foresee such an obvious need for the Church he promised to be with always, even until the end of the age?[216]

Catholics, knowing that the wisdom of Jesus is infinitely greater than that of any man, take note of the Petrine primacy and Petrine succession biblical verses earlier noted. They also read that, having given Peter that primacy, the risen Jesus told Peter and the other apostles to "go, therefore, and make disciples of all nations; baptize them .... Teach them to carry out everything I have commanded you, and know that I am with you always ...." The Catholic is thus given *biblical* assurance that, through the successor of Peter and the successors of the apostles united with him (i.e., bishops) the Catholic Church is protected from error in matters of faith and morals.

Popes know that they are sinners and go to Confession as all Catholics are called to do. As Hahn points out, in ages past a few "scoundrels" have held the office. Perhaps too busy with their scandalous personal lives, none of these promulgated any doctrine on faith and morals that is inconsistent with the entire fabric of Church teaching.[217]

Discussion Questions

1. How many churches did Jesus found and, through the apostles, promise to be with always? Approximately how many Christian denominations are there today, worldwide? Which one does the Bible indicate we should follow?

2. Martin Luther was an Augustinian monk. Why was he excom-

---

216 www.ewtn.com/library/scriptur/POPE.TXT
217 Dr. Scott Hahn is Founder and President of the St. Paul Center for Biblical Theology. The Center promotes life-transforming Scripture study in the Catholic tradition. www.salvationhistory.com

municated?

3. Why is *sola scriptura* incompatible with the teaching of the Catholic Church?

4. In *The Keys*, Martin Luther acknowledged that Jesus gave the keys of the kingdom to Peter alone. Why did Luther deny the authority of all later popes?

5. What Old Testament passage did Luther apparently overlook in regard to the keys Jesus said he would give to Peter?

6. Does the Bible state that believers are to rely on the Bible alone?

7. The Church did not decide on the *Canon*, the official list of books and letters of the Old and New Testaments, until the latter part of the fourth century. By that time the apostles and their successor bishops and priests had converted much of the known world. By what means did they accomplish this?

8. Do the biblical verses Jn 3:16, Jn 6:40 and Jn 6:47 provide a basis for Luther's *sola fide*? How can they be reconciled with the answer Jesus gave to the "rich young man"? Of what importance is it to consider the meaning of the root of the word *believe*? What is the meaning of the Canonical Greek word *pisteuon*? Why is it important in any discussion of *sola fide*?

9. Why do you think Luther wrote "let your sins be strong ..." in his letter to Melanchthon? Is such a view compatible with Catholic teaching?

10. The risen Jesus said to the apostles, "If you forgive the sins of any they are forgiven; if you retain the sins of any, they are retained." What does this mean for us today?

11. Jesus said "Unless you eat the flesh of the Son of Man and drink his blood, you shall have no life in you ...." Why do Catholics believe Jesus spoke these words not figuratively but literally?

12. Discuss Calvin's arguments against the Catholic interpretation of Mt 16:18, Mt 16:19 and Jn 21:15-17. Do you think that any of these arguments are substantive?

13. Paul said, "I opposed him [Peter] to his face." Does this mean

that Paul saw his apostolic authority as equal to, or greater than, that of Peter? Give the reasons for your interpretation of how Paul viewed his authority in comparison to that of Peter.

14. Why would Paul write, after fourteen years of preaching, "I went up [to Jerusalem] and I laid before them (but privately before those of repute), the Gospel which I preach among the Gentiles, lest somehow I should be running or had run in vain"?

15. Peter saw Paul as "our beloved brother …" (2 Peter 3:15). What does this indicate in regard to the Gospel as preached by Paul compared to the Gospel as preached by Peter and the other apostles?

16. Jesus said the prudent house builder digs deep and lays the foundation on rock (Luke 6:46-49). What does this mean in light of Jesus' appointment of Peter as the "Rock" on which he would build his Church?

17. In *The Institutes of the Christian Religion* Calvin writes as follows in regard to Jesus giving to Peter the keys of the kingdom of heaven: "But what he [Jesus] then promised to one [to Peter, in Mt 16:19] he elsewhere delivers, as it were hands over, to all the rest." Does Jesus actually say this in Mt 18:18, Jn 20:23, or in any other Gospel passage?

18. Calvin is correct when he states that, in Mt 18:18, Jesus invested the apostles "with a power of binding and loosing that is ratified in heaven." But in the same sentence Calvin stated, "the ministers of the Gospel are porters, so to speak, of the kingdom of heaven, *because they carry its keys*." [Emphasis added]. But, we must ask, *where in the Bible does Jesus duplicate for the other apostles the keys he promised only to Peter?* The larger question, of course, is: *Where in the Bible does Jesus duplicate the keys for ministers who would preach independently of Peter and the other apostles and, in many cases, preach a different set of requirements for salvation?* Since in the Bible Jesus promises the keys *only to Peter*, how should we view Calvin's claim of duplication of the keys?

19. What explanation can be given for Calvin's startling misstatement of Luke 11:32 in which Calvin claims that Jesus said that the *scribes and Pharisees have the key of the kingdom of heaven,* rather than the *key of knowledge,* as Jesus actually

stated?

20. Calvin properly notes that Peter exhorted his presbyters to feed the Church: "Tend the flock of God that is in your charge ..." (1 Pet 5:2). However, Calvin claims that, by this exhortation, "the right which Peter had received [i.e., as sole holder of the keys and primacy among the apostles] he communicated equally to others." Does the full context of *1 Peter* support this claim made by Calvin?

21. Why is it important to note that Jesus almost certainly spoke in Aramaic, his native language, when he said, "Thou art Peter and upon this Rock I will build my Church"?

22. How did St. Augustine of Hippo view those who sever their relationship with the Catholic Church? Based on the *Catechism of the Catholic Church,* 2nd Ed., what does the Church officially teach in regard to those who sever their relationship with the Church?

23. Why are Mt 28:20 and Isaiah 22:22 important biblical foundations for the teaching of the Church on apostolic succession and continuation of the (papal) primacy given by Jesus to Peter?

24. What was Jesus asking of the Father when he prayed "also for those who believe in me through their word [i.e., the word of the apostles], that they may all be one ..."? Do you think that Jesus is pleased, today, with the degree to which the world has maintained that original Church unity?

25. Some believe that Jesus spoke metaphorically when he said "Unless you eat my body and drink my blood you shall have no life in you" (Jn 6:53-54). Why does the Catholic Church teach that Jesus spoke literally? How are these words of Jesus related to what he said at the Last Supper? (Mt 26:26-28).

26. What is the "pillar and bulwark of the truth"? Why do so many today wrongly answer "Scripture"?

27. What did Jesus mean when he said "And I, when I am lifted up from the earth, will draw all men to myself" (Jn 12:32-33)?

28. Is salvation possible outside the Catholic Church? Discuss this in view of paragraphs 846 and 847 of the *Catechism* (Paragraph 847 of the *Companion to the Catechism of the Catholic Church,*

2nd Ed. is also relevant). Consider also the clarifying statements issued by Joseph Cardinal Ratzinger, Prefect of the Congregation for the Doctrine of the Faith, in *Dominus Iesus,* August 6, 2000: "Just as there is one Christ, so there exists a single body of Christ, a single Bride of Christ: 'a single Catholic and apostolic Church'" (IV 16; Vatican II, *Lumen Gentium*, 8).

29. Discuss Scott Hahn's reasoning in support of the continuing infallible interpretation of Scripture by the Church since the time of Christ.

30. In 2001 the *World Christian Encyclopedia* listed more than 33,000 separate Christian denominations worldwide, with many *contradictory sets of criteria for what is essential for salvation.* How does one discern which Church Jesus calls everyone to embrace?

31. In light of the primacy given to Peter by Jesus, how does "The Great Commission" of the eleven by Jesus (Mt 28:16-20) constitute a continuing assurance of the truth of Catholic doctrine?

32. The Church acknowledges that some Popes of history led scandalous personal lives. Is this a reason to remain outside the Catholic Church? Is it relevant that, as God, Jesus foresaw the sins of Peter, of each of his successors and those of the other apostles – as well as everyone else – for all time?

33. "Among all the religions of the world, Catholicism is unmatched in the peace of mind it offers to those who are faithful to it." On what basis does the author make this claim? Do you agree or disagree? Why?

Step 5. After giving Peter primacy, Jesus commissioned the apostles to make disciples of all nations

Having given primacy to Peter, the crucified, risen Jesus said "Go, therefore and make disciples of all nations, baptizing them in the name of the Father, and of the Son and of the Holy Spirit ... and teach them to observe all that I have commanded you" (Mt 28:18-20).

At this point every Christian should ask this vital question: *To whom was Jesus speaking when he gave this Great Commission?* The Bible clearly indicates that he spoke *only* to the eleven (all but Judas Iscariot); the same eleven to whom he said "I chose you and appointed you ..." (Jn 15:16).

As if to emphasize that Jesus gave authority to preach *only* to those apostles (and, in view of Mt 28:20, those whom they and their successors would so authorize), Paul writes: "And how are they to hear without a preacher? *And how can men preach unless they are sent?*" (Rom 10:14-15).

And in John 17 we read the prayer of Jesus to the Father at the Last Supper in which Jesus *consecrates* the eleven (Judas Iscariot had left) just before going out into the Garden of Gethsemane where he would be betrayed:

> [F]or I have given them the words which thou gavest me ... (Jn 17:8). As thou didst send me into the world, so I have sent them into the world. And for their sake I consecrate myself, that they also may be consecrated in truth (Jn 17:18-19).

Having prayed for and consecrated the eleven *and them only,* Jesus prays for *unity* among believers:

> I do not pray for these only, but also for those who believe in me through their word, that they may all be one; even as thou, Father, art in me, and I in thee ... (Jn 17:20-21).

Paul makes the same call to unity in response to factions even then developing:

> I appeal to you, brethren, by the name of our Lord Jesus Christ, that all of you agree and that there be no dissensions among you, but that you be united in the same mind and the same judgment (1 Cor 1:10).

And in what context was Paul calling believers to "be united in the same mind and the same judgment"? Clearly, to be in accord with the mind and judgment of the Church. As earlier noted, Paul affirms the

Church as "the household of God … the pillar and bulwark of the truth" (1 Tim 3:15).

And did Jesus himself not make it clear that the disciples to be made of all nations were to be united in his one *Church*? For example, did Jesus not say that if a brother sins against us and will not listen to us, or to others we later bring with us, that we are to "*tell it to the church*"?

Jesus continues, "[I]f he refuses to listen even to the church, let him be to you as a Gentile and a tax collector" (Mt 18:17).

Jesus then says to the disciples (later to become apostles), "Truly, I say to you, whatever you bind on earth shall be bound in heaven, and whatever you loose on earth shall be loosed in heaven" (Mt 18:18). Jesus thereby gives to the disciples / apostles a share in the authority he gave fully to Peter (to whom he also gave the keys of the kingdom of heaven) two chapters earlier in *Matthew*.

The Great Commission and Peter the Rock – difficulties with "The Purpose-D _ _ _ _ _ Life" and "The Roman Catholic controversy"

The popular book *The Purpose-D_ _ _ _ _ Life* is not without sound guidance in many aspects of Christianity. The author, Rev. Rick Warren, is founding pastor of Saddleback Church in Lake Forest, California. In this book he presents a 40-day journey to help each reader discern God's purpose for his life.

Unfortunately, *The Purpose-D_ _ _ _ _ Life* is problematic in at least two aspects. First, it fails to address the question noted at the outset of this step: ***To whom was Jesus speaking when he gave the Great Commission?*** Instead of acknowledging that Jesus personally gave the Great Commission (Mt 28:16-20) *only* to the eleven apostles – whom he had rigorously taught during his three-year ministry – ***Warren states emphatically that the Great Commission is the commission of each reader, apparently meaning every Christian.*** He does so at the beginning and end of Day 38, "Becoming a World Class Christian." [218]

To the Catholic this reinterpretation of *commission* would seem equivalent to that given by a general who makes available to every soldier the book, *How to Win the War,* and then sends each one off to battle with neither his direct leadership nor any mandate to follow those in his army who have been trained to lead them.

The second concern is Warren's unconventional method of quoting from the Bible. For example, Warren quotes Mt 7:24 from the NIV in

218 *The Purpose-D_ _ _ _ _Life* , 297.

its entirety: *"Everyone who hears these words of mine and puts them into practice is like a wise man who built his house on **the rock.**"* [emphasis added].[219]

However, when Warren quotes Mt 16:18 – in which Jesus identifies Peter as "the rock" on whom he will build his church – Warren *omits* the first thirteen words of Christ: *"Now I say to you that you are Peter (which means 'rock'), and **upon this rock** ... "* [Parenthesis in original New Living Translation text]. *Warren then quotes the remainder of that NLT verse beginning in mid-sentence, as if it were the entire verse:* **"I will build my church, and all the powers of hell will not conquer it.***"*[220]

In Appendix 3, Warren notes that, to make his point, he doesn't always quote *entire* biblical verses.[221] In this manner, he claims, he imitates Jesus and the apostles in the way they quoted the Old Testament.

It is one thing to quote selectively retaining the original meaning, but quite another to quote Mt 16:18 as Warren did. Readers of *The Purpose-D_ _ _ _ _ Life* might ask themselves if Jesus would approve of Warren's glaring omission of Peter – the very *subject* of Jesus' sentence in Mt 16:18 – the "rock" on whom Jesus promised to build his Church.

Among Protestant apologists opposing Catholicism one of the foremost is James R. White, Director of Alpha and Omega Ministries. His book, *The Roman Catholic Controversy*, includes a Scripture Index listing 232 biblical verses from *Genesis* to *Revelation* cited in his objections to Catholic teaching, including 26 verses from *Matthew.*[222]

It is quite revealing, it seems to me, that White chose not to include in this list Mt 28:18-20 – the "Great Commission." Jesus had told the apostles, "Truly, I say to you, whatever you bind on earth will be bound in heaven ..." (Mt 18:18). In Mt 28:18-20 the risen Jesus further directs the eleven, and their successors "to the close of the age," to "make disciples of all nations, baptizing them ..., teaching them to observe all

---

219 Ibid., 191. Scripture taken from the Holy Bible, New International Version®. Copyright © 1973, 1978, 1984 International Bible Society. Used by permission of Zondervan. All rights reserved.
220 Ibid., 132. Scripture quotations marked NLT are taken from the Holy Bible, New Living Translation, copyright 1996. Used by permission of Tyndale House Publishers, Inc., Wheaton, Illinois 60189. All rights reserved.
221 Ibid., 325.
222 *The Roman Catholic Controversy,* © 1996 by James R. White, 266-268, Bethany House Publishers, Minneapolis, MN.

I have commanded you ...."

Through *The Roman Catholic Controversy* and his many debates against Catholic apologists, White urges us to *reject* Christ's call to the one Church he founded, and to *reject,* rather than observe, much of what Christ commands through this apostolic Church.

In his effort to prevail against the one Church Christ personally founded and promised to remain with, at least Mr. White deserves credit for not attempting to misinterpret Mt 28:18-20, Christ's "Great Commission" of the eleven apostles and their successors, or pretending that Christ gave any such biblical mandate in support of Protestantism.

Clearly, The Bible calls all to the one Church founded by Christ upon Peter the "Rock," and established by the apostles and their successors; i.e., the Catholic Church and no other.

In *Faith of the Early Fathers* (Pre-Nicene and Nicene eras), V. 1, p. 421, in the Doctrinal Index, Fr. William A. Jurgens lists sixteen excerpts from the Early Church Fathers under the heading "Bishops are not less than the legitimate successors of the apostles."

Discussion Questions

1. To whom was the risen Jesus speaking when he gave "The Great Commission?" Through the "solemn laying on of hands through the ages" (consecration with apostolic authority originating with Jesus himself), who are the true holders of that apostolic authority today?

Note: Discussion of this topic should take into account relevant sections of Orthodox Christianity in Part III, and Paul's relationship to Peter as described under the heading, "How Calvin erred in denying that Jesus gave primacy to Peter alone" in Step 4.

Step 6. The Pope and Catholic bishops today – true successors of Peter and the apostles – continue to make disciples of all nations.

Those apostles and, with Peter's approval, Matthias and Paul, followed this directive of the risen Jesus. Through the *solemn laying on of hands* through the ages, their successors – the Pope and Catholic bishops of today – and the priests whom they have solemnly ordained, continue to carry out this mandate of Jesus.

As noted in Step 4, the Bible indicates that Jesus provided for papal and apostolic succession in Mt 28:20 and, In Mt 16:19, used the metaphor of the key, which, in Is 22:22, indicates authority transferable to a successor.

Each successor of Peter is elected through apostolic authority

For those who seek further biblical support for the papal authority of Peter's successors, we can point to the words of Jesus to the twelve in Mt 18:18: *"Truly, I say to you, whatever you bind on earth shall be bound in heaven, and whatever you loose on earth shall be loosed in heaven."* Later, the risen Christ told them (with the exception of the deceased Judas Iscariot) that he would be with them *always* ... (Mt 28:20). Clearly, Jesus intended that the authority he gave to *each* of them in Mt 18:18 would be transmitted by them to others whom they deemed worthy of it.

We know that the apostles exercised this authority in prayerfully selecting Matthias to replace Judas Iscariot (Acts 1:21-26). The authority Christ gave to those apostles was most recently in evidence April 19, 2005 when more than 100 of their successors – Cardinals – gathered in conclave in Rome and elected Joseph Cardinal Ratzinger – Pope Benedict XVI – as the 264th successor of Peter.

This is what is meant by the unbroken transmission of Christ's own authority through which the Church carries out the election of each successor of Peter. Clearly the authority Jesus gave to the eleven who chose Matthias was not lost upon the death of Peter, as some have claimed. There is always an *inter-regnum* – a period of time between the death of one successor of Peter and the election of another, which has been as long as several years. Similarly, it is through Christ's own continuing authority that bishops are consecrated and priests and deacons are ordained. Nor must the Pope reside in Rome. Beginning in 1309 with Clement V, for seventy years popes led the Church not from Rome but from Avignon, France.

As earlier noted, "The sole Church of Christ … subsists in the Catholic Church, which is governed by the successor of Peter and by the bishops in communion with him" (CCC par. 816).

Ignatius of Antioch was a contemporary of the apostle John and was probably a convert of John's. As Bishop of Antioch only about 60 years after Jesus' death, he led his flock during the persecution under Roman Emperor Domitian. He was later martyred – thrown to the lions – under Emperor Trajan. Seven of his letters, including those to believers in Ephesus and Smyrna, are accepted as authentic [the *short recension*, from which all the following quotations are taken] by biblical scholars and are available to us today. In these letters, Ignatius:

(a) Affirms the *virginity of the Mother of Jesus*:

He was truly the seed of David according to the flesh, and the Son of God according to the will and power of God, that He [Jesus] *was truly born of a virgin*, was baptized by John ….[223]

(b) Affirms the Eucharist as the *medicine of immortality.*
Ignatius exhorted the Ephesians to:

come together … in one faith … in Jesus Christ, obey the bishop and the presbyters, with an undivided mind, *breaking one and the same bread, which is the medicine of immortality* … which causes that we should live forever in Jesus Christ.[224]

(c) Affirms that *the Eucharist is the flesh of Jesus:*

They [heretics] abstain from the Eucharist and from prayer, because they confess not the Eucharist to be flesh of our Savior Jesus Christ ….[225]

(d) Provides the first known use of the term *Catholic* Church: *"wherever Jesus Christ is, there is the Catholic Church."*[226]

The term "the Catholic Church" is used many times by the Early Church Fathers. It is of interest, however, that this first known use dates back almost 2,000 years to the time of Ignatius of Antioch, a martyr and a hearer of John the apostle.

Discussion Questions
1. Why are the seven letters of Ignatius, Bishop of Antioch, important? What central teachings of the Church do they affirm?

---

223 The Epistle of Ignatius to the Smyrneans, I, **www.ccel.org/fathers2**
224 The Epistle of Ignatius to the Ephesians, XX, **www.ccel.org/fathers2**
225 The Epistle of Ignatius to the Smyrneans, VII, **www.ccel.org/fathers2**
226 The Epistle of Ignatius to the Smyrneans, VIII, **www.ccel.org/fathers2**

Step 7. There is no biblical "escape clause" to reject the one Church founded by Jesus

As a Protestant minister, Marcus Grodi was haunted by a dilemma:

Each Sunday I would stand in my pulpit and interpret Scripture for my flock, knowing that within a fifteen mile radius of my church there were dozens of other Protestant pastors – all of whom believed that the Bible alone is the sole authority for doctrine and practice – but each was teaching something different from what I was teaching .... There was also the knowledge – no, the gut-twisting certitude – that one day I would die and would stand before the Lord Jesus Christ, the Eternal Judge, and I would be required to answer not just for my own actions but also for how I led the people he had given me to pastor. "Am I preaching truth or error?" I asked the Lord repeatedly. "I think I'm right, but how can I know for sure?" Equally troubling was the knowledge that every Protestant pastor I knew had a different set of criteria that he listed as "necessary" for salvation.

After much reading, particularly of the Early Church Fathers and Karl Keating's *Catholicism and Fundamentalism,* Grodi realized that:

[T]he Protestant answer to church renewal was, of all things, unscriptural and ... the single most important issue was authority. All of this wrangling of how to interpret Scripture gets one nowhere if there is no way to know with infallible certitude that one's interpretation is the right one. The teaching authority of the Church in the magisterium centered around the seat of Peter.[227] If I could accept this doctrine, I knew I could trust the Church on everything else.[228]

Grodi and his wife Marilyn became Catholic. He founded the Coming Home Network International (800 664-5110) and can be seen on his weekly programs *The Journey Home* and *Deep in Scripture* on EWTN Global Catholic Television.

Interest in *The Coming Home Network International* on the part of

---

227 See "Peter and the Papacy," Chapter 17 of *Catholicism and Fundamentalism* for a detailed explanation of why, in Aramaic, the native language of Jesus, *Kepha / kepha* meaning *Rock / rock* can mean *only* the Catholic interpretation of Mt 16:18. Also see Chapter 18, "Infallibility of the Pope." The Doctrinal Index of *The Faith of the Early Fathers,* V. 1, lists 84 citations under "The Primacy" between about A.D. 80 (Pope St. Clement) and A.D. 382 (Pope St. Damasus).
228 *Surprised by Truth,* 38-54.

Protestants and other non-Catholics continues to increase at a remarkable rate. During 2007 the CHNI Web site, *htpp://www.chnetwork.org,* received a monthly average of 1,000,000 "hits." During 2007, 3,102 Protestants (compared to 1895 in 2005) contacted CHNI by phone, e-mail or letter to inquire about entering into full communion with the Catholic Church. Among them were 160 Protestant *ministers* - an average of more than 3 ministers per week. *Since the Network was founded in 1993 it has been instrumental in the conversion to Catholicism of almost 800 Protestant ministers.* Catholics have also contacted the Network and expressed an interest in returning to active participation in the Church. Grodi also hosts two other weekly programs, *The Journey Home Roundtable,* seen on EWTN[229] and the *Deep in Scripture* radio program.[230]

Jesus said there would be *one flock,* under *one shepherd* (Jn 10:16) and prayed *that all may be one as Jesus and the Father are one* (Jn 17:20-22). With the foreknowledge that Peter would deny him three times and abandon him at Calvary, still Jesus gave Peter primacy among the apostles as noted in 4 a, b, and c above. He promised to be with the One Church he founded always and that not even the Gates of hell ("the powers of death") would prevail against it (Jn 16:18).

Quoting St. Ignatius of Antioch, the *Catechism of the Catholic Church* states, "Where there is Christ Jesus, there is the Catholic Church." The *Catechism* continues, "In her subsists the fullness of Christ's body united with its head; this implies that she receives from him 'the fullness of the means of salvation' which he has willed: correct and complete confession of faith, full sacramental life, and ordained ministry in apostolic succession. The Church was, in this fundamental sense, catholic on the day of Pentecost and will always be so until the day of the Parousia."[231]

The Catholic Church teaches that, although elements of the means of salvation may be found in other religions, *it is only in the Catholic Church that we find the fullness of the means of salvation.*

Consider what something less than this "fullness" can mean today. Depending on whom one chooses to follow as a Christian, it can mean the condoning of sexual relations outside a valid marriage between one man and one woman, euthanasia and induced abortion, for example; matters that can result in the loss of one's eternal salvation.

---

229 www.ewtn.com/vcatalogue/pages/live_shows.asp?show=RT
230 www.deepinscripture.com/index.htm
231 CCC, par. 830.

The great importance of becoming and remaining Catholic is explained in the *Catechism of the Catholic Church,* 2nd Ed. (par. 846-848) and in the *Companion to the Catechism of the Catholic Church* (par. 847).

"Observe whatever they tell you, but not what they do," said Jesus in regard to those who sat "on Moses' seat" (Mt 23:2-3). Surely this applies to any in the Church whose scandalous behavior mocks their preaching. And what could be more sobering than these words of Jesus: *"It would be better for him if a millstone were hung round his neck and he were cast into the sea, than that he should cause one of these little ones to sin"* (Lk 17:2. Also see Mt 18:6 and Mk 9:42)?

Not all popes proved personally worthy of the office. But, as with Judas Iscariot, Jesus did not suppress the free will of Peter, other apostles, or their successor popes / bishops. But no pope has destroyed the fabric of *doctrine* of the One Church to which the Father, in the name of Jesus, sent the Holy Spirit (Jn 14:26; Acts 2:1-4).

Certainly, through the Bible, Jesus would have let us know if he intended the divided Christianity of today, with its more than 33,000 denominations, and, as Grodi noted, its *many contradictory teachings on matters on which one's very salvation may well depend.* And yet the most careful search of the Bible reveals nothing other than the following:

> *Other than those under the leadership of Peter, nowhere in the Bible does Jesus authorize anyone to "make disciples of all nations ..."* (Mt 28:18-20) *and the Bible includes no "escape clause" by which Jesus authorizes anyone to reject Peter or his successors to form, or join, a different Church; a Church other than the one Jesus promised to be with always.*

Paul has ominous words for those who preach a contrary version of the Gospel of Christ (Gal 1:6-9) as noted above. And, in the same vein, Peter wrote: "There are some things in them [in the letters of Paul] hard to understand, which the ignorant and unstable twist to their own destruction, as they do the other scriptures" (2 Pet 3:16).

In Part III we will address the difficulties regarding the claim that Islam, in the seventh century, superseded the Church founded by Christ, and that The Church of Latter-Day Saints – the Mormons – did so in the nineteenth century.

Discussion Questions

1. Consider the quandary of Protestant minister Marcus Grodi:

"Every Protestant minister I knew had a different set of criteria that he listed as necessary for salvation." Is this a situation that might have its roots in *sola scriptura*?

2. What do you think Jesus meant when he said that not even the gates of hell (the powers of death) would prevail against the Church he founded and promised to be with always?

3. Step 7 indicates that there is no biblical "escape clause" by which Jesus authorizes anyone to reject the only Church Jesus founded. And surely there is no biblical authorization to preach from the Bible independently of that one Church and draw believers away from that Church. Why does Mark 9:38, about the man casting out demons in Jesus' name, not constitute an escape clause? (Consider the great difference between allowing a man to cast out demons, apparently through strong faith and intense prayer, versus preparing him to preach the Gospel in its fullness. Also, consider the relevance of Mt 7:22-23: "[D]id we not ... cast out demons in your name ...?").

4. Why does Mt 18:20 ("Whenever two or three are gathered in my name ...") not constitute an escape clause? Is the granting of petitions by Jesus to the many groups gathered in his name equivalent to preparing and authorizing each petitioner to preach authoritatively the Gospel in its fullness?

5. The Catholic Church teaches that some sin is "mortal" and (having failed to repent) "those who die in a state of mortal sin descend into hell ..." (CCC 1035). The Catholic Church also teaches that it alone has "the fullness of the means of salvation." At the moment of your particular judgment before Christ, would you prefer to have lived as, (a) one who, loving God and neighbor, accepted this fullness of the means of salvation through the Catholic Church and strove to live accordingly, or; (b) one who rejected it? What difference do you think your choice would make in regard to your eternal salvation? Why?

6. Peter warned that there are some things in letters of Paul that are hard to understand [which some] "twist to their own destruction as they do the other scriptures." (2 Pet 3:16). Given this statement, do you think Peter would be in favor of *sola scriptura*, which is so widely accepted by our separated brethren since the Reformation? Why? Why not?

Where is the biblical basis for the Reformation?

The observations I have made under these seven steps lead me to draw the following conclusions:

(a) That, however well-intentioned they may have been, the reformers found no biblical basis for the Reformation;

(b) That a thorough study of the Bible, in particular Mt 16:13-19, Jn 21:15-17, Mt 28:20 and Is 22:22, leads us to the One Church Jesus founded on Peter, to whom he gave the keys of authority and the mandate to feed his sheep – the Church led today by Peter's papal successor, the Church against which the gates of hell will not prevail, and;

(c) Nowhere in the Bible does Jesus give us an "escape clause" i.e., his approval to leave the One Church he founded to found or join a different Church. Jesus gave us a number of prophesies in the Bible, e.g., he foretold the denial of Peter, yet gave him primacy in the Church. No one who believes that Jesus was God would deny that he foresaw those future popes who proved personally unworthy of the office. And still he gave his Church the EUCHARIST "without which you shall have no life in you," sent the Spirit to that Church, and, through the apostles, promised to be with that Church, *and no other,* always.

Surely many devout Christians who are spiritual sons and daughters of the reformers will have difficulty with these conclusions. In their place, I probably would also. My hope, however, is that this biblically-based call to Catholicism will encourage them to examine for themselves, and with their spiritual leaders, the *biblical basis* on which Luther, Calvin and others denied, or extended without biblical authorization, the authority Jesus *personally* gave to Peter *alone,* as noted above; authority transferable to his successors.

I encourage these separated brethren to read every line the reformers have written in regard to the three central Petrine primacy verses noted above. Where is the ***biblical*** basis for the Reformation? Let them read also what the Early Church Fathers have written on these subjects in books such as *Jesus, Peter and the Keys, The Faith of the Early Fathers,* and *The Complete Works of the Early Church Fathers* (Eerdmans) on CD-ROM or on the Internet.[232] Then, humbly … prayerfully … let them decide for themselves which Church the *Bible* points to as the one Jesus founded and promised to be with always.

---

232 **www.ccel.org/fathers2**

A Few Special Topics in Doctrine and the History of the Church

Misunderstandings about Mary, Mother of Jesus

For most Protestants, no aspect of Catholicism is more misunderstood than the teachings about the Mother of Jesus. But suppose at a Protestant service next Sunday the minister were to say,   "I'd like to suggest a series of meditations to help us to remember the Gospel message each day and help us to walk more closely with the Lord. It is based on key events in the life of Jesus":

1.   Mary answers the angel Gabriel saying she is the handmaid of the Lord and gives her consent to conceive and give birth to JESUS our Savior (Lk 1:20-38).

2.   Carrying JESUS in her womb Mary visits Elizabeth, who carries the precursor of JESUS in her womb (Lk 1:39-56).

3.   JESUS is born in Bethlehem (Lk 2:1-20, Mt 1:18-25).

4.   Mary and Joseph present the infant JESUS in the Temple (Lk 2:22-40).

5.   JESUS, at age 12, amazes the teachers in the Temple with his intelligence. He is found there on the third day by distraught Mary and Joseph (Lk 2:41-52).

6.   JESUS is baptized by John in the river Jordan (Mt 3:13-17, Mk 1:9-11).

7.   Having said, "My hour has not yet come," JESUS changes water into wine at the wedding feast at Cana of Galilee at the tacit request of his mother, Mary (Jn 2 1-11).

8.   JESUS proclaims the kingdom of God and calls all to holiness (Mt 4:23, Lk 4:14:30).

9.   JESUS is transfigured in the presence of Peter, James and John (Mt 17:2-8, Mk 9:2-8, Lk 9:28-36).

10.   JESUS initiates the *Eucharist.* "Jesus took bread, and blessed, and broke it …. Take, eat; this is my Body …. He took a cup, and when he had given thanks …. Drink of it, all of you, for this is my blood of the covenant, which is poured out for many for the forgiveness of sins" (Jn 6:54-56, Mt 26:26-29).

11.   Despite his agony in the Garden of Gethsemane, JESUS says to

the Father "Thy will be done …" (Mt 26:36-46, Mk 14:32-42, Lk 22:39-46, Jn 18:1-2).

12. JESUS is scourged (Mt 27:26, Mk 15:15, Jn 19:1).

13. JESUS is crowned with thorns (Mt 27:27-31, Mk 15:16-20, Jn 19:2).

14. JESUS carries his cross to Calvary (Mt 27:31-32, Mk 15:20-23, Lk 23:26-32, Jn 19:16-17).

15. JESUS is crucified and dies (Mt 27:35-56, Mk 15:24-41, Lk 23:33-49, Jn 19:18-37).

16. JESUS arises from the dead and is seen by more than five hundred people. (Mt 28:1-20, Mk 16:1-20, Lk 24:1-49, Jn 20:1-29, 1 Cor 15:6).

17. The risen JESUS ascends into heaven (Mk 16:19, Lk 24:50-52).

18. As promised by JESUS (Lk 24:49), the HOLY SPIRIT descends on the apostles (Acts 2:1-41).

"And" the minister concludes, "if we meditate often on these truths, they will serve to remind us of all the truths given to us through Jesus, our Savior." The Protestant congregation would surely welcome such a sermon.

But, except for two additional meditations, what we have in these eighteen events in the life of Jesus is exactly what Catholics meditate on as we pray the Rosary. The two additional meditations are:

19. The Assumption of the Blessed Mother into heaven, where she is with JESUS, as well as the FATHER and HOLY SPIRIT, for all eternity and;

20. The Coronation of Mary in heaven, certainly a glorious event even by heaven's standards, in the eyes of JESUS, as well as the FATHER and HOLY SPIRIT.

In regard to these last two meditations, the Bible tells us that God took Enoch, son of Cain, from this world while he lived. Elijah too was taken by God while he lived and, about 800 years later, Elijah appeared with Moses at the Transfiguration of Christ. Without any determination of whether Mary was dead or in a live but dormant state, the Church teaches that Mary too was taken bodily into heaven, to be with her son Jesus, as well as the Father and Holy Spirit.

The Coronation in heaven of Mary, mother of Christ, is consistent with the Old Testament in which the Queen was typically the Queen Mother, the mother of the king.

In honoring his mother as in these last two meditations, Jesus is surely acting in accordance with the fourth Commandment. When we honor Mary - not as God but as the mother of our divine Lord Jesus - we imitate Jesus. And we do so in full accord with the Bible, remembering the words of our Blessed Mother to her cousin Elizabeth: "For behold, henceforth all generations will call me blessed" (Luke 1:48).

Most Catholics who pray the Rosary pray just one of the four sets of mysteries each day, which takes about 20 minutes. On Mondays and Saturdays we meditate on the Joyful Mysteries. On Tuesdays and Fridays we meditate on the Sorrowful Mysteries, and on Wednesdays and Sundays, the Glorious Mysteries. On Thursdays we meditate on the Luminous Mysteries. The last of the Luminous Mysteries is the institution of the Holy Eucharist by Jesus at the Last Supper on Holy Thursday, the night before he died.

Is the Rosary vain repetition?

A number of non-Catholics, after observing Catholics pray the Rosary, have concluded that it is an exercise of vain repetition. Surely, after hearing so many repetitions of the Hail Mary, that thought is understandable. But the word *vain* comes from the Latin *vānus,* meaning *empty.* Is repetitious prayer necessarily *vain*? Not according to *Revelation* 4:8 and *Matthew* 26:44. However, if a Catholic were to not *pray* but simply *say* the Rosary as a mere outpouring of words, with his heart and mind empty of all thought of the life of Christ, that accusation would for him be valid. Instead, however, the Church encourages Catholics to let the Rosary take us back to the time of our Lord Jesus Christ and walk with him - as did our Blessed Mother Mary - throughout his life, death and – finally – his glorious Resurrection.

Let us welcome the gift of the Rosary as we strive to know, love and serve our Lord Jesus in this life so that we may be happy with him forever in heaven.

Over the past four centuries or so, the degree of praise and honor given to the Mother of Jesus by Catholics has been rejected by most Protestant churches. But, as noted above, it is certain that Jesus kept the Commandment "Honor thy Father and thy Mother." In giving special honor to Mary, then, are Catholics not imitating Jesus?

Catholics follow the example of Jesus in praying *The Lord's Prayer*, and they address a number of other prayers directly to the Father, Son, and Holy Spirit. Catholics also pray to Mary, but such prayers are made to her as a special *intercessor* – never as if she were God or had her own divine power to answer them.

To understand how Catholics pray to Mary, call to mind the last time you were deeply concerned for yourself or someone you love. In addition to your own prayers to God (Father, Jesus, Holy Spirit) you may have asked a friend to pray for you or your loved one. Catholics also ask others to pray for them at such times. But, in addition to their friends on earth, Catholics know that Mary is a friend in heaven, a very special friend. When Catholics pray to Mary, they remember the words of the angel Gabriel: *"Hail, full of grace, the Lord is with you!"* (Lk 1:28). Other than in reference to Jesus (e.g., Mt 4:11), nowhere in the Bible does an angel address anyone so deferentially, say that they are *"full of grace,"* or give equivalent praise.

God directed that the Ark of the Covenant, in which God himself would live, must be made of purest materials; it was so holy as to be untouchable except by the high priest. Similarly, Jesus was conceived by the power of the Holy Spirit and lived within Mary until birth. In anticipation of this is it unreasonable to believe, as Catholics do, that through a special grace of God Mary was immaculately conceived – i.e., conceived without Original Sin – and was preserved from actual sin?

Catholics remember the words of Mary upon meeting Elizabeth – the *Magnificat*:

> My soul magnifies the Lord, and my spirit rejoices in God my Savior, for he has regarded the low estate of his handmaiden. For behold, henceforth all generations will call me blessed; for he who is mighty has done great things for me, and holy is his name ... (Lk 1:46-49).

They remember the words of Mary to Jesus at the marriage feast at Cana: Did Mary speak to Jesus as if she had the authority and power of God? No. She spoke to her son as the intercessor or "Mediatrix" that Catholics see her as being even today: "They have no wine" (Jn 2:3). And, although his hour had not yet come, Jesus performed the miracle. The Catholic Church encourages devotion to Mary, not as an alternative to praying to God, but in her role as intercessor.

In praying to Mary, Catholics are, in effect, asking her to intercede for them or those they love as she did at Cana for that bride and groom: "Son, her child is dying." "Son, their country is being torn apart by war." "Son ...." "Son ...."

And, of course, in the *Hail Mary* Catholics say "Holy Mary,

Mother of God, *pray for us sinners* ....." No Catholic would say to Jesus *"pray for us sinners."* Said to Mary, however, such a prayer has proved most efficacious – particularly when we add the prayer to our Lord that he prayed at Gethsemane: "My Father, if it be possible, let this cup pass from me; nevertheless, not as I will, but as thou wilt" (Mt 26:39).

Mary: The official position of the Catholic Church

As stated elsewhere in this book, readers are encouraged to consult the *Catechism of the Catholic Church,* 2nd Ed. for the official Catholic position on virtually any subject. The interested reader, upon opening the *Catechism* to the Index, finds on page 782-83 a total of 52 paragraphs referring to Mary, the mother of Jesus. Regarding devotion to Mary we find in Paragraph 971:

> The Church rightly honors The Blessed Virgin with special devotion. From the most ancient times the Blessed Virgin has been honored with the title of "Mother of God," to whose protection the faithful fly in all their dangers and needs .... This very special devotion *differs essentially* from the adoration which is given the incarnate Word and equally to the Father and the Holy Spirit, and greatly fosters this adoration (Emphasis added).

Paragraph 972 notes that in the

> homeland at the end of her [the Church's] journey ... the Church is awaited by [Mary] the one she [The Church] *venerates* ... (Emphasis added).

The intensity of the devotion of some Catholics to Mary may give the impression that they see her authority as equal to that of God. However, no informed Catholic makes this error and nowhere in the *Catechism*, in the Early Church Fathers, or in any official publication of the Catholic Church, is there any indication that Catholics are to give adoration to Mary.

In Latin, the Church uses the term *cultus duliae* (veneration due angels and saints) and *cultus hyperduliae* (special veneration due Mary, Mother of Jesus). But to describe the adoration due to God alone the term is *cultus latriae*.

Empty cross or crucifix – which would Jesus prefer that we display?

Most Protestant denominations display only the Cross – sometimes ornate, sometimes austere – but rarely the Crucifix, i.e., the cross with the body of Jesus still nailed to it.

Many Protestants believe it is in poor taste for Catholics to show Jesus, scourged and about to die in agony, as many Catholic churches do. Why not the risen Jesus, or just the empty cross?

Many Catholic priests have accepted this view and have replaced most or all crucifixes in their churches with empty crosses or with some depiction of the risen Jesus with the empty cross in the background. Other priests, however, realize that the Crucifixion, horrible though it was, portrays Jesus in his ultimate expression of love for mankind. They know too that it was the crucifix that inspired so many of the great saints of the Church ever since the time of Christ. Did Paul say, "Let's be sure that we display only the empty cross"? No. He said "but we preach Christ crucified …" (1 Cor 1:23). And did Jesus say "And after I am removed from it, my empty cross will draw all men to me"? No.

Surely Jesus is pleased when we honor him through our use of the cross. But use of the crucifix – the fuller representation of Christ's ultimate sacrifice for us – has a sound biblical basis. Jesus said, "'[A]nd I, when I am lifted up from the earth, will draw all men to myself.' He said this to show by what death he was to die" (Jn 12:32-33).

Catholic ministry to those with same-sex attractions

In commissioning the apostles, the risen Jesus said, "Go, therefore and make disciples of all nations … teach them *all* I have commanded you …."

Could the Church carry out this mandate to preach the Gospel in its fullness to everyone if it were to disregard certain categories of individuals? Could it suppress certain passages of Scripture, ignorance of which could mean loss of eternal salvation for those individuals?

In ministering to homosexuals, for example, could the Church ever ignore 1 Cor 6:9 in order to be politically correct? Could it fail to make known to them Romans 1:18-32, 1 Timothy 1:10, verse 7 of Jude, Genesis 18:20 and 19:1-29, Leviticus 18:19-30 and 20:13?

Citing Matt 5:28 regarding the grave sinfulness of lustful thoughts, the *Catechism* states: "The tradition of the Church has understood the sixth commandment as encompassing the whole of human sexuality" (CCC 2336). In ministering to homosexuals, can the Church fail to take into account these ominous words of Christ?

Although some in the Church may at times fall short in ministering to certain categories of individuals, the Church is well aware of its responsibility in this regard. As earlier noted, Ezekiel 33:6, for example, describes not only how the Lord regards the one guilty of iniquity, but also any appointed watchman who fails to warn him.

Catholic teaching on this subject fully reflects the gravity of the above verses (e.g., CCC 2357) and calls homosexual persons to chastity as it does all unmarried persons.

Courage International, the Catholic apostolate founded by Fr. John Harvey of the Allentown Diocese (Pennsylvania) has been quite successful in ministering to those with same-sex attractions. Through its *Encourage* outreach, the organization also ministers to relatives and friends of those with same-sex attractions. *Courage* now has a total of about fifty chapters in the United States, Canada, South America, Australia and Europe and has been endorsed by the Pontifical Council for the Family.[233]

NARTH, the National Association for Research and Therapy of Homosexuality, represents a wide range of religious views and philosophies. They refute the claim that homosexuality is inborn and insist that, if the individual chooses, he or she has the right to receive therapy in the direction of his or her biological sexuality.[234]

AIDS prevention: Chastity / abstinence saves far more lives than condoms

The Catholic Church has been sharply criticized for refusing to approve condoms to prevent AIDS. In fact, Church-approved chastity / abstinence programs are not only morally correct – they can also save far more lives than the many condom-based programs now run by the UN Population Fund (UNFPA) and other organizations worldwide.

The Philippines has been one of the few countries to reject UNFPA and promote chastity and abstinence instead of the use of condoms. Thailand and the Philippines each reported its first AIDS case in 1984. In 1991 Thailand launched a "100 Percent Condom Use" AIDS prevention program. In 1991 the Philippines began "AIDS-Free Philippines," a chastity / abstinence program. *By 2003, as noted in the following table, AIDS had taken the lives of 125,000 in Thailand* (August), *but only 260 in the Philippines* (September). *As a percent of population, this loss in Thailand* (a country less than ½ % Catholic) *was more than six hundred times higher than in the Philippines* (83% Catholic).[235]

---

233 **http://couragerc.net**
234 **www.narth.com**
235 "Telling the Truth: AIDS Rates for Thailand and the Philippines;" Rene Josef Bullecer, M.D., Executive Director, Human Life International, Visayas, Mindanao,

Country	Population	Prevention Method	HIV/AIDS cases/deaths	Percent of population
Thailand	66,000,000	Condoms	**899,000 / 125,000**	0.013621 / 0.001894
Philippines	82,000,000	Chastity / Abstinence	**1,946 / 260**	0.000024 / 0.000003

The Inquisition; a brief comment

Fr. John Laux, eminent Church historian, notes that the "Inquisition" has been "much maligned." In his book *Church History*, Fr. Laux offers a historical perspective that should be of interest to every Catholic. Pope Innocent III (1198-1216) called heresy "high treason against God" and urged secular rulers to so charge offenders during the Albigensian heresy. However, in his legislation and in the Acts of the Fourth Lateran Council (1215) in regard to heretics, there is no mention of the death penalty. Fr. Laux notes, however, that Innocent III was the first Pope to make exclusive use of the secular arm against heresy "and the first to discover how difficult it is to call back the hounds of violence once they are unleashed." Pope Gregory IX opposed torture, but Pope Innocent IV and Pope Urban IV approved it as a means of discovering heresy.

Not commonly known today is the provision that the Church required the Inquisitors to offer a grace period of up to one month in each city they visited. Those who had been openly heretical but confessed during the grace period were exempt from the penalty of death or permanent imprisonment. Others who confessed then were "dispensed of all penalties or only given a secret and very light sentence." Obstinate heretics who were afterwards convicted "were handed over to the secular arm, which was equivalent to sentence of death by fire." However, Fr. Laux notes that Protestant historian H. C. Lea, in his *History of the Inquisition in the Middle Ages*, indicates that, of convicted heretics, probably not more than four percent suffered death by fire.[236]

Fr. Laux points out that although Pope Sixtus IV gave written consent to the Spanish Inquisition he did so wrongly believing it was to be an *ecclesiastical* Inquisition. After he learned otherwise he could do no more that object to its severity. In fact it was only with difficulty that the Pope rescued from the Inquisitors the Primate of Toledo,

---

http://www.hli.org/condom_facts_thailand_philippines_aids_rates.html
236 *Church History,* 357.

Cardinal Caranza.[237]

At this writing "The Inquisition," an excerpt from *Church History*, by Fr. John Laux, M.A., can be found on the Web page of J. Dominguez, M.D.[238]

The Da Vinci Code – the new Gnosticism

In the latter half of the last century modernism caused many to doubt the historicity of the New Testament. Now, at the outset of the third millennium, *Gnosticism* is causing a further erosion of faith in Jesus Christ as divine Savior and Redeemer.

Dan Brown's book *The Da Vinci Code*, published in 2003 by Doubleday (Random House, Inc.), has become phenomenally popular, with more than fifty million copies sold. It reportedly has been translated into more than forty languages. A film version of the book was released in 2006.

Under the thin veil of "fiction" *The Da Vinci Code* is a direct assault on the historical truth of the Gospels and thus on Christianity itself. In particular, the *Code*'s characters attack Catholicism, even claiming that members of the hierarchy have been complicit in murder to keep the world from learning the "truth" that Jesus was not God, that he married Mary Magdalene, and that she gave birth to their child.

For anyone reading the fictional *The Da Vinci Code*, the factual *The Da Vinci Hoax: Exposing the Errors in the Da Vinci Code* is essential to ensure an objective, history-based understanding of the Bible. In *The Da Vinci Hoax*, authors Carl E. Olson and Sandra Miesel write as follows about Brown's book: "Drawing deeply upon gnostic ideas about spirituality, Jesus Christ, Mary Magdalene, and the early Church, *The Da Vinci Code* weaves elements taken from that ancient belief system into a modern-day story of murder, intrigue, and conspiracy."[239]

The Catholic Encyclopedia notes that, while gnosticism flourished, far more gnostic literature than Catholic literature was produced. Gnosticism was "a collective name for a large number of greatly-varying and pantheistic-idealistic sects, which flourished from some time before the Christian Era down to the fifth century, and which, while borrowing the phraseology and some of the tenets of the chief religions of the day, and especially of Christianity, held matter to be a deterioration of spirit, and the whole universe a depravation of the

---

237 Ibid.
238 **http://biblia.com/islam/inquisit.htm**
239 *The Da Vinci Hoax*, 45.

Deity...."[240]

However, the anti-Christian story line of *The Da Vince Code* collapses in light of the actual writings of the Early Church Fathers and others of that era – documents long established as authentic by historians whom Dan Brown does not acknowledge or attempt to refute. Let's look at three central claims promoted by Teabing and Langdon, two of the *Code*'s Holy Grail authorities, and then at a few of the many authentic statements by Early Church writers that demolish Brown's house of cards:

Claim 1. Until 325, Christians believed that Jesus was a merely mortal prophet – not God.

Authentic history readily reveals the absurdity of this claim. For example, in Paul's letter to Titus, chapter 2, verse 13, about the year 60, he wrote: "awaiting our blessed hope, the appearing of the glory of *our great God and Savior Jesus Christ ....*"

Equivalent affirmations of Christ's divinity were written by St. Ignatius of Antioch about 110,[241] by St. Justin the Martyr about 150,[242] by St. Theophilus of Antioch about 181,[243] by Tertullian[244] and St. Clement of Alexandria[245] about 200, by Origen about the year 225,[246] by St. Cyprian about the year 250,[247] by Pope St. Dionysius in 262,[248] by St. Gregory the Miracle Worker about 270[249] and by Lactantius about 310.[250] Beyond the sense of the biblical "you are gods" reference to mere mortals (Jn 10:34; Ps 82.6), each of these early Church writers describes Jesus unequivocally as *God in his own right* in the context of the Trinity.

A particularly compelling source for the refutation of Brown's claim is *Detection and Overthrow of the Gnosis Falsely So-Called,* or *Against Heresies,* written about 180-199 by Irenaeus, the second Bishop of Lyons. In his youth, St. Irenaeus was a disciple of St. Polycarp, Bishop of Smyrna – a Christian martyr. Polycarp was a

---

240 **www.newadvent.com**, *The Catholic Encyclopedia* > Gnosticism.
241 *Letter to the Ephesians,* Introduction.
242 *First Apology,* 63.
243 *To Autolycus,* 2, 22.
244 *Apology,* 21, 13.
245 *Exortation to the Greeks,* 1, 7, 1.
246 *The Fundamental Doctrines;* 1, *Preface*, 4.
247 *Letter of Cyprian to the People of Thibar,* 58 (56), 10.
248 *Letter of Dionysius of Rome to Dionysius of Alexandria,*1, 3.
249 *The Creed.*
250 *The Divine Institutions,* 4, 29, 3.

hearer of John, the apostle of Jesus and author of the fourth Gospel.

In *Against Heresies*, Irenaeus wrote: "in order that to Christ Jesus, our Lord, and God, and Savior, and King, according to the will of the invisible Father, 'every knee should bow ....'"[251]

He also wrote of Jesus, "But that He is Himself in His own right, beyond all men who ever lived, God, and Lord, and King Eternal, and the Incarnate Word, proclaimed by all the prophets, the apostles, and by the Spirit Himself, may be seen by all who have attained to even a small portion of the truth."[252]

Irenaeus also affirms the oneness of the Church though it is found in many places:

> As I have already observed, the Church, having received this preaching and this faith, although scattered throughout the whole world, yet, as if occupying but one house, carefully preserves it. She also believes these points [of doctrine] just as if she had but one soul, and one and the same heart, and she proclaims them, and teaches them, and hands them down, with perfect harmony, as if she possessed only one mouth. For, although the languages of the world are dissimilar, yet the import of the tradition is one and the same. For the Churches which have been planted in Germany do not believe or hand down anything different, nor do those in Spain, nor those in Gaul, nor those in the East, nor those in Egypt, nor those in Libya, nor those which have been established in the central regions."[253]

The following quotation from *The Catholic Encyclopedia* further refutes Brown's claim that before A.D. 325 the Church believed that Christ was merely a mortal prophet. It is a literal translation of what was decided on this topic at the first Council of Nicea:

> We believe in one God the Father Almighty, Maker of all things visible and invisible; and in **one Lord Jesus Christ, the only begotten of the Father, that is, of the substance [*ek tes ousias*] of the Father. God of God, light of light, true God of true God ....** *Those who say: There was a time when He was not, and He was not before He was begotten; and that He was made out of nothing (ex ouk onton); or who maintain that He is of another hypostasis or another substance [than the Father], or that the Son of God is created, or mutable, or subject to change, [them] the Catholic*

---

251 *Against Heresies*, 1, 10, 1. **www.ccel.org**

252 *Against Heresies*, 3, 19, 2. **www.ccel.org**

253 *Against Heresies*, 1, 10, 2. **www.ccel.org**

Church anathematizes.

The Catholic Encyclopedia then notes the following, which indicates the near-unanimity of the bishops at Nicea on this matter and their conviction that it "contained the ancient faith ...."

> *The adhesion was general and enthusiastic.* ***All the bishops save five declared themselves ready to subscribe to this formula, convince[d] that it contained the ancient faith of the Apostolic Church.*** *The opponents were soon reduced to two, Theonas of Marmarica and Secundus of Ptolemais, who were exiled and anathematized. Arius and his writings were also branded with anathema, his books were cast into the fire, and he was exiled to Illyria.*[254]

Claim 2. At Constantine's direction, the bishops of the First Council of Nicea did two things: They proclaimed – for the first time – that Jesus was God. They also embellished the fourfold Gospel to falsely deify Jesus. Constantine burned all earlier "authentic" gospels – those presenting Jesus as a merely human prophet (Chapter 55).

The best way to promote a falsehood is to conflate it with well-established truth. Brown notes, correctly, that the Church did *formally declare* the divinity of Jesus Christ at the first Council of Nicea in 325, as stated above. ***However, Brown failed to explain to his readers that this was a necessary refutation of the Arian heresy – not a new doctrine.*** As noted under the refutation of claim 1, above, from its earliest days the Church had taught and wrote that Jesus was God.

Beginning with Nero, persecution by a number of Roman emperors failed to eliminate Christianity and its authentic writings. Surely many of the bishops at that Council in 325 were survivors of the 10-year attempt to crush Christianity begun by Diocletian, which ended in 312. Is it conceivable that these bishops, having weathered that storm with their faith and authentic writings intact, would *en masse* simply agree to Constantine's deception? Given Irenaeus' comment that authentic Christianity had spread throughout the then-known world, could Constantine hope to burn all copies of the early fourfold Gospel? If the earliest Christians did *not* believe that Jesus was God, Would Pope St. Sylvester I and all future popes, bishops and priests – many of them saints – have promulgated this egregious lie for the past seventeen centuries? As our friends in the U.K. would say to all three of these

---

254 **www.newadvent.com** > *The Catholic Encyclopedia* > The First Council of Nicea.

questions, "Not bloody likely!"

Claim 3. Jesus married Mary Magdalene by whom he had a child (Chapter 105).

This claim is equally bizarre in light of authentic early Church history and common sense. Theological considerations aside, If Jesus married, how can anyone explain the fact that there is *absolutely no mention* of his marriage – or his becoming the father of a child – by *any* of the Early Church writers who, through the apostles and successor bishops, followed Jesus, some to the point of martyrdom? If Jesus had married, his wife would certainly have been greatly honored. Any child – his own flesh and blood – would have been held in awe by every Christian, in particular, the above early Church writers. Their silence on this matter debunks completely the very foundation on which Brown spins *The Da Vinci Code* tale.

Brown deflects criticism by noting that his book is fictional. However, according to Olson and Miesel, "Brown claims that his book is based on facts and sound historical research."[255] Given this claim, it seems inconceivable that Brown was unfamiliar with these authentic, readily available early Christian writings that contradict his claims.

A Comment on the Arian heresy

Regarding the heretic Arius, it is true that he attended the First Council of Nicea. He promoted the idea that Jesus was not "of the same substance" (*homoousious*) as the Father and therefore not like God and not co-eternal. The bishops at this Council rejected Arius' view. Instead they reaffirmed the Church's historical view of Christ's full divinity, as brilliantly argued by the deacon Athanasius, who later became bishop of Alexandria.

Arius died in 336, but not before regaining the support of Constantine, who was baptized by an Arian bishop shortly before his own death in 337. As noted in *The Catholic Encyclopedia*, Constantine was inconsistent in his support of Catholic orthodoxy: "In the dedication of Constantinople in 330 a ceremonial half pagan, half Christian was used" and "Shortly before his death Constantine confirmed the privileges of the priests of the ancient gods."[256]

The storm of Arian and Semi-Arian heresy raged for several decades after the death of Constantine. During this time, "the Latin bishops were driven by threats and chicanery to sign concessions which

255 *The Da Vinci Hoax*, 28.
256 **www.newadvent.com**, *The Catholic Encyclopedia* > Constantine the Great.

at no time represented their genuine views."[257] In addition, *The Catholic Encyclopedia* notes that the Arian heresy did not subside until the Second General Council of Constantinople in 381. Much like Chillingworth, whose narrow view of early church history was refuted by Newman (Step 3, above), it would seem that Dan Brown placed undue emphasis on some of these coerced documents of the fourth century but failed to see the full context of Early Church writings.

Brown's neo-gnosticism may have a silver lining, however. His appalling distortion of early Church history will surely prompt many to read for themselves the authentic writings of the Early Church Fathers and the early Church councils. These sources have led countless seekers of truth to the one, holy, catholic and apostolic Church Jesus himself founded and promised to be with always.

If God loves us, why does he allow the innocent to suffer?

After a personal tragedy we may find ourselves thinking: "According to the Bible, God loves me, sees the future and is all-powerful. So God – if there is a God - foresaw the tragedy that struck me (or a loved one), *but did nothing to prevent it.* How can I go on believing in God?"

As our grief subsides, however, it is well for us to remember that God loves us beyond all human understanding: "*For God so loved the world that he gave his only Son, that whoever believes in him should not perish but have eternal life.*" (Jn 3:16). The phrase "*gave his only Son,*" of course, refers primarily to the horrific passion and crucifixion of Jesus; a death Father and Son - and Holy Spirit - foresaw but permitted for our redemption.

Only rarely does God intervene to prevent human tragedy by suspending the laws of nature or restraining the freely willed act of someone who would harm us. God granted the awesome gift of free will to the angels and to mankind. Without it we would be, as it were, programmed and unable to freely choose to love God and others. We humans would therefore be unable to gain *merit,* as we now can, through the *charity of Christ* as described in paragraphs 2006-2011 of the *Catechism of the Catholic Church.*

God respects our free will to do good *or evil* so profoundly that, rather than remove it from us – or annihilate us for our evil deeds - God permitted not only the Crucifixion of Jesus, but the persecution and murder of untold millions, including many prophets, most of the apostles, the many Christian lay martyrs and many missionaries throughout history who preached the Word in and out of season. God

---

257 **www.newadvent.com,** *The Catholic Encyclopedia* > Arianism.

did not prevent even the slaughter of the Holy Innocents, whose feast day as martyrs Catholics celebrate each December.

When tragedy strikes, we can also find some measure of consolation in books such as *Making Sense out of Suffering,* by Peter Kreeft, and in the words of our saints. For example: St. Catherine of Siena, *"Everything comes from love, all is ordained for the salvation of man, God does nothing without this goal in mind."* (Dialogue on Providence, ch. IV, 138); St. Augustine, *"For almighty God ..., because he is supremely good, would never allow any evil whatsoever to exist in his works if he were not so all-powerful and good as to cause good to emerge from evil itself"* (*Enchiridion* 3, 11:PL 40, 236); and St. Paul *"We know that in everything God works for good for those who love him (Rom 8:28)."* These saints are quoted in the *Catechism of the Catholic Church,* paragraphs 309-314, under the heading "Providence and the scandal of evil". A detailed commentary, primarily Thomistic, may be found under "Evil" in the *Catholic Encyclopedia,* Vol. 7, 1910 Ed., **www.newadvent.org**

The peace of mind of the faithful Catholic

Among all the religions of the world, Catholicism is unmatched in the peace of mind it offers to those who are faithful to it. Why? Because the faithful Catholic knows that if the present moment turns out to be his last on earth, he will meet Jesus: (a) as one who strove to follow the teachings of the One Church Jesus founded and promised to be with always – the Church led by the successor of Peter, the one to whom Jesus himself gave, and never took back, the keys of the kingdom of heaven; (b) as one who prayed fervently and strove to love God above all and to love his neighbor as himself in accordance with the Gospels; (c) as one who, in accordance with his state in life, participated fully in the sacraments, including Baptism, Confirmation, Penance (Reconciliation), and in the Eucharist, which Ignatius of Antioch described as *the Flesh of Christ ... the medicine of immortality.*

Ricardo Montalban affirmed this "peace of mind" from another perspective. In an article in *Be* magazine he remembers a physician – Chief of Staff at a hospital – who converted to Catholicism because he had watched Catholics die. He noted that for many (not all) non-Catholics, death is "agony" and they "struggle so." In contrast, the physician said, "So many Catholics, when they receive the last sacraments, die almost with a smile on their lips."[258]

---

258 Ricardo Montalban, "In the Heart of Tinseltown, a Faith Lived Deeply," *Be*

Discussion Questions

1   Many of our Protestant friends and neighbors wrongly believe that Catholics *worship* Mary. What can Catholics do to correct this misunderstanding?

2   What does the Church mean by *cultus duliae, cultus hyperduliae* and *cultus latriae*?

3   Is the Rosary primarily about Mary or about Jesus? Please explain.

4   Is there a biblical basis for the display of the crucifix in Catholic worship?

5   Why did Father John Laux write that the Inquisition (actually several different Inquisitions) has been much maligned?

6   What difficulties did Pope Innocent III and Pope Sixtus IV experience in regard to Inquisition practices?

7   Are there any categories of individuals to whom the Catholic Church is not obligated to preach the Gospel in all its fullness?

8   To what do you attribute the remarkable popularity of Dan Brown's *The Da Vinci Code?* Do you think such gnosticism-based books can undermine one's faith in Christ? Why? If gnosticism caused a friend to doubt that Jesus Christ is divine, what early Church writings could you cite to reassure that person of Christ's divinity?

9   Is there historical evidence indicating that Jesus was married and / or became the father of a child?

10 Do you think Catholicism is unmatched in the peace of mind it offers to those who are faithful to it? On what do you base your answer?

Magazine, March-April 2000, 7, Catholic Answers.

Part II

Revitalizing Faith in the Wake of Scandal and Dissent

Revitalizing Faith in the Wake of Scandal and Dissent

In the wake of the ongoing sexual molestation and other scandals in the Church in the United States, Catholics – and others – are looking for answers. Surely no Catholic columnist of our day – and few non-Catholic columnists – have been silent on the subject. Paul Likoudis of the weekly Catholic newspaper *The Wanderer,* Michael S. Rose, George Weigel, Fr. Benedict Groeschel, C.F.R. and many others have had books published on the subject.

Kenneth D. Whitehead has written a very informative article on this topic and dissent in the Church: *The Catholic Bishops and the Scandals: How Could They Have Done This?*[259] This is one of twenty-seven scandal-related articles listed on the CatholiCity Web site.[260]

Ideas abound about how so many of our bishops could have allowed such widespread sexually predatory acts to be committed for so long by priests under their direction, and about what must be done now to prevent recurrence.

"In the first few months of 2002, The Catholic Church in the United States entered its greatest crisis in history ...."
So begins *The Courage to be Catholic; Crisis, Reform and the Future of the Church,* written by George Weigel, the well-known Catholic author-journalist and biographer of Pope John Paul II. Given some of the great threats to its very existence the Church has faced in its long history, some might disagree. But there is no denying that many of our clergy have broken their vows, sinned gravely and, in the eyes of many Catholics, criminally betrayed their sacred trust.

"This is a crisis of *fidelity,*" Weigel states on page six of his Introduction. He identifies the major components of the crisis as priestly identity, episcopal leadership and discipleship, which can be traced in large part to the "Truce of 1968."

As noted In Step 3, In July, 1968 Pope Paul VI issued *Humanae Vitae,* his encyclical reaffirming the Church's ban on artificial contraception; Catholics with good reason to defer having children were limited to natural methods of accomplishing this. In the storm of dissent that followed, priests, religious and theologians led the charge. In overwhelming numbers, the laity soon followed.

Tacit though it was, the nature of the "truce" was that priests, religious and theologians learned that they could publicly *defy* the Pope

---

259 www.wf-f.org/02-3-Bishops-Scandals.html
260 www.catholicity.com/scandals.html

on a key doctrinal matter without consequence. On the contrary, many dissenters found themselves selected for positions of power throughout the Church.

Having seen the apparent success of certain outspoken clergy in the United States in challenging the Pope on artificial contraception, many priests, religious and lay Catholics began to see *all* Church teaching as optional, and the *Cafeteria Catholic* came into being.

This "faithful dissent" described by Weigel soon took root within the priesthood at large. By the late 1960s it became rampant in seminaries in the U.S. and elsewhere. Weigel alludes to the same doctrinal dissent and sexual activity of various kinds in seminaries that Michael S. Rose documents in his devastating book *Goodbye, Good Men.*

In the last three chapters of his book, Weigel outlines an agenda for reform and the book closes on a hopeful, prayerful note.

Perhaps Weigel's most insightful comments are in regard to the root cause of the scandal:

> *The deepest root of the crisis of episcopal misgovernance, however, is theological – bishops having failed to live the truth of who and what they are. And they have failed to do that because they have not believed, with sufficient life-transforming power, the truth of what the Catholic Church teaches they are.*[261]

In cases where such bishops and priests have "*failed to live the truth*" could it be that those bishops and priests *no longer believe the truth* – that is, no longer *believe* in the Jesus of the Gospels? As we saw in Step 3, the predominant late-date / no eyewitness view of the Gospels has done much to erode the faith of many Catholics.

Admittedly, in addition to this widespread historical blurring of the Gospels, Catholics have seen many changes in the Church since Vatican II.

Fr. G. H. Duggan attributes the erosion of faith and moral collapse among Catholics in large part to Neo-Modernism, in which the predominant streams of thought are:

[T]he Kantian Existentialism of Karl Rahner,[262] the Evolutionary

---

261 *The Courage to be Catholic*, 96

262 Fr. Duggan noted, for example, that Fr. Rahner rejected the Church teaching that we have a soul that is separate from our body and rejected the doctrine of Transubstantiation; "The Collapse of the Church in the West," 21-22, *Christian Order*, January, 2003.

Pantheism of Teilhard de Chardin ... and the Existentialist exegesis of Rudolf Bultmann, which influenced the 'scientific' biblical work of Raymond Brown. The Neo-Modernists have been far more successful that their Modernist predecessors (Embedded quotation marks in the original).

Fr. Duggan added that sound catechetics based on The *Baltimore Catechism* in the United States and the *Penny Catechism* in England and Wales gave way to *experiential* catechesis that has left several generations of Catholics with little knowledge of our faith. He also expressed concern about the abuses that have followed the implementation or the *Novus Ordo,* "[which] is of course a valid rite and, celebrated reverently, can be edifying." Not so, he adds, such innovations as "rock Masses" and "clown Masses."[263]

Given all of these negative influences and more, still, as earlier noted, it seems to me that the root cause of the loss of faith among Catholics has been the late-date historical blurring of the Gospels that has its roots in fifteenth century Humanism and can be traced through Descartes, Reimarus, Hume, Kant, Hegel, Baur, Strauss, and Bultmann. Surely this placing of a "Doubtful Historicity" label on the Gospels paved the way for all the faith-eroding notions that have since afflicted the Church.

Will anyone deny that a strong faith in the Jesus of the Gospels is vital for all Catholics and in particular for our priests? When one no longer sees the Body, Blood, Soul and Divinity of Jesus our risen Savior and Redeemer writ large across those ancient pages, can one long retain the Grace to pray from the depths of one's very *soul*? Embracing the modernist view that ours is a God of Mercy but no longer of Justice and that, ultimately, all go to heaven, is one likely to fight heroically to resist an inclination to grave sin, including sin that may involve the Church in scandal?

Can such an individual pray with fervent conviction: *"O my God, I am heartily sorry for having offended thee, and I detest all my sins because I dread the loss of heaven and the pains of hell. But, most of all, because I offend thee my God, who are all good and deserving of all my love. I firmly resolve, with the help of thy Grace, to confess my sins, to do penance, and to amend my life. Amen"*?

In recent decades, incidents of sexual molestation of youths by

---

263 "The Collapse of the Church in the West," 18-27, *Christian Order*, January, 2003.

priests increased substantially, based on information made public in 2002. This scandal has occurred in most dioceses in the United States and in other countries as well. Well over one thousand priests have been accused of this crime in the United States.

Is it merely coincidental that a historically hazy view of the Gospels has been widely promoted in a number of Catholic seminaries since Vatican II?

If not, perhaps this suggests an essential component of Church revitalization to those charged with that awesome responsibility.

As we saw in Step 3, the reading of just one small book can do much to reestablish the reality of Jesus – as made known to us in the Gospels – in the heart and mind of every bishop, priest, religious and lay Catholic. That book is *The Birth of the Synoptic Gospels*, by Fr. Jean Carmignac.

Of equal value is *The Hebrew Christ*, by Claude Tresmontant, also earlier noted. This book gives many examples of Semitisms which strongly indicate redaction of *Matthew*, *Mark* and *John* in a Semitic language and the redaction of *Luke* based on Semitic documents, primarily Hebrew, thus strongly indicating early date / eyewitness origin.

In regard to the catechesis of youth, during the last decade the United States Conference of Catholic Bishops and others among the 108 Catholic national / regional councils of the world began to require that publishers bring new religious formation texts into line with the *Catechism of the Catholic Church,* 2nd Ed. Will these new texts strengthen the belief of young Catholics in Jesus as he is described throughout the Gospels? Will they be able to explain their Faith, graciously and with confidence, to those in the Church who express doubt about various aspects of the Gospels? Will they be prepared to resist attractive Christian and non-Christian alternatives to Catholicism? Time will tell.

In any case, it seems clear that immediate steps are needed to rescue great numbers of Catholics (and former Catholics) from the faith-eroding effects of biblical speculation.

Becoming familiar with the analytical methods used by the early-date / eyewitness biblical scholars as outlined in Step 3, in contrast to the subjectivity of their late-date / no eyewitness colleagues, can greatly strengthen the historical foundation of one's faith. Surely such information, widely promulgated, would revitalize the faith of many Catholics, result in an increase of vocations for the priesthood and religious life, prompt the return of former Catholics and breathe new life into the

Catholic New Evangelization initiative as well as Ecumenical activities.

Many changes have come about within the Catholic Church since the Second Vatican Council (1962-1965). Most were not mandated but were permitted by the Council, subject to the approval of the local bishop, e.g., the removal of altar rails; the moving of the tabernacle to a place other than the front and center of the church; that the priest is to say Mass facing the people, and so on.

Of concern, however, are the distortions of approved Church doctrine that Catholic priests not infrequently make in homilies, in publications, in statements to the media and elsewhere that are improperly attributed to Vatican II.

Catholic deacons, priests and even some bishops today may be seen as falling into two categories: (a)   Those who "preach the Gospel in all its fullness" in complete accord with Church doctrine as summarized in the *Catechism of the Catholic Church,* 2nd Ed., and do so in loyalty to the Pope and Magisterium in keeping with their vows of ordination or consecration, and; (b)   Those who, at times, fall short of this requirement.

The lay Catholic may say, "Why should it matter to me or my family which type of priest I have for a pastor? It's all the same Catholic Church, isn't it?" The answer is *yes* and *no*."

It is *yes* in the sense that all Catholic parishes continue to make available Mass and all seven sacraments, and continue the various ministries proper to the Church. However, in many parishes today throughout the world, the answer may be *no* in some very important respects, particularly in regard to how the faith is being imparted in homilies, written materials, special programs, and especially how it is being taught to young Catholics.

The following are some of the more popular ideas presented directly or indirectly to the faithful ***in error*** by more than a few members of the Catholic clergy, and, in brackets, the applicable paragraph of the authoritative *Catechism of the Catholic Church,* 2nd Ed.:

(a)   Jesus never intended to found a religion [CCC 881];

(b)   Many "miracles" attributed to Jesus probably never happened; they were added much later by those who edited the Gospels [CCC 124-127];

(c)   Hell is probably just a metaphor. If it exists, few if any souls are there, none permanently [CCC 1033-1037, 1861];

191

(d)   At worst, hell is simply an eternal separation from God, with no equivalent of physical pain or discomfort [CCC 1034-1036];

(e)   The Pope is simply the "first among equals" among all the bishops of the world; the Pope has no actual authority outside Rome [CCC 880-885];

(f)   The Eucharist is just symbolic; it is not *really* the body and blood of Christ [CCC 1333, 1374];

(g)   The *Catechism of the Catholic Church* was never intended for those in the pews [Introduction by Pope John Paul II; Section 3, pp. 5-6];

(h)   Homosexual acts are not sinful; they may, in fact, be legitimate ways of expressing love [CCC 2357-59];

(i)   Unless the Pope speaks *ex cathedra*, the faithful are free to ignore him. Encyclicals and other directives given by the Pope are simply his suggestions, or just matters for discussion [CCC 882].

The obligation to preach (and teach) responsibly is set forth in Scripture, perhaps nowhere more forcefully than in regard to one made a "watchman for the house of Israel":

> If I say to the wicked, 'You shall surely die,' and you give him no warning, nor speak to warn the wicked from his wicked way, in order to save his life, that wicked man shall die in his iniquity; but his blood I will require at your hand. But if you warn the wicked and he does not turn from his wickedness, or from his wicked way, he shall die in his iniquity, but you will have saved your life (Ezekiel 3:18-19).

Members of the clergy and Catholic educators who promote dissent may take exception to being seen as undermining the teaching of the Church as it given to the faithful through the Pope and Magisterium. They may respond: "What I have said is affirmed by recognized Catholic theologians and biblical scholars." For others, the response may be that they spoke in the "Spirit of Vatican II" in keeping with the intentions of Pope John XXIII. *However, in his opening remarks at that Council Pope John XXIII stated his intention that it "transmit pure and integral doctrine, without attenuation or distortions."* All the matters listed above represent attenuation or distortions.

In presenting the list above, which is by no means complete, I judge no one; I simply invite all readers, as an aid to *discernment* (Mt 18:15-

17), to refer to the *Catechism of the Catholic Church,* 2nd Ed. and, using the Index or the CCC Internet search engine, refer to these and any other relevant topics as we continue on our spiritual journey.

Where it seems apparent that a statement made by a priest, educator or other person is inconsistent with the *Catechism of the Catholic Church,* 2nd Ed., Catholics are encouraged to respectfully ask the priest or other person for clarification. It may be that the person misspoke, or that you, the listener or reader, misunderstood. The *Catechism* offers guidance on this matter (CCC par. 907). Note, however, that some subjects found in the *Code of Canon Law* [1983],[264] the *General Instruction of the Roman Missal* [2003],[265] recent papal encyclicals, or other Church documents may not be addressed in the *Catechism,*[266] but should not be inconsistent with it.

If the priest or other person insists on a view that is contrary to that in the *Catechism,* you might respond:

> If I accept what I read in the *Catechism*, I know I will be following
> the successor of Peter on whom Jesus himself founded his Church.
> If I accept this contrary interpretation, who will I be following?

If it seems that the priest doubts the historical authenticity of the Gospels, ask if he is familiar with the compelling case for eyewitness testimony made by Fr. Carmignac and others as outlined in Step 3 of this book.

Most who oppose or are indifferent to the Pope also have little regard for the Mother of Jesus. But some, who want to continue gravely sinful acts, see Mary as their ticket to heaven. These individuals know what Jesus said about the fate of those who say, "Lord! Lord!" but make no serious effort to keep the Commandments. But they somehow believe that if they simply say "Mary! Mary!" she will intercede and they will be saved. No Catholic doctrine supports this view for such unrepentant sinners. [CCC 2092] To see the Byzantine rite *Troparion* as supporting such a view would be to misinterpret it [CCC par. 966].

Catholic educators declare independence from the authority of the Pope and Magisterium

In 1967, presidents of the largest Catholic universities in the United States met at Land O'Lakes, Wisconsin and declared their intention to act independently not only of their bishops but also of the Pope:

---

264 www.intratext.com/X/ENG0017.htm
265 www.nccbuscc.org/liturgy/current/GIRM.pdf
266 www.scborromeo.org/ccc.htm

[T]he Catholic university must have a true autonomy and academic freedom in the face of authority of whatever kind, lay or clerical, external to the academic community itself (Excerpt from par. 1).[267]

Most other Catholic colleges and universities soon followed suit. Pope John Paul II, aware of the vital importance of truly Catholic higher education, included a mandate to that effect in the revised *Code of Canon Law* (1983). And in 1990 he issued *Ex Corde Ecclesiae,* an encyclical that included the following requirements for all Catholic Universities: (a) A competent ecclesiastical authority must determine the Catholic credentials of a university; (b) A Catholic theologian must have a mandate from his or her bishop to teach Catholic theology and; (c) University officials should ensure the appointment of a predominantly Catholic faculty.

In his comprehensive article, James Tunstead Burtchaell, C.S.C., noted that in 1999, nine years after the encyclical – even though U.S. Supreme Court and other court decisions have now removed all significant legal obstacles to its implementation – most Catholic colleges in the U.S. continue to resist implementing the canon law and *Ex Corde Ecclesiae.*[268]

On May 3, 2000, the National Conference of Catholic Bishops (now United States Conference of Catholic Bishops) approved the *mandatum* described above, with the provision that it would have the force of particular law for the United States on May 3, 2001.

More than seven years have passed since the May 3, 2001 implementation date and, with few exceptions, resistance to the mandatum continues among those who teach on Catholic campuses. A *National Catholic Register* online editorial dated October 20-26, 2002, states that, since the *mandatum* as received from Rome was undefined, the U.S. Bishops defined it. However, in the words of the *Register* Editor, the definition they developed has resulted in a *mandatum* "that is not always required, may be kept secret, and has no penalties if ignored."[269]

Fr. Benedict J. Groeschel, who recently called the general state of religious education in Catholic higher education "appalling" and most books used for religious education "unbelievably superficial,"[270]

---

267 **http://catholic.arhives.nd.edu/episodes/visitors/lol**
268 *Crisis,* July/August, 1999, 11-35.
269 **www.ncregister.com/Register_News/102202edi.htm**
270 *From Scandal to Hope,* 36.

summarized the problem as follows:

> *The principal problem in Catholic education at the present time [2002], from kindergarten to university, is that it is undermined by a spirit of dissent .... People teaching Catholic religious doctrine are allowed to decide for themselves when and how to dissent .... Many's the priest, religious or layperson who has suffered disdain, rejection or ridicule for refusing to countenance dissent.*[271]

Selecting a Catholic college or university

As Fr. Groeschel indicates, selecting a truly orthodox Catholic college or university to attend in North America can be a challenge today. *The Collegiate Guide,* based on a survey by *The National Catholic Register* and *Faith and Family* magazine provides guidance on this important matter. This *Guide* includes the answers given by the twenty-one Catholic institutions of higher learning in the U.S. and Canada that responded to the following questions in 2006: (a) Did the president make the public profession of faith and take the oath of fidelity? (b) Is the majority of the board of trustees Catholic? (c) Is the majority of the faculty Catholic? (d) Do you publicly require all Catholic theology professors to have the mandatum? (e) Did all Catholic theology professors take the oath of fidelity? (f) Is the head of campus ministry Catholic? (g) Do you exclude advocates of abortion, euthanasia or cloning as commencement speakers or recipients of honorary degrees? (h) Do you exclude sponsoring pro-abortion campus groups? (i) Do you exclude coed dorms? (j) Do your student health services exclude referrals to abortion clinics?

Fifteen of the twenty-one schools that responded gave an unqualified "yes" in answer to the mandatum requirement for all Catholic theology professors. Only seven of the twenty-one gave an unqualified "yes" to all ten of these questions. Details about the questionnaire and the answers given by each school can be viewed on the NCR Web site.[272]

Another important aid in choosing a Catholic college is the *Newman Guide to Choosing a Catholic College,* published November 1, 2007 by the Cardinal Newman Society. The Society was formed in

---

271 *From Scandal to Hope,* 79-80.
272 *NCR* and *Faith & Family* are not suggesting that the only institutions actively committed to Catholic orthodoxy are those that replied. Those who wish to better assess the commitment of any particular school are free to use the questions in the *Collegiate Guide.* **http://ncregister.com/info/2006_collegiate guide**

1993 by Founder and President Patrick J. Reilly for the preservation of Catholic higher education. The *Guide* lists a total of 21 Catholic Colleges / Universities in three categories: *Joyfully Catholic, Born from the Crisis*, and *Fighting the Tide*. Here is an excerpt from the CNS Web site:

> ***The Newman Guide to Choosing a Catholic College: What to Look For and Where to Find It*** is the first college guide to show students where they can learn and grow in a genuine Catholic environment without the nonsense that has overtaken even some of the most well-known Catholic universities. It includes detailed profiles of schools, essential data on each institution, and practical advice from eminent Catholic thinkers, including Father Benedict Groeschel, Father C. John McCloskey and Dr. Peter Kreeft, on how to approach the college decision process. It also tells prospective pupils where to look to find an array of unique and specialized programs.
>
> Based on two years of extensive research and hundreds of interviews, and with complete fidelity to the heart of the Church, *The Newman Guide to Choosing a Catholic College* is an indispensable tool for students and parents looking to pursue a Catholic college education today.

For further information and to order the *Guide*, see the CNS *The Newman Guide* Website.[273]

Does God love us "unconditionally?"

Not infrequently, Catholics hear in homilies that "*God loves us unconditionally.*" I submit that, without clarification, this statement has prompted many Catholics to begin thinking as follows:

> Why should I make all the sacrifices necessary to live morally, truly loving God and neighbor and keeping the Commandments, if God loves everyone unconditionally and, at death, welcomes *everyone* – saints and grave sinners alike – into heaven?

Consider this fictional but fact-based conversation between a priest (**P**) and a typical Catholic (**C**):

P: "If I say that God loves each of us unconditionally, what do you think that means in regard to your salvation?"

C: "Well, if there are no conditions to God's love, it must mean that

---

273 **http://thenewmanguide.com/Home/tabid/324/Default.aspx**

even if I die unrepentant in a state of mortal sin, I will be saved."

P: "No, I'm afraid that is not what the Church teaches. As we read in the *Catechism,* if we die unrepentant in a state of mortal sin, we will go to hell" (CCC par. 1035).

C: (With perplexed expression) "Well, then, God's love is not unconditional, is it? Haven't you just stated a condition – that to be saved, at the moment of death I must have repented of any mortal sin?"

P: "No, God's love really is unconditional. Even though you would remain in hell for eternity, God would continue to love you. He would love you as a parent loves a delinquent runaway child who – by freely choosing to offend his parents gravely and without repentance – irrevocably separates himself from them and no longer abides in their love ...."

C: "But after I've been condemned to suffer in hell for eternity, of what benefit to me is God's "unconditional" love"? Clearly, it was of benefit to me only during my earthly life and would have been to my benefit had I gone to heaven. Also, if I went to hell having heard only that God loves me "unconditionally," it seems to me that priests and others in the Church who failed to explain that *God's love for us does not mean our unconditional salvation,* would bear some responsibility for my being there."

I might mention here a thought on one's "freely choosing hell" that Fr. Mitch Pacwa, S.J., shared on an EWTN program. We may think of our soul as a lump of clay. We are called by Jesus, through the Church, to shape the clay suitably by living a virtuous life, but have free will and can shape it as we please. We do so knowing that at some point – possibly instantly and without warning – we will die. At the moment of death our clay is "fired" i.e., hardened permanently. The fired clay – our immortal soul – will then be judged by Jesus as suitable for heaven, purgatory or hell depending on the final shape we ourselves gave it.

This metaphor of the clay reminds me of my concern for the soul of an airline pilot whose plane went down some years ago. His last words on the cockpit voice recorder were not "Oh God!" but "Oh _ _ _ _!" (the four letter "s" word). We can only hope that in that last split-second before death his final thought – and that of all of his passengers and crew – was a repentant plea for God's mercy. Afterward I asked myself what my final thought might be in such a situation. Would it be a prayerful, repentant plea for God's mercy? I hope and pray that it would be.

For those who wish to read the documents noted in the *Catechism* (Early Church Fathers, papal encyclicals, documents of the various Church Councils, quotations of saints, etc.), an excellent resource is *The Companion to the Catechism of the Catholic Church.* As earlier noted, Internet users will find the Early Fathers of the Church on the Web page of *Christian Classics Ethereal Library* at Wheaton College.[274]

The "Conscience not guided by Church teaching" error

Those who see the Pope as simply the Bishop of Rome generally hold the following erroneous beliefs:

(a)   Because the Pope has no more authority than any other bishop or national council of bishops, (and, according to some dissidents, no more than a theologian), the *Catechism* is not authoritative and;

(b)   Each person's conscience reigns supreme, period.

Item (a) is addressed in detail in Part I. Item (b) is a very subtle and spiritually dangerous error, and calls for careful explanation.

I had a chance conversation a few years ago with a Catholic nearing completion of the Deaconate program in an upstate New York diocese. Our conversation turned to pro-life matters and I asked how he would counsel an unmarried Catholic who planned to abort her baby but who sought his counsel on the matter.

He said he would do his best to encourage her to have the baby. However, if she said her conscience was telling her to have the abortion, his final advice would be along these lines: "We all have an obligation to follow our conscience."

Astonished, I asked if he would not tell her that *we have an obligation to first form our conscience in accordance with Church teaching* (which, of course, condemns abortion as a grave evil). That obligation seemed alien to him, however, and he appeared not to accept it.

This "conscience alone" error stems from the "*Winnipeg Statement*" which was issued in September 1968, by the Canadian Conference of Catholic Bishops in response to *Humanae Vitae,* the encyclical of Pope Paul VI (July 25, 1968) which banned artificial methods of

---

274 www.ccel.org/fathers2

birth control. In part, the statement refers to persons who have "tried sincerely" but without success to follow Church teaching, and it includes:

> [W]hoever honestly chooses that course which **seems right to him** does so in good conscience.[275]

This statement of the CCCB was soon widely quoted in Catholic publications and media and accepted by many priests and lay persons throughout the world. It still appears in some materials used to teach those studying to become Catholic. What is generally not revealed to the faithful by those who promulgate the above statement, however, is that five years later (December, 1973) the Canadian bishops issued a clarification which included:

> A believer has the absolute obligation of conforming conduct first and foremost to what the Church teaches ....[276]

Unfortunately, their clarification was never widely disseminated. In addition to Canada, nine other national hierarchies, eight in Western Europe and one in Indonesia, made similar decisions regarding contraception. In contrast, the *Catechism of the Catholic Church,* 2nd Ed. explains as follows the obligation to form one's conscience:

> A human being must always obey the certain judgment of his conscience. If he were deliberately to act against it, he would condemn himself. Yet it can happen that moral conscience remains in ignorance and makes erroneous judgments about acts to be performed or already committed [par. 1790].

> This ignorance can often be imputed to personal responsibility. This is the case when a man "takes little trouble to find out what is true and good, or when conscience is by degrees almost blinded through the habit of committing sin" [*Gaudium et Spes,* par. 16]. In such cases, the person is culpable for the evil he commits [par.1791].

Imagine a scene in which one doomed soul in hell says to another: "*I said to St. Peter: 'But I always let my conscience be my guide.' St. Peter replied: 'Your guide lacked a sense of direction.'*"

Humorous though this may seem at a glance, every informed Catholic knows that these words mask a consequence too horrible to

---

275 **www.catholicinsight.com/humanae/winnipeg_html**
276 **www.catholicinsight.com/humanae/choose_html**

contemplate – the eternal consequence that is the result of grave, unrepentant sin.

But how are we to receive the *guidance* that will ensure the sound sense of direction that is essential for every conscience?

> In the formation of conscience the Word of God is the light for our path (Cf. Ps 119:105); we must assimilate it in faith and prayer and put it into practice. We must also examine our conscience before the Lord's Cross. We are assisted by the gifts of the Holy Spirit, aided by the witness or advice of others and *guided by the authoritative teaching of the Church* (Emphasis added) [par. 1785].

The *Catechism* further states:

> One may never do evil so that good may result from it [par. 1789].

Isn't it probable that, after much deliberation, it *seemed right* to Judas Iscariot to lead the band of abductors to Jesus, to say "Hail, Rabbi" and betray him with a kiss?

Rejecting the Church because of a hypocrite

Speaking of Judas, I sometimes wonder about those, two thousand years ago, who began to follow Jesus through him. When they learned that Judas betrayed Jesus, did they reject Christianity forthwith – without seeking out any of the remaining apostles; all of whom throughout their lives would proclaim all that Jesus taught; most, according to tradition, to the point of martyrdom? Surely the advice Jesus gave regarding the Scribes and the Pharisees who sat "on Moses' seat" (Mt 23:2-3) he intends for us today, as earlier noted: "Observe whatever they tell you, but not what they do." Surely this applies to any in the Church whose scandalous behavior mocks their preaching.

In hell, can there be any souls more pathetic than those who rejected the teachings of Jesus because they heard them proclaimed by a hypocrite and looked no further?

Abortion

And how many abortions *seem right* to a conscience not guided by the authoritative teaching of the Church? But, in his words to Jeremiah, the Lord affirmed that what is in the womb is in every sense a human person: ***"Before I formed you in the womb I knew you, and before you were born I consecrated you ..."*** (Jer 1:5).[277]

---

277 A medical records-based study in eight European countries found that abortion, especially of a first child, is the best predictor of breast cancer; in England / Wales and Scotland an increase of about 40% is expected within 20 years. "The Breast Cancer

The Roman Catholic Church teaches that deliberate abortion is a sin so grave it results in *latae sententiae* (automatic) excommunication:

> Formal cooperation in an abortion constitutes a grave offense. The Church attaches the canonical penalty of excommunication to this crime against human life. "A person who procures a completed abortion incurs excommunication *latae sententiae* by the very commission of the offense, and subject to the conditions provided by Canon Law" [CCC, par. 2272].

> "Certain particularly grave sins [including formal cooperation in an abortion] incur excommunication, the most severe ecclesiastical penalty, which impedes the reception of the sacraments and the exercise of certain ecclesiastical acts, and for which absolution consequently cannot be granted, according to canon law, except by the Pope, the bishop of the place or priests authorized by them. In danger of death any priest ... can absolve from every sin and excommunication" [CCC par. 1463].[278]

Although an exception is made for those in danger of death, as indicated, excommunicated Roman Catholics may no longer receive the sacraments, including the Eucharist (to willfully continue to receive the Eucharist is to commit a grave sacrilege (See 1 Cor 11:27-29). However, excommunicated Catholics are encouraged to continue to attend Mass and are urged to see their pastors without delay to request reinstatement in the Church. Perhaps the most sobering verse in the entire Bible for those who have made a "pro-choice" decision regarding abortion is: ***"For with the judgment you pronounce you will be judged, and the measure you give will be the measure you get"*** (Mt 7:2). On line, an excellent Catholic resource is **www.priestsforlife.org/**

Natural Family Planning

In regard to *Humanae Vitae,* George Sim Johnson wrote a noteworthy commentary in 1995. It reads, in part:

"The best kept secret in the Church today is Natural Family Planning (NFP) .... But there are married Catholic couples who know better. My wife and I are among them. [NFP is not] the old rhythm method which was the only way of spacing births when *Humanae Vitae*

Epidemic ..." P. S. Carroll, *Journal of American Physicians and Surgeons*, Fall, 2007.

278 Note the exceptions to penalties listed in Canon Law, par. 1323-1325. These include a person who "was, without fault, ignorant of violating the law or precept; inadvertence and error are equivalent to ignorance;" and one who "has not completed the sixteenth year of age." **www.intratext.com/X/ENG0017.htm**

appeared ....

"NFP is free (once you buy your thermometer and charts), and it's *about 99% effective, the same as the Pill* .... There is nothing like periodic restraint to keep a couple's sex life interesting.

"NFP is *like going on a honeymoon every month,* which is why even non-Catholics use it and don't understand why more couples aren't in on it. NFP also gives the peace of mind that comes from living in accordance with the will of God ... the rewards of NFP easily outweigh the sacrifices ....

"The divorce rate among couples who use NFP is under 3%, while the divorce rate among couples who use contraceptives is well over 50% .... Catholic catechism and pre-Cana programs are not getting out the message that NFP makes for happier marriages.

"It's time for Catholic educators to sit down and read, prayerfully, *Humanae Vitae*. It has turned out to be one of the prophetic documents of our age"[279] (Emphasis added).

It may come as no surprise to see NFP so highly praised by George Sim Johnson, a Catholic. But surely many were surprised to find NFP similarly praised by syndicated ethics and religion columnist Mike McManus, who is not Catholic. At this writing this column (#948; October 30, 1999) can be read on his *Marriage Savers* Web site.[280] McManus notes that some restraint is involved – but only about one week per month – and that NFP "is as effective as the Pill or IUDs, but completely without their possible side effects ... is almost free, and almost eliminates the possibility of divorce!" He concludes this re-markable column by wondering why NFP is not promoted by Planned Parenthood, magazines for women, and others who express concern about divorce or population trends.

For information on NFP see such Web sites as The Couple to Couple League[281] and the Billings Ovulation Method.[282]

Affirmation of NFP comes from another, non-Catholic, source: *Open Embrace; a Protestant Couple Rethinks Contraception, by* Sam and Bethany Torode (Eerdmans). The book was the subject of an article by Carl E. Olson in *Envoy* Magazine, Volume 6.4 (January, 2003). Bethany had this to say: "NFP refers to the married couple as beings made in the image of God, instruments for creation, vessels of love. It

---

279 *National Catholic Register,* July 16, 1995.
280 **www.marriagesavers.org**
281 **www.ccli.org**
282 **www.billingsmethod.com/bc_home.htm**

acknowledges the spiritual depth that accompanies all our physical acts, and in doing so sanctifies our lovemaking."[283]

The Post-Conciliar period – Cardinal Ratzinger expresses concern

Without mentioning the name of any order of priests Joseph Cardinal Ratzinger, Prefect of the Vatican's Congregation for the Doctrine of the Faith (now Pope Benedict XVI), spoke as follows during an interview in 1985: "Under the onslaught of the post-Conciliar period, the great religious orders have vacillated, have undergone grave hemorrhages, and have seen new admissions reduced to levels never experienced before, and they still seem to be shaken by an identity crisis …. It has often been the traditionally most 'educated,' the intellectually best equipped orders that have undergone the gravest crises."[284]

Clearly, Cardinal Ratzinger was referring to more than one religious order. However, In light of the above comment, a news release a decade later by Catholic News Service may be of interest. CNS noted that the 34th General Congregation meeting of Jesuits in its more than 450-year history was held in Rome from January 5 through March 22, 1995.

According to the press release the 223 delegates, under the leadership of Fr. Peter-Hans Kolvenbach, Superior-General of the Society of Jesus, the group approved a revision of the Jesuits' mission in the Church and society.

One of the documents addressed the situation regarding the vow professed Jesuits take – a fourth, special vow that they will be obedient to the Pope – and its applicability in circumstances in which the Jesuit is inclined, intellectually and academically, to speak or write critically of the official teaching of the Church.

The CNS article noted that the Order desires to remain faithful to the "hierarchy" and to the "Magisterium," but at times the individual Jesuit may feel an obligation to make known a contrary view even if the probable result will be harsh sanction by Rome. In such cases, under the revised rules, it appears that the Jesuit will no longer be seen by the Order as being disobedient. The article goes on to speak of fidelity to God, truth and a well-formed conscience and appears to redefine the special vow of obedience to the Pope as simply applying to

---

283 **www.envoymagazine.com**
284 *The Ratzinger Report, 55.*

the church [lower-case 'c'] and hierarchy.

News releases do not always present the full picture. Statements may be misleading and important details are sometimes omitted. It is well known, however, that in more than a few instances priests of this order have been numbered among the many ordained and non-ordained Catholics who, in recent decades, have seen fit to make know views contrary to the teaching of the Pope and Magisterium as summarized in the *Catechism of the Catholic Church.*

Ann Roche Muggeridge commented with sadness in 1990 on problems in regard to the vows taken by many Catholic nuns.

Muggeridge noted that within the movement of Catholic feminism, made up mostly of nuns, activities are carried out that appear to be blasphemy, including a ritual "blessing" of the bread and the wine, accompanied by dancing.[285]

The spiritual demise of so many orders of nuns is just one of many topics in *The Desolate City.* In her book *Ungodly Rage*, Donna Steichen documents in breathtaking detail the effect of modernism on so many orders of nuns who have been transformed by its force, in contrast to the exemplary few, such as The Missionaries of Charity, founded by Mother Teresa, who have not.

Dr. William Coulson offers some insight into how disregard of vows on such a scale could come about. Dr. Coulson was an associate of influential psychologist Carl Rogers who promoted humanistic (self-centered rather than God-centered) "nondirective" therapy. In a 1995 interview by Dr. William Marra, published in *The Latin Mass,* Coulson looked back with regret on the widespread spiritual harm Rogers, Coulson and many associates unwittingly inflicted on dozens of Catholic religious organizations soon after Vatican II. They did their first workshop at a Jesuit University in 1965: "I don't know whether you remember," Coulson said, "but in 1967 the Jesuits had a big conference at Santa Clara and there was a lot of talk about the Third Way' among the Jesuits .... The first two ways are faithful marriage and faithful celibacy. [The third way was the] idea that priests could date."

Fr. Benedict Groeschel notes that Eugene Kennedy, an ex-priest, originated the "third way." It meant that "those vowed to chastity could have warm, close, emotionally expressive relationships with members of the opposite sex and nothing would happen." The third way was promoted in the book *The Genius of the Apostolate: Personal Growth*

285 *The Desolate City; Revolution in the Catholic Church,* 139.

in the Candidate, the Seminarian and the Priest, by Eugene Kennedy and Paul F. D'Arcy (Sheed and Ward, 1965).[286]

Coulson recommends the book *The Re-Formed Jesuits*, by Fr. Joseph Becker, which reviews the collapse of Jesuit training between 1965 and 1975 while under the influence of Carl Rogers. But Coulson adds:

> I think the Jesuits are capable of bouncing back because they had such strong traditions of their own, and God willing they will.

Coulson said that Rogers, a man of principle, really cared about his clients. He adds that Rogers, depressed [because of the great number who had left their religious orders after learning to emphasize self, thereby de-emphasizing God], said the following in 1976:

> Yes I started this thing, and now look where it's carrying us. Where is it going to carry us? And did I start something that is in some fundamental way mistaken, and will lead us off into paths that we will regret?[287]

As earlier noted, the story of the Second Vatican Council, and the influence of forces opposed to the successor of Peter and the Magisterium, is told in great detail and with a wealth of documentation by Ann Roche Muggeridge in *The Desolate City*, as well as by Msgr. George Kelly in *Battle for the American Church* and *Battle for the American Church Revisited.*

The Documents of Vatican II are important and address a wide spectrum of issues. However, as Msgr. George A. Kelly indicated, the Council documents include a number of statements that lend themselves to different interpretations. Factions within the Catholic Church have interpreted such statements to suit their own agendas.[288]

(Ven.) John Henry (later Cardinal) Newman provided a historical parallel in his *Apologia:* "How had the Arians drawn up their Creeds? Was it not on the principle of using vague ambiguous language, which to the subscribers would seem to bear a Catholic sense, but which, when worked out on the long run, would prove to be heterodox?"[289]

---

286 *From Scandal to Hope*, 22.
287 *The Latin Mass*, Special Edition, December, 1995: "We overcame their traditions; we overcame their faith," Interview by Dr. William Marra, 17-21. Also see "Defending the Faith: The Story of a Repentant Psychologist,"**www.cfpeople.org/Apologetics/page51a080.html**
288 *The Battle for the American Church*, 20.
289 *Apologia Pro Vita Sua*, Ven. John H. Newman, Chapter II, par. 65,

Documents of Vatican II to be interpreted by the Catechism of the Catholic Church

These ambiguities were certainly on the minds of the Bishops in 1985. It was in that year, at an extraordinary Synod, that it was decided – with the approval of Pope John Paul II – that a new catechism would be written for the entire Church worldwide, a task that had not been undertaken in 400 years.

The *Catechism of the Catholic Church,* 2nd Ed. is introduced by the Pope as a *"sure and authentic reference text for teaching catholic doctrine …."* *Many* references to the *Documents of Vatican II* are included in the vast scope of the *Catechism* [The *Catechism* includes more than 800 references to *The Documents of Vatican II*; more than any of the other sixteen Ecumenical Councils, including Trent].

In *Crossing the Threshold of Hope,* Pope John Paul II explained that all post-Vatican II teaching – of which the *Documents of Vatican II* are certainly foremost – is to be interpreted in light of the *Catechism of the Catholic Church,* 2nd Ed.:

> The Catechism was also indispensable, *in order that all the richness of the teaching of the Church following the Second Vatican council could be preserved in a new synthesis and given a new direction.* Without the Catechism of the universal Church this would not have been accomplished (Italics in the original).[290]

Clearly, then, it is the intention of the Pope and Magisterium that the faithful are to look with confidence to the *Catechism* as an authoritative source for resolving any differences of opinion that may arise from reading the *Documents of Vatican II.*

The Pope is the spiritual and historical successor of Peter. Even those who question the exact sequence of who led the Church in the first few centuries acknowledge that Pope John Paul II was elected Pope in 1978 by the prayerful vote of the College of Cardinals. Each Cardinal, through the solemn laying on of hands through the ages derives his authority – through the apostles – from Jesus himself, as does every Catholic bishop and priest.

Coming from this rich spiritual and historical background, how does the credibility of the *Catechism of the Catholic Church,* 2nd Ed. compare to that of the authoritative statements of faith offered by other religions? Each believer of whatever religion is encouraged to make his

---

www.fordham.edu/halsall/mod/newman/apologia1.html
290 *Crossing the Threshold of Hope,* 164.

or her own comparison. The *Catechism* has become a best seller; a remarkable achievement for a religious work.

One feature of the *Catechism* of special interest to Protestants and others is the Index of Citations in the back of the book (Included in the hard cover and soft cover second editions published in 2000 by the United States Catholic Conference, but omitted in some other editions). There we find in sequence every chapter and the great majority of the verses of all the books of the New Testament and much of the Old, with the paragraph number of the *Catechism* where the verse is addressed. Using this Index, the reader can quickly find the Catholic interpretation regarding verses of particular interest.

One might expect that every bishop and priest throughout the world would encourage every Catholic to get a copy of the *Catechism of the Catholic Church,* 2nd Ed. Using its subject index (or taking the time to read it from cover to cover), the faithful could readily become fully aware of virtually all approved teaching of the Church and live accordingly, under the guidance of their parish priest.

Is the Pope's mandate for this *Catechism* being reflected in Sunday homilies (sermons), diocesan newspapers, Catholic magazines, seminars and other Church media throughout the world?

While many bishops and priests encourage the faithful to read the *Catechism*, many other bishops and priests appear to be indifferent to it, at best. Why? Because, in the Catholic Church today, as earlier noted, there are reports of many priests and some bishops who tacitly or openly oppose one or more of the official teachings of the Church. Msgr. George A. Kelly wrote in 1995:

> One would have to be a Rip Van Winkle not to know that, within a generation, vital Catholic teachings have been redefined at lower levels of the Church, contrary to the teachings represented by the *Catechism of the Catholic Church,* 2nd Ed. The Catholic faith has also been compromised by the frequent appeal, even by bishops, to pastoral practice over against dogmatic or moral principle. As if deliberately disbelieving or directly doing evil can ever be legitimized by casuistry or compassion. It is one thing after the fact to "suffer with" the sinner, especially in the confessional or the rectory office; quite another to mount a pulpit or write a column or a letter which leaves parishioners feeling that God so understands their personality and circumstances that, for them, doing wrong is believing or doing right.[291]

---

291 *The Battle for the American Church Revisited,* 124.

Although the *Catechism* has come into wider use in recent years, in their comprehensive book *Flawed Expectations: The Reception of the Catechism of the Catholic Church*; Msgr. Michael J. Wrenn and Kenneth D. Whitehead describe in detail how so many dissidents within the Church, with the support or indifference of a number of bishops, did so much to undermine the credibility of the *Catechism of the Catholic Church,* 2nd Ed., as well as the authority of the Pope and Magisterium, in the years before and immediately after its publication.[292]

The Episcopal Conference cannot be a substitute for the persons of the bishops

In 1966, in the Motu Proprio *Ecclesiae Sanctae*, Pope Paul VI called for the establishment of Episcopal Conferences where none had by then been established.

The Code of Canon Law in 1983 provided norms for the establishment, membership, functioning, powers and objectives of these Conferences (Canons 447-459).[293]

Joseph Cardinal Ratzinger, Prefect of the Vatican's Congregation for the Doctrine of the Faith, spoke as follows on this subject in a 1985 interview:

> We must not forget that episcopal conferences have no theological basis, they do not belong to the structure of the Church, as willed by Christ, that cannot be eliminated; they have only a practical, concrete function .... The collective, therefore, does not substitute for the persons of the bishops, who are the authentic teachers and instructors of the faith for the faithful entrusted to their care .... No episcopal conference, as such, has a teaching mission; its documents have no weight of their own save that given to them by individual bishops .... It must once again become clear that in each diocese there is only one shepherd and teacher of the faith in communion with the other pastors and teachers and with the Vicar of Christ.[294]

In *Apostolos Suos,* an apostolic letter released July 23, 1998, the Pope further clarified the doctrinal and juridical limits of the episcopal conferences of the world which, at this writing, number 108. Two examples indicate why, in the interest of Church unity, such papal

---

292 *Flawed Expectations,* Msgr. Michael J. Wrenn and Kenneth D. Whitehead.
293 **www.intratext.com/X/ENG0017.htm**
294 *The Ratzinger Report,* 59-60.

intervention was necessary: Most Catholics are aware that – contrary to official Church doctrine – norms produced independently by the South African bishops' conference made it possible for President William J. Clinton to receive the Holy Eucharist in a Soweto church. Also, the Vatican required the National Conference of Catholic Bishops here in the United States to issue a clarification of *Always Our Children* – which was promulgated by an NCCB (now USCCB) committee – because it did not fully convey the Church's approved teaching that "Homosexual persons are called to chastity" and the concern of the Church for the eternal salvation of those who fail to heed that call.

The Sacrament of Penance (Reconciliation)

Many pre-Vatican II Catholics, including this author, initially welcomed the changes that followed Vatican II. Few realized then that the pendulum that began at a point of reverence and solemnity would quickly swing to an extreme of liberalism unimaginable to Catholics of the '50s. Consider, for instance, the Sacrament of Penance. In pre-Vatican II days, when we violated the Commandments in any serious way our consciences were soon troubled and we joined the long line of repentant Catholics at the confessional to receive the Sacrament of Penance. After confessing our sins the priest would offer words of understanding and encouragement (he went to confession too) and then asked that we say the Act of Contrition:

> O my God, I am heartily sorry for having offended thee, and I de-test all my sins because I dread the loss of heaven and the pains of hell. But, most of all, because I offend thee my God, who art all good and deserving of all my love. I firmly resolve, with the help of thy Grace, to confess my sins, to do penance, and to amend my life. Amen.

The priest, representing Jesus (Jn 20:22-23), then said: "I absolve you in the name of the Father, the Son and the Holy Spirit; go, and sin no more." To conclude, the priest then gave us our penance, generally asking us to say the "Our Father," the "Hail, Mary" and the "Glory be to the Father ..." one or more times. We would do so, generally before leaving the Church, and, knowing we were in the State of Grace, felt cleansed and again pleasing in the eyes of God.

Vatican II never mandated any changes in the Act of Contrition, but those who decide what will be in missals, First Communion materials, adult Catholic formation and other Catholic literature discarded the above form even before this Council.

Most modern versions of this prayer exclude any thought of

209

heartfelt sorrow for having offended the God who created us, redeemed us and is truly deserving of the full measure of our love. The true concept of sin, and an understanding of why it should not just be regretted but "detested," is quite foreign to a generation of Catholics who have been taught that to sin is merely to fail to show enough love, primarily toward our neighbor.

As earlier indicated, the possibility of being barred from heaven and spending eternity in hell for sinning gravely without repentance is simply inconceivable to most Catholics today. Too often young Catholics are taught that, if hell exists at all, it has few if any inhabitants. Many post-Vatican II Catholics, based on what they have been taught, think along these lines:

> Surely nothing I am doing, like my sexual relationship ... the abortion I had ... that lie I told that resulted in such a grave injustice ... nothing like that would ever cause our loving God to send me to hell. On second thought, even if hell exists, which I doubt, and God did send me there, life would not be so bad. We know the "fire" of hell is just a metaphor, and surely I would not be there forever, In fact, to be in hell probably wouldn't be much different than the separation from God that I'm experiencing right now, and that suits me just fine.

> To resolve to confess my sins and do penance is one thing, but what's this about firmly resolving with the help of thy Grace to amend my life? I know what it means to firmly resolve to do something. I've done exactly that in getting good grades in school, excelling in sports, getting the job and promotions I wanted, working out regularly .... But if "resolving to amend my life" means really trying to abide by the letter and spirit of all ten Commandments, and to "Love one another as I have loved you" and to do all this in accordance with the *Catechism of the Catholic Church*, forget it; I'd lose all my friends. And why should I make such a sacrifice when God is going to welcome me into heaven anyway?

For Catholics who know their faith such thinking is beyond comprehension. We have a God of Mercy but also of Justice and – as the Bible indicates and the Church confirms – if we die as unrepentant fornicators, adulterers, sexually active outside of a valid marriage between a man and a woman, drunkards or other "workers of iniquity," we can expect to suffer the pains of hell forever (e.g., Mt 7:21-23, 13:47-50, 25:31-46, Mk 9:41:49, Lk 16:19-31, Jn 5:28-29, Rom 1:28, 1 Cor 6:9 and Jude 6-8). In paragraph 1035 of the *Catechism* we read:

The teaching of the Church affirms the existence of hell and its eternity. Immediately after death the souls of those who die in a state of mortal sin, descend into hell, where they suffer the punishments of hell, "eternal fire."

For more than a quarter-century, many priests and others in the Church have been reluctant to promote "the Gospel in all its fullness" as noted earlier by Msgr. George Kelly. The effects of the preaching of the watered-down Gospel are everywhere apparent. The promotion of the "seems right" conscience – so often preached to Catholics in recent years – has had its effect. What seems morally right to society as a whole is hardly distinguishable from what seems morally right to the great majority of Catholics. The problem is that today, with respect to the Commandments, the morality of society as a whole is in free-fall.

However, as we begin the new millennium, it appears that within the Catholic Church the tide may be turning. Fr. Vernon J. Schaefer notes that when the teachings of the Church are presented in a manner that is gentle, but with nothing watered down, Catholics respond. And, he adds:

> The best Catholics are beginning to vote with their feet, abandoning their parishes in favor of the papist parish whose pastor has demonstrated his unswerving loyalty to the Holy Father and the Magisterium.[295]

Pope reasserts definitive articles of Faith; dissenters subject to "just penalties"

Priests and bishops everywhere who teach the faith "with nothing watered down" certainly welcomed *Ad Tuendam Fidem* (*To Defend the Faith*), an apostolic letter issued June 30, 1998 by Pope John Paul II. Directed primarily at Catholic theologians, the *letter* noted the addition to Canon Law of the provision that "Each and everything definitively proposed by the Magisterium of the Church regarding faith and morals ... also must be firmly accepted and held; one who denies the propositions which are to be held definitively opposes the doctrine of the Catholic Church" and is subject to a "just penalty."

In an accompanying commentary, Joseph Cardinal Ratzinger (now Pope Benedict XVI) gave examples of such definitive truths and made it clear that anyone denying them would no longer be in communion with the Catholic Church, and that those who "obstinately" doubt Church teachings would fall "under the censure of heresy." As noted

---

295 "A Papist Priest Prospers," *Homiletic & Pastoral Review,* October, 1997, 22-25.

above, then-Cardinal Ratzinger was then Prefect of the Sacred Congregation for the Doctrine of the Faith.[296]

Penalties or not, and scandals notwithstanding, Catholic orthodoxy in the U.S.A. and in most of the world continues under siege from powerful heterodox forces within the Church.

I received an e-mail in July, 2002, from a friend whose daughter at that time attended a Catholic university not far from St. Peter's Basilica in Rome. Her daughter's theology textbook suggested, erroneously, that there is no historical basis for the Resurrection of Jesus and that the Bible is the word of the Lord in the same way that the myths of pagan religions are the words of their gods.

Clearly, these are desperate times for Catholicism; Catholic parents must wait no longer to ensure that their children can confidently answer the question, "Why be Catholic?"

The Gospels reemerge as authentic history – a clear call for the revitalization of Catholicism.

In view of the doubt cast on the historicity of the Gospels by Catholic and other exegetes during the last half-century, as well as the acceptance of that flawed view of biblical history by many of our theologians, it is not surprising that dissenting views have surfaced and have had their devastating effect on the faith of so many of the faithful.

My hope and prayer for the Church is that the well-documented work of the many early-date / eyewitness scholars, as outlined in Step 3, will soon become widely known throughout the Church. Surely the long-awaited revitalization of Catholicism worldwide will soon follow.

The primary purpose of this book will have been achieved if those who read it:

(a) are able to answer clearly and confidently when asked the question: "Why should anyone be a Catholic, rather than practice some other religion or none?";

(b) can recognize aberrations and omissions in Catholic teaching, in contrast to the "Gospel preached in all its fullness" as summarized in the *Catechism of the Catholic Church,* 2nd Ed.;

(c) have gained an understanding of the compelling case for the Gospels as *sound history*, based on the studies of early-date / eyewitness scholars such as Fr. J. Carmignac and C. Tresmontant,

---

296 *The Wanderer*, July 9, 1998, 1. Article by Paul Likoudis.

as well as those of C. Thiede and others;

(d)   have a fuller appreciation of the tremendous gift Jesus gave to mankind – *unique in all of history*; his dying on the cross to redeem us and founding his One Church through which – under the leadership of Peter and his successors in the papacy – all may receive the graces necessary to live as Jesus taught us in this life and be happy with him forever in the next.

Discussion Questions

1.   What effect do you think the molestation of youths by priests, now widely publicized, has had on the faith of the average Catholic? To what extent do you think this scandal has affected the faith of young-adult Catholics who typically are not very well grounded in their faith?

2.   To what extent do you think dissent on the part of some priests and Catholic educators in recent decades has affected the faith of Catholics?

3.   George Weigel attributes the crisis to a failure of *fidelity;* that the bishops involved in this scandal *"have not believed, with sufficient life-transforming power, the truth of what the Catholic Church teaches they are."* Do you agree or disagree? If Weigel's analysis is correct, what factors might have undermined the fidelity of those involved? What might the Church do to correct this problem?

4.   What are some of the spiritual effects on parishioners when a pastor fails to "preach the Gospel in all its fullness," e.g., ignores or glosses over such topics as: (a) fornication, adultery or other sexual acts forbidden by Church teaching; (b) induced abortion; (c) the reality of hell and purgatory; (d) artificial birth control and the approved Natural Family Planning alternative; (e) the fullness of the teaching of the Church in regard to homosexual acts; (f) after grave sin, the requirement for confession with a firm purpose of amendment before receiving the Eucharist and; (g) the fact that God's unconditional love does not mean unconditional salvation?

5.   What does the Church teach in regard to each of the following, according to the authoritative *Catechism of the Catholic Church,* 2nd Ed.? (a) Did Jesus intend to found a religion? (b)

Does hell exist? If so, does the Church teach that souls who go there will remain there forever? (c) Can a person who dies, unrepentant, in a state of mortal sin, avoid hell simply by choosing to go to heaven (or purgatory) at the moment of judgment by Jesus? (d) Are souls in hell simply separated from God, much as we seem to be here on earth? Aside from separation, do these souls also suffer? (e) Among the Catholic bishops, is the Pope simply "The first among equals?" (f) Is the Eucharist truly the Body and Blood of Christ, or is it merely symbolic? (g) Is the *Catechism of the Catholic Church,* 2nd Ed. intended for all Catholics and for interested non-Catholics? (h) Are Catholics free to ignore the teachings of the Pope (e.g., as made known to us in the *Catechism* and in his encyclicals) except when he speaks *ex cathedra*? (i) To act in the "Spirit of Vatican II" sounds commendable. However, are such actions always in keeping with authentic Church teaching?

6. How might we respond graciously if we find that our pastor's preaching or personal spiritual guidance contradicts Church teaching as found in the *Catechism of the Catholic Church,* 2nd Ed.?

7. Is it true that a human being must always obey the certain judgment of his conscience? In forming our conscience we must be guided by what authoritative source?

8. Do you think that some have rejected Catholicism because of hypocrites in the Church? How widespread a problem do you think this is? What might be done to address this problem?

9. What does the Church teach in regard to a person who procures a completed abortion or formally cooperates in an abortion?

10. What does the Church advise excommunicated Catholics to do?

11. What are some of the factors that might constitute "good reason" for a married couple who wish to postpone having children through the use of Natural Family Planning?

12. What concern did Joseph Cardinal Ratzinger (now Pope Benedict XVI) express in 1985 in regard to certain religious orders?

13. What concerns did Ann Roche Muggeridge and Donna Steichen express in regard to certain religious orders?

14. What influence did psychologist Carl Rogers have on certain Catholic religious orders according to his colleague, William Coulson?

15. Writing in 1979 about the documents of Vatican II, Msgr. George Kelly noted: "[T]he Council Documents include a number of statements that lend themselves to different interpretations .... Factions within the Catholic Church have interpreted such statements to suit their own agendas." In the view of Pope John Paul II, in what way is the *Catechism of the Catholic Church,* 2nd Ed. intended to address this problem?

16. In the *Catechism,* of what value is the "Index of Citations?"

17. In 1995 Msgr. George Kelly wrote, "vital Catholic teachings have been redefined at lower levels of the Church, contrary to the teachings represented by the *Catechism of the Catholic Church.* The Catholic faith has also been compromised by the frequent appeal, even by bishops, to 'pastoral practice' over against 'dogmatic or moral principle'" Why do you think Msgr. Kelly expressed such concern?

18. What concern is expressed in *Flawed Expectations* in regard to the *Catechism?* Based on your own experience, to what extent do you think Catholics have been encouraged to make use of the *Catechism of the Catholic Church* by their Bishops? By their pastors?

19. In *The Ratzinger Report,* what did Cardinal Ratzinger have to say about episcopal conferences?

20. What does the *Code of Canon Law;* 1983, say in regard to episcopal conferences?

21. What is *Apostolos Suos* and why was it written?

22. What aspect of the *Act of Contrition* is de-emphasized or omitted in more recent revisions compared to the pre-1960 version quoted in this book? Why does that aspect remain very important?

23. How has the prevailing understanding of sin and the possible loss of salvation changed among Catholics since Vatican II, compared to pre-Vatican II teaching on these matters? What does the Church officially teach on both subjects as stated in

the *Catechism of the Catholic Church,* 2nd Ed.*?*

24. What was the central concern addressed by Pope John Paul II in his apostolic letter *Ad Tuendam Fidem*? Why do you think he found it necessary to write it?

25. What was the Land O' Lakes agreement? What effect has it had on the teaching of Catholicism in most Catholic universities in the United States (and, indirectly, elsewhere)?

26. What is *Ex Corde Ecclesiae* and why do many Catholic Colleges in the U.S.A. and elsewhere continue to resist it and the mandate (*mandatum)* it requires from the local bishop?

Part III

Other Religions

Orthodox Christianity

It is commonly believed that the Great Schism between Eastern and Western Christendom took place in 1054. It is true that legates of Pope Leo IX excommunicated Patriarch Michael Cerularius in Constantinople on July 16 1054, and that this was followed by a declaration by Cerularius on July 24 that the Pope was anathema.

However, it is problematic for at least two reasons to state that Great Schism *occurred* in 1054: (a) The bull clearly did not excommunicate the Eastern Churches. It specifically excommunicated only "Caerularius, Leo of Achrida and their adherents" and stated that "the emperor (Constantine IX, who was excessively annoyed at the whole quarrel), the Senate, and the majority of the inhabitants of the city were 'most pious and orthodox.'"[297] (b) Pope Leo IX died in Rome April 19, 1054, about three months before the bull of excommunication was issued by his legate, Cardinal Humbert, and about one year before the election of his successor, Pope Victor II, on April 13, 1055.

The *Catholic Encyclopedia* goes on to explain that the "quarrel" need not have gone any further. Unfortunately, over a period of time, the Patriarchs of all the other Eastern Churches, of their own volition, chose to join Cerularius in the schism. The final separation of the Orthodox Churches from Rome did not occur until about 1450, only about 70 years before the Protestant Reformation.

On December 7, 1965 a joint declaration mutually nullifying the excommunications / anathemas of 1054 was issued by Pope Paul VI and Athenagoras, Ecumenical Patriarch of Constantinople. Reconciliation with all the autocephalous Patriarchates of the Orthodox Churches remains elusive, however. About one week after this joint declaration it was rejected by Metropolitan Philaret as "treason against Orthodoxy [which would] ... provoke a schism in the Orthodox world." Metropolitan Philaret was at that time President of the Synod of Bishops of the Russian Orthodox Church Outside of Russia.[298]

As explained in considerable detail in the *Catholic Encyclopedia*, there were many schisms between Rome and Constantinople in the first nine centuries of Christendom, all of which led to an increasing sense of disunity:

> From the beginning of the See of Constantinople to the great schism in 867 the list of these temporary breaches of communion

---

297 *Catholic Encyclopedia,* **www.newadvent.org/cathen/13535a.htm**
298 **www.orthodoxinfo.com/ecumenism/philaret_lifting.aspx**

is a formidable one. There were fifty-five years of schism (343-98) during the Arian troubles, eleven because of St. John Chrysostom's deposition (404-15), thirty-five years of the Acacian schism (484-519), forty-one years of Monothelite schism (640-81), sixty-one years because of Iconoclasm. So of these 524 years (343-867) no less than 203 were spent by Constantinople in a state of schism. We notice too that in every one of these quarrels Constantinople was on the wrong side; by the consent of the Orthodox, too, Rome in all stood out for right. And already we see that the influence of the emperor (who naturally always supported his court patriarch) in most cases dragged a great number of other Eastern bishops into the same schism.

In contrast to the Protestant Reformation of the sixteenth century, the Eastern Churches that rejected papal authority already had their own validly ordained and consecrated bishops. This meant that not only the original schismatic Eastern bishops, but also the bishops they would consecrate and the priests they would ordain would continue to be recognized by Rome as validly ordained and consecrated. For this reason the Catholic Church affirms that when during the Mass the Eastern Orthodox clergy say, "This is my Body … This is the cup of my Blood …" the bread and wine truly become the Body and Blood of Christ.

In his informative work *Religion in the Twentieth Century*, George P. Fedotov noted that, after Constantinople fell in 1453, all orthodox Balkan countries were brought under the rule of Turkey. Through the Sultans, they came under the jurisdiction of Constantinople's Greek Patriarch.

But Fedotov points out that in the nineteenth century Balkan Christians (Serbs, Greeks, Rumanians and Bulgarians) gradually became liberated from Turkish domination. The result was a number of independent states and, within these states, national churches.[299]

By the middle of the nineteenth century the Orthodox Church had become a free alliance of independent and partially independent individual churches linked by similar liturgy, creeds, traditions and theology. Fedotov added that, despite these similarities, no common unifying entity existed.[300]

The autonomous nature of the each Orthodox entity continues today, as indicated by Ernest Dawson, writing in *The Catholic World*

---

299 *Religion in the Twentieth Century*, 176.
300 Ibid.

Report in 1996 (Dawson notes that he relied heavily on the book *The Eastern Churches,* By Fr. Ronald Roberson):

> Today the Orthodox world generally recognizes 13 'autocephal-ous,' or self-governing, independent churches, each with its own hierarchy. Among these the Russian Orthodox Church is by far the largest, with 50 million believers. But the Ecumenical Patriarch of Constantinople, who presides over his own church of 3.5 million Greek Orthodox believers, remains the 'first among equals' within the Orthodox Hierarchy.[301]

Today, according to *Wikipedia,* the number of autocephalous churches is fifteen; fourteen in the opinion of those who do not ac-knowledge that designation for the *Orthodox Church in America.*

Fedotov notes that in the eighteenth century the tsars appointed the bishops – members of the synod who led the Orthodox faithful in lands under Russian rule. A similar synod-based arrangement became effective in Greece. The difficulty is that, in the Churches of the East, there is no single voice that can speak with ultimate infallible authority on matters of doctrine.[302]

The Filioque – now less of an obstacle to unity?

The Orthodox Church venerates Mary the Holy Virgin, the Saints, and administers all seven sacraments. The *Filioque* in the Nicene Creed, [We believe in the Holy Spirit, the Lord, the giver of life, who proceeds from the Father *and the Son*], was rejected by the Orthodox Church in the past, but this difficulty appears to have lessened, at least in the Russian School of Orthodoxy, where some have acknowledged that on this matter there was diversity of opinions among the fathers of the ancient, undivided Church.

Other obstacles to unity

But Fedotov indicates that the Orthodox Church (a) rejects the doctrine of Purgatory [after death the soul undergoes a particular judgment, then remains in a middle state between heaven and hell until the Second Coming and last judgment] and; (b) rejects the Immaculate Conception [they believe Mary was cleansed of original sin at the Annunciation] and, particularly, rejects the Infallibility of the Pope.[303] The Orthodox prefer to leave the divine mysteries veiled rather than attempt to explain them logically.

---

301 *The Catholic World Report, April,* 1996, 36
302 *Religion in the Twentieth Century,* 180.
303 Ibid., 182.

Fedotov calls our attention to the fact that Eastern Orthodoxy was transfixed in wonderment before the inexplicable: God had become man. In contrast to the Church of the West, it did not emphasize the pain and anguish Jesus experienced during his ministry.[304]

But is the Roman Catholic Church really so ill advised in its emphasis on Christ's Passion? Consider the words of Pope John Paul II:

> The veneration of the Christ's Cross has shaped the history of Christian piety and has inspired the greatest saints emerging over the centuries from the heart of the Church .... The Eastern Church attributes great importance of the Feast of the Transfiguration. The saints of the Orthodox Church give outstanding expression to this mystery. The saints of the Catholic Church often received the stigmata, beginning with Saint Francis of Assisi. They bore on their own bodies the sign of their similarity to Christ in His Passion [305] ....

For an overview of Catholic / Orthodox differences from an Orthodox perspective, see the Web-based-article, "What are the differences between Orthodoxy and Roman Catholicism?" by (Orthodox) Fr. Michael Azkoul, St. Catherine Mission, St. Louis, MO. (1994).[306]

Is common Orthodox Christian-Roman Catholic Eucharistic celebration within reach?

In the *Catechism of the Catholic Church,* 2nd Ed., paragraph 838, we read:

> Those "who believe in Christ and have been properly baptized are put in a certain, although imperfect, communion with the Catholic Church" [From *Unitatis redintegratio*, 541]. With the Orthodox Churches, this fullness is so profound "that it lacks little to attain the fullness that would permit a common celebration of the Lord's Eucharist" [From Paul VI, Discourse, 12/14/75; cf. *Unitatis redintegratio* 13-18].[307]

The words of Pope John Paul II and Pope Paul VI – and certainly the intent of Pope John XXIII in convening the Second Vatican Council – make abundantly clear the close bond the Roman Catholic Church feels for its sister church, the Orthodox. Although there have been some

---

304 Ibid., 183-4
305 *Crossing the Threshold of Hope,* 75-76.
306 **www.ocf.org/OrthodoxPage/reading/ortho_cath.html**
307 *Catechism of the Catholic Church,* par. 838.

difficulties along the way, bonds of friendship and mutual respect have been sought by both sides, especially in the last quarter-century.

In *Crossing the Threshold of Hope*, Pope John Paul II states "[T]he gap between the Catholic and Orthodox Church is not very wide .... The very fact that we are able to come together and pray is very significant. Some years ago this was absolutely unthinkable"[308]

Interviewed recently by a reporter from the Russian newspaper *Trud*, Cardinal Christoph Schönborn, Archbishop of Vienna, expressed his belief that "Catholic and Orthodox beliefs are in accord 'on almost every theological issue.'" He stressed the need for unity and the importance of Christians speaking with one voice, in particular "to oppose abortion, euthanasia and embryonic stem-cell research, and to promote respect for the dignity of human life."[309]

We can expect that the Orthodox Christian will agree with the first three steps of *The 7-Step Reason to be Catholic,* 2nd Ed. The difficulty may begin with the fourth: "The Bible indicates that Jesus founded only ONE Church ...." Until unity is reestablished, steps four through seven – and in particular the words of Jesus himself to Peter in Mt 16:18-19 and Jn 21:15-17 – cannot help but be unsettling to the devout Orthodox Christian.

Discussion Questions

1. What was the "Great Eastern Schism?" Was it the only Eastern schism?

2. Does the Catholic Church recognize the authority of the Orthodox Christian churches to consecrate bishops and ordain priests? Why?

3. Within Orthodoxy there are a number of *autocephalous* churches. What is the meaning of autocephalous? How does this differ from the Catholic Church which has Maronite, Melkite, Chaldean, Ruthenian and other rites in addition to the Roman rite?

4. What is the *filioque*?

5. Pope John Paul II stated, "The gap between the Catholic and Orthodox Church is not very wide." What do you think the Pope meant by this?

---

308 *Crossing the Threshold of Hope,* 148.
309 "Cardinal optimistic on Catholic-Orthodox talks," *The Catholic World Report,* May, 2007, 14.

Judaism

Introductory Comments

It seems to me that a question somewhat similar to the following cannot be uncommon among devout Jews today:

> We have been waiting well over 2,500 years for the Messiah. Christians believe the words of our prophets have been fulfilled. The Sanhedrin rejected the Messianic claims of the Nazarene forthwith, as does our *Talmud*. But now almost 2,000 years have passed since Jesus died on the cross. Where is our prophesied Messiah?

For Orthodox Jews,[310] the principal authoritative book is not the Hebrew Bible,[311] but the *Talmud*, a collection of Rabbinic statements in sixty-three books interpreting the *Torah*[312] and based on a tradition said to have originated with the God of Israel at Sinai at the time of Moses, but *unwritten until several centuries after Christ* [This, of course, would have required the precise oral transmission of the equivalent of more than 2,000 pages of text from generation to generation for about 1,700 years].

The first part of the *Talmud,* the *Mishna* ("instruction") is said not to have been written until more than 200 years after the time of Christ. The second part, the *Gemara* ("completion"), is of Babylonian and Palestinian origin. The Babylonian elements were not written until about six hundred years after Christ and are considered more authoritative. Important codifications of the Talmud were the *Mishneh Torah* by Moses Maimomedes (1135-1204);[313] the *Beyt Yosef* and its popular condensation the *Shulhan 'Arukh* by R. Yosef Karo in the late 1500s. Important twentieth century codifications are the *Mishnah Berurah* and the *Talmudic Encyclopedia*.[314]

The *Mishna* is fundamentally at odds with the teachings of Christ in

---

310 Excluding Ethiopian Jews, Karaite Jews and others for whom the Talmud does not supersede the Hebrew Bible.
311 "The Hebrew Bible includes the entire Old Testament [except] the seven deutero-canonical books, Tobias, Judith, Wisdom, Ecclesiasticus (Sirach), Baruch, I and II Maccabees, and the deuterocanonical portions of Esther (x, 4 to end) and Daniel (iii, 24-90; xiii; xiv)." Source: *Catholic Encyclopedia,* **www.newadvent.com**
312 The first five books of the Bible; the *Pentateuch.*
313 *The American Heritage Dictionary of the English Language, Fourth Edition, Copyright © 2006 by Houghton Mifflin Company.*
314 *Jewish History, Jewish Religion,* Israel Shahak, 51-52.

the New Testament (some *Mishna* teachings *egregiously* so) and with the Catholic and other Christian interpretation of many aspects of the Old Testament. At this writing, further information can be found at the Chabad-Lubavitch "Noah's Covenant" Web site.[315]

The *Mishna* carries forward a number of the criticisms of Christ's teaching by Pharisees recorded in the four Gospels of the New Testament, in which are found Jesus' responses to the charges directly made against him.

We read in the *Jewish Encyclopedia* that certain passages of the Talmud were considered "reprehensible from a Christian point of view." Condemnation and even confiscation and burning of the Talmud occurred under various Popes, individuals or religious orders acting under the authority of the papacy in 1264, 1415, 1553, 1559, 1565, 1593, and 1757.[316]

It seems to me that Catholics and other Christians who endeavor to enter into conversation with Orthodox Jews about religion may well become perplexed as follows:

> It would seem that we should hold in common *the preeminent work of Jewish history*, the Old Testament, as translated into the *Septuagint*,[317] more than one hundred Messianic prophecies of which Christ fulfilled. Why, instead, do our Jewish friends give priority to the *Talmud*?

> And why would they place more confidence in what is claimed to be a parallel but *conflicting* tradition (i.e., in conflict with the Old Testament) that remained *unwritten for about 1700 years,* until several centuries after the time of Christ?

> If both the written Old Testament and long-unwritten Talmud originated with Yahweh at Sinai at the time of Moses as claimed, when did they begin their ultimate sharp incompatibility regarding Messianic prophecy?

> At about the time of Christ, surely Gamaliel, Shammai, the Great Hillel and all the Sanhedrin would have been well aware of any unwritten tradition originating with Yahweh at Sinai at the time of Moses that was in conflict with the written Testament in Hebrew that had served as the basis for the Greek Septuagint translation.

---

315 www.noahide.com/yeshu.htm
316 www.jewishencyclopedia.com/view.jsp?artid=32&letter=T#149
317 The *Septuagint* is the Greek translation of the ancient Hebrew books of Scripture completed in the second/third century B.C. by about seventy of the most prestigious Hebrew scholars of that era.

But if these esteemed Rabbis knew of such a contrary unwritten tradition *that was of greater importance than the written Testament in Hebrew,* surely they would have used it instead of the Testament written in Hebrew. But where is the evidence that they set aside the written Testament?

Given this history, it is only with great resolve that our Orthodox Jewish brethren will be able to consider objectively the case for accepting Jesus as **Prophet, Messiah** and **Servant of Yahweh** – the fulfillment of the threefold hope of Sacred Scripture.

One Jewish woman who set out to learn about Christianity – to better *refute* it – was Rosalind Moss. What she learned led to her become Protestant and then Catholic. With Christine Franklin, she co-hosted the weekly TV program "Household of Faith" on EWTN and is now a well-known apologist on the staff of Catholic Answers.[318]

Marty Barrack, author of *Second Exodus,* is a convert from Judaism to Catholicism. He wrote the book, "so that a Jew in search of Christ would realize that in becoming Catholic he completes a journey he has already begun." His Web site is a valuable resource for information on this topic.[319]

———————————

Almost two thousand years ago, a child known as Jesus of Joseph was born in Bethlehem of Judea. There are reports of extraordinary events surrounding his birth (*Matthew*, chapters 1 and 2; *Luke*, chapters 1 and 2). In just the first two chapters of these Gospels Christians see the fulfillment of Psalm 72:10; Isaiah 9:5 and 60:5; Hosea 11:1; Jeremiah 31:15. [Based on the *Septuagint*, the Greek translation of the Old Testament by "The Seventy" Jewish scholars in the third century B.C. See later comments on this in comparison to the Palestinian Canon].

Another unusual event occurred in Jerusalem after Passover when Jesus was age 12. Luke reports that, unknown to Mary and Joseph, Jesus remained in the Temple with the teachers for three days, and that all who heard him were amazed at his answers and his understanding (Lk 2: 41-51). Luke does not tell us the names of the teachers, but at about that time the great Rabbi Hillel taught regularly in the Temple. Is it possible that Hillel was among those so impressed by the understand-ing of Jesus? Shammai too was a well-known rabbi then[320] and Gama-

———————————

318 **www.catholic.com/seminars/moss.asp**
319 **www.secondexodus.com**
320 *Y'shua,* 79.

liel may also have been among those who heard Jesus at that time. It was Gamaliel, who – after the death of Jesus – asked the Sanhedrin to let the apostles alone; if their activity was of human origin it would not long survive Christ's death; but if it were from God, they would be fighting God himself [Acts 5:33-39]. After that event in the Temple and his return with Mary and Joseph to Nazareth, we are told nothing more about Jesus until his thirtieth year.

Yochanan ben Zechariah

By the time Jesus began his public ministry at age thirty, many Jews acknowledged Yochanan ben Zechariah, "John the Baptist," as a true prophet. It was he who proclaimed "I am the voice of one crying in the wilderness, Make straight the way of the Lord" (Jn 1:23). Christians identify John as the Precursor of whom Isaiah spoke:

A voice cries: "In the wilderness prepare the way of the Lord, make straight in the desert a highway for our God!" (Isaiah 40:3).

Was Jesus, in fact, the one of whom it was prophesied:

But you, Bethlehem-Ephrathah, too small to be among the clans of Judah, from you shall come forth for me one who is to be ruler in Israel .... He shall stand firm and shepherd his flock by the strength of the Lord (Micah 5:1-3). He shall come to Zion a redeemer to those of Jacob who turn from sin, says the Lord (Isaiah 59:20).

Like a lamb led to the slaughter ... oppressed and condemned ... though he had done no wrong nor spoken any falsehood ... surrendered himself to death ... pierced for our offenses, crushed for our sins ... counted among the wicked ... And he shall take away the sins of many, and win pardon for their offenses (From Isaiah 53:1-12).

Lamb of God?

John the Baptist had no doubt that Jesus was the one who fulfilled these prophecies:

The next day he [John the Baptist] saw Jesus coming toward him, and said, "Behold, the Lamb of God, who takes away the sin of the world!" (Jn 1:29).

Was this Jesus the "Lamb of God?" Was he the long-awaited Messiah who would free the Jewish people from bondage? Because of the awesome power of his miracles, he was perceived by many to be their deliverer, and many of the people urged him to become their King. He said he had indeed come to deliver them from bondage; not from the bondage of rulers who oppressed them – but from the bondage of sin. His entire ministry was based on the Decalogue. He enhanced it only by his message of love, as in this example:

> [L]ove your enemies, pray for your persecutors …. This will prove that you are sons of your heavenly Father … (Mt 6:44-45).

Jesus affirmed three times by a voice from heaven

In the New Testament witnesses reported hearing a voice from heaven affirming Jesus. It happened after his baptism by John the Baptist: "And when Jesus was baptized, he went up immediately from the water, and behold, the heavens were opened and he saw the Spirit of God descending like a dove, and alighting on him; and lo, a voice from heaven, saying, *'This is my beloved Son, with whom I am well pleased.'*" (Mt 3:16-17).

The phenomenon is reported again at the Transfiguration: "[A] bright cloud overshadowed them and a voice from the cloud said, *'This is my beloved Son, with whom I am well pleased; listen to him.'*" (Mt 17:1-8). The third instance occurred in the Temple in Jerusalem after Jesus had raised Lazarus from the dead and after Jesus had ridden triumphantly into Jerusalem: In this case, it seems that The Father responds to the request of Jesus:

> "Father, glorify thy name." Then a voice came from heaven, "I have glorified it, and I will glorify it again." The crowd standing by heard it and said that it had thundered. Others said, "An angel has spoken to him." Jesus answered, "This voice has come for your sake, not for mine. Now is the judgment of this world, now shall the ruler of this world be cast out; and I, when I am lifted up from the earth, will draw all men to myself." He said this to show by what death he was to die (Jn 12:28-32).

Jesus considered a blasphemer

By that time, it appears that most of the Sanhedrin regarded Jesus as a blasphemer. But the New Testament indicates that at least two members of the Sanhedrin, Joseph of Arimathea and Nicodemus, had become his followers (Jn 19:38-39).

Did Jesus fulfill the words of David at his Crucifixion?

My God, my God, why hast thou forsaken me? (Ps 22,1; [21,1]).

My God, my God, why hast thou forsaken me? (Mt 27:46).

All who see me mock at me, they make mouths at me, they wag their heads ... (Ps 22:7).

And those who passed by derided him, wagging their heads and saying, "You who would destroy the temple and build it in three days, save yourself!" (Mt 27:39-40).

He committed his cause to the Lord; let him deliver him ... (Ps 22:8).

He trusts in God; let God deliver him now ... (Mt 27:43).

[T]hey have pierced my hands and feet – I can count all my bones ... they divide my garments among them, and for my raiment they cast lots (Ps 22:16-18).

When the soldiers had crucified Jesus they took his garments and made four parts, one for each soldier; also his tunic. But the tunic was without seam, woven from top to bottom; so they said to one another, "Let us not tear it, but cast lots for it to see whose it shall be" (Jn 19:23-24).

In Isaiah we read that there is one on whom the Lord "has laid ... the iniquity of us all":

But he was wounded for our transgressions, he was bruised for our iniquities; upon him was the chastisement that made us whole, and with his stripes we are healed. All we like sheep have gone astray; we have turned every one to his own way; and the Lord has laid on him the iniquity of us all (Is 53:5-6).

And in the *Letter to the Hebrews* (Heb 8:10) we find Jeremiah quoted *verbatim* in linking the Old Covenant to the New Covenant (Mt 26:26-30) established by Jesus at the Last Supper:

But this is the covenant which I will make with the house of Israel after those days, says he Lord: I will put my law within them, and I will write it upon their hearts; and I will be their God, and they shall be my people (Jer 31:33).

And, as noted above, the Rabbi Gamaliel addressed the Sanhedrin after the death of Jesus in defense of the accused Peter and the apostles.

In his book *Y'shua, The Jewish way to say Jesus,* Moishe Rosen examines many prophecies from Jewish Scripture that predict the coming of the Messiah, the one who would redeem the world from evil. His conclusions that Jesus alone fulfilled these prophecies seem most persuasive. Rosen's examination of those prophecies provides compelling reading for Jew and Gentile alike.

In the Gospels, Jesus had harsh words for those of the Sanhedrin who opposed him in his mission to take the Decalogue – given to Moses at Sinai – and inscribe it in the hearts of men (Jer 31:33, Heb 8:10, Rom 2:15).

Many in Israel rejected Jesus' message of love and forgiveness based on the Law of Moses while he lived. But how much more grievously is Jesus rejected when one like me – *a believer* – rejects him by committing a sin? But his is a message of forgiveness. He forgives when we ask for his forgiveness with true repentance in our hearts.

Was Jesus the "Word of God" prophesied by Isaiah?

"For as the rain and the snow come down from heaven, and return not thither but water the earth, making it bring forth and sprout, giving seed to the sower and bread to the eater, so shall my **word** be that goes forth from my mouth; it shall not return to me empty, but it shall accomplish that which I purpose, and prosper in the thing for which I sent it" (Is: 55:10-11).

"In the beginning was the **Word**, and the **Word** was with God, and the **Word** was God. He was in the beginning with God; all things were made through him ..." (Jn 1:1-3).

"Jesus answered them, 'Is it not written in your law, *I said, you are gods?*'"[321] If he called them gods to whom the **word** of God came (and scripture cannot be broken) do you say of him whom the Father consecrated and sent into the world, 'You are blaspheming,' because I said, 'I am the Son of God'? If I am not doing the works of my Father, then do not believe me; but if I do them, even though you do not believe me, believe the works, that you may know and understand that the Father is in me and I am in the Father" (Jn 10:34-38; emphasis added).

Words of Jewish historian Flavius Josephus

As noted in Step 3, Flavius Josephus – Pharisee, Jewish historian and near-contemporary of Jesus, documented the Crucifixion and Resurrection of Jesus in *The Jewish Antiquities.* According to histori-

---

[321] "I say, 'You are gods, sons of the Most High, all of you; nevertheless, you shall die like men, and fall like any prince.'" (Ps 82:6).

ans, he wrote that Jesus was "the Messiah," who, after crucifixion, "appeared to them live again at the third day as the divine prophets had foretold" (See full text under Step 3, "History Affirms the Biblical Jesus").

Although he is not accepted as the prophesied Messiah, there are a number of references to Jesus in works of Jewish history. So often today we read of someone who, years later, was found to have been wrongly convicted of a crime. In the religious and political turmoil of that time, is it possible that Jesus' claim to be the Messiah was not examined as thoroughly as it might have been by the Sanhedrin in the light of Scripture?

Was he really just the son of a carpenter, this worker of wonders? Or was he the prophesied Messiah – born in Bethlehem of Ephrathah to the virgin Miriam, fulfilling the prophesies of Micah 5:1-3 and Isaiah 7:14? (Rosen concludes that Isaiah could only have meant "virgin" when he used the Hebrew term "almah"). [322]

Did Jesus work his miracles through the power of Satan as some claimed? If so, why did he oppose Satan in his every word and deed? Or was he truly what he said he was – The Lamb of God, the Messiah who came to redeem us all, Jew and Gentile alike, through the Jews, God's chosen people?

In Genesis, *God* in Hebrew is not *Eloah,* the masculine singular form, but *Elohim,* the masculine *plural.* For example, "In the beginning God [*Elohim*] created the heavens and the earth" (Gen 1:1).

Later, instead of "I will make man in my image," we read "Let *us* make man in *our* image ..." (Gen 1:26). With plurality of Divine Persons in the One God implied, the dialogue between Abraham and the Lord intermingled with Abraham's dialogue with the three mysterious visitors (Gen 18:1-33) may be seen as prefiguring the God of Three Persons of which Jesus speaks in Mt 28:19: "baptizing them in the name of the *Father,* and of the *Son* and of the *Holy Spirit* ...."

And Jesus is unequivocal in his public claim to be the Messiah (e.g., Jn 4:25-26) who, as prophesied, "like a lamb that is led to the slaughter ... was wounded for our transgressions ... numbered with the transgressors ... cut off from the land of the living ... yet he bore the sins of many, and made intercession for the transgressors" (Is 53:4-12). And, in Zechariah; "[T]he inhabitants of Jerusalem ... when they look on him whom they have pierced, they shall mourn for him .... On that day there shall be a fountain opened for the house of David and the

---

322 *Y'shua,* 17.

inhabitants of Jerusalem to cleanse them from sin and uncleanness" (Zech12: 10-14, 13:1).

Jesus said "[B]efore Abraham was, *I am*" (Jn 8:57-58), and "I and the Father are one" (Jn 10:30). But Jesus also said "When you have lifted up the Son of man, then you will know that I am he, and that I do nothing on my own authority but speak thus as the Father taught me" (Jn 8:28). And it was the Father who gave him authority to judge each of us after our death (Jn 5:22-23).

During his agony in the garden of Gethsemane the night before his crucifixion he prayed: "My Father, if it be possible, let this cup pass from me; nevertheless, not as I will, but as thou wilt" (Mt 26:39). On the Cross he exclaimed, "My God, my God, why hast thou forsaken me?" (Mt 27:46, Ps 22:1[21:1]). And, as he was about to die, he said, "Father, into thy hands I commit my spirit!" (Lk 23:46).

The Catholic Church teaches that, as the second person of the Blessed Trinity, Jesus is equal in divinity to the Father, even though full understanding of what this means is beyond human comprehension – a mystery. But Gospel passages such as the above in which Jesus prayed to the Father, was given authority by the Father, and committed his spirit to the Father, are no less firmly held as Church doctrine.

Of particular interest to the Jewish reader may be the words Jesus addressed to Jews in Solomon's Portico who were about to stone him after he said, "I and the Father are one." (Jn 10:30). Jesus called their attention to Psalm 82:6: "You are gods, sons of the Most High, all of you ...." And Jesus continued:

> If I am not doing the works of my Father, then do not believe me; but if I do them, even though you do not believe me, believe the works, that you may know and understand that the Father is in me and I am in the Father (Jn 10:37-38).

In his book *Y'shua,* Moishe Rosen lists more than 150 Old Testament prophecies fulfilled by Jesus.[323] Some maintain that Isaiah Chapter 53, "the Suffering Servant," was never considered Messianic prophecy. Rosen points out, however, that in the *Targum of Jonathan* it *was,* at least in part, regarded as Messianic prophecy.[324] In Isaiah 53 alone (Septuagint) we find at least fifteen prophetic verses fulfilled by Christ.[325]

---

323 *Y'shua,* 141.
324 A *targum* is an Aramaic translation of all or parts of the Hebrew Bible (the *Tanakh*).
325 Ibid., 143.

Does it not seem to require quite a stretch of symbolic abstraction to hold that Israel or any *nation,* or *person* other than Jesus, fulfills such prophecies? On the other hand, to see how Jesus fulfills those prophecies, one need only read the New Testament, supported in non-biblical history by the Early Church Fathers.

One of the Internet resources mentioned earlier, *Dr. Scott Hahn Links Page,* provides an excellent overview of the Old Testament and its relevance to the New Testament: *One Holy Tribe; One Holy kingdom; One Holy Nation* are just three talks from Dr. Hahn's highly informative series on Salvation History. His article in *This Rock* magazine, "The Hunt for the Fourth Cup," provides a fascinating parallel between the four cups of the Jewish Passover and the (incomplete) Passover meal – the "Last Supper" – that Jesus had with his apostles the night before he died on the cross.[326] These topics are also included in Dr. Hahn's book *A Father who keeps His Promises – God's Covenant Love in Scripture.*

The Septuagint – comparisons with the Palestinian Canon

As earlier noted, the *Septuagint* is the Greek translation of the Old Testament by "the seventy" Jewish scholars in the second or third century before Christ. It had stood the test of time, having been in use for more than 200 years before the time of Christ. It seems that the first Christians were Palestinian Jews whose native language was Aramaic (similar to Hebrew) and, in general, they would have used the Hebrew Scriptures. Jews who read Greek may also have used the Septuagint. When non-Jewish Greeks in great numbers became interested in what Paul, Silas, Barnabas and others were teaching it would have been the Septuagint they studied.

What were they looking for? Surely, after hearing the claims of Paul that Jesus was the long-awaited Messiah, it would have been the Messianic prophecies they examined most closely; well over one hundred of them, according to Christian belief. Paul was phenomenally successful in drawing people into the Church, of course, and the Septuagint played an important part in those conversions. As earlier noted, in the days of Christ the Septuagint presented a problem for the Jewish leaders who saw more and more of their number converting to Christianity. The destruction of the Temple in A.D. 70 virtually eliminated the priestly class in Jerusalem, but a remnant – primarily Pharisees – survived and:

---

326 **www.catholic.com/thisrock/1991/9109fea1.asp**

Toward the end of the first century A.D. at Jamnia, they decided that their Bible consisted only of books written up to the time of Ezra, when prophecy was deemed to have ceased; and this criterion, though not applied uniformly, excluded the books of more recent origin which were on the whole less in accord with the Pharisaic outlook ... they also not long afterward condemned the Greek Septuagint translation as inaccurate.[327]

The Greek Septuagint translation was produced by prestigious Jewish Scripture Scholars who studied their Bible intensely and could surely quote much if not all of it from memory. With this in mind, it seems to me that the Jewish reader of today might ask this question regarding the Septuagint:

> *What is the probability that not just one or two, but about seventy of the best Jewish Scripture scholars of that era produced a Bible that was inaccurate and deserving of condemnation?*

And if "The Seventy" were in error on the points changed at Jamnia about 300 years later, *why did their equally distinguished successors for almost three centuries – including Gamaliel, Shammai, the great Hillel and the entire Sanhedrin during the time of Christ – fail to call attention to these errors?*

It seems to me that reflection on such historical incongruities might shed important light on Y'shua the Nazarene – the one so much of the world now accepts as the Messiah.

Discussion Questions

1. As noted, for Orthodox Jews the principal authoritative book is not the Hebrew Bible but the *Talmud*. To what extent do you think emphasis on the Talmud rather than the Hebrew Bible complicates dialogue between Orthodox Jews and Catholics? To what extent do you think it might complicate interreligious dialogue between Orthodox Jews and Muslims?

2. Events recorded in the first two chapters of *Matthew* and *Luke* represent the fulfillment of what Old Testament prophecies?

3. What Rabbi asked the Sanhedrin not to persecute the apostles after the death of Jesus? What reason did he give?

4. What did John the Baptist mean when he said, "Make straight

---

327 *The Holy Bible*; RSV Catholic Edition, Ignatius, vii.

the way of the Lord"? John was then echoing the words of a prophet who lived about 700 years earlier. What was his name?

5. The prophet Mica also lived about 700 years before Christ. Where did he say would be born "one who is to be ruler in Israel ...," one who "shall stand firm and shepherd his flock by the strength of the Lord"?

6. What prophet wrote, "Led like a lamb to the slaughter ... surrendered himself to death ... he shall take away the sins of many and win pardon for their offences"?

7. Seeing Jesus approaching, why did John the Baptist say, "Behold the Lamb of God ..."?

8. Matthew and John, apostle-eyewitnesses to the ministry of Jesus, record a total of three occasions on which a voice from heaven affirmed Jesus and his ministry. What were those occasions and why were they important?

9. What two members of the Sanhedrin became followers of Jesus? How do you think the other members of the Sanhedrin regarded them after this became known?

10. Consider the parallels between the Messianic prophecies of David and Isaiah, written hundreds of years earlier, and the Crucifixion accounts of *Matthew* and *John*. After the death of Jesus, how do you think Annas, Caiaphas and others who opposed Jesus regarded the Crucifixion in light these and other Messianic prophecies?

11. Why do you think the author of *Hebrews,* in chapter 8, verse 10, quoted Jeremiah 31:33?

12. At the time of Christ, there was an expectation of a powerful king in the line of David who would deliverer the Jews from their earthly oppressors (e.g., Jeremiah 23:1-6). Is it possible that Annas, Caiaphas and others *chose* not to consider the other equally well-documented prophecies of the Messiah as a "suffering servant"; a sacrificial "Lamb of God who takes away the sins of the world?"

13. What is the significance of the word *elohim* rather than *eloah* in Genesis and elsewhere in the Old Testament?

14. In what sense are we made in God's image?

15. In responding to the Jews who questioned him, Jesus said, "Before Abraham was, I AM" and "I and the Father are one." What meaning would these statements have had to his listeners? How did they react upon hearing them?

16. On the Cross Jesus exclaimed (in his native Aramaic), "My God, my God, why hast thou forsaken me?" Where in the Old Testament and Hebrew Bible do we find these words?

17. What is the *Septuagint* and why was it important in the early Church?

18. What occurred in Jamnia toward the end of the first century, A.D.? What effect do you think this event had on the spread of Christianity?

Hinduism

Hinduism differs from most religions in that its founder is unknown. It traces its origin to the combination, in about 1500 B.C., of the religion of the Aryans and the various religions of India of that time. The word *Hindu* is said to be of Persian origin meaning the *Indus,* the river, although the term *Hinduism,* designating the religion, did not come into use until the early nineteenth century.

At this writing more than a third of a million Web sites appear in my browser in response to the entry "Hinduism." Among the most popular are "The Hindu Universe – Hindu Resource Center"[328] *and* "The Directory of Hindu Resources Online," a public service of Himalayan Academy, publishers of *Hinduism Today* Magazine.[329]

The introductory paragraph of the latter Web site answers the question, "Who is a Hindu?" with the following definition by B. G. Tilak:

> Acceptance of the Vedas with reverence; recognition of the fact that the means or ways to salvation are diverse; and the realization of the truth that the number of gods to be worshiped is large, that indeed is the distinguishing feature of the Hindu religion."

On July 2, 1995, India's Supreme Court referred to the above as an "adequate and satisfactory formula."[330] For a Catholic view of Hinduism see *The Catholic Encyclopedia.*[331]

In his introduction to *The Bhagavad Gita,* [Published by Penguin] Juan Mascaro notes the great variety of Sanskrit literature, including the *Vedas*, the *Upanishads*, the *Bhagavad Gita,* the *Mahabharata* and more. But Mascaro points out that this literature is filled with a yearning for spiritual vision. He then calls our attention to the *Gayatri,* a prayer from the *Vedas,* quoted below from another source, which Hindus and those practicing its antecedent religions, in vast numbers, have prayed each morning for more than three millennia:

Om Bhur Buvaha Suvaha
Thath Savithur Varenyam
Bhargo Devasya Dheemahi
Dhiyo Yonaha Prachodayath

---

328 **www.hindunet.org**
329 **www.hindu.org.**
330 **www.hinduismtoday.com/archives/2001/3-4/24_from_the_vedas.shtml**
331 **www.newadvent.org/cathen/07358b.htm** Also see **www.ourladyswarrors.org/ dissent/defbrahm.htm**

> *We contemplate the glory of Light illuminating the three
> worlds: gross, subtle, and causal.
> I am that vivifying power, love, radiant illumination, and divine
> grace of universal intelligence.
> We pray for the divine light to illumine our minds.*[332]

Mascaro tells us that the one who wrote these words so long ago was looking toward the future, searching for enlightenment and truth. He adds that this search for light and truth characterizes India to this day. About 1,000 years after the unknown poet wrote the above words, Jesus said:

> *I have come as light into the world …* (Jn 12:46).

When Jesus said those words he was speaking to the Indian people, then and now. He is the light of the entire world, of course. But, although they call God by other names, surely Jesus has a special place in his heart for the people of the Indian subcontinent who pray so fervently using the *Rig Veda* (e.g., II. 28 1-9) and other Vedic writings.

In Christ, the light so long sought by the fervent, prayerful people of India and others who practiced Hinduism and its antecedent religions had come. He came as a flesh-and-blood person and, unique in all of history, *Jesus Christ ALONE (a) proved by his works that he spoke with the authority of the Creator; (b) acknowledged that he was God and; (c) arose from death.*

Because Jesus willed it the blind saw, the lame walked, dead persons came to life. And Jesus himself arose from death on the third day. And Jesus fulfilled more than one hundred prophecies of the Old Testament.

If anyone comparable to Jesus had ever lived among the Indian peoples his miracles and teachings would surely have been passed down by word of mouth through the ages of antiquity. But, about such a flesh-and-blood person, ancient Sanskrit literature is silent.

And the Light of the World told his apostles to go and make disciples of all nations, baptizing them in the name of the Father, the Son and the Holy Spirit. He said "Teach them all I have commanded you." But what was it that Jesus commanded?

When the rich young man asked what he must do to gain eternal salvation, Jesus replied "Keep the commandments." In the *Catechism,*

---

332 Source: International Sai Organization, **www.sathyasai.org/devotion/prayers/ gayatri.html**

the Church explains the meaning of this verse in the context of the sacrificial death of Jesus for our sins – without which no one could have been saved – our need to repent of our sins, and related teachings.

Of particular interest to the Hindu is the first Commandment, "I am the Lord your God, who brought you out of the land of Egypt, out of the house of bondage. You shall have no other gods before me" (Ex 20:2-3, Deut 5:6-7). Jesus taught that there are three persons in the one God: Father, Son, and Holy Spirit (Mt 28:19). Jesus also said "no one comes to the Father, but by me" (Jn 14:6).

Today many Hindus accept Christ insofar as his benevolent teachings are concerned. However, Hinduism rejects the fullness of the teaching of Jesus as recorded in the New Testament and rejects the Church he founded.

But is it not prudent, in light of our mortality, for each of us to ask in regard to our spirituality: *Who am I following and why? What manifestations did he (she) exhibit to indicate that he spoke with the authority of the Creator and will call me to account for my life after I take my last breath on earth?*

As noted above, no one knows the ancient founder(s) of what is now known as Hinduism, including the origin of belief in reincarnation, which, of course, is incompatible with Catholic teaching that each person lives but once and after death is immediately judged by Christ (i.e., the *Particular Judgment,* to be followed by the *General Judgment* when Christ returns in glory).

For Christ, however, as outlined in Step 3, there is sound historical evidence that he acknowledged that he was God, uniquely manifested the awesome authority of the Creator and said that no one comes to the Father but through him.

Discussion Questions

1. B. G. Tilak's definition of Hinduism includes: "the realization of the truth that the number of gods to be worshiped is large …." Of what importance is this fact in interfaith dialogue?

2. Consider the *Gayatri*. Although the author is unknown, what does it tell us about the ancient predecessors of Hindus and the Hindus of today?

3. Jesus said "I have come as light into the world." Why should these words be of particular interest to those of the Hindu religion?

4. It is not known with whom the *Rig Veda*, the *Bhagavad Gita* and other ancient Vedic writings originated. However, ancient Sanskrit literature provides no historical indication of any flesh-and-blood Savior and Redeemer who manifested supernatural power and authority as Jesus did. If you were asked to organize a Hindu-Catholic interfaith dialogue, would you include in-depth discussion of these differences in belief in the agenda? Why? Why not?

5. Why is the first Commandment of special relevance in regard to Hindus and others who have many gods?

Buddhism

In "The Karma of the Gospel," an article in the March 27, 2000 issue of *Newsweek* magazine, the Dalai Lama indicated that, in his view, Christ is either a being who has been fully enlightened, or a *bodhisattva* whose spiritual realization is quite high. [333] The Dalai Lama goes on to note the similarities he sees between Buddhism and Christianity.

It would seem commendable to call attention to such similarities; many books have been written which do so. However, as important as it may be for us to understand the similarities between Buddhism and Christianity, it is at least as important to understand the fundamental differences.

Buddhism has been described as an agnostic reformation of Hinduism. It shares with Hinduism a belief in reincarnation – transmigration of the soul – but Buddhism taught that the right-living believer could reach *Nirvana* with fewer reincarnations than is required in the Hindu religion.

Buddhism originated with Prince Siddhartha Gautama who was born in what is now Nepal about 560 years before Christ. His father was a feudal lord or "king," one of many in that part of the world at that time, and Gautama grew up in luxury. At age 16 he married Yasodhara, a princess from the region. They had a son they named Rahula. His father succeeded in shielding the young Gautama from a full awareness of sickness, death and other negative aspects of life. However, in his mid-twenties, Siddhartha became aware of such difficulties and was deeply troubled by them.

In his 29th year, Gautama left his wife and child in what has become known as his "Great Going Forth"; dressed in the clothes of a peasant, with shaved head he entered the forest in search of enlightenment. After about six years of searching, including time spent with Hindu masters, Prince Siddhartha's meditations became deeper and deeper, finally, it is said, penetrating the secrets of the universe. Thus he experienced the "Great Awakening." His followers believe that his being was transformed in the process and he emerged the Buddha, which, in Sanskrit, means "the awakened one."

After preaching his message all over India for about 45 years, the Buddha died of dysentery in 483 B.C. It is said that Buddha himself left nothing of his teachings in writing and that almost 150 years passed

---

333 A *bodhisattva* is one who, in order to save others, foregoes *Nirvana*.

before the first written records. By then partisan schools had come into existence, some of which wanted to emphasize Buddha's break with Hinduism while others wished to minimize it.[334]

These key points emerge from a brief overview of Buddhism:

(a)   Through the Aryan invasions and trade routes of the time, Buddha may have known something about the beliefs of the Jews and possibly even their expectation of a Messiah. But he died about five centuries before Christ.

(b)   Through the ages Buddha has been portrayed lovingly, but in a legendary manner, by his authoritative spokespersons, according to religious historian Huston Smith. Buddhist apologists do not claim that Buddha performed miracles. Jesus performed many.

(c)   After teaching for about 45 years, Buddha died. I found no claim that he rose from death. There are strongly supported claims that Jesus rose from death after his Crucifixion and entombment.

(d)   Buddha taught that there is no such entity as a personal God, but that there is an impersonal "Godhead"; something Unborn, not formed or created.[335] In contrast, Jesus spoke of a triune personal God of Mercy and Justice – Father, Son and Holy Spirit – who loves all mankind without limit but who, according to the Bible, requires repentance for all *mortal* sins before death as a condition for eternal salvation.

(e)   Buddha believed in an abstract kind of *causality* from one life to the next. But he denied the existence of the *soul* as Christians would later come to understand that term, and he denied that any spiritual equivalent of *self* survives after death. Jesus, in contrast, taught that each human being has an immortal soul which Jesus himself judges immediately after death. No soul "goes 'round" more than once.

Born about 563 B.C., Buddha may have been aware of the Old Testament writings available in his time, as noted above. But suppose Buddha had been born during the time of Christ and that his six-year search for Truth had brought him not only to the Hindu masters and the ascetics, but also to the Holy Land during the time of Jesus. What would he think of the Sermon on the Mount and the other teachings and

---

334 *The World's Religions,* 112.
335 *The World's Religions,* 114.

miracles of the one who said he was the *Way,* the *Truth* and the *Life* (Jn 14:6)? Surely his heart would have been touched by the parable of the Good Samaritan (Lk 10:25-37) and the love Jesus showed for the poor and disadvantaged.

Suppose, instead of the rich young man, it was Prince Siddhartha who approached Jesus and said: "Teacher, what good deed must I do, to have eternal life?" (Mt 19:16). To the rich young man, Jesus replied, "If you would enter life, keep the commandments." And Jesus added, "If you would be perfect, go, sell what you possess and give to the poor, and you will have treasure in heaven; and come, follow me" (Mt 19:21).

Prince Siddhartha had already given up all he had, not unlike Jesus had done. When Jesus said, "Follow me" would he have resisted? I believe Prince Siddhartha would have accepted the invitation of Jesus. I know this is just speculation. But it seems to me that Prince Siddhartha – having already made such great sacrifices in search of Truth – might well have become an exemplary follower of Jesus.

If today Buddha could send us a message from the hereafter, would he urge us to follow the teachings he formulated never having known Christ? Or, now that he knows that Jesus is the Second Person of the Blessed Trinity, would he exhort us to waste no time in embracing the teachings of Jesus and the Church he founded?

Many have called our attention to the common ground between Buddhism and Christianity. But all that has been written and said about these two faiths comes down to this:

> *Do we have a "soul," a spiritual self, which, after we live only one life on earth, is judged at death and, ultimately, rewarded in heaven or punished in hell for eternity?*

The answer of Buddha was: **No**
The answer of Jesus was: **Yes**

We can follow Buddha or we can follow Jesus. To follow one is to reject the other. Of the two, only Jesus, through his teachings and his miracles – in particular his power over death – gave evidence that he spoke with the authority of the Almighty Creator and acknowledged that he was God. As great as he was, no such claims are attributed to Buddha. Is it not prudent, then, for the Buddhist to look more closely at the teachings of Jesus and the Church he founded?

Discussion Questions

1. Did Buddha believe in a personal God? Did he believe in the soul as a spiritual equivalent of self that survives after death?

2. Do the authoritative spokespersons for Buddhism claim that Buddha rose from death or was otherwise comparable to Jesus in manifesting the supernatural power and authority of the Creator?

3. The author speculates that if, 600 years later, Buddha could have met Jesus as did the rich young man, Buddha might have become an exemplary follower of Jesus. Do you agree or disagree? Why?

4. As with the other non-Christian founders of a religion, the author calls the reader to decide whom it is more prudent to follow – Buddha or Jesus. What is your opinion?

Islam

Introductory Comments

On September 10, 2001 the World Trade Center towers were standing tall and the Pentagon was intact. The following day the towers were brought down and the Pentagon was burning, with great loss of innocent lives.

President George W. Bush immediately launched the "War against Terrorism;" a war not against Islam, but against the *militant Islamic groups* seen as responsible for the carnage.

Within Islam as well, international terrorism has been condemned. Although they saw Palestine as a separate case, **The Organization of Islamic Conferences declared, "We unequivocally condemn acts of international terrorism in all its forms and manifestations ..."** (#7; Kuala Lumpur, 1-3 April, 2002).[336]

The Indonesia-based Liberal Islam Network promotes inter-religious brotherhood, including non-discrimination on the basis of religion, ethnicity, social status, political status and gender.[337] Of special interest in regard to world peace is "The Theological Basis of Inter-Religious Brotherhood," an on-line article by Budhy Munawar-Rachman. The Republic of Indonesia has a Muslim population of about 200 million; more Muslims than any other country in the world.

There are more than seventy separate, independent Islamic religious organizations worldwide.

Are earliest copies of the Koran "harmonious with the New Testament?"

The July 28, 2003 issue of *Newsweek* was banned in Pakistan because it included a brief article about a book by "Christoph Luxenberg," a pseudonym, which was to be published in English.

The book, *Die syro-aramaeische Lesart des Koran (The Syro-Aramaic Reading of the Koran)*, was published in German in 2000 by Das Arabische Buch. An extensive scholarly review in English of *Die syro-aramaeische Lesart des Koran* by Robert R. Phenix, Jr. and Cornelia B. Horn of the University of St. Thomas, St. Paul, Minnesota, was published in the scholarly journal *Hugoye: Journal of Syriac*

---

336 **www.oic-oci.org**.
337 **www.islamlib.com**

Studies; Vol. 6, no. 1 (2003). At this writing the review may be read at the Beth Mardutho / Hugoye Web site.[338]

Many other authors have offered novel interpretations of the Koran. Variant copies of it exist today – even though Uthman, the third Caliph (A.D. 644-656), i.e., the third successor to Muhammad, ordered the destruction of all other copies after having a standardized copy made. In his commentary, "The Uthmanic Recension of the Qur'an," John Gilchrist noted that Uthman ordered the destruction of manuscripts of the entire Koran which had been transcribed by those close to Muhammad himself. Gilchrist asks why Uthman would have done this to those revered copies of what Muslims believed was the very word of God if Uthman's recension did not differ substantially from the copies he destroyed.[339]

In their review of Luxenberg's book, Phenix and Horn state that it is unique in the history of exegetical commentary on the Qur'an and that it brings to a "critical turn" exegesis of the Qur'an. They conclude that "Scholars of the first rank" must now set aside long-held assumptions about the Qur'an; from now on they will find it essential to take Luxenberg's philology-based conclusions into account.

According to Luxenberg, Arabic – long considered the original language of the written Koran – was not a developed written language during the lifetime of Muhammad. Instead, Syro-Aramaic or Syriac, a language similar to Aramaic, was the primary means of written communication in that part of the world at that time. Phenix and Horn state that, according to Luxenberg's analysis, the Koran was originally

> *[a]* ***call to participate in the Divine Liturgy, the eucharistic commemoration*** *.... If Luxenberg's analysis is even in broad outline correct, the content of the Qur'an was substantially different at the time of Muhammad and Uthman's redaction played a part in the misreading of key passages. Were these misreadings intentional or not?* ***The misreadings in general alter the Qur'an from a book that is more or less harmonious with the New Testament and Syriac Christian liturgy and literature to one that is distinct, of independent origin***[340] (Emphasis added).

---

338 **http://bethmardutho.cua.edu/hugoye** > Volume Index > Volume 6 Number 1 > Book Reviews, Christoph Luxenberg.
339 **http://answering-islam.org.uk/Gilchrist/Jam/chap2.html**
340 **http://bethmardutho.cua.edu/hugoye** > Volume Index > Volume 6 Number 1 > Book Reviews; Christoph Luxenberg.

Phenix and Horn also note in their review Luxenberg's conclusion that, *instead of "dark, wide-eyed (maidens)" believed to await Muslim males in heaven, the more precise translation of the Koran would be: "[W]hite grapes"* (or *"white raisins" according to other scholars) are among the fruits of heaven*.

In his enlightening article, "What is the Koran?" Toby Lester tells of the finding in Yemen in 1972 of very early manuscripts during restoration of The Grand Mosque of Sanaa. Workers stuffed them into about twenty potato sacks. Qadhi Isma'il al-Akwa', who was at that time president of the Yemeni Antiquities Authority, realized their importance. In 1979, through a visiting German scholar, arrangements were made for a restoration project financed by the German government. Photographs of those Koranic manuscripts were the central focus of these studies. Lester was executive editor of Atlantic Unbound, the *Atlantic Monthly* Web site.[341] The article was published in the *Atlantic Monthly;* January 1998; Volume 283, No. 1; pp. 43-56.

This subject was also addressed by Alexander Steele in "Scholars Scrutinize the Koran's Origin," an informative article that appeared in the *New York Times* and the *International Herald Tribune* March 4, 2002.[342]

Steele notes Luxenberg's view that for centuries the Koran, having been mistranslated, was misread. The article indicates that for about the past quarter century scholars have been doing philological studies of the earliest known manuscripts of the Koran which were written without diacritical marks or vowels – essential for clear translation – but which were not yet used in the language of The Koran.

Luxenberg and other such scholars base their clarifications on many factors, including the predominant written language of the region at that time and careful study of the context of the Koran. Steele begins his article by noting that Muslims regard the Koran as the actual word of God spoken to Muhammad through the Angel Gabriel and, as stated at the outset of the first sura, The Cow, "This book is not to be doubted."

In the Islamic world, death threats have been made, and carried out, against some scholars and others accused of doubting the Koran. But is Luxenberg really *doubting* the Koran? Is he not actually attempting to remove any doubt about the Koran? Here is Luxenberg's explanation, in part, as he gave it to interviewer Christoph Burgmer:

---

341 www.theatlantic.com/issues/99jan/koran.htm
342 www.corkscrew-balloon.com/02/03/1bkk/04b.html

The existence of the Koran is a historical fact. It is now a question of seeing this historical fact in its historical context, which also means seeing it historically and subjecting the text to critical examination from that point of view. But critically does not mean that I want to disparage the Koran. I only want to understand it correctly on the basis of historio-linguistic findings. What people make of my interpretation is beyond my influence. That depends entirely on Muslim theologians. In many passages the Koran is immutable, and thus it is also the word of God. I never claim that it is not the word of God. Nevertheless, one must reach the conclusion that in the course of history this word of God was changed – particularly through misreadings and the wrongly-placed diacritic signs. So it is not the word of God itself that was changed; it was erroneously interpreted by human beings.[343]

Luxenberg points to what for Muslims is unthinkable – that the Koran today is substantially different from the Koran as it was dictated by Muhammad. Surely every Muslim who learns of the conclusions of *The Syro-Aramaic Reading of the Koran* and the high scholarly praise it has earned will not rest until Muslim philologists skilled in Syriac investigate the claims of Luxenberg and resolve the matter in a manner satisfactory to the religious leaders of Islam. As noted below, a team of Islamic scholars is conducting their own independent study of the Yemeni manuscripts.

Muslim scholars seek Koran as uttered by Muhammad

At least one additional effort is under way to develop a reading of the Koran that more closely approximates that uttered by Muhammad, this one by Muslim scholars. That group is led by Moncef ben Abdeljelil, Professor of Literature and Human Science at Sousse University in Tunis. As reported by Jim Quilty in 2003, Abdeljelil, his colleagues and a number of other scholars, including one representing Luxenberg's views, attended a conference in Beirut on that subject.

Luxenberg's thesis is "quite separate" from the critical study of the Koran as undertaken by Abdeljelil and his Tunisian group. However, although the Tunisians have expressed skepticism in regard to what Luxenberg has concluded, "they support his method." Quilty quotes Abdeljelil as follows:

---

343 "The Koran as Philological Quarry; A Conversation with Christoph Luxenberg," Christoph Burgmer, "Fikrun wa Fann/Art & Thought" No. 80, May, 2005, 29-36, **www.goethe.de/ges/rel/prj/ffs/ori/en1184094.htm**

"As an approach we [the Tunisians] are not bothered by what Luxenberg has proposed, nor with his premise that there are languages that had an impact upon Arabic. In fact we would go so far as to encourage it."

Abdeljelil is in agreement with Luxenberg and others that when Uthman, the third Caliph, ordered the definitive recension of the Koran, diacritical marks and short vowels – essential for precise understanding – were not yet in use in Arabic and, two centuries after the death of Muhammad, "the Aramaic loan words were misread as Arabic." Abdeljelil and his group use textual criticism, the method widely used to study the bible and, as noted by Quilty, "[T]he impact of the critical edition will be profound." He then quotes Abdeljelil as follows:

In the Sana'a [Yemeni] parchments we found a radically different method of transcription, a different way of reading the Koran. It could change some sharp interpretations of the text, and will lead to another way of thinking about the Koran.[344]

Sunni, Shiite and other Islamic spiritual leaders surely took notice in 2000 when *The Syro-Aramaic reading of the Koran* was published in German and received high scholarly praise. But imagine their concern upon learning that a group of *Muslim* Koranic scholars not only agreed with Luxenberg's method but, using the same Yemeni parchments and method, began a translation of the Koran that, as noted above, "*will lead to another way of thinking about the Koran.*"

I would ask that every reader pray for these Islamic spiritual leaders as each makes his courageous decision regarding this Muslim retranslation effort. I say courageous because *any* decision will be criticized. Leaders who approve of the new translation effort will be called betrayers of Allah, as well as of The Prophet and the traditional Koran. Leaders who are silent or oppose the retranslation will be criticized by Muslims who believe that these scholars are doing Allah's will in providing a retranslation that may well be "*more or less harmonious with the New Testament and Syriac Christian liturgy and literature*" (as was said of Luxenberg's translation by Phenix and Horn), and could result in peace among nations far surpassing any the world has known.

The observations in the remainder of this section are based on the Koran as currently accepted by Muslims.

---

344 "Giving the Koran a history: Holy Book under scrutiny; Critical readings of the Muslim scripture offer alternative interpretations of well-known passages," Jim Quilty, The Daily Star - Lebanon Wire, July 12, 2003. **www.lebanonwire.com/0307/ 03071213DS.asp**

Islam came into existence about 600 years after Christ. It came in the form of messages attributed to Allah, the Almighty Creator, and, it is claimed, given by the angel Gabriel to Muhammad, who dictated them to others. The compilation of these messages is known as the *Koran* or *Qur'an*. Those who practice the religion of Islam are known as Muslims, which means "submitters" to the will of Allah.

At a glance, the Koran may seem compatible with the Bible. For example, the Koran indicates that *Allah sent Jesus and gave him the Gospel in which there is light and guidance* (sura 5:46);[345] that Jesus was an upright man (6:85); that Satan is a deceiver, cursed by God, who leads believers to hell (4:117-121); that believers, Jews, Sabaens and Christians – whoever believes in God and the Last Day and does what is right – shall have nothing to fear or regret (5:69); the Koran confirms the Scriptures and explains them fully (10:37); that Muslims are to forgive the People of the Book (Christians and Jews) who attempt to convert them (2:109); let those who follow the Gospel judge according to what God has revealed therein (5:47).[346]

But the Koran also teaches emphatically that: (a) Jesus was *not* God and *not* the Son of God (4:171), (b) Jesus was just one of many prophets leading up to Muhammad, *the* Prophet; (4:163, 2:136) and; (c) Jesus was *not* Crucified but simply taken back to heaven by Allah (4:157-159). The Koran also states that wine is one of Satan's abominations (5:90) [wine became the Blood of Christ when consecrated by Jesus at the Last Supper (Mt 26-29) and does so today when consecrated by the priest at Mass].

More than just denying the divinity of Jesus, the Koran takes on an ominous tone in regard to Christians who, in worshiping Jesus as God, greatly offend Allah. The Koran defines as among the "unbelievers" those who worship the Messiah, who was born of Mary (Isa ibn Maryam) (5:16).

And Allah calls on Muslims to take up arms against "the unbelievers" until they shall cease their idolatry and Islam shall be triumphant (8:40, 9:73). After the four sacred months are over, Muslims are to slay idolaters wherever they are found; they are to be taken into custody; brought under siege; ambushed. Those who repent, begin to pray and

---

345 Except as noted, all are based on *The Koran*, translated by N.J. Dawood. Numbers of all verses are approximate.

346 **http://etext.lib.virginia.edu/koran.html** Verses tolerant of non-Muslims are generally attributed to Muhammad's Meccan (early) period. Such verses are often considered *abrogated*, i.e., suppressed and superseded by less tolerant verses of Muhammad's Medinan (later) period.

pay the alms levy (*jizya*) may be released (9:5). To unbelievers, those who follow Muhammad are ruthless, but among themselves they show mercy (48:29).

However, in regard to such aggression and violence, it seems that some Muslim apologists believe that Allah was referring only to certain Christians of history with whom the Muslims were then at war – not to all Christians for then on. In any case, Christians reading the Koran are struck by such statements in comparison to those of Jesus who, stating that he said and did nothing that was not the will of the Father, said "Love your enemies and pray for those who persecute you ..." (Mt 5:44).

In the *Hadith* (sayings Muslims believe originated with Muhammad himself), we read that at the time of the Resurrection a multitude will seek, in the following sequence, an Intercessor: Adam, Abraham, Moses, Jesus and Muhammad. Each in turn, *including Jesus,* will say they themselves are unworthy and refer the multitude to the next person. Jesus, declaring his unworthiness, refers the multitude to Muhammad, who humbly but successfully accepts the role of Intercessor [*Volume 9, Book 93, Number 601*].[347]

Upon reading this in the *Hadith*, the Catholic or other Christian seeking to understand *Islam* will be, to say the least, puzzled. Given all that is known about Jesus and Muhammad, on what basis could any Christian not, in that context, see Jesus, our Savior and Redeemer, as the supreme *Intercessor*? On the other hand, if this moment of "Resurrection" were what followers of Jesus call the "Last Judgment," then Jesus would be no longer our Intercessor but would instead be our *Judge,* as at the Particular Judgment (Mt 25:31-46).

It would seem that apologists for Islam have a difficult task as they attempt to reconcile the many apparent discrepancies between the Bible – particularly the New Testament – and the Koran, which came about six centuries later, as well as between the Bible and the Hadith.

Did Muhammad fulfill biblical prophecies?

Of interest to Catholics and other Christians is the belief of a number of Islamic apologists that Muhammad and the Koran were foretold in the Bible. The following are some of the passages they cite, as well as some extra-biblical claims, and my responses as a Catholic.

1.   God promised to make of Ishmael a great nation.

---

347 **www.usc.edu/dept/MSA/fundamentals/hadithsunnah/bukhari/093.sbt.html #009.093.601**

God's promise to Abraham that God would make of him a great nation predates the birth of both Isaac and Ishmael (Genesis 12:2). God also referred to Ishmael by name, saying that God would make him fruitful and would make of him a great nation (Genesis 17:20).

J. G. Response:

God did indeed promise to make of Abraham a great nation (Gen 12:2) and God heeded Abraham's prayer to bless Ishmael: "I will bless him and make him fruitful and multiply him exceedingly; he shall be the father of twelve princes, and *I will make him a great nation*" (Gen 17:20, cf. Gen 21:13-20).

But, through Abraham's wife Sarah, God made a similar promise in regard to Isaac: "I will bless her, and moreover I will give you a son by her, and she shall be a mother of nations; kings of peoples shall come from her." (Gen 17:16, cf. Gen 26:24).

However, the key question is not one of giving rise to a nation but of receiving a *covenant* from God. On which of the two sons of Abraham did God's favor rest in regard to establishing a covenant? The answer is Isaac, as we see in the biblical passage that immediately follows God's promise to make Ishmael the father of twelve chieftains:

> **But I will establish my covenant with Isaac**, whom Sarah shall bear to you at this season next year (Gen 17:21).

Ishmael was then 13 years of age. Ishmael had been born of Hagar, Egyptian handmaid of the elderly and childless Sarai (Sara or Sarah). Sarai had given Hagar to her husband Abram (Abraham), with his consent, so that at least they would have children by her handmaid (Gen 16:2-16).

It is Isaac's son Jacob who is renamed Israel after He contends with an angel (Gen 32:23-31, Gen 35:9-12, Hos 12:5.). Jacob / Israel was a progenitor of Moses, not of Muhammad. In regard to the covenant established with Isaac, and later with Isaac's descendant Moses (Deuteronomy 5:2), we find no parallel in the Bible in regard to Ishmael or Muhammad.

2. Abraham was neither Jew nor Christian (3:67). He was not a polytheist, but believed in, and submitted to, only one God. The word Muslim means one who submits to the one God – Allah. Since Allah / God's first prophet was, in essence, a Muslim, the Muslim faith supersedes the faith of both Jews and Christians, all of whom are called by Allah / God to return to the one true faith practiced by Muslims – Islam.

252

J. G. Response:

By this definition, anyone who "submits to one God" is Muslim. But one of the great prayers of Judaism is "Hear O Israel, the Lord our God is One Lord ...." Surely no one would claim that all Jews are, therefore, Muslims. Christians too worship that same "One God," but – through the revelation of Jesus Christ – Christians believe that this one God is, in fact, three Divine persons: Father, Son and Holy Spirit. Certainly no one would claim that, because of this belief in "One God," all Christians are therefore Muslims.

The New Testament is almost 2,000 years old. The Old Testament (largely what for Jews is the Hebrew Testament) penetrates far deeper into antiquity, and includes the events surrounding the life of Abraham about 1700 to 1800 B.C. The devout Muslim may believe with all his heart that Islam predated all other religions and was the only one that truly originated with Allah / God. To credibly make this case to non-Muslims, however, he must; (a) produce a body of authentic manuscripts at least 3,000 years old; (b) convince scholars that these ancient manuscripts supersede or invalidate the Old and New Testaments and; (c) show clearly that these manuscripts, presently unknown to scholars, specifically support Islam. Given the solid historical / philological foundation of the New and Old Testaments, the burden of proof rests with the Muslim. (Gnostic Marcionist documents, which postdate the New Testament by more than 100 years, fall far short of any scholarly test of authenticity or antiquity).

3. *Muhammad was the "Prophet like Moses" foretold in Deuteronomy.*

In Deuteronomy 18:18 we read that God would *raise up a great prophet like Moses*, and that God would put God's own words in his mouth; a prophecy that Muslims believe Muhammad fulfilled.

J. G. Response:

In the Bibles to which I referred, Deut. 18:18 does indeed indicate that God would raise up a great prophet. But when we read this in context we find:

> And the Lord said to me [Moses] "They have rightly said all that they have spoken. I will raise up for them a prophet like you *from among their brethren*; and I will put my words in his mouth and he shall speak to them all that I command him" (RSV, CE).

Other translations state that this prophet will be "of thy nation" and;

"from among your own kinsmen." In the Bible there are eighteen prophetic books, all of which were written later than Deuteronomy. Prophets such as Isaiah, Jeremiah, Ezekiel, Mica, Daniel, Micah and Zechariah wrote them – and, of course, we have the prophecy of John the Baptist. As Hebrew prophets, all of these could be called "brethren" of Moses and each could be considered "great."

In regard to Muhammad, great though he may have been in the eyes of his followers, how can he be seen as coming from the brethren / nation / kinsmen of Moses?

The differentiation of the descendants of Jacob / Israel from those of his brother Ishmael was firmly established well before the time of Moses. It was Jacob / Israel's son Joseph who was sold into slavery by his brothers to "Ishmaelites" whose caravan was going from Gilead to Egypt (Genesis 37:25-27).

And so the Christian is puzzled by the suggestion that Deuteronomy 18:18 applies to Muhammad who was born about 2,000 years after Moses and who was a descendant not of Moses and the Israelites but of Ishmael.

In the New Testament Moses and Elijah, in a glorified state, appeared to Peter, James and John in the *Transfiguration* (Mt 17:1, Mk 9:2, Lk 9:28). The central figure in this awe-inspiring event is, of course, the transfigured Jesus. If Sacred Scripture points to anyone as "The Prophet" foretold by Moses, surely, based on this event, it can only be Jesus.

4. Muhammad was "like Moses" in that he was the only other law-giving Prophet.

For this reason, as well as the one above, some Muslims claim that Muhammad is "The Prophet" foretold by God in Deut 18:18.

J. G. Response:

As noted in the previous response, the one who would fulfill God's prophecy in Deut 18:18 would have been an Israelite. Though he may be seen as a law-giver, having dictated the Koran, Muhammad was not an Israelite. How, then, could he be the Prophet foretold in Deut 18:18?

5. Muhammad fulfilled the "fiery law" prophecy of God in Deuteronomy 33:2-4.

Some Islamic apologists interpret the words of Moses in Deut 33: 2-4 along these lines:

The Lord came from Sinai (a reference to Moses); rose up from Seir to them (a reference to the conquest of Seir by David); that the

Lord shone forth from Mount Paran (Hijaz), the ancient name of the land of Ishmael, progenitor of Muhammad; advanced with (or from) ten thousand saints; and that a fiery law went forth for them from the right hand of the Lord (Deuteronomy 33:2). These Islamic apologists hold that this prophecy was fulfilled by Muhammad – and only Muhammad – who gave the world the law (*baida'*), and who marched triumphantly into Makkah with ten thousand saintly followers.

J. G. Response:

The first difficulty with this claim is the apparent absence of any *prophecy* in the above passage. If Moses did, in fact, state that the Lord *shone forth* from Mount Paran with a flaming law in his right hand, Moses referred to an act *already accomplished* by the Lord, not something to be done by someone else in the future.[348]

Genesis refers to mount Paran as the territory of Ishmael. But 2,000 years would pass before Muhammad would receive the Koran, and, although it includes references to hell, as do the Gospels, its primary emphasis is on gaining salvation in heaven forever with Allah. And so it would seem difficult to categorize the Koran as a "fiery" law.

In any case, let us look more closely at Deuteronomy 33:2-4. For the law given to Moses on Mount Sinai, we have no doubt of its fiery origin:

> And Mount Sinai was wrapped in smoke, because the Lord descended upon it in fire; and the smoke of it went up like the smoke of a kiln, and the whole mountain quaked greatly (Exodus 19:18. RSV Catholic Edition).

And, of course, this was preceded by the deliverance of the Israelites from Egypt, after which we read:

> And the Lord went before them by day in a pillar of cloud to lead them along the way, and by night in a pillar of fire … (Exodus 13:21-22. RSV Catholic Edition).

However, among the sources of the Koran listed in Islamic literature (Allah Himself, the Holy Spirit, angels, and the angel Gabriel), none would seem to provide the basis for calling the Koran "fiery" in origin.

If the Law given to Moses is the only one that we can describe as

---

348 Of fifteen online Bibles consulted by J. Gilmartin, only five refer to a fiery or flaming *law* in the right hand of the Lord. Of the five, three are versions of the King James Bible.

"fiery," it appears that another interpretation of Deuteronomy 33:2-4 may be more credible. The passage begins: "The Lord came from Sinai ... (a clear historical reference to the Law already given to Moses on Sinai [Exodus 19 and 20]); and from Seir he rose up to us." Seir may be a reference to David, who would be born an estimated 300 years later (Book of Samuel).

We might then interpret the remainder of the passage to mean that, although the Lord gave the fiery law only to Moses (in keeping with God's covenant with Moses and the Israelites [Ex 19:3-8], rather than to a descendant of Ishmael), the Lord's coming forth from mount Paran with "a fiery law" in his right hand may well mean that the Law given to Moses is intended to apply equally to the descendants of Ishmael.

The "ten thousand saints" may symbolize the many descendants of Ishmael who would accept and follow the Law given to Moses. If we remember that Deuteronomy preceded the time of Muhammad and the Koran by an estimated 2,000 years, and an additional 1400 years have since passed, this interpretation should not seem at all unreasonable. The reader may wish to compare the reference to Moses and the Commandments in the Koran with those noted above (Sura 7:143-146 in the N. J. Dawood translation).

6. *Muhammad was the biblical Comforter / Holy Ghost.*

Jesus told the apostles he would pray and the Father would "give you another Counselor, to be with you for ever, even the Spirit of truth ... (Jn 14:16). "When the Spirit of truth comes, he will guide you into all the truth ..." (Jn 16:13). The claim of at least one Islamic apologist is that Jesus could not have been referring to the Holy Ghost because the Holy Ghost had already come to men (e.g., to John the Baptist before his birth (Luke 1:41) and to Jesus at his baptism (Luke 3:21-22); and "that he [the Holy Spirit] may abide in you forever" is interpreted to mean that Muhammad, identified as the Holy Spirit, will be the last Prophet.

J. G. Response:

Is it probable that these and other biblical references to the Holy Spirit refer to Muhammad, a man who was not born until about 600 years after the time of Jesus? Or, as Christians believe – is it more probable that they refer not to Muhammad but to the Third Person of the Blessed Trinity?

Let us begin by examining the above Islamic view in the context of Jn 16:13. In Jn 16:14-15 Jesus adds "He [the Spirit of truth] will glorify me, for he will take what is mine and declare it to you. All that the

Father has is mine ...."

Surely any reader of the Koran would be hard pressed to maintain that the Koran meets this test. In the Koran Jesus is recognized as a prophet, but is not "glorified" or presented as one who has "all that the Father has" (and, of course, the Bible is suppressed in most Muslim countries).

In regard to Jn 14:16, the Holy Ghost, or Holy Spirit, is noted in Scripture well before the time of Jesus. About 700 years before Christ we find the following: "There shall come forth a shoot from the stump of Jesse, and a branch shall grow out of his roots. And the *Spirit of the Lord* shall rest upon him ..." (Isaiah 11:1-2). And the following was written about 500 years before Christ: "for I am with you, says the Lord of hosts, according to the promise that I made you when you came out of Egypt. *My Spirit* abides among you; fear not" (Haggai 2:4-5). Among Christians, of course, aside from at the baptism of Jesus, the best-known manifestation of the Holy Spirit is at Pentecost, "the 'fiftieth' day at the end of the seven weeks following Passover (Easter in the Christian Dispensation)" (CCC *Glossary*):

> When the day of Pentecost had come, they were all together in one place. And suddenly a sound came from heaven like the rush of a mighty wind, and it filled all the house where they were sitting. And there appeared to them tongues as of fire, distributed and rest-ing on each one of them. And they were all filled with the Holy Spirit and began to speak in other tongues, as the Spirit gave them utterance (Acts 2:1-4).

From these examples, it would seem clear that not every manifesta-tion of the Holy Spirit is the same, nor does the Spirit's coming to a particular person mean that the Spirit has thereby come to all mankind with the same gifts, to the same degree, or inspiring them to begin the same mission or other activity.

Let us suppose, for the sake of discussion, that the various manifes-tations of the Holy Spirit throughout the Old and New Testaments were, in fact, actually the spirit of Muhammad long before his birth. Why, then, in Isaiah 11:1-2, did Muhammad / Holy Ghost not add a caveat, such as, "Although he [Jesus] will be in error in his claim to be the Son of God, My Spirit will be upon him"? And in Haggai 2:4-5, Muhammad / Holy Ghost might have added that an Israelite – Jesus – would one day be born and would wrongly claim the authority to send the Spirit, or Comforter, to his twelve followers. Certainly Muhammad / Holy Ghost would have known that Jesus would be accepted by many as the Messiah (Koran 9:31) and would be a true prophet (Koran 2:135-138), *but that many would believe his "false" claim to be the Son of God. This "false" claim ultimately would lead billions of people to further "erroneous" beliefs about Jesus (e.g., his crucifixion in atonement for the sins of mankind and his Resurrection from the dead), rather than what Muslims see as the truth that would be later told in the Koran by Muhammad.*

Why, then, did Muhammad / Holy Spirit not forewarn us in Haggai or in other biblical prophecies that this Jesus would have some rather exaggerated notions regarding his divine authority and nature, was simply one of many prophets leading up to Muhammad, the ultimate Prophet, and would *not* die on the cross in atonement for the sins of mankind?

And surely Muhammad / Holy Spirit would have foreseen Jesus' affront to Allah by his misuse of Allah's power at Cana of Galilee, when Jesus changed water into wine at the wedding feast, – the Koran would later describe wine as one of the abominations of Satan (5:90).

And, in what may be Jesus' ultimate affront to Allah – one that in the centuries to come would overspread the entire Christian world – at the Last Supper, *Jesus instituted the Mass, telling his followers drink wine in remembrance of Jesus and saying that this wine was the Blood of Jesus!* Surely, each time Mass has since been said by Catholic priests – many thousands of times per day – Allah, in the view of Muslims, must be greatly offended. Again, why did Muhammad / Holy Spirit not preclude this by forewarning those who would consider following Jesus – particularly during the 600 years between the time of Jesus and the time Muhammad would receive the Koran?

And if it really was Muhammad / Holy Ghost / Comforter / Spirit of Truth who descended upon the apostles at Pentecost, how is it possible that it was *the Gospel of Jesus* the apostles then began to preach with such zeal to all – a message that includes fundamental contradictions of the Koran – as we have seen? In particular, how could Peter, after Pentecost, have spoken of Jesus as follows to the Sanhedrin:

> This [Jesus] is the stone which was rejected by you, the builders, which has become the corner stone. Neither is there salvation in any other. For there is no other name under heaven given to men by which we must be saved (Acts 4:11-12)?

7. Jesus was simply a prophet of Islam and a "unitarian" (God is One, there is no Trinity). Early Church censorship and distortion of his message gave rise to the "pseudo-religion" called Christianity.

Paul promoted this "false Christianity."

Among apologists for Islam some claim that, in the early centuries, the Church censored, repressed and distorted the message that would later be given in the Koran, resulting in the *pseudo-religion* of Christianity.

Following the "disappearance" of Jesus the new Church soon split into two opposing factions. The first faction was made up of Peter and the apostles other than Paul [Mathias having replaced Judas Iscariot]. Peter's faction held the "correct" *unitarian* view in accordance with the later Koran.

The other faction, led by the apostle Paul, proclaimed the *erroneous* view of Jesus as the Son of God who was Divine, who was crucified to redeem mankind, who rose from death on the third day, ascended into heaven and will one day come to judge everyone, living and dead.

However, because of Paul's zeal, the *erroneous* Pauline version soon eclipsed the *"correct"* unitarian teaching of Peter and the other apostles.

These Islamic apologists claim that the New Testament we read today is *erroneous* in claiming Jesus as the Divine Savior and Redeemer, crucified and risen.

They attribute this to *deception* at the time of the Church Councils that agreed upon the Canon of the Bible in the fourth century. This deception (by unnamed persons) supposedly resulted in the bishops rejecting *"authentic"* documents that denied the divinity of Christ and, among the many early Christian-era documents, authorizing only *"erroneous"* documents that affirmed Christ's divinity – those Christians know today as the New Testament.

J. G. Response:

Many pages have been written in affirmation of the decisions of the early Church Councils. Rather than attempt to summarize the able work of others, let me begin by referring the reader to the latter part of Step 3 of this book which refers to the Early Church Fathers and the "Semitisms" and other indications that affirm early dates of the Gospels

This *Gospel according to Matthew* – promulgated within a few decades after the Resurrection – by Matthew the tax collector / apostle, unequivocally proclaims not only the Divinity, Crucifixion and Resurrection of Jesus, but also the appointment of Peter to head the Church. *Matthew* was among the four approved by the Early Church Councils (and later at Trent).

Many eyewitnesses to Jesus were alive when Matthew promulgated his written Gospel and would have vehemently refuted it if it were inaccurate. But all four Gospels passed muster by great numbers of eyewitness to Jesus and the children of those eyewitnesses to whom the facts about Jesus would surely have been told. Many in those times chose to die as martyrs rather than deny what we read today in the Gospels.

And if Paul's Gospel was not that preached by Peter and the other apostles why – after Paul had preached for three years – in *Arabia* and *Damascus* (Syria) – did Peter (Ce'phas) allow Paul to spend fifteen days with him? (Gal 1:17-18). And why, after preaching for fourteen years, did Paul write: "I went up [to Jerusalem] by *revelation*; and *I laid before them* (but privately before those of repute) *the gospel which I preach among the Gentiles, lest somehow I should be running or had run in vain"* (Emphasis added; Gal 2:2). Finally, if in Peter's eyes Paul were a heretic, why would Peter describe Paul as "our beloved brother" (2 Peter 3:15)?

8. Contrary to Paul, Barnabas preached the "correct" unitarian message of the merely human Jesus.

Some Islamic apologists promote Barnabas as one who wrote accurately about Jesus [and his lack of divinity] and fault the Church for excluding the letters of Barnabas from the Canon of Scripture. Their supposition is that Barnabas parted company with Paul because: (a) Barnabas wanted to promote the "authentic" (unitarian) teaching of the merely human Jesus, while Paul was preaching an *erroneous* view that declared Jesus as crucified and risen and affirmed his divinity and; (b) Barnabas realized that it was futile to spread to Gentiles what Jesus had intended *only for Jews*.

Using a line of reasoning that includes no small measure of speculation, these Islamic apologists conclude that Paul's teachings about redemption and atonement are simply false, since they are based on the erroneous belief that Jesus was crucified and resurrected.

Christians should therefore reject the letters of Paul and the rest of the New Testament and instead accept Barnabas as the primary authentic source of Jesus' teaching.

J. G. Response:

Surely the Christian reading the above charge against the Church will feel as if he has stepped through the looking glass. Perhaps the simplest way to refute it is to read what Barnabas actually wrote on these points. If Barnabas believed Jesus was not God, why did he write the following?

For the Scripture says concerning us, while He [God the Father] speaks to the Son, "Let Us make man after Our image, and after Our likeness; and let them have dominion over the beasts of the earth, and the fowls of heaven, and the fishes of the sea."[349]

And, if Barnabas did not believe Jesus was crucified, why did he write the following?

Give good heed. [You see] "one upon the altar, and the other accursed;" and why [do you behold] the one that is accursed crowned? Because they shall see Him then in that day having a scarlet robe about his body down to his feet; and they shall say, Is not this He whom we once despised, and pierced, and mocked, and crucified? Truly this is He who then declared Himself to be the Son of God.[350]

And if Barnabas believed that Jesus intended his teaching only for Jews, why did he write as follows:

What, then, says He to Abraham? "Because thou hast believed, it is imputed to thee for righteousness: behold, I have made thee the father of those nations who believe in the Lord while in [a state of] uncircumcision."[351]

And again, the prophet says, "Behold, I have appointed Thee as a light to the nations, that Thou mightest be for salvation even to the ends of the earth, saith the Lord God that redeemeth thee."[352]

Based on the above verses, it would seem that the Early Church would have included the writings of Barnabas in the Sacred Canon. Perhaps they were excluded because of statements such as these:

"Thou shall not eat the hyena." He means, "Thou shall not be an adulterer, nor a corrupter, nor be like to them that are such." Wherefore? Because that animal annually changes its sex, and is at one time male, and at another female.[353]

Attend, my children, to the meaning of this expression, "He finished in six days." This implieth that the Lord will finish all things in six thousand years, for a day is with Him a thousand years. And

---

349 *Epistle of Barnabas*, Chapter VI, **www.ccel.org/ccel/schaff/anf01.toc.html**
350 Ibid., Chapter VII
351 Ibid., Chapter XIII
352 Ibid., Chapter XIV
353 Ibid., Chapter X

He Himself testifieth, saying, "Behold, to-day will be as a thousand years." Therefore, my children, in six days, that is, in six thousand years, all things will be finished."[354]

In any case, based on the verses quoted above that affirm Jesus as the crucified Son of God, it is difficult to understand how we could reconcile the views of Barnabas with the Koran.

9. *Irenaeus, Origin and Tertullian did not believe in the Divinity of Christ.*

J. G. Response:

If this claim were true, why would these early Church writers have written as follows:

Irenaeus:

3. First of all it [faith] bids us bear in mind that we have received baptism for the remission of sins, in the name of God the Father, and in the name of Jesus Christ, the Son of God, who was incarnate and died and rose again, and in the Holy Spirit of God.[355]

40. Thus then the Word of God [Jesus] in all things hath the pre-eminence; for that He is true man and Wonderful Counselor and Mighty God; calling men anew to fellowship with God, that by fellowship with Him we may partake of incorruption.[356]

47. So then the Father is Lord and the Son is Lord, and the Father is God and the Son is God; for that which is begotten of God is God.[357]

Origen:

[L]et us take an instance, which, although it does not describe the subject of which we are treating either fully or appropriately, may nevertheless be seen to be employed for this purpose only, to show that the Son of God, who was in the form of God, divesting Himself (of His glory), makes it His object, by this very divesting of Himself, to demonstrate to us the fulness [fullness] of His deity.[358]

---

354 Ibid., Chapter XV
355 *The Demonstration of the Apostolic Preaching*, 3 Christian Classics Ethereal Library **www.ccel.org/ccel/irenaeus/demonstr.preaching_the_demonstration_of_the_apostolic_preaching.html**
356 Ibid., 40
357 Ibid., 47
358 De Principiis, Book I, Chapter 2, 8. New Advent, translated by Kevin Knight. ©

And while we thus briefly demonstrate the deity of Christ, and (in so doing) make use of the prophetic declarations regarding Him, we demonstrate at the same time that the writings which prophesied of Him were divinely inspired ....[359]

Tertullian:

We should note that Tertullian, after initially accepting the teaching of the early Church, in about A.D. 212 separated himself and became a Montanist. But he left *not* because he rejected the divinity of Jesus or the Holy Spirit, but because he denied that the Church had the authority to forgive the sin of adultery. His objections on this matter are found in *De pudicitia* (On purity), one of his last writings, which he wrote after accepting the rigors of Montanism. Even as a Montanist, Tertullian affirmed the Trinity, as indicated in *Against Praxeas,* in which he writes, "[F]or the Unity is distributed in a Trinity. Placed in order, the three are Father, Son and Spirit."[360]

And so the idea that these three well-known early writers of the Church were "unitarians" who rejected the Trinity as well as the divinity of Jesus appears difficult to justify in light of what they actually wrote.

10. The prophecy of Isaiah 29:12 was fulfilled by Muhammad

Isaiah wrote: "And when they give the book to one who cannot read, saying, 'Read this,' he says, 'I cannot read'" (Is 29:12). Some Islamic apologists conclude that this can only refer to Muhammad, who was illiterate.

J. G. Response:

When we read this verse in context, a quite different meaning emerges. Only six verses later Isaiah wrote: "In that day the deaf shall *hear* the words of a book. And out of their gloom and darkness the eyes of the blind shall see. The meek shall obtain fresh joy in the Lord, and the poor among them shall exult in the *Holy One of Israel*" (Is 29:18). Further along, Isaiah again speaks of "The Lord God, the Holy one of Israel" (Is 30:15; emphasis added).

If God were referring to Muhammad, or to his progenitor Ishmael, why would Isaiah write "the Holy one of Israel?" As it is, does it not appear that the book the Lord is referring to is the Bible, which comes

---

2007 by Kevin Knight. All rights reserved. **www.newadvent.org/fathers/04120.htm**
359 Ibid., Book IV, From the Greek, Chapter I, 6.
360 Against Praxeas, 2, 4; *The Faith of the Early Fathers,* V.1, 154

from Israel, and which was *preached* to countless numbers who were illiterate – particularly in the 1,300 years that separated Isaiah from Muhammad? We should add that not all Islamic historians agree that Muhammad was illiterate. According to some accounts, because he had run a business he probably had some ability to read and write.

11. The prophecy of Isaiah 42:1-13 was fulfilled by Muhammad

God's "chosen one" prophesied in Isaiah 42:1-13 is Muhammad. This passage makes reference to Kadar, the second son of Ishmael (Gen 25:13) from whom Muhammad descended, and Isaiah 42:1-4 notes that God will send his chosen one to "bring forth justice to the nations." As a descendant of Kedar and the "chosen one" to whom God gave his Law (the *Koran*), Muhammad fulfilled this prophecy.

J. G. Response:

It is true that Muslims consider Kedar, the second son of Ishmael (Gen 25:13), an ancestor of Muhammad, and Isaiah 42:1:13 does mention "the villages that Kedar inhabits."

When we read Is 42:1-13 in its entirety, however, we see that this "messenger" is not *from* the people of Kadar, or from Sela, mentioned in the same verse, but stresses that his universal message is *for* these and other peoples of "the nations," including "the coastlands ... the desert and its cities ... [and again] the coastlands." The key question, however, is who best meets the criteria given for this *universal* messenger, Muhammad or Christ?

This passage states that God will send his servant who will "establish justice in the earth ... who will open the eyes that are blind ... my glory I give to no other." But Muslims have never claimed that Muhammad was in any way comparable to Christ in manifesting the glory of the Father, e.g., giving sight to one born blind, raising Lazarus from the dead, his own Resurrection from the dead after his Crucifixion. In particular, the Crucifixion and Resurrection of Christ are rejected in the Koran, of course, but the historical authenticity of the Gospels in regard to these and all other manifestations of the divinity of Jesus – "my glory I give to no other ..." – is thoroughly documented in Part I, Step 3. Objective readers will surely question how Muhammad, rather than Christ, can be seen as the "universal messenger" prophesied in Isaiah 42:1-13.

Authoritative apologists for Islam readily admit that Muhammad never claimed to be without sin, and they make no claim that anyone ever witnessed Muhammad perform a miracle such as raising Lazarus after four days in the tomb, giving sight to one born blind, healing lepers, as Jesus did in the presence of many witnesses.

Many legends have arisen regarding Muhammad (e.g., he cast no shadow; from his perspiration the rose was created; his finger split the moon; he became so heavy while receiving spiritual messages several men could not lift him). It has also been said that in some manner Muhammad, during his life, experienced a brief ascent into heaven. I found no claim or documentation to the effect that such an event, if it happened, was witnessed by anyone. If it happened, of course, Muhammad would have been the *object* of a miracle rather than the one performing it.

The Ascension of the risen Christ, on the other hand, was witnessed by the eleven who – after this culmination of Christ's three-year public ministry and the descent on them of the Holy Spirit at Pentecost - were so convinced of the divinity of Jesus and the truth of his Gospel message that none would ever again question or deny his divinity and most would later give their lives as martyrs proclaiming his divinity and his teachings.

In any case, no recognized Islamic apologist claims that Muhammad experienced a bodily resurrection as recorded in all four Gospels in regard to Christ, and it is well established in historical accounts that Muhammad died in Medina in June, A.D. 632, at age 63, having made no provision for a successor. His tomb is in the Prophet's Mosque in Medina in what is now Saudi Arabia.

Anyone who spends a little time reading the Koran and the New Testament will quickly be at a loss to attribute both to the same supernatural source. For example, as earlier noted, sura 5:46 points out that in the Gospel there is light and guidance, and that *it was Allah himself who gave Jesus the Gospel.* But why, then, would Allah have permitted Matthew, Mark and Luke to include the following verses in the Gospel – verses that would surely cause the reader to look upon Muhammad, who is associated with the desert – with great suspicion?

> For false Christs and false prophets will arise and show great signs and wonders, so as to lead astray, if possible, even the elect. Lo, I have told you beforehand. So, if they say to you, "Lo, he is in the wilderness [in some translations *in the desert*]," do not go out … (Mt 24:24-26; also Mk 13:21-23, Lk 21:8-9).

When Muhammad began relating the messages of the Koran in about A.D. 610, the Bible used by the Christian "People of the Book" was well established. Each of the books and letters of the Old and New

Testaments had been approved by the Church more than 200 years earlier, as previously noted. Among the letters included in "The Book" was Paul's letter to the Galatians, which warns the faithful not to be misled, *even by an angel:*

> But even if we, or an *angel* from heaven, should preach to you a gospel contrary to that which we preached to you, let him be accursed (in some translations *anathema*) (Gal 1:8-9).

About five and one-half centuries later, in the Arabian *desert* country about 750 miles southeast of Jerusalem, Muhammad, The Prophet, began relating the messages that would become the Koran. Muslims believe that these messages originated with Allah and were given to Muhammad by an *angel.*

As God, surely Allah knew that the Church had approved these words of Paul – so damaging to the cause of Islam – about two centuries earlier. Why did Allah allow Paul to write them? Or, in the messages that became the Koran, why did Allah not reject them?

No true Christian would desire that anyone of any faith be *accursed,* or declared *anathema,* irrevocably, with no possibility of repentance, and thus be forever barred from heaven. In the Catholic Church today the equivalent word would be *excommunicated.* As earlier noted, an excommunicated Catholic may not receive the Eucharist or other sacraments, but is encouraged to retain his or her bond with the Church in other ways, especially by attending Mass. The hope is that such a person will repent and be returned to full membership in the Church. Surely Paul would have intended that any anathema lead the offender to, or back to, the Church. There can be no doubt that Paul remembered that no one was more deserving of anathema than he when, as Saul of Tarsus, he was a staunch persecutor of Christians.

In regard to persecution, another prophecy of Christ seems most relevant today. At the Last Supper, after Judas departs, Jesus tells the eleven apostles that they will be put out of the synagogue and:

> [I]ndeed the hour is coming when whoever kills you will think he is offering a service to God. And they will do this because they have not known the Father, nor me (Jn 16:2-3).

In any case, although respect for all founders, proclaimers and believers of all faiths is essential, we cannot escape the conclusion that *as religions,* Islam and Christianity are incompatible. We can either

(a) **accept Muhammad and the Koran,** which means that we **deny** the divinity of Jesus as well as his death on the cross and Resurrection *or:*

(b)   *accept Jesus and the Bible,* which means that, contrary to the *Koran,* we *accept the* divinity of Jesus as well as his death on the cross and Resurrection

There is no middle ground.

Jesus or Muhammad. Of the two, Jesus performed many public miracles with a multitude of witnesses, acknowledged that he was God, raised the dead, was himself raised from death on the third day, said he would be our ultimate Judge and said that no one comes to the Father except through him. There is a wealth of historical documentation from contemporaries (in the New Testament) and near-contemporaries of Jesus (Early Church Fathers and others) supporting these biblical claims. Muhammad, according to his authoritative apologists, did nothing comparable to these things.

Of the two, then – Jesus or Muhammad – which one would seem more credible in his claim that he spoke on behalf of the Almighty Creator?

Which one would seem to be in the best position to keep, in the hereafter, the promises he made to us – *including the promise of everlasting happiness in heaven for those who are faithful to his teachings?*

Islam and Christianity; the importance of a broad historical perspective

In keeping with the purpose of this book, we have focused on the religious aspect of Islam in comparison to that of Christianity, and Catholicism in particular. In view of world events in recent years, however, it is also important to seek an understanding of Christian / Islamic interaction in a broad, unvarnished, historical context. The following is an excerpt from the online version of the *Catholic Encyclopedia* on the New Advent Web site:

> After Mohammed's death Mohammedanism aspired to become a world power and a universal religion. The weakness of the Byzantine Empire, the unfortunate rivalry between the Greek and Latin Churches, the schisms of Nestorius and Eutyches, the failing power of the Sassanian dynasty of Persia, the lax moral code of the new religion, the power of the sword and of fanaticism, the hope of plunder and the love of conquest – all these factors combined with the genius of the caliphs, the successors of Mohammed, to effect

the conquest, in considerably less than a century, of Palestine, Syria, Mesopotamia, Egypt, North Africa, and the South of Spain. The Moslems even crossed the Pyrenees, threatening to stable their horses in St. Peter's at Rome, but were at last defeated by Charles Martel at Tours, in 732, just one hundred years from the death of Mohammed.

This defeat arrested their western conquests and saved Europe. In the eighth and ninth centuries they conquered Persia, Afghanistan, and a large part of India, and in the twelfth century they had already become the absolute masters of all Western Asia, Spain and North Africa, Sicily, etc. They were finally conquered by the Mongols and Turks, in the thirteenth century, but the new conquerors adopted Mohammed's religion and, in the fifteenth century, overthrew the tottering Byzantine Empire (1453). From that stronghold (Constantinople) they even threatened the German Empire, but were successfully defeated at the gates of Vienna, and driven back across the Danube, in 1683.[361]

Another view is offered by Serge Trifkovic in his book *The Sword of the Prophet; Islam – History, Theology, Impact on the World.* In his informative review of this comprehensive book, after noting that Trifkovic writes of "countless Jihads against unbelievers," Paul Eidelberg wrote:

> Chapter 3, "Jihad Without End," demonstrates that the goal of Islamic *jihad* is world conquest, and that willingness of Muslims to sacrifice their lives to this end "is neither extreme nor even remarkable from the standpoint of traditional Islam."[362]

The Crusades; a brief comment

The Crusades of the eleventh and twelfth centuries are often cited as examples of Christian hostility toward Muslims. However, as noted by Jimmy Akin in *Islam, a Catholic Perspective,* the Crusades began only after half the Christian world had been conquered by Muslims who had begun to hinder Christian pilgrimages to the Holy Land.[363] Akin asks if the situation had been reversed and Christians were deterring Muslims from going on the *Hajj* to Mecca, would Muslims not have mounted the equivalent of a Crusade against those Christians?

---

361 **www.newadvent.org/cathen/10424a.htm**
362 Freeman Center for Strategic Studies: **www.freeman.org/m_online/aug03/eidelberg.htm**
363 A *Catholic Answers* booklet by Jimmy Akin; **www.catholic.com**

Perhaps the darkest hour of the Crusades was the redirection of the Fourth Crusade against the Christian cities of Zara and Constantinople in the year 1204, about 150 years after the Great Eastern Schism began.

An outraged Pope Innocent III, who had authorized the Fourth Crusade against the Saracen followers of Muhammad and whose threat of excommunication did not deter those who led the unauthorized redirection of those Christian forces, "thundered" against the crusaders thus: *"You vowed to liberate the Holy Land but you rashly turned away from the purity of your vow when you took up arms not against Saracens but Christians .... The Greek Church has seen in the Latins nothing other than an example of affliction and the works of Hell, so that now it rightly detests them more than dogs."*[364]

"The Crusades 101," an informative article by *Catholic Answers* apologist Jimmy Akin on the eight Crusades (1095-1270), as well as articles on this topic by Thomas F. Madden, James V. Schall, S.J., Vince Ryan, James Hitchcock, Janet E. Smith and Gerard V. Bradley appeared in the January / February 2002 issue of *Catholic Dossier* and can be seen online.[365]

Vatican seeks true religious freedom for Christians in the Middle East

In "The Church and Islam. *La Civiltà Cattolica* Breaks the Cease-fire," an article posted on the web site of *Chiesa*, the Italian Catholic news agency, columnist Sandro Magister calls attention to the much firmer approach the Vatican has taken toward Islam in the past few years. In this *Chiesa* article, Magister includes an extensive excerpt from an article by Giuseppe De Rosa, S.I., published in the October 18, 2003 edition of the magazine *La Civiltà Cattolica*. This magazine is edited by Jesuits in Rome. Although not an official publication of the Vatican, it is reported that, before publication, *La Civiltà Cattolica* articles are reviewed by the Vatican Secretary of State. Magister summarizes the central thesis of De Rosa's article as follows:

> In all of its history, Islam has shown a warlike and conquering face; that "for almost a thousand years, Europe lived under its constant threat," and that what remains of the Christian population in Islamic countries is still subjected to "perpetual discrimination," with episodes of bloody persecution.[366]

---

364 http://en.wikipedia.org/wiki/Fourth_Crusade
365 www.catholic.net/rcc/Periodicals/Dossier/2002-02/article3.html
366 "The Church and Islam. *La Civiltà Cattolica* Breaks the Ceasefire," by Sandro Magister, including an excerpt in English from "Christians in Islamic Countries," by

An article in the July 5, 2006 issue of *Our Sunday Visitor* includes the following, indicating the position Pope Benedict XVI is taking in regard to Islam:

> Again and again, the pope and other Vatican officials have reiterated the need for Muslims to grant the same rights of religious freedom to Christians living in the Middle East that they demand for themselves in the West – the right to build places of worship, to pray openly and freely and to pass on their faith to their children. And Pope Benedict's refusal to remain silent on the subject, both in public and in private, marks a distinct departure from the days of Pope John Paul II.[367]

On September 12, 2006 in Regensburg, Germany, Pope Benedict XVI gave an academic address entitled "Faith, Reason and the University; Memories and Reflections." In it the Pope quoted 14th century Byzantine Emperor Manuel Paleologos II as follows:

> Show me just what Mohammed brought that was new, and there you will find things only evil and inhuman, such as his command to spread by the sword the faith he preached …. The emperor, after having expressed himself so forcefully, goes on to explain in detail the reasons why spreading the faith through violence is something unreasonable. Violence is incompatible with the nature of God and the nature of the soul. 'God', he says, 'is not pleased by blood – and not acting reasonably (σὺν λόγω) is contrary to God's nature. Faith is born of the soul, not the body. Whoever would lead someone to faith needs the ability to speak well and to reason properly, without violence and threats …. To convince a reasonable soul, one does not need a strong arm, or weapons of any kind, or any other means of threatening a person with death ….

In the days following, newspapers worldwide carried threats on his life and front page stories with such headlines as, "Pope's comments spark Muslim outrage." The Pope later said he was "deeply sorry" that Muslims had been offended by his reference to the words of Paleologos II and that they did not express the Pope's personal thoughts, but he did not retract them or deny they were historically well-founded.

Giuseppe De Rosa S.I., that was published in *La Civiltà Cattolica,* no. 3680, October 18, 2003. **www.chiesa.espressonline.it/dettaglio.jsp?id=6985&eng=y**
367 "Pope Benedict holds tougher line in Catholic Church dialogue with Islam" *Our Sunday Visitor,* July 5, 2006, **www.osv.com; www.catholic.org/international/ international_story.php?id=20410**

Bat Ye'or is the pseudonym of the author of *Eurabia; The Euro-Arab Axis*. The author, a French woman now living in Switzerland, has also written several other books and numerous articles on the emergence in recent decades of a strong Islamic influence in Europe. On three occasions she testified at U.S. congressional hearings on this subject.[368] In well-documented detail, Ye'or describes in *Eurabia* how – to the detriment of Christianity and Judaism – Islamic influence has become a dominant force at the highest political, religious, economic, educational, social, and cultural levels throughout Europe.

Robert Spencer is the author of *Islam Unveiled* and *Onward Muslim Soldiers,* as well as co-author with Daniel Ali of *Inside Islam: A Guide for Catholics*. Spencer endorsed Ye'or's book *Eurabia* as follows:

> Bat Ye'or is one of the only analysts in the world with the courage and insight necessary to state clearly what is happening in Europe today [2005]. Her account of the betrayal by the European powers of their own identity and history will stand for future historians as a cautionary tale of cultural suicide.

These grim assessments should prompt all – Muslims and Non-Muslims alike – to look with hope to Luxenberg's *The Syro-Aramaic Reading of the Koran* and his forthcoming work in English, as well as to the anticipated results of the study by Abdeljelil and the Tunisian scholars.

Will Muslim leaders reject these studies and reaffirm the long-accepted Uthmanic Recension? Or, as Phenix, Jr. and Horn suggest regarding Luxenberg's work, will these studies provide compelling evidence that the *true* Koran – *as received from The Prophet himself* – is *"more or less harmonious with the New Testament and Syriac Christian liturgy and literature"*?

For the sake of world peace for this and future generations, let us hope and pray for an auspicious resolution of this matter.

Discussion Questions

1. Explain the importance of differentiating between (a) the many Muslims worldwide who practice their faith peacefully and without violence toward non-Muslims and; (b) Muslims who promote violence against non-Muslims.

---

368 http://mypage.bluewin.ch/ameland/CV.html

2. According to Phenix, Jr. and Horn, Luxenberg's *The Syro-Aramaic Reading of the Koran* indicates that the *original* Koran was "*more or less harmonious with the New Testament and Syriac Christian liturgy and literature.*" If Muslim scholars agree, what effect do you think this will have on world peace?

3. Give some examples of verses of the Koran that appear to support the Bible.

4. Give examples of verses of the Koran that are incompatible with the Bible.

5. Why would a Muslim consider the worship of Jesus as God an affront to Allah?

6. Jesus said that we are to love our enemies and do good to those who persecute us. How does this compare to some of the verses of the Koran?

7. What is the *Hadith*, and why is it important in Islam? Discuss the reference to Jesus in relation to Muhammad in V. 9, Book 93, Number 601 of the *Hadith*.

8. Some Islamic apologists believe the Comforter / Spirit of Truth sent at the request of Jesus was Muhammad. Is this a reasonable view?

9. Some Muslims believe that the fourth-century bishops who selected the books and letters that constitute the New Testament Canon were misled. Otherwise they would *not* have selected books and letters affirming the divinity of Jesus. What do you think, and why?

10. Did Muhammad meet the criteria described in Deuteronomy 18:18 for "a great prophet like Moses?" Did he satisfy the criteria for the "law-giving" prophet in this passage of Scripture?

11. Did Muhammad fulfill the "fiery law" prophecy of Deuteronomy 33:2-4?

12. In the opinion of some Muslims, Barnabas did not regard Jesus as God. In view of what Barnabas wrote, what is your opinion?

13. Did Irenaeus believe in the divinity of Jesus? On what do you base your answer?

14. Consider the quotation of Origin from *de Principiis*, Book II,

IX. 4. Does it appear that Origin believed in the divinity of Jesus?

15. Some Islamic apologists maintain that Tertullian did not believe in the divinity of Jesus. Is there a basis in Tertullian's writings for saying that Tertullian *did* believe in the divinity of Jesus?

16. Sura 5:46 notes that Allah gave Jesus the Gospel. But the Gospel, written more than 500 years earlier, includes a warning against following future prophets in the wilderness or desert who will lead the faithful astray. Can these seemingly conflicting statements be reconciled? If not, in view of one's eternal salvation, which is it more prudent to accept and why?

17. In your opinion, who best fulfills the criteria for the "chosen one" prophesied in Isaiah 42:1-13, Muhammad or Jesus? Explain your answer.

18. Muhammad died in 632 having made no provision for a successor. What effect has the lack of agreement upon a single line of succession and authority had on Islam since then?

19. In your opinion, can the Koran and Bible be attributed to the same supernatural source? Explain your answer.

20. Consider the power and authority of the Creator as manifested by Jesus compared to that manifested by Muhammad. Of the two, who would seem more likely, in the hereafter, to be able to keep his promises to us?

21. In September, 2006 Pope Benedict XVI quoted 14th century Byzantine Emperor Manuel Paleologos II. The Pope's remarks were followed by outrage in some Islamic countries. Do you think those Muslims were justified in their outrage? Do you think the Pope and other Christian leaders should make such public references to Islam and its history?

22. Why were the Crusades undertaken? Other than the Fourth Crusade, which was shamefully redirected against Christians in Zara and Constantinople, do you think they were justified? If there had never been a Crusade or equivalent Christian action, in what ways if any, do you think Europe and the Middle East might be different today?

23. An article in *Our Sunday Visitor* noted that Pope Benedict XVI

and other Vatican officials "have reiterated the need for Muslims to grant the same rights of religious freedom to Christians living in the Middle East that they demand for themselves in the West." To what extent, if any, do you think this call for true religious freedom for Christians in Muslim lands will be successful? Why?

Jehovah's Witnesses

Charles Taze Russell founded the organization known today as the Jehovah's Witnesses in Pittsburgh in 1872. In evaluating the credibility of Mr. Russell as the founder of a religion, it seems we must take into account the following concerns raised by William J. Whelan.

It seems that the thought of the reality of hell disturbed Russell and he became convinced that the true meaning of the Hebrew word *Sheol* was not *hell* but *grave*. When he began to preach in 1872 he found that his teaching that no one experienced hell drew many to his new religion.

Whelan also relates that two events hampered the early progress of Russell's ministry. In a suit for divorce, his wife claimed, among other things, that he was cruel and unfaithful. Russell made five unsuccessful attempts to contest the divorce decree. Then, to avoid paying alimony, Russell reportedly transferred his assets to businesses over which he had control.

An additional event that damaged Russell's credibility was his participation in a "phony $60-a-bushel 'Miracle Wheat' promotion."[369]

Are there explanations – possibly extenuating circumstances – that may exonerate Mr. Russell of these and other accusations reported in *Separated Brethren*? Possibly. However, the real difficulty is that Jehovah's Witness beliefs differ so radically from those of the Church Christ founded. For example, they insist that there is no Trinity, that Jesus was and is simply an exalted spiritual being; that Jesus was not God, that he was not immortal, and that he did not rise from death; i.e., that there was no Resurrection.

There are a number of other differences that are well documented and readily available for those interested. But those listed above should serve to show the wide gulf between the religion founded by Charles Taze Russell and that founded by Jesus.

To no avail, I have spent many hours giving the Catholic response on particular scriptural questions to well-meaning Jehovah's Witnesses who were invariably kind and pleasant. It seems to me that it might be more productive to respond along the following lines, in view of all that I have written in this book regarding Jesus:

> To embrace the religion founded by Charles Taze Russell means to reject the religion founded by Jesus Christ who: (a) acknowledged that he was God (Jn 20: 28-29); (b) said he would judge each per-

---

369 *Separated Brethren*, 199.

son after death (Jn 5:22-23); (c) said that no one comes to the Father but by him [in some translations through him] (Jn 14:6); (d) founded his Church on Peter only (Mt 16:18); (e) gave to Peter only the keys of the kingdom of heaven (Mt 16:19); (f) to Peter only said "Feed my lambs .... Tend my sheep .... Feed my sheep" (Jn 21:15-17) and, (g) his three-year ministry was filled with supernatural manifestations that affirmed his claim that he spoke with the authority of the Almighty Father.

All of these statements are solidly based on biblical and extra-biblical history. No Jehovah's Witness claims that Mr. Russell or any of his successors was in any way comparable to Jesus in manifesting the authority of the Creator. Why, then, would any prudent person deny Christ in his divinity and in the Church he founded and follow the merely human Mr. Russell and his successors?

The Catholic Answers Web site includes many articles and other resources addressing virtually the entire religious spectrum.[370] Articles on the faith of Jehovah's Witnesses include these: "Talking to Jehovah's Witnesses," "Shunned by Kingdom Hall," "Pastor Russell, the founder of the Jehovah's Witnesses and the purveyor of "Miracle Wheat," "How many true Gods are there anyway? Is the Father the only true God? That's what Jehovah's Witnesses say ..." and "You can't be right, You can't be right – A Jehovah's Witness confronts the Truth."

Other informative articles can be found at the Web site of Dr. Jeffrey Schwehm and his wife Kathy.[371] Dr. Schwehm was raised as a Jehovah's Witness from early childhood. At age 8 he gave his first talk in Kingdom Hall. He served in the JW World Headquarters in Brooklyn, NY in 1987-1988. For reasons explained on their Web site, he left the Jehovah's Witnesses in 1996 and became a Catholic in 2003. His wife Kathy was raised Catholic until her teenage years when her mother joined the Jehovah's Witnesses. Kathy joined as well in her early twenties, but left in 1996 and returned to the Catholic Church in 2003.

At this writing their Web site includes sixteen articles, including these by Dr. Schwehm: "Understanding the Fundamental Doctrine of the Jehovah's Witnesses," "Witnessing to Jehovah's Witnesses at your door," "Discussing the Trinity with Jehovah's Witnesses," "Second Class Citizens of the Watchtower," and "Welcome to the Universal

---

370 **www.catholic.com**
371 **www.catholicxjw.com**

(Catholic) Family of God."

Discussion Questions

1. Founder Charles Taze Russell, beginning in 1872, denied the divinity of Jesus and the existence of hell. In doing so Mr. Russell, in effect, said that all the Christian Bible scholars of the past were wrong on these essential points and that he alone, after nineteen centuries, finally got it right. How does the Bible-based authority of Mr. Russell compare to that given by Jesus to the apostles in the Great Commission?

2. In view of all the Bible-based reasons to embrace Catholicism in this section [items (a) through (g)], on what basis would anyone instead accept the novel interpretation of the Bible and the other beliefs promoted by Mr. Russell and his successors?

The Church of Latter-Day Saints – The Mormons

As with most religions, Mormonism has a number of different denominations (approximately twelve) with corresponding variation in some elements of belief. The observations in this section do not necessarily apply to all Mormon denominations.

The Mormon Web site, **www.lds.org**, includes an Index to help answer questions about that religion. Unfortunately, at this writing, it does not appear to address certain beliefs antithetical to Catholic teaching such as the following on the Web site of the Christian Study Center [372]:

- On another planet, God was once a man. *Mormon Doctrine, p. 321. Joseph Smith, Times and Seasons,* Vol. 5, pp. 613-614; *Orson Pratt, Journal of Discourses,* Vol. 2, p. 345, *Brigham Young, Journal of Discourses,* Vol. 7, p. 333.

- God is married. He and his goddess wife have children who are spirits. *Mormon Doctrine,* p. 516.

- The sacrifice of Jesus on the cross cleansed us from most sin, but not from that of adultery that is repeated, or murder. *Journal of Discourses,* Vol. 3, p. 247, 1856.

- God the Father did not always exist; he had a Father; *Joseph Smith, History of the Church,* Vol. 6, p. 476; *Heber C. Kimball, Journal of Discourses,* Vol. 5, p. 19; *Milton Hunter, First Council of the Seventy, Gospel through the Ages,* p. 104-105.

In any case, the Utah or Brighamite group of The Church of Latter-Day Saints (the largest of its sects), known as the Mormons, accept *Jesus Christ as the Divine Savior of the world, and believe that through His atonement all mankind may be saved by obedience to the principles of the Gospel.* However, the Mormon interpretation of this statement is quite different from that of the Catholic Church.

The Church of Latter Day Saints was founded by Joseph Smith. Smith reported that in 1827, when in his teens, he was visited at his home near Palmyra, N.Y. by the angel Moroni.

According to Smith, the angel told him that the Church founded by Jesus had fallen into apostasy not long after the last apostle died. Smith

---

372 **www.christianstudycenter.com/modules.php?name=News&file=article&sid=104**

claimed that both Jesus and the Father appeared to him in 1829 and through him restored not only the authority of the priesthood, but the true Church itself.

The Golden Plates

In conjunction with Smith's mission to reestablish the true church and the priesthood, Mormons believe the angel Moroni allowed Smith to unearth a box of golden plates at the top of Hill Cumorah near Palmyra. On the plates was written the *Book of Mormon.*

Smith claimed that the angel gave him a pair of magic spectacles or "peepstones" [supposedly the Urim and Thummim of the Old Testament] which were needed to read the "caractors" of the unknown language on the plates that Smith called Reformed Egyptian.

Did any disinterested party see the Golden Plates?

However, according to William Whalen, there may be reason to question the authenticity of the golden plates. After receiving them from the angel, Smith, then age twenty-two, employed several people to take down his spoken words in writing. One who did so was Oliver Cowderly, who had been employed as a school teacher. However, as indicated below, it seems that Smith may have dictated the *Book of Mormon* with a blanket separating him and the plates from the person taking the notes.

The *Book of Mormon* supposedly describes the lives of those who originally lived in what was later called North America from about six hundred years before Christ to about A.D. 421. Christ is described as appearing among the Nephites during this period, selecting twelve indigenous (Native American) apostles and establishing a church equivalent to the one in Jerusalem. The son of the defeated Nephite General Mormon, Moroni, took the golden plates and buried them. Whelan notes that the *Book of Mormon* includes extended word-for-word passages of the New Testament, and uses many King James idioms, although it would be eleven centuries before that Bible would be written.[373]

Whalen also notes that the *Book of Mormon* is full of contradictions and anachronisms, including the prophecy that Mary would give birth to the Son of God *at Jerusalem.*

After Smith used the special spectacles to translate the Reformed Egyptian, he reportedly returned both the plates and the spectacles to the angel, and no one has seen them since.

---

[373] *Separated Brethren,* 187-188.

There is a report that Smith copied some of the "caractors" he had supposedly seen on the plates for examination by a Columbia College linguist. Whelan notes that the linguist could not identify them as coming from any known language.

Plates seen "with eyes of faith" – while they were covered.

Whalen's further comments seem to make Smith's story of the plates even more implausible: Eleven witnesses testified that they had seen Smith's "Golden Plates" and none later admitted that, in so doing, he or she had committed perjury or been misled. However, one witness testified some years later that he saw the plates through "faith" although they were then under a cloth.[374]

Whalen goes on to say that of the witnesses five were Whitmers and three were Smiths including Harris, the Prophet's father. Whalen adds that Cowdery and David Whitmer eventually apostatized, and that eighty Mormons signed a complaint accusing them of being counterfeiters and thieves and drove them out of Missouri.[375]

In addition to the above difficulties, residents of Palmyra who knew the Smiths reportedly made a public statement which included the following:

> We, the undersigned, have been acquainted with the Smith family for a number of years …. They were particularly famous for visionary projects; spent much of their time in digging for money, which they pretended was hid in the earth ….[376]

Joseph Smith and his brother Hyrum were imprisoned at Carthage, Illinois when a mob stormed the prison and both were shot and killed. Smith died at age 39, only 17 years after he dictated the Book of Mormon. Brigham Young succeeded him.

Does the Book of Mormon conflict with the Gospels?

Does the book of Mormon, translated from the plates, conflict with the teachings found in the Bible? It is evident that, on certain central questions of faith, it does. For example, in the Gospel, Jesus speaks as follows: "And I say to you: whoever divorces his wife, except for unchastity, and marries another, commits adultery" (Mt 19:9, Lk 16:18 and Mk 10:11).

---

374 *Separated Brethren,* 187-188.
375 *Separated Brethren,* 187.
376 *The Millennial Harbinger,* New Series, Vol. VI, No IX, Alexander Campbell, ed. Bethany, VA, September, 1842.
www.mun.ca/rels/restmov/texts/acampbell/tme/TME01.HTM

If, as the Bible states, Jesus condemned as adultery a marriage after a divorce, how much graver the adultery if the man marries one or more additional times while *retaining* all wives?

Divine authorization for plural marriages?

In 1843 Mr. Smith explained that in 1843 he received a revelation that approved the doctrine of plural marriages, but was silent about the conflict with the teaching of Jesus on this matter.[377] Did Mr. Smith "test the spirit" from whom he received this revelation? I found no indication that he did so. According to news reports, some fundamentalist Mormons do practice polygamy despite the Edwards Law of 1882 and other laws against bigamy. The Missouri contingent of Mormons, on the other hand, denies that Joseph Smith practiced or authorized polygamy; they claim that this is a clear sign that the Church in Utah, the followers of Brigham Young, does not constitute the true Mormon Church.[378]

Death does not end a marriage

A further difficulty is found in the belief that a Mormon marriage does not end with death, but continues after death.[379] This, of course, contradicts what Jesus said to the Sadducees about marriage ending with death: "For in the resurrection they neither marry nor are given in marriage, but are like angels in heaven" (Mt 22:30).

Living persons may bring about a vicarious marriage of the dead

Even more startling to non-Mormons is the Mormon belief that marriages may be made *vicariously* by the living for the dead.[380] This contradicts the words of Jesus in Mt 22:30 and, possibly, the prohibition against attempting to communicate with the dead.

Even if, contrary to the Gospels, God were to permit such marriages, how can we know that the deceased person would wish to be bound in a celestial marriage? How is consent obtained from the dead person? How is the marriage consummated? Even if a deceased person expressed such a wish before death, how can we know that this person has not changed his or her mind now that they are in a realm unimaginable to us still here on Earth? How can the earth-bound proxies be sure that the prospective spirit-spouses, now with a vastly broader outlook on all matters, are not looking down saying "No!" as the marriage vow

---

377 *Religion in the Twentieth Century,* Cowles, 291.
378 *The Protestant Churches of America,* 164-165.
379 *Religion in the Twentieth Century*, Cowles, 300.
380 Ibid.

is given by proxy? *Wikipedia* notes that Mormons believe that, as in marriage among the living, proxy *sealing* in marriage of the dead is voluntary on the part of those in the afterlife. But, aside from religious considerations, such proxy marriages would seem problematic in regard to such matters as inheritance, insurance, and determining who one's relatives are.

Although Mr. Smith may have believed he was acting with the best of intentions in cooperating with his spirit contact, such difficulties remain.

By what authority did Mr. Smith change Christ's teachings?

If Mr. Smith's revelations were true, then as God Jesus would have foreseen that the Church he founded on Peter would soon fall into apostasy and that, eighteen centuries later, he and the Father would reestablish his church through Joseph Smith. It would seem, then, that the same questions must be raised as have been asked in regard to other non-Catholic religions: (a) Why did Jesus not foretell these events through the Gospels, instead of giving us the warnings about false prophets and saying that he would be with the Church he founded on Peter always? (b) Why did Smith not manifest some supernatural signs that he was truly acting with God's authority as he amended the Commandments?

Aside from the plates and peepstones, the authenticity of which are so seriously challenged, I found no indication that Mormon apologists credit Smith with any clear manifestations of divine authority.

Important teachings of Joseph Smith clearly *contradict* the teaching of Jesus Christ. A believer can follow one or the other, but not both. The supernatural signs indicating that Jesus truly was what he said he was – including Messiah, Redeemer, God and Son of God – are found throughout the New Testament and in extra-biblical sources. The biblical warnings about false prophets and false messiahs – "even an *angel*" – noted in the section on Islam must be noted here as well (Gal 1:8-9). In Step 3 we outlined the compelling case for the solid historicity of the Gospels.

Does DNA evidence contradict the Book of Mormon?

The Web site of Ontario Consultants on Religious Tolerance includes an article indicating that DNA studies cast serious doubt on the authenticity of the Book of Mormon.[381] The author, B. A. Robinson, cites an article that appeared in the *Los Angeles Times* in 2002 calling

---

381 **www.religioustolerance.org/lds_migr1.htm**

attention to Simon Southerton's book, *Losing a Lost Tribe: Native Americans, DNA and the Mormon Church*. Southerton, an Australian plant geneticist, is one of a number of scientists who conclude that the results of DNA studies of Native Americans are so seriously in conflict with the Book of Mormon that belief in that book is no longer possible.[382]

The difficulty is that the Book of Mormon – the authoritative source of Mormon doctrine – has long been presented as a historically accurate account of God's interaction with Israelites who sailed across the "Great Waters" to the virtually uninhabited Americas as early as 2247 B.C.

Laman was the eldest son of Lehi, who sailed to the Americas in about 600 B.C. The Book of Mormon indicates that, of these Israelites, only the Lamanites survived and, primarily from them, descended the Indians of the Americas. [383]

However, when DNA sampling was done in recent years among the Native American population, instead of the expected high proportion of Native Americans whose mitochondrial DNA should have matched Israelite DNA, researchers found almost none. Instead, the DNA of Native Americans was far more indicative of Asian and Polynesian ancestry.

FARMS (the Foundation for Ancient Research and Mormon Studies) and others are attempting to reconcile the DNA findings with the Book of Mormon, but, at this writing, the controversy continues.

For the Mormon who has long been faithful to the teachings of this denomination it will certainly not be easy to reexamine them based on these difficulties. In contrast, in view of the history of the Bible addressed in an earlier section, there are solid historical reasons to believe that Jesus, (a) founded his Church on Peter, (b) promised to be with that one Church always, (c) promised that not even the Gates of hell would prevail against it, and: (d) warned against future false prophets.

For the Mormon engaging in missionary activity, it might be well to carefully consider all these concerns. Jesus said that each of us will one day be called before him to be judged by him (Jn 5:22-23). Is Jesus then likely to say to the Mormon:

Well done, my good and faithful servant; you have lived faithfully

---

382 William Lobdell and Larry B. Stammer, "Mormon Scientist, Church Clash Over DNA Test; Anthropologist may be ousted for questioning teachings about Native American ancestry," *LA Times*, December 8, 2002, **www.latimes.com/news**
383 *The Book of Mormon,* Introduction, (2006); *http://scriptures.lds.org/en/bm*

according to the Commandments as revised through Joseph Smith and his successors, and you have drawn many away from the Church I founded upon Peter and promised to be with always....

Or is Jesus more likely to see such accomplishments in a different light?

Discussion Questions

1. Discuss the beliefs attributed to Mormonism by the Christian Study Center. What are some of the difficulties for Mormon-Catholic interfaith dialogue if these beliefs are, in fact, currently held by Mormons?

2. Author William J. Whelan notes that the *Book of Mormon* is "full of contradictions and anachronisms ...." Do you agree? If so, to what extent do you think this affects its credibility as a basis for religious belief?

3. How should an objective reader consider the documentation reported by the late Fr. Hardon regarding the "visionary projects" of the Smith family (e.g., "peepstones," pretense of finding buried money, and metal plates "gotten up" by a black-smith)?

4. In light of Catholic teaching, what can be said of the Brigha-mite belief (prohibited since 1882 by the Edwards Law) that allows a man to have several wives?

5. What can be said of the belief that a living Mormon may arrange a marriage – a "sealing" – of the dead?

6. In comparison to Jesus, what supernatural manifestations of the power and authority of the Creator do Mormons attribute to Joseph Smith?

7. Should the reports of failure of DNA testing to confirm Israelite ancestry of native Americans cause Mormons to lose confidence in the Book of Mormon?

Confucianism

The most important name in Chinese culture is K'ung-fu-tzu - Kung the Master – best known to us as Confucius. He was born about 551 B.C. in the principality of Lu (now Shantung province) and died at age 73 in 479 B.C. He was raised in poverty by his mother after his father died before he was three.

As a tutor in his early 20s, he began to earn a reputation for his personal qualities and his practical wisdom. It was his intention to apply these principals to government and, from age fifty to sixty-three, he traveled widely, offering unrequested suggestions to various persons in authority on how they could better govern their people.

Although biographies written by some would indicate that Confucius had some degree of success, Huston Smith indicates otherwise. Smith notes that those in power were uneasy with his frankness and honesty and for that reason did not place him in any position of real authority.[384]

Confucianism – religion, or ethical-philosophical system?

We are told that Confucius did not set out to found a religion; the primary focus of his writings was on the right ordering of society. In ancient China the dead were worshiped, we are told, and Confucius did make references to the gods. According to Huston Smith, Confucius wrote that if we offend them we have no one to whom we can pray.[385]

But it appears that, great as was his contribution to Chinese culture for over two millennia, we must look to Confucius as one who led his followers more toward an ethical-philosophical consciousness-raising than the formation of a new form of worship or an enhancement of an existing religion. In his article in *Religions of the Twentieth Century*, Dr. Chan Wing-Tsit indicates that, as the word "religion" is commonly understood by those in the West, there is no basis for considering Confucianism a religion. It is not called a "religion" by the Chinese, he says, and adds that there is no organized body of priests, no equivalent of the Bible, no creedal formula and no agreed-upon designation of "gods" as such.[386] However, Chan Wing-Tsit also indicates that Confucians not only worship parents and other ancestors but do so in all seriousness.[387]

---

384 *The World's Religions*, 155-156.
385 *The World's Religions*, 186.
386 *Religions of the Twentieth Century*, 99-100.
387 Ibid., 104.

"Worship" of ancestors?

The late Malachi Martin noted that by the 1600s Jesuit missionaries had created a multimillion member Church in China. At that time the Jesuits had made accommodation within Catholic services for acknowledgment of the Emperor, Confucius and one's forefathers. This resulted in a controversy in Rome.

One faction claimed that the Chinese were giving worship to these entities as gods and thus violating the first Commandment. However, Martin notes that Jesuits carefully studied all the written characters of Chinese and determined that in their religious services *they did not worship as gods* their ancestors, Confucius, or their Emperor. Instead, they merely honored forefathers, Confucius and their Emperor without deifying them.[388]

Initially, in 1704, they were overruled by Pope Clement XI and required to discontinue the accommodations, which resulted in decimation of the Catholic population. However, in 1939 those Jesuits were vindicated. In that year Pope Pius XII issued an authorization that allowed Catholics to participate in these services.[389]

In keeping with the emphasis of this book, however, the question the Confucian must ask is this:

> What supernatural signs, if any, did Confucius manifest that indicate that he, rather than Jesus, spoke and acted with the authority of the Creator?

The answer, of course, is none. To my knowledge, no Confucian apologist has ever claimed otherwise. Jesus died on the cross to redeem us, arose from death on the third day, and said that each of us will one day stand before him to give an account of our stewardship. Is it prudent, then, to accept Confucius, thereby rejecting Jesus and the Church he founded on Peter, "the Rock" – the Church Jesus promised to be with always?

Discussion Questions

1. Are there sound historical or other reasons to consider Confucianism a religion?

2. What supernatural manifestations of the power and authority of the Creator are attributed to Confucius?

---

388 *The Jesuits,* 211.
389 Ibid., 210-212.

Taoism

Scholars tell us that they are uncertain of the identity of the person or persons who, in about the fourth century B.C., wrote the slim volume known as *Tao Te Ching* or *The Way and its Power* – the "bible" of Taoism. It is generally attributed to one named Li who was later given the honorary title of Lao Tzu, meaning "old philosopher."

Huston Smith relates the tradition that the man who would become known as Lao Tzu, saddened by the lack of natural goodness among his people left, on his water buffalo, for Tibet.

A gatekeeper, sensing something special about the man, convinced him to write his beliefs for the people he was about to leave. Lao Tzu went away and, on the third day, came back with a small booklet entitled *The Way and the Power (Tao Te Ching),* a book that continues to be regarded as the primary written work of Taoism.[390]

Smith adds that he then left his country, without any attempt to promote his system of thought or answer questions. We know nothing more about him and even this, based on tradition, is uncertain.

In his article on Taoism, Dr. William James Hail noted that most Chinese saw the universe as having heaven as the ultimate power, at times of greater superiority that the various deities. But Hail tells us that the *Tao Te Ching* rarely refers to heaven, and to God only once, saying that the Tao may have preceded God (I:4:2b;3).[391]

Both Hail and Smith give comprehensive overviews of the complexities of Taoism and a number of references for further study. "The Great Tao" is described as a latent power in the universe that in some way begins to unfold and move irresistibly forward, somehow bringing into existence gods, spirits and human beings. The word "Tao" means "way" or "road," but it can also mean the power that exists throughout the universe and the evolution of the universe. Smith tells us that Taoism became a full-fledged Church, but Hail notes that Taoist priests were relegated to ministering to the ignorant and superstitious of China after so many of their fellow priests left Taoism for Buddhism.[392]

Lao Tzu – "Old philosopher," or one with divine authority to found a religion?

But our primary focus here is the evidence, if any, of supernatural authority of the founder of each religion, as best we can discern it,

---

390 *The World's Religions,* 197.
391 *Religion in the Twentieth Century,* 85-86.
392 *Religion in the Twentieth Century,* 91.

compared to Christ. By this measure should we reject Jesus and follow the "Old Philosopher," the enigmatic Lao Tzu, who believed "The Way" may have existed before God and may have brought gods into existence? Or, based on all that we know about Jesus, does it appear that he is the one who has greater credibility as the one who spoke with the authority of the Almighty Creator in founding his Church?

Discussion Questions

1. The *Tao Te Ching,* the foundational book of Taoism, states that the Tao – the latent force in the universe – may have *preceded* God. What does this indicate in regard to the Taoist versus the Christian concept of God?

2. Whom would it seem more prudent to follow: Jesus, or Li, the enigmatic "Old Philosopher"? Why?

Baha'i

William J. Whalen in *Separated Brethren* tells us that Baha'i began as a sect of Islam and, although it has become westernized – with an important temple in Wilmette, Illinois – it retains its Islamic flavor and believers must submit to a central religious authority in Haifa.

Jesus – just one of many prophets?

Baha'i claim their religion does not deny the older religions; it fulfills them. It has been doing so gradually, over the centuries, through what believers call *manifestations,* i.e., persons considered prophets, such as Adam, Abraham, Moses, Krishna, Zoroaster, Buddha, Jesus and Mohammed. For the Baha'i, the most recent of these manifestations is Bahá'u'lláh (1817-1892). Though seen by many as incompatible, it is claimed that the teachings revealed by such manifestations have been inexorably pointing to the one ultimate divine truth, as people grow in their capacity to accept that truth. Properly understood, according to Baha'i, all the religions of the world are thus not incompatible but integral since all originate from the same divine source.

Baha'i therefore teaches full inter-faith compatibility of the central elements of the great religions and that these religions have the same purpose. These religions differ only in what Baha'i consider secondary aspects and are, in fact, steps in the "spiritual evolution" of humanity.[393] This evolution is not only spiritual. As we read on the official Baha'i Web site, it is of primary importance that all peoples everywhere realize that they are *one*, and work to bring about that divinely-willed unity in the world.[394]

The chronology of Baha'i may be outlined as follows, according to Wikipedia:

1844 – Iranian Siyyid `Ali-Muhammad became the self-proclaimed proclaimed *Gate* (*Bab* in Arabic). Claiming the inspiration of Scripture, he prophesied the coming of a kind of Messianic leader whom God himself would reveal.

1863 – Mirza Husayn Ali of Nur, who had been a follower of the Bab, discerned that it was he to whom the Bab's prophecy applied. He assumed the title Baha'u'llah (Arabic: "Glory of God") and, according to *Wikipedia*, in his writings claimed to be the symbolic convergence of the Messianic figures of

---

393 *Separated Brethren,* 231.
394 Baha'i Topics, **http://info.bahai.org**

Judaism, Christianity, Zoroastrianism, Shi'a Islam, Sunni Islam and Babism.

1892 – Baha'u'llah died in that year, having willed his title and position to his son, Abdul-Baha, who led the faithful, at times in prison and in exile, until his own death in 1921. Baha'i has since been led not by a single religious leader but by a governing organization that includes both elected and appointed members.

The Baha'i faith has no professional clergy. In their worship services they read from sacred books of various religions, including *The Bible*, *The Koran* and *Bhagavad-Gita*. Their temples are nine-sided representing the nine major religions of the world. Monasticism is prohibited and the reality of "original sin" is denied, as is the existence of Satan. The Baha'i do not formally attempt to describe the state of the soul after death, except to say that heaven is the state of a soul close to God, whereas hell is the state of a soul that is far from God. The idea of hell as a place or state of *eternal* punishment for a soul who dies unrepentant in grave or "mortal" sin seems alien to Baha'i belief, at least as explained on their Web site.

Jeffery Huffines, the United States Baha'i representative to the United Nations, noted in effect that, in order to ensure peace in the world, Baha'i favors some form of global governance and that, although the United Nations may have its flaws, it has no equal as an international body through which nations may strive for global peace.[395]

There is, of course, much more to the history and practices of the Baha'i faith; interested readers may want to read *Separated Brethren*, *Al Kitah Al-Aqdas* ("The Most Holy Book") or other books on the subject, or use the Internet.

Does Baha'i fulfill, and not deny, other religions?

The claim is made that Baha'i does not deny the older religions; it fulfills them. However, this claim cannot withstand even casual analysis. If Baha'i accepts the Christian belief in the divinity of Jesus and in his crucifixion and Resurrection, it thereby unequivocally rejects Islam, which flatly rejects all three of these Christian beliefs. If Baha'i accepts the Hindu and Buddhist belief in reincarnation – transmigration

---

395 "US Baha'i community urges strong support for the United Nations – including full US funding." **www.onecountry.org/e112/e11209as.htm**

of souls – it thereby unequivocally rejects the Christian and Islamic teaching that we live one life only; after that one life comes death and judgment and, ultimately, either heaven or hell for all eternity.

Surely Baha'i believers profess their faith with reverence and only the best intentions. However, such believers and anyone considering joining Baha'i face an insurmountable difficulty: Given that Baha'u'llah and his son Abdul-Baha died, as all mere mortals do, what rationale can be give for following them and their administrative successors rather than the *risen* Christ, as described in the Bible interpreted by the one apostolic Church Christ founded and promised to remain with?

Discussion Questions

1. Shoghí Effendí Rabbání, head of the Baha'i faith from 1921 until his death in 1957, wrote that the central teachings of all the great religions are essentially compatible, and that they differ only in nonessentials. Do you agree or disagree? Why?

2. Discuss the claim that Baha'i does not deny the older (pre-nineteenth century) religions; it fulfills them. Is this claim defensible? Explain.

Freemasonry

It may come as a surprise to many to find Freemasonry listed as a religion. However, John Ankerberg and John Weldon present this view in emphatic terms in *The Secret Teachings of the Masonic Lodge – a Christian Perspective*. The authors claim that Freemasonry turns men away from Christ in at least five ways:

(1) Freemasonry deliberately deletes the name of Christ from its prayers and Scripture quotations; (2) Freemasonry requires a Christian to disobey Christ by officially prohibiting all discussion of Christ from Lodge activities; (3) Freemasonry blasphemously offers the titles and offices of Christ to unbelievers; (4) Freemasonry denies the deity of Christ; and (5) Freemasonry purposely downplays the unique role of Christ as Savior, e.g. by teaching that the Christian message of divine redemption is merely a revival of earlier pagan stories.[396]

Catholic Freemasons may not receive Holy Communion

The *Catholic Encyclopedia* lists sixteen papal pronouncements against Freemasonry since 1738: Clement XII (1738); Benedict XIV (1751); Pius VII (1821); Leo XII (1825); Pius VIII (1830); Pius IX (1846, 1849, 1864, 1865, 1869, 1873); and Leo XIII (1882, 1890, 1894 [twice], 1902).[397]

In addition, Joseph Cardinal Ratzinger (now Pope Benedict XVI) stated the position of the Roman Catholic Church November 26, 1983. In a *Declaration on Masonic Organizations* approved by Pope John Paul II, he said that Catholics who join such organizations are in a state of serious sin; they may not receive Holy Communion.[398]

Worship of Baal?

A major concern of Ankerberg and Weldon is that in the Royal Arch Degree [18th Degree, Scottish Rite] Masons actually worship three "Gods" simultaneously: Jehovah; Baal, the Canaanite / Babylonian god from which was derived the Satanic name Baalzebub or Beelzebul; and, (probably) the Egyptian god Osiris.[399] This is done, the authors indicate, when the Mason undergoing the Royal Arch Degree is

---

396 *The Secret Teachings of the Masonic Lodge,* 126.
397 **www.newadvent.org/cathen/09771a.htm**
398 See Canon 916 of the *Code of Canon Law* promulgated in January, 1983, which applies to those "conscious of grave sin": **www.intratext.com/IXT/ENG0017/_P37. HTM.**
399 *The Secret Teachings of the Masonic Lodge,* 119-125.

told that the true name for the God he has been praying to *throughout the different degrees of Masonry* is "Ja-bul-on."

The authors quote *Coil's Masonic Encyclopedia*, indicating that Coil himself states that "bul" or "bal" refers to the Babylonian god Baal. Author W. J. Whalen, also states that Masons worship Baal as described by Ankerberg and Weldon.

If he finds that these authors are correct, can the Freemason / Christian avoid the conclusion that his salvation may be in jeopardy because he is willfully violating God's first Commandment?

Authors Ankerberg and Weldon note that a 1975 issue of *Masonic Square* admitted a connection between English Masons and Rosicrucianism. Ankerberg and Weldon describe Rosicrucianism as a mystical brotherhood stressing personal development of occult powers, spirit contact, and the cultivation of altered states of consciousness. The name derives from the order's symbol, a combination of a rose and a cross.

For the reader who is a Freemason, do you not feel obligated in conscience to find out for yourself what truth there may be in the statements made by Whelan, by Ankerberg and Weldon, Crow, Coil, and others?

The need to "Choose whom you will serve"

For the Freemason in business or other endeavor who has come to depend on the advantages of Masonic membership, a decision to leave Freemasonry as a matter of conscience could mean giving up very much indeed, according to the sources I quote in this chapter. Masons hold many influential positions in almost every walk of life, of course, and Whalen notes that, within American Freemasonry, there is no larger group than the Royal Arch.[80] Certain elements of the Royal Arch oath egregiously violate fundamental principles of law, justice and conscience, as well as federal and state employment regulations and the oath one takes upon becoming a judge, juror or law enforcement officer:

> I furthermore promise and swear, that I will employ a Companion Royal Arch Mason in preference to any other person of equal qualifications …. I furthermore promise and swear, that I will assist a Companion Royal Arch Mason when I see him engaged in any difficulty, and will espouse his cause so far as to extricate him from the same, whether he be right or wrong.[400]

---

400 *Duncan's Masonic Ritual and Monitor*, Royal Arch or 7th Degree, Malcolm C.

Nor is the Royal Arch oath to be taken lightly, according to the accompanying penalty for violation: "to have my skull smote off, and my brains exposed to the scorching rays of the meridian sun, should I knowingly or wilfully [sic] violate or transgress any part of this my solemn oath or obligation of a Royal Arch Mason. So help me God, and keep me steadfast in the due performance of the same."

Except for what I have learned from the references indicated, I claim no knowledge at all about Freemasonry. Based on these reports, however, it appears that no Christian – certainly no Catholic, in good conscience, can be a Freemason or a member of any of its affiliate organizations.

As announced by Cardinal Ratzinger in 1983 with the approval of Pope John Paul II, Catholics who join such organizations are in a state of serious sin; they may not receive Holy Communion.

An extensive eight-part history of Freemasonry from the *Catholic Encyclopedia* is listed on the New Advent Web site.[401]

Discussion Questions

1. Freemasonry has a long history of philanthropy in the United States and elsewhere. Needy Catholics have been among the many who have received the benefit of the generosity of various Masonic lodges and the auxiliary organizations affiliated with them. In light of this benevolence, many rank-and-file Freemasons are perplexed at the stand of the Catholic against Freemasonry. The fact is that there have been sixteen papal pronouncements against Freemasonry since 1738. Why has the Church taken this stand against Freemasonry?

2. Consider the view of authors Ankerberg and Weldon that Freemasons worship a kind of "trinity." Do you agree or disagree?

3. Do the claims that Freemasons worship Baal appear substantive? Why?

4. Define Rosicrucianism. Authors Ankerberg and Weldon associate Freemasonry with Rosicrucianism. Do you believe their claim is substantive? Why?

Duncan (1866). **www.sacred-texts.com/mas/dun/dun08.htm**
401 **www.newadvent.org/cathen/09771a.htm**

5. Marty Barrack states that the fraternity of Freemasonry deliberately deceives Master Masons [in regard to the Blue Degrees] and that "Men who wear the Masonic ring have no idea that they are mocking Christianity." Do you find it credible that such deception, if it occurs, could persist for very long without the Master Masons becoming aware of it and in some way objecting? On what do you base your answer?

6. In *Declaration on Masonic Organizations,* what did Joseph Cardinal Ratzinger write about Catholics who are Freemasons?

New Age

The influence of *New Age* as an alternative to traditional religions may be best seen by walking into your local bookstore. Due to their popularity, there may well be more books in the New Age section than books about *all* mainstream Christian and non-Christian beliefs in the Religion section.

New Age has become a catchall title for a bewildering array of quasi-religious and occult / Satanic beliefs. The one belief totally dismissed by New Age is monotheism. In particular, it rejects Christianity.

The New Age movement is said to have its roots in Theosophy, which originated with Helena Petrovna Blavatsky (1831-1891). Those who engage in occult practices hold her main work, *The Secret Doctrine*, in high regard.

The Secret Doctrine is a cleverly written two-volume work strewn with such terms as *Swastika, Gnostic Ophites, Arhats, Agathodaemon, Kakodaemon* and *Anubis.* The *Serpent* is presented as something to be adored and admired for its great intelligence. God, however, rather than being all good, is said to be both good *and evil.*

However, like a slick gothic video game, the credibility of *The Secret Doctrine* collapses when given even the most basic reality check. In the Introduction, Blavatsky refers to the law of probability through which, by joining with others, she claims we can transform doubt into near certainty. She gives the example of a person who has only a 50 percent level of certitude regarding occultist claims. Thanks to the law of probability, she asserts, this person need only find nine others with the same 50 percent level of confidence in the occult to somehow reach a combined level of certitude of 1023/1024 – virtual certainty.

Given the peer pressure among the young, this gross misapplication of probability mathematics surely lures many into the occult. That her claim is erroneous is quite evident to any teen who ever saw his or her high school football team lose to a team considered a pushover, or to a group of ten adults who would go to the racetrack each 50% certain that the one horse they would all bet on would win.

A further example of Blavatsky's twisted reasoning is her *Kabala*-based claim that, in the Genesis account of the fall, *the Serpent and God are really the same person* and *Jehovah and Cain are the same person.*[402]

---

402 *The Secret Doctrine,* Vol. 1, 414, **www.theosociety.org/pasadena/sd/sd1-2-11.htm**

It would seem that Blavatsky gives her readers little credit for intelligence, or at least for the prudence to check her claim against what Genesis actually says. Upon doing so, we find that Blavatsky would have us believe that; (a) *The Lord God created himself:* **"Now the serpent was more subtle than any other wild creature that the Lord God had made."** (Gen 3:1) and; (b) *The Lord God cursed himself:* **"The Lord God said to the serpent, 'Because you have done this, cursed are you …'"** (Gen 3:14). And, in banishing Cain, God again cursed himself: **"and now you are cursed from the ground …"** (Gen 4:11).

Anyone familiar with the Bible knows that, from beginning to end, it presents Satan as the archenemy of God. And the Bible presents God not only as distinct from Satan and superior to him in every way, but as Satan's Creator. Clearly, then, the Kabalistic "key" Blavatsky puts forth – that Satan and Cain are identical with the Lord God – simply won't open the lock.

I wonder if, sitting around a sulfurous campfire toasting whatever demons toast, they shake their heads in amazement, thinking:

> How can these otherwise intelligent human *adepts* and *novices* so easily swallow our clever lies tinged with truth that draw them ever nearer to The Father of Lies, who *despises* them, and ever farther from Truth personified, who died on the cross out of love for them?

In the early 1900s Theosophy was promoted by Alice A. Bailey (1880-1949) who, in 1922, founded the *Lucifer* Publishing Company in New York City. (The following year she renamed it the *Lucius* Publishing Company). Bailey wrote more than twenty books of revelations she claimed to have "channeled" from a deceased Tibetan "spiritual master."[403]

As noted elsewhere in *7-Step Reason,* we are free to believe as we wish. In regard to beliefs of the New Age movement I simply ask: **"Who says so, and with what evidence that he or she spoke with the authority of the Creator?"** Where is the evidence that Blavatsky, Bailey and other leaders of the New Age Movement manifested the authority of the Creator – *including power over death itself* – as Jesus did? The answer, of course, is nowhere. Why, then, would anyone believe that after death the fate of New Agers will be any different from

---

403 Lee Penn; "Beware! The New Age Movement is more than Self-Indulgent Silliness," *New Oxford Review,* July-August 2000.

that of so many others who reject God and his Commandments?

As noted in the following section on Satanism, the dark power of the occult is no match for the power and authority of Jesus, who said, "I am the light of the world; he who follows me will not walk in darkness, but will have the light of life" (Jn 8:12).

We can choose to walk in the labyrinth of New Age darkness or emerge into the light of Christ. The choice – with its eternal consequences – is for each reader to make.

The book *Catholics and the New Age,* by Fr. Mitch Pacwa, is an informative overview of Jungian psychology, the Enneagram, Astrology and other aspects of New Age belief. Readers will find a number of informative articles on New Age by Fr. Mitch Pacwa, S.J., and others on the *Catholic Pages* Web site."[404] Another book giving sound Catholic insight into New Age deception is *The New Age Counterfeit: A Study Guide for Individual and Group Use,* by Johnnette S. Benkovic who hosts "The Abundant Life" on EWTN television, as well as the "Living His Life Abundantly" and "Moments of Truth Live" programs on EWTN Radio.

Discussion Questions

1. Is New Age belief compatible with Catholic belief in Christ?

2. In what belief is New Age said to have its roots?

3. What do you think about the author's characterization of demons around a sulfurous campfire and their thoughts about their human followers?

---

404 **www.catholic-pages.com/dir/new_age.asp**

Satanism

Those who practice Satanism apparently believe that by paying homage to Satan they gain an ominous power over people and situations. Whereas most believers endeavor to avoid hell and its eternal suffering, Satanists want to go there to be with the one they serve.

There is strong aversion to anything having to do with Jesus or his Mother, and the Commandments are not only broken but also ridiculed. With abhorrence for the holy days of Christmas and Easter, they celebrate the unholy night – *All Hallow E'en* (the night before All Saints Day) – which our children celebrate as "Halloween." It seems to me that the Satanist may want to ask himself or herself:

When all is said and done, do I want to be a winner, or a loser?

As earlier noted, there is overwhelming historical evidence affirming the astonishing supernatural power of Jesus; power that far exceeds that of Satan. From beginning to end, Holy Scripture – backed by extensive extra-biblical history – is filled with accounts in which God is the winner and Satan the loser:

Satan the loser – thrown out of heaven for defying God, after being created Lucifer; "Light Bearer"; the most beautiful of angels (Rev 12:7:9, Jn 8:44).

Satan the loser – failing in his effort to tempt Jesus in the desert (Mt 4:1-10).

Satan the loser – in the humiliation of his demons before Jesus as he expelled them from the possessed man (Mt 8:29).

Satan the loser – as these exorcized demons plead with Jesus: *"Have you come to torture us before the appointed time?"*

Satan the loser – as these exorcized demons begged Jesus to let them "possess" a nearby herd of pigs. Doesn't that strike you as pathetic?

Satan the loser – couldn't even manage to stop the escape into the desert of the Woman Clothed with the Sun, and her Child. After her escape, "the dragon was angry with the woman, and went off to make war on the rest of her offspring, on those who keep the commandments and bear testimony to Jesus" (Rev. 12:17).

[Addressing the Satanist directly now]
If you saw a strong man beating a 2-year-old would you:

    (a) help the man beat the child, or;
    (b) stop him and get help for the child?

In "making war on the rest of her offspring" is the powerful Satan not acting toward us as the man who was beating the small, defenseless child? Is this Satan *really* a leader whom you are proud to follow?

In Mt 8:29, above, the demons spoke of their punishment. When the **appointed time of punishment** comes for Satan and his demons, do you not think they will become enraged? At that time, i.e., after the Second Coming of Christ (Rev. 20:1), upon whom will the tortured demons be able to vent their rage? Do you really think that, in the grip of God's eternal punishment, they will bring you milk and cookies, fluff your pillow, adjust the air conditioning and say, "sleep well, my little human-soul friend?"

As a loyal follower of Satan, are you not expected to offend God greatly in order to please your evil leader? How, then, can you hope to avoid your own share of punishment that Jesus promised would befall those who die, unrepentant, in grave sin? Do you really believe that Satan – himself "thrown into the lake of fire and brimstone where the beast and the false prophet were, and they will be tormented day and night for ever and ever." (Rev. 20:10) – would wish to alleviate your torment rather than increase it to match or exceed his own?

Even if Satan wanted to help you, on what basis can you anticipate that, all of a sudden, Satan would be given the power to override God's decree of punishment for him and his demons and for you and other condemned sinners? Is Satan not inferior to God, who created him? Who, then, could make Satan superior to God?

Are you one of those who want to go to hell because "all my friends will be there" and believe it will be one unending party? Consider the parable of the rich man and Lazarus, the beggar whom the unnamed rich man had denied even the scraps from his table (Lk 16:19-31). After being denied even a drop of water to ease his torment, "for I am tortured in these flames" does the rich man settle back and say; "Well, at least I will soon have the companionship of my brothers." No. Instead he begs God, unsuccessfully, to send someone to warn his five brothers so they will repent and *not join him* in hell. Does this sound like a man who can go to the refrigerator for a cold drink?

Since hell is not a place of benevolence, the rich man's motive may have been to avoid even greater suffering at the hands of those brothers. To the extent they imitated the rich man, they might well see him as partly responsible for their own loss of salvation.

In any case, suppose you are the first in your group to die and enter hell, expecting that your friends will one day join you there. How will you feel if your friends, learning from your mistakes, reform their lives and enter heaven, waving a final farewell to you across that great chasm? According to Scripture, you will have eternity in hell to consider that you could have been with them at the eternal "party" – the eternal banquet, in heaven.

Through his followers, Satan will promise much to you in return for rejecting Jesus and following him. You are not stupid. But how smart are you, really, if you continue to believe the "Father of Lies" and do his bidding?

> *But I took an oath transferring lordship and possession of my soul from "The Ancient Enemy" to the hands of the "All Power-ful" Lucifer. I sealed that oath with my own blood! It's impossi-ble for me to reject Satan now!*

Such resolve is music to the ears of Satan. But is it valid? Suppose you acquired a car under a standard lease agreement. You might be foolish enough to allow a malevolent third party to drive the car wherever he wished with you as a passenger. But suppose you said to your evil driver, "I hereby give this car to you." Would your words make him the owner of the car? They would not, of course; the car would still belong to the one who leased it to you.

Even if you accepted a substantial sum of money – or important favors – from the third party for the car, it would not become his. Even sealing your statement with your own blood – dramatic though it may appear – would not convey ownership to your evil driver. Why? Because the true owner of the car – the one who leased it to you alone – never authorized you to transfer ownership to another.

What is true of that leased car is true of your soul and mine. The one who created our souls never authorized us to transfer ownership to anyone else (e.g., "Behold, all souls are mine" Ez 18:4).

An oath of loyalty to Lucifer / Satan is gravely sinful. Clearly such an oath, and the sins that would follow, would place one firmly on the path to hell. But in Isaiah 1:18 we read: *"though your sins are like scarlet, they shall be as white as snow …."*

Would "sins like scarlet" not include a blood-sealed oath to Lucifer / Satan? Jesus, of course, gave us many assurances that our sins can be forgiven. Do you still doubt that you can leave the path to hell and begin to run toward heaven? If so, stop reading now. Find a Bible, go to a quiet place and read Lk 15:11-32: The Parable of the Prodigal Son. He was "dead, and is alive; he was lost, and is found." And so it can be with you. You need only take the first few steps in his direction and your *true* Father will run to meet you, throw his arms around your neck and kiss you.

You were lost, but are found.

Discussion Questions

1. "What is the meaning of the term *All Hallow E'en*?

2. Throughout the Bible Satan is clearly "the loser" in his opposition to Jesus. Give some examples of this.

3. In hell, can Satan be expected to ease the suffering of humans who loyally did his bidding during their lives on earth? Explain.

4. Does it make any sense to desire hell because "All my friends will be there?" Explain.

5. Taking a blood-oath in an attempt to transfer lordship and possession of one's soul to Satan *does not* doom one to hell. Why not?

6. What does Ezekiel 18:4 tell us about the soul?

7. What do Isaiah 1:18 and Luke 15:11-32 tell us about God's love and forgiveness?

New World Order; One World Religion?

Just about everyone has seen the cartoon of the three fish of increasing size. The first and smallest is swimming happily along, unaware that behind it is a much larger fish about to devour it. The second, in turn, is unaware that a huge fish is about to devour it as well as the first fish. I was unable to find the name of the cartoonist, who deserves high praise for a depiction that can so readily be applied to the ominous movement toward One World Religion.

The first fish may be seen as the Catholic citizen of the United States today who, taking the Constitution and Bill of Rights at face value, assumes that he retains in full measure the freedom of speech and of religion provided for by the founding fathers in those documents. Catholic citizens of most free world countries are in a similar situation.

The second fish represents government, both Federal and State. While bringing about much that is good, legislation and judicial decisions increasingly run roughshod over the doctrines of the Catholic Church.[405] In an increasing number of jurisdictions a Catholic, other Christian, or Jew can now be prosecuted for quoting passages from the Bible that a homosexual chooses to consider offensive. "Love speech," in the sense of loving one's neighbor enough to attempt to ensure his / her eternal salvation, can now be considered "hate speech."

The third fish – the huge one about to devour the other two – is, sad to say, the United Nations. Much has been written in recent years about the progress being made by the U.N. in regard to global sovereignty and its key component, One World Religion.

Mary Jo Anderson, who has written extensively on the subject for *Crisis* Magazine and *WorldNetDaily.com,* summed up the problem as follows in September 2002:

> A great vise is closing upon American Christians. On the one hand Christians are pressured by their own nation where liberal judges increasingly outlaw in public expression of faith while legalizing every form of immorality. On the other hand, the global juggernaut gathers military muscle and legal powers of crushing scope.[406]

---

405 e.g., induced abortion, euthanasia, ubiquitous pornography, same-sex marriage, artificial birth control paraphernalia and training made available to children despite parental objection, embryonic (as opposed to non-embryonic) stem cell research.
406 "Neo Gnostics at the End of the Age," *WorldNetDaily.com*, September 25, 2002.
http://petersnet.net/research/retrieve_full.cfm?RecNum=4635

The centerpiece of the One World Religion is The Earth Charter. This Charter can be accessed through the Web site of The Green Cross, an organization headed by Mikhail Gorbachev, one of the principals responsible for its development.[407]

The Earth Charter, which would subordinate all religious teaching to the needs of "our mother the earth," is being presented as a document that would appear to supersede the Ten Commandments.

On the morning of January 24, 2002 The Earth Charter, ensconced in an ornate, 200-pound "Ark of Hope," crafted to resemble the Ark of the Covenant (even to being carried between two poles), was exhibited in U.N. headquarters in New York City during a meeting in preparation for the World Summit on Sustainable Development, i.e., a meeting to consider the many methods of *limiting* world population. The new "Ark" has been ceremoniously presented in several countries during the past two years.[408] The true Ark of the Covenant contained, among other sacred objects, the tablets on which **I AM** inscribed the Ten Commandments given to Moses (Ex 40:20).[409]

In October, 2001, Belgian priest Fr. Michel Schooyans wrote as follows in regard to the thrust of the U.N. "One World Religion" initiative:

> Religions in general, and above all the Catholic religion, figure among the obstacles that have to be neutralized .... Strongly influenced by the New Age, this [U.N. 'United Initiative of Religions'] project aims, in the end, at the creation of one unique new world religion that would entail right away the prohibition of proselytism on the part of all other religions ... crimes against the "new rights" of man could be judged by the International Criminal Court established at Rome in 1998. For example, to the extent that abortion remained illegal in this or that state, the state in question could be excluded from the "global society"; to the extent that a religious group opposes homosexuality or euthanasia, that group could be condemned by the International Criminal Court for attacking the "new rights of man."[410]

In his 283-page book *La face cachée de l'ONU* (The Hidden Face

---

407 **www.gci.ch/GreenCrossPrograms/earthcharter/earth.html**

408 **www.gci.ch/DigitalForum/digiforum/articles/article2002/earth charter.html**

409 The Earth Charter page; Bill Jacobs, Catholic Conservation Center, **http://conservation.catholic.org/Earth%20Charter.htm**

410 "Globalization's Dark Side," *Inside the Vatican*, October, 2001, **www.petersnet.net/browse/4026.htm**

of the United Nations),[411] Fr. Schooyans describes in considerable detail the primary philosophical foundation of the U.N. [the philosophy of Hans Kelsen (1881-1973)], the changes brought about through its many conferences, the plans and steps already taken to bring about a "World Government" and the means by which it seeks to deal with "Christian Dissent." This book is the subject of a most informative article by Philip Vickers, in which he referred to an anti-Catholic *See Change* effort within the U.N. (the UNO) aimed at the Holy See, as well as at Protestants and Muslims.[412]

In September 2002, Mary Jo Anderson sounded the alarm about the attempted criminalization of Catholicism and about the possibility that the Pope may one day be brought before the International Criminal Court:

> The Church is now experiencing ominous threats from various world bodies. Recently, with the advent of the International Criminal Court (ICC), the United Nations and its affiliated systems have openly spoken of the "criminal" intent of Catholic teachings and policy. It jabs the Church for failing to ordain women and suggests that policy is a violation women's rights. The same "criminal" language is used in regard to the Church's teaching on all life issues
> ....
>
> Some fear that the ICC, whose mandate is to prosecute "Crimes against humanity," will some day charge the Vatican with "hate crimes" because it preaches against homosexuality. Or, charge the Church with "crimes against humanity" for preaching against abortion which the UN views as an obstruction of "human rights." If the case is made that that a 'violation' affects millions of people, then the magnitude of the number trips the ICC jurisdiction and we could have a pope hauled before the ICC for defending life in the womb.[413]

The forces arrayed against the Catholic Church, as well as against Judaism, Islam and other religions, are formidable. Lest we be unduly optimistic, Anderson cautions us not to believe there will be a quick and easy resolution of the matter. The course of action she proposes in her *WorldNetDaily.com* article of September 2002 is one that should be a wake-up call for every Catholic: ***"Reconvert paganized America or***

---

411 Published in French, in 2000, by Le Sarment, Fayard.
412 "The Hidden Face of the UNO," Philip Vickers, *Christian Order,* April, 2003.
413 Neo Gnostics at the End of the Age; *WorldNetDaily.com*, September 25, 2002,
http://petersnet.net/research/retrieve_full.cfm?RecNum=4635

be persecuted by it."

In describing the second fish as unaware of the third, I erred; at least in regard to the U.S. Supreme Court. In a 2003 AP news article Gina Holland noted that, despite the concern of a few members of that Court – in particular Justice Antonin Scalia – a majority of the Justices appear to be taking a more global view of law and its interpretation.[414]

In some instances, of course, the laws of particular countries have a direct bearing on cases to be decided by the U.S. Supreme Court. However, it seems that Holland is expressing the broader concern that, to the extent that our Supreme Court justices give increasing weight to international (and foreign intra-national) court decisions, they reduce their reliance on the U.S. Constitution, contrary to their oath of office. The deeper concern, of course, is that this may lead to serious compromise of U.S. sovereignty. Will the appointment to the Court of Justices John G. Roberts, Jr. and Samuel A. Alito, Jr. diminish this concern? Time will tell.

To the three fish described at the outset of this chapter can be added a fourth. It is the "Fish" that ultimately overtakes each of us at the moment of our own personal death. This all-encompassing force is Jesus Christ. It was Jesus who said, "The Father judges no one, but has given all judgment to the Son" (Jn 5:22) and, "I am the way, the truth and the life; no one comes to the Father but by me" (Jn 14:6).

Discussion Questions

1. Do you agree or disagree with the author's statement that "While bringing about much that is good, legislation and judicial decisions increasingly run roughshod over the doctrines of the Catholic Church"? Explain.

2. Do you believe, as Mary Jo Anderson does, that "A great vice is closing on American Christians?" If so, what examples of this, if any, have you seen or become aware of?

3. Imagine that a one-world religion of the kind described by Mary Jo Anderson and Fr. Michel Schooyans was mandated globally. In what ways, if any, do you think life would change for Catholics, for other Christians, and for those of other religions? How do you think clergy of the various faiths might be affected?

---

414 "Ginsburg: Int'l Law Shaped Court Rulings;" Gina Holland; Associated Press; August 2, 2003, **http://news.yahoo.com/news?tmpl=story2&cid=558&u=/ap/ 20030803/ap_on_go_su_co/ginsburg_3&printer=1**

4. Go online and read the latest version of the Earth Charter. In what ways do you believe it is compatible with the beliefs of Catholics and other Christians? In what ways does it seem in conflict with these beliefs?

5. An "Arc" intended to represent the biblical Ark of the Covenant has been used to promote the Earth Charter. How do you think devout Jews and Christians should regard this method of promoting the Earth Charter?

6. Abortion is one of the principal means by which *Sustainable Development* is to be achieved. Mary Jo Anderson expressed concern that, because the Catholic Church strongly opposes abortion, "we could have a pope hauled before the ICC for defending life in the womb." Do you share her concern?

7. What effect, if any, do you think an international perspective, reflected in decisions of the U.S. Supreme Court, would have on the ability of Catholics and other Christians to freely practice their faith?

The seven steps described in these pages may be seen as paving stones across an expanse of very muddy ground. Test them by means of the various sciences. Test the Semitism-based studies of the many early-date / eyewitness Scripture scholars against the popular view that the Gospels are doubtful, historically, due to presumed late-date / no eyewitness origin. Test these steps against the claims made by authoritative spokespersons for other Christian and non-Christian faiths. With Mt 23:2-3 in mind ("[O]bserve whatever they tell you, but not what they do ....") test them in light of the reported instances of sexual scandal among Catholic clergy. Test them against the prohibitions and "liberties" initiated by both jaws of "the great vice closing upon American Christians."

Most importantly, let us test them – on our knees before God – for their usefulness in leading us to the Church that will guide us as we make the choices that will determine how we will spend eternity.

Let us then reflect on the question asked by Jesus after he said, "For whoever would save his life will lose it; and whoever loses his life for my sake and the gospel's will save it":

For what does it profit a man, if he gain the whole world, but suffer the loss of his own soul? (Mk 8:36-37).[415]

---

415 Confraternity of Christian Doctrine; *The New Testament* – a revision of the Challoner-Rheims version. Benziger Brothers, Inc.

Bibliography of Primary Sources and Recommended Reading

Ahmed Deedat Abul-Qasim; *What the Bible says about Muhummed* (Peace be upon Him), Ahmed Deedat Abul-Qasim Publishing House (Saudi Arabia, Jeddah, 1979).

Ali, Daniel and Spencer, Robert. *Inside Islam: A Guide for Catholics* (West Chester: Ascension Press, 2003).

_____. *The American Heritage Dictionary of the English Language, Fourth Edition* (Boston: Houghton Mifflin Company, 2006).

Ankerberg, John and Weldon, John. *The Secret Teachings of the Masonic Lodge: A Christian Perspective* (Chicago: Moody Publishing, 1989, 1990).

_____. *Apologetics Concordance.* Single two-sided laminated sheet; More than five hundred biblical verses in more than 50 categories; (San Juan Catholic Seminars, P.O. Box 5253, Farmington, NM, 1999, 2003).

_____. Augustine of Hippo. *The Confessions of Saint Augustine;* Translated, with introduction and notes, by John K. Ryan (New York: Image Books, Doubleday / Random House, 1960).

Behe, Michael J. *Darwin's Black Box* (New York: The Free Press / Simon & Schuster, 1996).

Belloc, Hilaire. *The Great Heresies* (London: Sheed & Ward 1938; Rockford: TAN, 1991).

Belloc, Hilaire. *How the Reformation Happened* (New York: R. M. McBride 1928; Rockford: TAN, 1992).

Benkovic, Johnnette S. *The New Age Counterfeit: A Study Guide for Individual or Group Use,* Revised Edition (Emeryville, CA: Faith Publishing Company / Alibris, 1997)

Bennett, Rod. *Four Witnesses: The Early Church in Her Own Words* (San Francisco: Ignatius Press, 2002).

_____. *The Bhagavad Gita*; Mascaro, Juan, translator (London: Penguin Books, 1962).

Brown, (Rev.) Raymond E.; Donfried, Karl P. and Reumann, John, editors. *Peter in the New Testament*, The Lutheran-Catholic Dialogue;

Minneapolis: Augsburg; New York: Paulist Press, 1973. (Quoted in *Jesus, Peter and The Keys*, p. 16).

Brown, (Rev.) Raymond E.; *Biblical Exegesis and Church Doctrine,* Copyright © 1985 by Raymond E. Brown, S.S.; Paulist Press, Inc., New York / Mahwah, NJ. www.paulistpress.com

Brown, (Rev.) Raymond E. *Biblical Reflections on Crises Facing the Church*; Copyright © 1975; the Missionary Society of St. Paul the Apostle in the State of New York; Paulist Press, Inc., New York Mahwah, NJ www.paulistpress.com

Brown, (Rev.) Raymond E. *The Birth of the Messiah*; Copyright © 1977, 1993; the Associated Sulpicians of the U.S.; Anchor Bible Reference Library; Doubleday (Random House, Inc.), New York, NY.

Brown, (Rev.) Raymond E. *101 Questions and Answers on the Bible*; Copyright © 1990 by Raymond E. Brown, S.S., Paulist Press, Inc., New York / Mahwah, NJ. www.paulistpress.com

Brown, (Rev.) Raymond E. *An Introduction to the New Testament,* Copyright © 1997, Associated Sulpicians of the U.S.; (New York: Doubleday / Random House).

Brown, (Rev.) Raymond E. *An Introduction to New Testament Christology*; Copyright © 1994; Associated Sulpicians of the U.S.; Published by Paulist Press, Inc., New York / Mahwah, NJ. www.paulistpress.com

Bultmann, Rudolf. "New Testament and Mythology," in *Kerygma and Myth*, ed. Hans Werner Bartsch (London: S.P.C.K. 1964) vol. 1, 39.

Butler, Alban. *The Lives of the Saints*; Complete Edition, edited, revised and supplemented by Herbert Thurston, S.J. and Donald Attwater (New York: P. J. Kenedy & Sons 1956).

Butler, Scott; Dahlgren, Norman; Hess, David. *Jesus, Peter and the Keys: A Scriptural Handbook on the Papacy* (Santa Barbara: Queenship, 1996).

Calvin, John. *Calvin: Institutes of the Christian Religion,* in two volumes, W. L. Jenkins, translated and indexed by Ford Lewis Battles, edited by John T. McNeill (Philadelphia: The Library of Christian Classics, Westminster Press, 1960).

Calvin, John. *Calvin's Commentaries; A Harmony of the Gospels, Matthew, Mark and Luke*; Vol. II; translated by T. H. L. Parker (Grand Rapids: Eerdmans, 1972).

Campbell, Joseph. *The Hero's Journey: The World of Joseph Campbell,* Phil Cousineau and Stuart L. Brown (HarperSanFrancisco, 1990).

Campbell, Joseph. *The Masks of God: Creative Mythology,* (New York: Viking Press, 1968).

Carmignac, Rev. Jean. *The Birth of the Synoptic Gospels* (Quincy, IL: Franciscan Press [Formerly Franciscan Herald Press] 1987).

_____. *Catechism of the Catholic Church,* English; 2nd Ed., Publication no. 5-109; ISBN 1-57455-109-4, Hardcover (Washington: United States Catholic Conference, Inc., 1994, 1997, 2000).

_____. *The Catholic Encyclopedia,* (Robert Appleton Co., 1911), Online Edition, K. Knight (2003) www.newadvent.com

_____. *The Catholic Light*, Official newspaper of the Diocese of Scranton; Catholic Light Publishing Co., Scranton.

_____. *The Catholic Resources Network,* Trinity Communications, Manassas.

_____. *The Catholic World Report,* Published monthly (bimonthly August / September). (San Francisco: Ignatius Press).

Ceruti-Cendrier, Marie-Christine. *Les Evangiles sont des reportages: n'en déplaise à certains (The Gospels are the work of Reporters: too bad if that upsets some people)* (Paris: Tequi, 1997).

_____. *Code of Canon Law,* Code of Canon Law Society Trust (Grand Rapids: Eerdmans, 1983).

Collins, Francis S. *The Language of God: A Scientist Presents Evidence for Belief* (New York: Free Press / Simon & Schuster, 2006).

_____. *Companion to the Catechism of the Catholic Church* (San Francisco: Ignatius Press, 1994).

_____. *Compendium; Catechism of the Catholic Church* (Washington: The United States Conference of Catholic Bishops, exclusive U.S.A. licensee. English translation copyright © 2006 *Libreria Editrice Vaticana.*

Connor, Fr. Charles P. *Defenders of the Faith in Word and Deed* (San Francisco: Ignatius Press, 2003).

Cranston, Ruth. *The Miracle of Lourdes,* © 1955 by Ruth Cranston;

Renewed 1983 by Jean Cranston Taneyhill; © 1988 by Bureau M'edi-cal (New York: Image / Doubleday / Random House).

_____. *Crisis Magazine* (Washington).

Crow, W. B., Witchcraft, *Magic and Occultism* (North Hollywood: Wilshire Book Company, 1968).

Dawson, Christopher. *The Dividing of Christendom* (New York: Sheed & Ward, 1965).

Dembski, William A. *The Design Revolution: Answering the Toughest Questions About Intelligent Design* (Nottingham, U.K., IVP Books, 2004).

Dembski, William A. and Wells, Jonathan. *The Design of Life: Discovering Signs of Intelligence in Biological Systems.* Foundation for Thought and Ethics, Richardson, TX, 2007).

Dungan, David Laird. *A History of the Synoptic Problem: The Canon, the Text, the Composition, and the Interpretation of the Gospels* (New York: Anchor Bible Reference Library / Doubleday / Random House 1999. Rights: Yale University Press, 2007).

Dubay, Fr. Thomas. *The Evidential Power of Beauty: Science and Theology Meet* (San Francisco: Ignatius Press, 1999).

_____. *The Early Years of the Church.* Catholic Information Service; Knights of Columbus (New Haven).

_____. *Encyclopedia Judaica* (Israel, Jerusalem: Keter Publishing House 1972).

_____. *The Essential Catholic Survival Guide* (San Diego: Catholic Answers, 2005).

Eusebius, Bishop of Caesarea (Circa AD 260); *The History of the Church from Christ to Constantine* (Baltimore: Penguin Books, 1965).

Farmer, William R. *The Synoptic Problem* (Macon: Mercer University Press, 1981).

Farmer, William R. *The Gospel of Jesus: The Pastoral Relevance of the Synoptic Problem* (Philadelphia: Westminster / John Knox Press, 1994).

Farmer, William R. "The Present State of the Synoptic Problem," Paper produced for the Synoptic Problem Seminar at SNTS, (Copenhagen, Denmark, 1998).

_____. *The Five Gospels: the search for the authentic words of Jesus;* Robert W. Funk, Roy W. Hoover and the Jesus Seminar (New York: Polebridge / Macmillan, 1993).

_____. *The Florida Catholic*; Diocese of Orlando.

Grodi, Marcus C. *How Firm a Foundation* (Zanesville: Coming Home Resources International, 2002).

Groeschel, C.F.R., Fr. Benedict J. *From Scandal to Hope* (Huntington: Our Sunday Visitor, 2002).

Hahn, Scott. *A Father Who Keeps His Promises: God's Covenant Love in Scripture,* Scott Hahn (Ann Arbor: Charis / Servant, 1998).

Hahn, Scott and Kimberly. *Rome Sweet Home* (San Francisco: Ignatius Press, 1993).

Hardon, S.J., John. *The Protestant Churches of America.* The Missionary Society of Saint Paul the Apostle in the State of New York (New York: Image / Doubleday / Random House, 1969).

_____. *The Holy Bible:* Revised Standard Version; Catholic Edition; Prepared by the Catholic Biblical Association of Great Britain. New Testament, © 1965; Old Testament, Incorporating the Apocrypha, © 1966; by Division of Christian Education of the National Council of Churches of Christ in the United States of America. Published by Thomas Nelson Publishers, Camden, for Ignatius Press, San Francisco.

_____. *Homiletic & Pastoral Review,* (monthly); Kenneth Baker, S.J., Editor, San Francisco.

_____. *Irenaeus, Proof of the Apostolic Preaching,* Translated and annotated by Joseph P. Smith, S.J. (Westminster, MD: Newman Press, 1952).

_____. "The Jewish Antiquities," *The Complete Works of Flavius Josephus; The Celebrated Jewish Historian,* translated by William Whiston, A.M. (Philadelphia: John E. Potter & Co., 1936).

_____. *The Jewish Encyclopedia;* New York / London: Funk and Wagnalls, 1905).

John Paul II; *Crossing the Threshold of Hope*; Arnoldo Mondadori Editor (New York: Albert A. Knopf / Random House, 1994).

Johnson, Phillip E. *Darwin on Trial.* (Downers Grove, IL: Intervarsity Press. 1991, 1993).

Jonson, Luke Timothy. *The Real Jesus: The Misguided Quest for the Historical Jesus and the Truth of the Traditional Gospels* (San Francisco: HarperSanFrancisco, 1996).

Jurgens, Rev. William A. *The Faith of the Early Fathers.*, The Order of St. Benedict, Inc. (Collegeville, MN: The Liturgical Press, 1970).

Keating, Karl. *Catholicism and Fundamentalism,* (San Francisco: Ignatius Press, 1988).

Kelly, Msgr. George A. *The Battle for the American Church* (New York: Doubleday / Random House, 1979. Rights: St. John's University, New York).

Kelly, Msgr. George A. *The Battle for the American Church Revisited* (San Francisco: Ignatius Press, 1995).

Kelly, Msgr. George A. *The New Biblical Theorists: Raymond E. Brown and Beyond* (Ann Arbor: Servant Books, 1983).

Ker, Rev. Ian. *Healing the Wound of Humanity: The Spirituality of John Henry Newman* (London: Darton Longman Todd, 1993).

Kreeft, Peter. *Fundamentals of the Faith: Essays in Christian Apologetics* ((San Francisco: Ignatius Press, 1988).

Kreeft, Peter. *Making Sense out of Suffering* (Ann Arbor: Servant, 1986).

_____. *The Last Two Million Years* (London: Reader's Digest Association, Ltd 1973; London: Reader's Digest Association, Inc. 1973; Philippines: Reader's Digest Association, Far East Ltd., 1977).

_____. *The Latin Mass* Magazine (Fort Collins, CO).

Laux, Fr. John. *Church History: a Complete History of the Catholic Church to the Present Day* (New York: Benzinger Brothers 1930, 1945; Rockford, IL: TAN Books and Publishers, 1989).

_____. *Lives of Saints,* From authorized sources including *Butler's Lives of the Saints*; Editorial supervision by Fr. Joseph Vann, O.F.M. (New York: John J. Crawley & Co., 1954).

Luther, Martin. *The Keys*; in Conrad Bergendoff, ed, trans. Earl Beyer and Conrad Bergendoff, *Luther's Works*, vol. 40 (Philadelphia: Fortress, 1957).

Luther, Martin. "A Letter From Luther to Melanchthon," Letter no. 99. Translated by Erika Bullman Flores for Project Wittenberg (Fort Wayne, IN: Concordia Theological Seminary).

Luxenberg, Christoph (pseudonym). *Die Syro-Aramaeische Lesart des Koran* [*The Syro-Aramaic Reading of the Koran*] (Berlin: Das Arabische Buch, 2000).

Madrid, Patrick, Ed., *Surprised by Truth: 11 Converts Give the Biblical and Historical, Reasons for Becoming Catholic* (San Diego: Basilica Press, 1994).

Maier, Gerhard. "The Church in the Gospel of Matthew: Hermeneutical Analysis of the Current Debate," trans. Harold H. P. Dressler, in D.A. Carson Ed., *Biblical Interpretation and Church Text and Context*, (Flemington Markets, NSW: Paternoster Press, 1984).

Martin, Malachi. *The Jesuits – The Society of Jesus and the Betrayal of the Roman Catholic Church.* (New York: Simon and Schuster, 1987).

McBirnie, William Steuart. *The Search for the Twelve Apostles* (Wheaton, IL: Published by Pyramid Publications for Tyndale House Publishers, 1973).

Muggeridge, Ann Roche. *The Desolate City: The Revolution in the Catholic Church* (San Francisco: HarperCollins, 1990).

_____. *The New American Bible,* The New Catholic Translation (Nashville: Thomas Nelson, 1983).

_____. *New Living Translation* (NLT), Holy Bible, Tyndale Charitable Trust, (Wheaton, IL: Tyndale House Publishers, 1996, 2004).

Newman, (Ven) John Henry. *An Essay on the Development of Christian Doctrine* (New York: Image / Random House, 1960).

Newman, (Ven.) John Henry. *Apologia Pro Vita Sua;* Edited by David J. DeLaura (New York: W.W. Norton & Company, 1968).

Oatis, Gregory. *Catholic Doctrine In Scripture; A Guide To the Verses That Are Key To Affirming the Faith* (Zanesville, OH: Coming Home Resources, 2003).

Olson, Carl E. and Miesel, Sandra. *The Da Vinci Hoax: Exposing the Errors in the Da Vinci Code* (San Francisco: Ignatius Press, 2004).

_____. *Origen: On First Principles*; Translated by G. W. Butterworth (New York: Harper Torchbooks / Harper and Rowe, 1966).

Ott, Ludwig. *Fundamentals of Catholic Dogma.* Translated from German by Patrick Lynch, Ph.D. Edited in English by James Canon Bastible, D.D. (Rockford, IL: TAN Books and Publishers, 1974).

Pacwa, S.J., Mitchell C. *Catholics and the New Age: How Good People are Being Drawn Into Jungian Psychology, the Enneagram and the Age of Aquarius* (Ann Arbor MI: Servant Publications, 1992).

Quasten, Johannes. *Ancient Christian Writers*; V. 28; *Tertullian on Penance and on Purity;* translated by William P. Le Saint, S.J., S.T.D. (Westminster, MD: The Newman Press, 1959).

Quasten, Johannes. *Patrology,* Volume I, *The Beginnings of Patristic Literature* (Westminster, MD: The Newman Press / Utrecht-Brussels: Spectrum Publishers, 1950).

Quasten, Johannes, and Plumpe, Joseph C. *Proof of the Apostolic Preaching; Ancient Christian Writers*; v. 16; Translated by Joseph P. Smith, S.J. (Westminster, MD: The Newman Press, 1952).

Ratzinger, Joseph Cardinal. *Foundations and Approaches of Biblical Exegesis.* The annual Erasmus Lecture, January 7, 1988. Sponsored by the Rockford Institute's Center on Religion and Society, *Origins,* Vol. 17: No 35, February 11, 1988 (Washington: Catholic News Service / USCCB).

_____. *The Ratzinger Report*; An exclusive interview of Joseph Cardinal Ratzinger on the state of the Church; by Vittorio Messori (San Francisco: Ignatius Press, 1985).

_____. *Religion in the Twentieth Century*; George Petrovich Fedotov (New York: The Philosophical Library, 1948).

Robinson, John A. T. *Redating the New Testament* (London: S.C.M. Press, 1976).

Rose, Michael S. *Goodbye, Good Men* (Washington: Regnery Publishing / Eagle Publishing, 2002).

Rosen, Moishe. *Y'shua* (Chicago: Moody Publishing, 1982).

Ross, Hugh. *The Fingerprint of God* (Orange, CA: Reasons to Believe / Promise Publishing Company, 1989, 1991).

Schönborn, Cardinal Christoph, *Chance or Purpose?: Creation, Evolution and a Rational Faith,* (San Francisco: Ignatius Press, 2007).

Shahak, Israel. *Jewish History, Jewish Religion* (Brooklyn, NY: Published for Baruch Spinoza Press by Moshe Lieberman, 1994).

Sheler, Jeffery L. *Is the Bible True?: How Modern Debates and Discoveries Affirm the Essence of the Scriptures* (San Francisco: HarperSanFrancisco / Zondervan, 1999).

Simmons, M.D., Geoffrey. *What Darwin Didn't Know* (Eugene, OR: Harvest House Publishers, 2004).

Smith, Huston. *The World's Religions* (New York: HarperCollins, 1991).

Steichen, Donna. *Ungodly Rage – The Hidden Face of Catholic Feminism* (San Francisco: Ignatius Press, 1991).

Strauss, David Friedrich. *The Life of Jesus Critically Examined;* Edited by Peter C. Hodgson; Translated by George Eliot (Philadelphia: Fortress Press, 1972).

_____. *Teaching About Evolution and the Nature of Science,* National Academy of Sciences (Washington: National Academy Press, 1998).

St. Thérèse of Lisieux. *Story of a Soul, The Autobiography of St. Thérèse of Lisieux*, 3rd ed. (Washington: ICS Publications, 1997).

Thiede, Carsten Peter and d'Ancona, Matthew. *Eyewitness to Jesus* (New York: Doubleday / Random House 1996. Rights: Yale University Press, 2007).

Thiede, Carsten Peter and d'Ancona, Matthew. *The Jesus Papyrus* (London: Weidenfeld and Nicholson, 1996).

Thiering, Barbara. *Jesus and the Riddle of the Dead Sea Scrolls* (San Francisco: HarperSanFrancisco / Harper Collins, 1992).

St. Thomas Aquinas. *Summa Theologica,* Translated by Fathers of the English Dominican Province (New York: Benzinger Brothers, 1947).

Tresmontant, Claude. *The Gospel of Matthew, Translation and Notes* (Front Royal, VA: Christendom Press, 1996).

Tresmontant, Claude. *The Hebrew Christ* (Quincy, IL: (Franciscan Press, Quincy, IL, 1989, formerly Franciscan Herald Press).

Trifkovic, Serge. *The Sword of the Prophet: Islam – History, Theology, Impact on the World* (Boston: Regina Orthodox Press, 2002).

_____. *Vatican Council II, Vol. 1: The Conciliar and Post Conciliar Documents,* New Revised Edition, Rev. Austin Flannery, O.P., General Editor (Northport, NY: Costello Publishing Company, 1975, 1986, 1992, 1996).

_____. *The Wanderer* (published weekly) (St. Paul, MN: Wanderer Printing Co).

Warren, Rick. *The Purpose-D_ _ _ _ _ Life* (Grand Rapids, MI: Zondervan, 2002).

Weigel, George. *The Courage to be Catholic; Crisis, Reform, and the Future of the Church* (New York: Basic Books / Perseus Books Group, 2002).

Wenham, John. *Redating Matthew, Mark, and Luke* (London: Hodder and Stoughton, 1991).

Whalen, William J. *Christianity and American Freemasonry* (Huntington, IN: Our Sunday Visitor, 1958, 1987).

Whalen, William J. *Separated Brethren* (Huntington, IN: Our Sunday Visitor, 1979).

Wiker, Benjamin D. and Dembski, William A.; *Moral Darwinism: How We Became Hedonists* (Downers Grove, IL: Intervarsity Press, 2002).

Woods, Thomas E., Jr. *How the Catholic Church Built Western Civilization* (Washington: Regnery Publishing, 2005).

_____. *World Christian Encyclopedia,* 2nd Edition (Oxford, UK: Oxford Press, 2001).

Wrenn, Msgr. Michael J., and Whitehead, Kenneth D. *Flawed Expectations* (San Francisco: Ignatius Press, 1996).

Ye'or, Bat (pseudonym). *Eurabia: The Euro-Arab Axis* (Cranbury, NJ: Fairleigh Dickinson University Press / Associated University Presses, 2005).

Appendix A – Summary – English

Download this free summary in English, Spanish, French, Russian, Chinese, Arabic and Indonesian at http://7step.catholic.org (Other languages planned).

The 7-Step Reason to be Catholic, 2nd Ed.:
Science, the Bible and History point to Catholicism

A Summary of Part I of this three-part book

Part II addresses scandal and dissent within Catholicism today.
Part III addresses key points of incompatibility with other faiths.

© 2001, 2008 by Jerome D. Gilmartin
jdgilmartin@hotmail.com

*An important supplement to
Catholic teaching in:*

- Catholic universities
- Home schooling
- Catechesis
- Bible study
- Evangelization

- High schools
- Campus ministry
- RCIA
- Apologetics
- Prison ministry

Imprimatur: + *Most Rev. Joseph F. Martino, D.D., Hist. E.D.*
Bishop of Scranton
October 29, 2007

Nihil Obstat: Father Charles P. Connor, *Censor Librorum*
October 22, 2007

Unlimited copying of this summary is authorized

CCC = *Catechism of the Catholic Church*, 2nd ed.

From the book, *The 7-Step Reason to be Catholic, 2nd Ed.:
Science, the Bible and History point to Catholicism.* Imprimatur.
© 2008 by Jerome D. Gilmartin. ISBN: 978-0-615-21197-8
416 pp., 6" x 9" trade paperback, (English only),. $19.95 U.S. + S&H.
View Contents and sample pages at **http://7step.catholic.org**
Publisher: 7 Steps to Catholicism, 171 Hickory Ridge Road,
Greenfield Township, PA, 18407-3514
To order book, call toll-free in the U.S.: 1- 866 578-4077.
Customer Service: 570 650-1327

Call for a PowerPoint ® talk / workshop by the author.

The 7-Step Reason to be Catholic

1. *Strong scientific evidence points to the Intelligent Design of the universe.*

At this writing in May, 2008 more than 600 scientists have challenged Darwinian Theory by signing this *Scientific Dissent from Darwinism* statement posted on the Discovery Institute Web site:

"We are skeptical of claims for the ability of random mutation and natural selection to account for the complexity of life. Careful examination of the evidence for Darwinian Theory should be encouraged." http://www.dissentfromdarwin.org/

The Institute further states, *"The list is growing and includes scientists from the U.S. National Academy of Sciences, Russian, Hungarian and Czech National Academies, as well as from universities such as Yale, Princeton, Stanford, MIT, UC Berkeley, UCLA, and others."*

Science does not deny that God exists. The National Academy of Sciences states "Science can say nothing about the supernatural. Whether God exists or not is a question about which science is neutral" (*Teaching About Evolution and the Nature of Science; FAQ;* © 1998) **http://search.nap.edu/reading room/books/evolution98/evol5.html**

The Catholic Church does not deny the possibility that scientists may some day conclude, beyond reasonable doubt, that evolution played some part in how we came to be. To do so convincingly, however, they will have to overcome the formidable challenges to macroevolution presented by Intelligent Design scientists like astrophysicist Hugh Ross, Ph.D. (astonishing evidence of design, from atom to cosmos); biochemist Michael Behe, Ph.D. (cellular systems of *irreducible complexity*); and biologist Jonathan Wells, Ph.D. (Ten warning labels for biology textbooks). Wells has also refuted *exaptation, t*he adapting of something for a use other than that for which it apparently evolved. An important Intelligent Design Web site is **www.arn.org**. Also see: **www.doesgodexist.org/Charts/ Evidence-ForDesignInTheUniverse.html**

Can a marble statue wave?

*"*It [The Intelligent Design Movement] may well be the most important intellectual movement to occur in the last 200 years, if not the last half-millennium.*"* So wrote Benjamin D. Wiker **in his informative two-part article "Does Science Point to God?"** (Crisis, April

7, 2003; July 9, 2003).

Richard Dawkins, author of *The Blind Watchmaker: Why the Evidence of Evolution Reveals a Universe Without Design* (© 1986), is one of the foremost opponents of Intelligent Design. In "Does Science Point to God?" Wiker has this to say about Dawkins' understanding of probability: "Dawkins believes that anything can be explained by chance, even a miracle."

Wiker then quotes from *The Blind Watchmaker* (pp. 159-160) Dawkins' claim that *the hand of a marble statue could actually wave,* if all the molecules of the marble hand were to simultaneously move in one direction and then in the opposite direction. Dawkins acknowledges that the odds against this far exceed what we can imagine, but insists on the *possibility* that in this way a marble statue could "wave."

Dawkins may be on to something. Perhaps in a back issue of *Le Monde* we will find the headline, "Venus de Milo loses arms attempting to wave to tourists." Or maybe not. Wiker's two-part article may be read on the *Crisis* Web site:

www.crisismagazine.com/april2003/feature1.htm
www.crisismagazine.com/julaug2003/feature1.htm

Benjamin D. Wiker is a senior fellow at the Discovery Institute and the author of *Moral Darwinism: How We Became Hedonists*. He is a lecturer in theology and science at Franciscan University of Steubenville.

Lee M. Spetner, author of *Not by Chance; Shattering the Modern Theory of Evolution* (© 1998), earned a Ph.D. in physics from M.I.T. in 1950 and from 1951 to 1970 was a member of the staff of the Applied Physics Laboratory of Johns Hopkins University.

In "The Watchmaker's Blindness," Chapter 6 of his book, Spetner notes that Dawkins is not alone in failing to make a convincing case for the spontaneous origin of life – an "army of research scientists" failed as well, he observed, though they have worked on the problem for the past generation (p. 166).

For a spirited exchange of scientific views on the B-cell hypermutation model, information content of proteins and more, see the Lee Spetner / Edward Max Dialogue: *www.trueorigin.org/spetner2.asp*

Intelligent Design: Other Informative Web Sites:

www.creationsafaris.com/crevnews.htm
www.arn.org/docs/insight499.htm
www.reasons.org/about/index.shtml?main

www.lassp.cornell.edu/sethna/KinkTunneling/KinkTunneling.html
www.origins.org/articles/ross_modgoliath.html
www.world-of-dawkins.com/Catalano/box/behe.htm#reviews
www.arn.org/behe/mb_response.htm
www.discovery.org/crsc/fellows/MichaelBehe
www.iconsofevolution.com
http://ist-socrates.berkeley.edu:7521/projects/IB160/VDG/
Fall94/Wells/Wells.html
www.nmsr.org/text.htm#preface
www.actionbioscience.org/evolution/nhmag.html
www.nationalreview.com/comment/comment-west121702.asp
www.nationalreview.com/comment/comment-winnick101802.asp
www.arn.org/wells/jwhome.htm

The Church teaches that "Every spiritual soul is created immediately by God .... The account of the fall in Genesis 3 uses figurative language, but affirms a primal event, a deed that took place at the beginning of the history of man" (CCC par. 366; 390).

In *Fundamentals of the Faith*, Peter Kreeft suggests skeptics pray as follows: "God, if you are really out there, please ... somehow ... let me know ... I want to know."

2.   Other than I AM of the Old Testament, no other founder of a religion is comparable to Jesus.

True respect for others is important, regardless of what religion they practice. However, it is important that students and others become aware of this: ***With the exception of Jews (and Christians) who speak of I AM of the Old Testament – the Messianic prophecies of which Jesus fulfilled – no authoritative spokesperson for any non-Christian religion claims that its founder or reformer is comparable to Jesus in the way he manifested the authority of the Creator – including his power over death.***

Other than I AM, of all founders of a religion Jesus Christ alone manifested the authority of the Creator; only Jesus did *all* of the following: (a) fulfilled the many Messianic prophecies of the Old Testament (*Y'shua;* Moishe Rosen); (b) proved by his works that he had the authority of the Creator; (c) acknowledged that he was God (Jn 20: 28-29); (d) died on the cross to redeem us and make possible our salvation; (e) rose from death on the third day, appeared to many, and ascended into heaven; (f) said he would judge us after death (Jn 5:22-23) and; (g) said no one comes to the Father except through him

(Jn 14:6). *http://bible.gospelcom.net*

3. *History affirms the Jesus of the Bible*

Until about three decades ago, the historical reliability of the Gospels was widely accepted – including the *apostle-eyewitness* authorship of *Matthew* and *John,* which include the primary biblical / historical foundation of the Church and the Papacy: Mt 16:18-19, Mt 26:26-29, Mt 28:16-20 and Jn 21:15-17.

About two centuries ago, however, some scholars began an effort to cast doubt on the Gospels as reliable sources of historical truth about Jesus and his ministry.

These scholars virtually ignore the extrabiblical testimony of Early Church Fathers and other near-contemporaries of Jesus. They also ignore the compelling evidence for early-date Gospel authorship which so clearly points to the historical truth of the Gospels.

Instead, despite lack of evidence for their claim, these scholars continue to promote the idea that all four Gospels originated between A.D. 68 and 100 and that all are therefore historically doubtful.

These scholars also make dubious assumptions in their use of the historical-critical method and make minimal use of Hebrew and Aramaic, contrary to the requirements of *Divino Afflante Spiritu.* They also virtually ignore recent scholarly studies that strongly indicate:

(a) early authorship of the *Gospel according to Matthew* in Hebrew or Aramaic;

(b) early authorship in Hebrew or Aramaic of the *Gospel according to Mark* (possibly by Peter himself);

(c) that the Greek of the *Gospel according to John* is the Greek of translation from a Hebrew or Aramaic original and;

(d) that the sources of the *Gospel according to Luke* were written in Hebrew or Aramaic; or that the entire *Gospel according to Luke* was translated from a Hebrew or Aramaic original except the introduction.

Fr. Jean Carmignac has shown that these early date / eyewitness conclusions cannot be refuted by attributing them to the author's attempt to imitate the Septuagint or to the influence of the author's native language.

Late-date conjecture notwithstanding, the evidence for early-date Gospel authorship is formidable and compelling. This evidence, as outlined in *The 7-Step Reason to be Catholic,* 2nd Ed.,

provides a rock-solid foundation for the faith in the biblical Jesus held by Christians for the past 2,000 years.

- "Contemporary Catholic Biblical Scholarship: Certitudes or Hypotheses?;" Msgr. Michael J. Wrenn: *www.ewtn.com/library/SCRIPTUR/CERTHYPO.TXT*

- "The Dates of the Gospels;" *Fr. George H. Duggan: www.catholic.net/rcc/Periodicals/Homiletic/May97/gospels. html*

- *The Birth of the Synoptic Gospels;* Fr. J. Carmignac; © 1987 by Franciscan Herald Press, Chicago; (Franciscan Press, Quincy, IL) ISBN 0-8199-0887-8.

- *The Hebrew Christ;* Claude Tresmontant, © 1989 by Franciscan Herald Press, Chicago; (Franciscan Press, Quincy, IL), ISBN 0-8199-0876-2.

Carsten P. Thiede concluded that *during the 60s* the Gospels of Matthew and Mark had already been copied from scrolls onto codices [*Eyewitness to Jesus,* p. 16; © 1996, Thiede / d'Ancona; Doubleday (Random House, Inc.)].

Cardinal Ratzinger, in his 1988 Erasmus Lecture, was critical of liberal Catholic and Protestant biblical scholars alike. The Cardinal said that, in addition to their great achievements, they had "*brought forth great errors.*" He then stated that **texts must be viewed "in light of the total movement of history and in light of history's central event, Jesus Christ"** (Origins).

Emphasis on authentic biblical / extra-biblical history is essential in Catholic education at all levels as well as in Catholic seminaries. Compromise of such history has been associated with heresy and scandal (See *Goodbye, Good Men*; © 2002, Michael S. Rose, Regnery).

In response to criticism of Early Church Fathers, Ven. John Henry Newman, while an Anglican priest, wrote as follows in *An Essay on the Development of Christian Doctrine* (1845): **"History is not a creed or a catechism. It gives lessons rather than rules; still no one can mistake its general teaching in this matter, whether he accept it or stumble at it. Bold outlines and broad masses of colour rise out of the records of the past. They may be dim, they may be incomplete, but they are definite. And this one thing at least is certain; whatever history teaches, whatever it omits, whatever it exaggerates or extenuates, whatever it says or unsays, at least the Christianity of history is not Protestantism ... and Protestantism has ever felt it so.... To be deep** *in history is to cease to be a Protestant"* (Image Books © 1960). *www.newmanreader.org/works/development/introduction. html* (Web site of Bob Elder). Newman became a Catholic – and an esteemed Cardinal. *www.newadvent.org/fathers*

4. Jesus founded, and protects from error, one Petrine Church.

God loves all his children, including our separated brethren (CCC par. 822), many of whom pray and practice their Christian faith with great fervor. But did Jesus not pray *"that all may be one"* (Jn 17:17-23) and say, *"there shall be one flock, one shepherd"* (Jn 10:16)?

Clearly, the Bible indicates that Jesus founded only One Church, and Jesus: (a) *founded his Church on Peter alone* (Mt 16:18, Lk 6:46-49); (b) *gave the keys of the kingdom of heaven to Peter alone* (Mt 16:19); (c) *said "Feed my lambs…. Tend my sheep…. Feed my sheep"* to Peter alone (Jn 21:15-17); *(d) provided for papal and apostolic succession* (Isa 22:22), in which the key indicates authority transferable to a successor and; *(e) protects his Church from doctrinal error* (CCC par. 888-892).

www.ewtn.com/library/scriptur/POPE.TXT (Scott Hahn).

When Jesus said, "Thou art Peter and upon this Rock I will build my Church" (Mt 16:18), he would have spoken in *Aramaic*, his native language. In Aramaic, the *only* meaning this statement can have is the Catholic interpretation. On this, linguistic scholars of all faiths are in virtually unanimous agreement.

In the full light of history, to be a true "Bible Christian" is to be Catholic.

5. After giving Peter primacy, Jesus commissioned the Apostles to make disciples of all nations

Having given primacy to Peter, the risen Jesus commissioned the eleven apostles (all but Judas Iscariot): "Go, therefore and make disciples of all nations, baptizing them in the name of the Father, the Son and the Holy Spirit … and teach them all I have commanded you" (Mt 28:18-20).

Do the important differences between Catholic and non-Catholic teaching mean *different gospels* are preached? Note Paul's words on this (Gal 1:6-9).

6. The Pope and Catholic bishops – successors of Peter and the apostles – continue to make disciples

of all nations

Those apostles and, with Peter's approval, Matthias and Paul, followed this directive of the risen Jesus. Through the solemn "laying on of hands" through the ages, their successors – the Pope and Catholic bishops of today – continue to carry out this mandate of Jesus. "The sole Church of Christ ... subsists in the Catholic Church, which is governed by the successor of Peter and by the bishops in communion with him." (CCC par. 816).

7. *There is no biblical escape clause to reject the one Church founded by Jesus*

Protestant minister Marcus Grodi was haunted by a dilemma: *"Each Sunday I would stand in my pulpit and interpret Scripture for my flock, knowing that within a fifteen-mile radius of my church there were dozens of other Protestant pastors – all of whom believed that the Bible alone is the sole authority for doctrine and practice – but each was teaching something different from what I was teaching."* Especially troubling for Grodi was the knowledge that ***"Every Protestant minister I knew had a different set of criteria that he listed as 'necessary' for salvation."*** After much reading, particularly of the Early Church Fathers and Karl Keating's *Catholicism and Fundamentalism*, Grodi realized that *"the Protestant answer to church renewal was, of all things, unscriptural,"* and that *"the single most important issue was authority"* (*Surprised by Truth*; pp. 38-51). Grodi and his wife Marilyn became Catholic. He founded the Coming Home Network ***www.chnetwork.org*** (800 664-5110) and hosts *The Journey Home* weekly call-in program on EWTN.

With the foreknowledge that Peter would deny him three times and abandon him at Calvary, Jesus gave Peter primacy among the apostles as noted in 4 a, b and c above. Jesus promised to be with the One Church he founded always; not even the Gates of hell would prevail against it.

Certainly, through the Bible, Jesus would have let us know if he intended the divided Christianity of today, with its more than 33,000 denominations and its **many contradictory teachings on matters on which one's very salvation may well depend.** And yet the most careful search of the Bible reveals nothing other than this:

Other than those led by Peter, nowhere in the Bible does Jesus authorize anyone to "make disciples of all nations" (Mt 28:18-20) **and the Bible includes no "escape clause" by which Jesus authorizes anyone to reject Peter or his successors to form, or join, a different Church.** *The exorcist in Mk 9:38 did not preach a "contrary gospel."*

Nor do "two or three" embrace such a gospel if truly gathered in his name (Mt 18:20, Mt 7:21-23). Paul has ominous words for those who preach a "gospel" contrary to that of Christ (*Gal* 1:6-9). In Proverbs we are told we must not rely on our own insight (or understanding) (Prov 3:5) and Peter warned against *private interpretation* of Scripture (2 Pet 3:16) which has led to the proliferation of non-Catholic Christian denominations we see today.

For each of us, life on earth will one day end. ***Except for that of Jesus (and I AM), the tomb of every founder / reformer of a religion is occupied, or will be,*** as someone has said. Do we close our eyes rather than prayerfully seek the Church to which Jesus calls us?

Doesn't it make sense to belong to the One Church founded by Jesus, knowing that ***Jesus himself will judge us at death, affirming our ultimate choice of heaven or hell based not on the decisions we might then wish we had made, but on the decisions we actually made during our life on earth?*** (See CCC par. 1033; 1020-1050).

The false idea that God's *everlasting love* for us (e.g., Is 54:8) guarantees our salvation is widely believed. But the clear teaching of the Church is that God's love for us is no guarantee of our eternal salvation. (CCC par. 1035).

The *fullness* of the means of salvation – i.e., all seven sacraments including the EUCHARIST, "without which you shall not have life in you (Jn 6:53-59)," as well as the spiritual leadership of the successor of Peter – is found only in the Catholic Church.

Consider what something less than this "fullness" can mean today. Depending on whom one chooses to follow as a Christian, it can mean the condoning of sexual relations outside a valid marriage, euthanasia and induced abortion, for example; matters that can result in the loss of one's eternal salvation.

The great importance of becoming and remaining Catholic is explained in the *Catechism of the Catholic Church,* 2nd Ed. (par. 846-848) and in the *Companion to the CCC* (par. 847).

"Observe whatever they tell you, but not what they do," said Jesus in regard to those who sat "on Moses' seat (Mt 23:2-3). Surely this applies to any in the Church whose scandalous behavior mocks their preaching. Not all popes proved personally worthy of the office. But, as with Judas Iscariot, Jesus did not suppress the free will of Peter, other apostles, or their successor popes / bishops. But no pope has destroyed the fabric of ***doctrine*** of the One Church to which the Father, in the name of Jesus, sent the Holy Spirit (Jn 14:26; Acts 2:1-4).

In *Crossing the Threshold of Hope*, Pope John Paul II states that ***the Documents of Vatican II are to be interpreted using the authoritative Catechism of the Catholic Church***: *"The Catechism was also indispensable in order that all the richness of the teaching of the Church following the Second Vatican Council could be preserved in a new synthesis and be given a new direction. Without the Catechism of the universal Church this would not have been accomplished"* (p. 164; Knopf; © 1994). **CCC Search Engine: www.scborromeo.org/ccc.htm**

When asked to consider another religion ...

The first question you might ask is: **"Who was the founder of your faith, or the first to promote or reform it?"** If that person *was not* Jesus, ask:

(a) "What signs did he (she) manifest to show that he had the authority of the Creator, and how do those signs compare with those of Jesus?" Other than for **I AM** of the Old Testament, the Messianic prophecies of which Jesus fulfilled, *no authoritative apologist for any other religion claims that their founder manifested signs comparable to those of Jesus.* See Step 2, (a) through (g) above and "Other Religions." In the Old Testament Hebrew, God is *Elohim* (masculine plural, meaning "the strong ones") implying plurality, not *Eloah*, the singular form. Similarly in Gen 1:26, "Let *us* make man in *our* image."

(b) "Did your founder / reformer indicate or acknowledge that he / she was God, as Jesus did?" (Jn 20:28-29). Even if some others may have made this claim, *their tombs are all occupied, or will be,* as someone has said. "Wonder workers" are found in all cultures, but history could never remain silent about another like Jesus.

(c) And finally, ask: *"Does it make sense, really, to follow someone other than Jesus, the ONLY ONE who manifested the power to keep, in the hereafter, the promises he made to us?"*

If the founder *was* Jesus, note Steps 3 to 7 above. Then ask:

(a) "What is the pillar and bulwark of the truth?" Paul's answer is not "Scripture," but "the Church of the living God" (1 Tim 3:15).

(b) "On whom did Jesus found his Church?" On Peter alone (Step 4). Jesus differentiated between the "foundation" (Himself), and the "Rock" on which the foundation is laid (Lk 6:48-49, and Mt 7:24-27). Refer to Step 3 to affirm the historical authenticity of the Gospels.

(c) "To whom did Jesus give the keys of the kingdom of heaven?" To Peter alone (Mt 16:19). Luther affirmed this Catholic position long after his excommunication, but denied the papal authority of Peter's successors. Calvin, attempting to duplicate "the keys," *misquoted Jesus in Luke.* Show how Isaiah 22:22 and Mt 28:20 indicate apostolic / papal succession.

(d) Ignatius – Bishop of Antioch, martyr and hearer of John the apostle – described the *Eucharist* as *"the flesh of Christ ... the medicine of immortality."*

(e) Note that there is no biblical "Escape Clause" to reject the One Church Jesus founded and promised to be with always. Against it, even the gates of hell will not prevail. By encouraging a Catholic to leave that Church, or discouraging anyone from joining it, is that person not attempting to "prevail against it" (Mt 16:18)?

Next, I suggest that you and your well-meaning non-Catholic friend explore together the *Catechism of the Catholic Church,* 2nd Ed. Using the index, you can quickly find the answer to virtually any question about what the Church teaches. Extensive footnotes provide the biblical basis for these teachings. *http://bible.gospelcom.net*

Old Testament / New Testament, or Koran?

God made a *covenant* with Abraham (as with Adam, Noah, Moses and David – preceding the New Covenant of Jesus (Mt 26:26-28)) and promised to establish it with Isaac (Gen 17:21). Although God made no *covenant* with Ishmael, he was conceived after Sarai (Sarah) gave Hagar to Abraham "as a wife" (Gen: 16:3). God named Ishmael ("God hears") (Gen 16:11), blessed him (Gen 17:20) and promised to make him a great nation (Gen 17:2).

Isaac and Ishmael went their separate ways, but their bond as sons of Abraham endured. When Abraham died, at age 175, together these half brothers buried him next to his wife Sarah (Gen 25:7-10). *True descendants of Abraham / Isaac – and of Abraham / Ishmael – strive to come together in peace as sons and daughters of a common father.*

About 2,400 years later, in about A.D. 610, Muhammad began to dictate *The Koran (Q'uran)* – messages he believed came from Allah through an angel. It is said that the ancestry of Muhammad can be traced to Ishmael through Kedar, his second son (Gen 25:13). Today there are more than 70 separate Islamic denominations.

Several suras of the Koran appear to refer favorably to the Bible, Jews and Christians, e.g.: Allah sent Jesus and gave him the Gospel in which there is light and guidance (5:46); Muslims are to forgive the People of the Book (Christians / Jews) who attempt to convert them (2:109); Jesus was a prophet (2:86, 136) with whom Allah made a covenant (33:7). Muslims honor Jesus as a prophet.

In contrast to the Koran, however, are the following biblical words and acts of Jesus: **(a)** turned water into wine (forbidden; sura 5:90) at the wedding feast (Jn 2:1-11); **(b)** said of a cup of wine "Drink of it, all of you; for this is my blood (forbidden; 5:3) of the covenant ..." (Mt 26:27); **(c)** warned his followers not to follow future desert prophets (a veiled reference to Muhammad?) (Mt 24:24-26); **(d)** said, "I and the Father are one" (Jn 10:30) and "Before Abraham was, I AM" (Jn 8:58), implying equality with the Father / Allah; **(e)** replying to Thomas, Jesus acknowledged that he was God (Jn 20:28-29) and; **(f)** unique in world history, Jesus manifested the power and authority of the Creator (Step 2).

The following suras cause Catholics and other Christians to reject the Koran as Divine revelation: *(a) Jesus was not God and not the Son of God* (4:171); *(b) Jesus was just one of several prophets preceding Muhammad, The Prophet* (4:163, 2:136) *and; (c) Jesus was not crucified* (4:157-159).

Clearly, one must choose: Bible or Koran? – Jesus or Muhammad? *One's eternal salvation may well depend on making the right choice and living accordingly.* **Why? Because Jesus said unequivocally that he would be our ultimate judge and said no one comes to the Father except through him (See *Baptism;* CCC par. 1213-1284).** By what standard will Jesus judge us? *To gain eternal life, Jesus said we must keep the commandments (Mt 19:16-17; 22:36-39). We must love all, including our enemies. God will forgive us only if we forgive others* (Mt 5:43-44, 6:15); *and we must forgive "from the heart"* (Mt 18: 35). How will Jesus judge those who engage in violence toward innocent Jews, Christians, Muslims and others? Within Islam as well, such acts have been condemned. Although they saw Palestine as a separate case, *The Organization of Islamic Conferences declared, "We unequivocally condemn acts of international terrorism in all its forms and manifestations ..."* (#7; Kuala Lumpur, 1-3 April, 2002). *www.oic-oci.org*.

The Indonesia-based Liberal Islam Network, *www.islamlib.com* promotes inter-religious brotherhood, including non-discrimination on the basis of religion, ethnicity, social status, political status and gender. Of special interest in regard to world peace is "The Theological Basis of Inter-Religious Brotherhood," an on-line article by Budhy Munawar-Rachman. The Republic of Indonesia has a Muslim population of about 200 million; more Muslims than any other country in the world.

Do earliest copies of the Koran support Christianity?

In 1972, the oldest known copies of the Koran were found in Yemen. **Careful philological (source language) study of these early manuscripts convinced some scholars that *The Koran, as recited by Muhammad, supported Christianity, and even encouraged participation in the "eucharistic commemoration."* They also conclude that, instead of "dark, wide-eyed (maidens)," Muhammad would have recited that "white grapes" or "white raisins" are among the fruits of heaven.**

These are among the findings documented in the book, *Die syro-aramaeische Lesart des Koran* (*The Syro-Aramaic Reading of the Koran*) by "Christoph Luxenberg," a pseudonym. It was published in German in 2000 by Das Arabische Buch and will soon be published in English. A scholarly review acclaiming this book, in English, is posted on the "Hugoye" Web site below. The July 28, 2003 issue of *Newsweek,* which included an article about this book, was banned in Pakistan.

Quite the opposite of doubting the Koran, which the Koran forbids, Luxenberg and other philologists are confident that their studies <u>clarify</u> it, providing a more accurate account of the Koran as it was first recited by Muhammad himself. Done in good faith, It would seem that Muslims would consider such an endeavor pleasing to Allah and to all Muslims sincerely seeking truth.

One scholar observed that a new translation of the Koran based on these findings (approved and made known worldwide by authoritative Islamic spokespersons), could result in greater Islamic tolerance of Christianity and Judaism based on a new awareness of Islam's close ties to both religions. Dare we imagine what this could mean in terms of religious freedom, prosperity and world peace? Further information on this subject can be found on the following Web sites:

www.theatlantic.com/issues/99jan/koran.htm;
www.corkscrew-balloon.com/02/03/1bkk/04b.html
http://bethmardutho.cua.edu/hugoye > Volume Index > Volume 6 Number 1 > Book Reviews; Christoph Luxenberg
http://answering-islam.org.uk/Gilchrist/Jam/chap2.html

Hear "Catholic Answers Live" on your computer:
http://www.catholic.com/radio/calive.asp

Questions? EWTN, *www.ewtn.com/vexperts/search.asp*. *Catholic* Answers: *www.catholic.com* (619 387-7200). Jimmy Akin, CA staff apologist, has his own excellent Web page: Nazareth Resources Library, *www.cin.org/users/james*. *Or* call Catholics United for the Faith toll free: **1 800 – MY FAITH** or *www.cuf.org*. The following Web sites are also highly recommended: Patrick Madrid, *www.surprisedbytruth.com;* Steve Ray, *www.catholic-convert.com;* John Martignoni, *www.biblechristiansociety.com;* Pope John Paul II Society of Evangelists, *www.pjpiisoe.org/index.htm;* The National Catholic Bioethics Center, *www.ncbcenter.org* and Dave Armstrong, *www.biblicalcatholic.com*. *The Bible Gateway* Web site is a very helpful biblical resource: *http://bible.gospelcom.net*.

All Bible quotations are from the *Revised Standard Version, Catholic Edition*, © 1965, 1966 by NCCC, USA. All rights reserved (See NCCC Web page).

Appendix B – Wallet Outline – English

The 7-Step Reason to be Catholic

Evangelize as a Card-Carrying Catholic™ in 12 languages!

Download this wallet outline free as a card, or on paper, in English, Spanish, French, Russian, Chinese, Arabic, Indonesian, Portuguese, Hindi, Bengali, Tamil and Telugu. Download summary, about 9 pages, in the first seven of these languages: http://7step.catholic.org/

1. **Strong *scientific* evidence** points to the intelligent design of the universe.[1]

2. In all of history, only **Jesus manifested the power of the Intelligent Designer/Creator**, including power over death, and fulfilled the Messianic prophecies.[2]

3. **Evidence for the very early origin and authenticity of the Gospels** includes writings of Early Church Fathers and others, ancient papyrus fragments and many underlying *Semitisms*, which account for the "ear-grating" Greek in the Gospels.[3]

4. **Jesus founded one Church**, said there shall be *one flock, one shepherd* and prayed for the *unity* of all believers.[4]

5. Having instituted the *Eucharist* and given primacy in his Church to Peter, the risen **Jesus commissioned the apostles to make disciples of all nations.**[5]

6. **The Pope and Catholic bishops today are the spiritual and historical successors of Peter and the other apostles.**[6]

7. Although denied by Peter, betrayed by Judas Iscariot, abandoned by all apostles but John and scandalized by some of the ordained and consecrated, including a few popes of history, *Jesus gave us no biblical "escape clause" to reject the one Church he founded and, through the apostles, promised to be with always.*[7]

To be a true "Bible Christian" is to be a Catholic.

1 600+ scientists have signed the "Scientific Dissent from Darwinism Statement." www.dissentfromdarwin.org. See 21 ID-related Web sites in free 9-pg. Summary at http://7step.catholic.org/

2 In the Gospels, Jesus tells us what we must do to enter heaven and that *he will judge each of us after we die* (Jn 5:22).

3 www.catholic.net/rcc/Periodicals/Homiletic/May97/gospels.html/ (Fr. G. Duggan). www.ewtn.com/library/SCRIPTUR/CERTHYPO.TXT/ (Msgr. Michael J. Wrenn). *The Birth of the Synoptic Gospels*, Fr. Jean Carmignac, © 1987, ISBN 0-8199-0887-8.

4 Mt 16:18; Jn 10:6; Jn 17:17-23. Today 33,000+ Christian denominations do not agree on *requirements for salvation.*

5 Mt 16:18-19; Lk 6:46-49; Jn 21:15-17; Mt 28:18-20.

6 Is 22:22; Early Church Fathers; *Catechism of the Catholic Church*, par. 816.

7 Prov 3:5; Gal 1:6-9; 2 Pet 3:16: Mt 23:2-3; Mt 7:21-23.

From the book, ***The 7-Step Reason to be Catholic, 2nd Ed.: Science, the Bible and History point to Catholicism.*** *Imprimatur.* © 2008 by Jerome D. Gilmartin, jdgilmartin@hotmail.com. ISBN: 978-0-615-21197-8

417 pp., 6" x 9" trade paperback (English only). $19.95 U.S. + S&H. View Table of Contents & sample text: **http://7step.catholic.org** Publisher: 7 Steps to Catholicism, 171 Hickory Ridge Road, Greenfield Township, PA, 18407-3514

To order book, call toll-free in the U.S.: 866 578-4077. Customer Service: 570 650-1327

Call for a PowerPoint ® talk / workshop by the author.

http://quod.lib.umich.edu/r/rsv/ (Revised Standard Version).
http://bible.gospelcom.net/languages/

Appendix C – Summary – Spanish

SIETE PASOS DE UNA RAZON PARA SER CATOLICO, 2nd ed.

Un resumen de la Primera Parte de este libro en tres partes
que pronto será publicado

La Segunda Parte del libro se dirige al escándalo y la disención dentro del catolicismo actualmente. La Tercera parte del libro se dirige a puntos doctrinales principales y su incompatibiliad con otras fes.

© 2001, 2008 por Jerome D. Gilmartin
jdgilmartin@hotmail.com

Traducido por Jorge A. Topete, Ph. D.

Ofrecido con la fe de que un católico verdaderamente ecuménico es el que puede explicar amable y concisamente la importancia de ser católico.

Un importante suplemento para una educación católica universitaria y en la escuela preparatoria, así como para programas diocesarnos y paroquiales en la catequesis, el rito de iniciación católica para adultos, ministerio universita-rio,ministerio en las prisiones, estudios bíblicos y otros pro-gramas para educación de jóvenes y adultos.

Una introducción a la apologética católica.

Nihil Obstat e Imprimatur otorgados para el texto inglés de este libro.

Se autoriza hacer una cantidad ilimitada de copias de este resumen.

CCC = Catecismo de la Iglesia Católica, 2a. edición.

7 PASOS DE UNA RAZON PARA SER CATOLICO

1. La ciencia no niega que Dios existe – El "Diseñador Inteligente"

La ciencia no niega que Dios existe. La prestigiosa Academia Nacional de Ciencias declara: "La ciencia no puede decir nada sobre lo sobrenatural. Si Dios existe o nó es una cuestión ante la cual la ciencia es neutral."(Teaching About Evolution and Nature Science; FAQ; © 1998.
http://search.nap.edu/readingroom/books/evolution98/evol5.html

La Iglesia Católica no niega la posibiliad de que los científicos un día puedan concluir, sin ningún género de duda, que la evolución jugó alguna parte en cómo llegamos a ser. Sin embargo, para hacer esto de manera convincente, tienen que vencer los formidables desafíos presentados por El Diseño Inteligente de científicos como el astrofísico Hugh Ross, Ph. D. (asombrosa evidencia del diseño, desde el átomo hasta el cosmos); el bioquímico Michael Behe, Ph. D. (sistemas celulares de irreducilbe complejidad); y el biologista Jonathan Wells, Ph. D. (Diez títulos admonitorios para textos de biologia) Wells también refuta la exaptación.) [El portal del Diseño Inteligente es *www.arn.org* Ver también:
www.doesgodexist.org/Charts/EvidenceForDesignInTheUniverse.html

¿Puede una estatua de mármol agitar las manos?

"[El Movimiento del Diseño Inteligente] puede ser el más importante movimiento intelectual que ha ocurrido en los últimos doscientos años, si no en la última mitad del milenio pasado."

Así escribió Benjamin D. Wiker en su informativo artículo en dos partes "¿La ciencia señala a Dios?" (Crisis, 7 de abril de 2003; Julio 9 de 2003).

Richard Dawkins, autor de *The Blind Watchmaker: Why the Evidence of Evolution Reveals a Universe Without Design* (© 1986) [El relojero ciego: ¿Por qué la evidencia de la Evolución revela un universo sin designio] es uno de los más importantes oponentes del Designio Inteligente. En Does Science Point to God? [La ciencia señala a Dios?] Wiker dice esto a lo que

336

Dawkins entiende como probabilidad: "Dawkins cree que todo puede ser explicado por la casualidad, aún un milagro."

Wikers luego cita de *The Blind Watchmaker* [El fabricante ciego] (págs. 159-160) la afirmación de Dawkins que **la mano de una estatua de mármol puede moverse realmente,** si todas las moléculas de la mano de mármol se mueven en una dirección y luego en la dirección opuesta. Dawkins reconoce que las probabiidades contra esto exceden por mucho lo que podemos imaginar, pero insiste en la posibilidad de que de esta manera la estatua de mármol pueda "saludar."

Dawkins puede saber algo. Tal vez en un ejemplar viejo de *Le Monde* encontremos un titular que dice: "La Venus de Milo pierde sus brazos al intentar saludar a los turistas." O tal vez no. El artículo en dos partes de Wiker puede ser leído en el Website de Crisis: *www.crisismagazine.com/april2003/feature1.htm www.crisismagazine.com/julaug2003/feature1.htm*

Benjamin D. Wiker es un socio antiguo en el Discovery Institute y el autor de *Moral Darwinism: How We Became Hedonists*. Es un conferenciante en teología y ciencia en la Universidad Franciscana de Steubenville.

Lee M. Spetner, autor de *Not by Chance; Shattering the Modern Theory of Evolution* (© 1998) [No por casualidad; Destruyendo la moderna teoría de la Evolución]. Recibió su Doctorado en Filosofía en Física del M. I. T. en 1950 y de 1951 a 1970 fue un miembro del equipo técnico del aboratorio de Física Aplicada de la Universidad Johns Hopkins.

En The Watchmaker's Blindness [La ceguera del fabricante de relojes], capítulo 6 de su libro, Spetner nota que Dawkins no está solo en haber fallado en hacer un caso convincente del espontáneo origen de la vida – un "ejército de cientificos investigadores" también fallaron, observó, aunque han trabajado en el problema toda la generación pasada (pág. 166).

Para un animado cambio de puntos de vista científico sobre el modelo de la hipermutación de la Célula B, información sobre el contenido de las proteinas y más, ver el Diálogo entre Spetner y Edward Max: *www.trueorigin.org/spetner2.asp*

Diseño Inteligente: Otros Websites informativos:

www.creationsafaris.com/crevnews.htm
www.arn.org/docs/insight499.htm
www.reasons.org/about/index.shtml?main

www.lassp.cornell.edu/sethna/KinkTunneling/KinkTunneling
.html
www.origins.org/articles/ross_modgoliath.html
www.world-of-dawkins.com/Catalano/box/behe.htm#reviews
www.arn.org/behe/mb_response.htm
www.discovery.org/crsc/fellows/MichaelBehe
www.iconsofevolution.com
http://ist-socrates.berkeley.edu:7521/projects/IB160/
   VDG/Fall94/Wells/Wells.html
www.nmsr.org/text.htm#preface
www.actionbioscience.org/evolution/nhmag.html
www.nationalreview.com/comment/comment-west
   121702.asp
www.nationalreview.com/comment/comment-winnick
   101802.asp
www.arn.org/wells/jwhome.htm

La Iglesia enseña que "Cada alma espritual es creada inmediatamene por Dios .... La narración de la Caída en el capítulo 3 del Génesis usa lenguaje figurativo, pero afirma un evento primordial, un hecho que tuvo lugar al principio de la historia del hombre." (CCC 366; 390).

En "Fundamentos de la Fe," Peter Kreeft sugiere que el escéptico rece así: "Dios, si tú realmente estas allí, por favor ... de alguan manera ... déjame conocer ... yo quiero saber."

2. Excepto "YO SOY"del Antiguo Testamento, ningún otro fundador de una religión es comparable con Jesucristo.

Un verdadero respeto por otros es importante, cualquiera que sea la religión que practiquen. Sin embaro, es importante que estudiantes y otros se den cuenta de la siguiente verdad: Con la excepción de judíos (y cristianos) que hablan de "YO SOY" del Antiguo Testamento cuyas profecías mesiánicas cumplió Jesucristo.

Ningún portavoz autorizado de una religión no cristiana puede pretender que su fundador o sus reformadores son comparables con Jesucristo en la manera cómo él manifestó la autoridad del Creador – incluyendo su poder sobre la misma muerte.

Excepto "YO SOY." de todos los fundadores de una religión, sólo Jesucristo manifestó la autoridad del Creador – Sólo Jesús hizo todas las siguientes cosas: (a) cumplió las numerosas profecías mesiánicas del Antiguo Testamento; (*Y´shua;* Moishe

Rosen); (b) probó con sus obras que tenía la autoridad del Creador; (c) confesó que era Dios (Jn 20:28-29); (d) murió en la cruz para redimirnos y hacer posible nuestra salvación; (e) resucitó el tercer día, se apareció a muchos y subió a los cielos; (f) dijo que iba a ser nuestro juez después de la muerte (Jn 5:22-23); y (g) dijo que nadie va al Padre sino a través de él. (Jn 14: 6-7) *http://bible.gospelcom.net/languages*

3. La historia afirma al Jesús de la Biblia

Hasta hace tres décadas, la veracidad histórica de los Evangelios era generalmente aceptada – incluyendo como autores a los *Apóstoles y testigos oculares* Mateo y Juan, que incluye el fundamento primario bíblico-histórico de la Iglesia y del Papado: Mt 16:18-19,Mt 26:16-20 y Jn 21:15-17.

Sin embargo, hace unos dos siglos, algunos eruditos comenzaron un esfuerzo en poner en duda a los Evangelio como fuentes veraces de la verdad histórica de Jesús y su ministerio.

Estos eruditos virtualmente ignoran el testimonio extrabíblico de los Primeros Padres de la Iglesia y otros casi contemporáneos a Jesús. También ignoran la fuerte evidencia sobre la temprana escritura de los Evangelios que señala claramente la verad histórica de los Evangelios.

En su lugar, a pesar de falta de evidencia sobre lo que declaran, esos eruditos continúan promoviendo la idea de que todos los cuatro Evangelios se originaron entre los años 68 y 100 A. D. y que por lo tanto son históricamente dudosos.

Estos eruditos también hacen afirmaciones dudosas en su uso del método histórico-crítico y hacen un uso mínimo del hebreo o del arameo, contrario a los requerimientos de *Divino Aflante Spiritu.* También virtualmente ignoran estudios eruditos recientes que indican fuertemente:

(a) La temprana escritura del Evangelio de Mateo en hebreo o en arameo;

(b) La temprana esritura del Evangelio de Marcos (posiblemente por el Mismo Pedro);

(c) Que el griego del Evangelio de Juan es una traducción al griego de un original hebreo o arameo y;

(d) Que las fuentes del Evangelio de Lucas fueron escritas en hebreo o en arameo; o que todo el Evangelio de Lu-

**cas fue traducido de un original en hebreo o arameo ex-
cepto la introducción.**

Jean Carmignac ha mostrado que esas conclusiones tem-
pranas de testigos oculares no pueden ser refutadas atribuyén-
dolas al intento del autor de imitar a la Septuaginta o a la in-
fluencia de la lengua nativa del autor.

A pesar de conjeturas sobre fechas tardías, la evidencia de
que los Evangelios fueron escritos tempranamente es formidable
y convincente. Esta evidencia, como se señala en Siete Pasos
de una Razón para Ser Católico, 2ⁿᵈ ed., prove un fundamento
sólido como una roca para la fe en el Jesús bíblico sostenida por
los Critianos por los pasados dos mil años.

1. "Contemporary Catholic Biblical Scholarship:
   Certitudes or Hypotheses;" Msgsr.Michael J. Wrenn:
   www.ewtn.com/library/SCRIPTUR/CERTHYPO.TXT

2. "The Dates of the Gospels;" Fr. George H. Duggan:
   ***www.catholic.net/rcc/Periodicals/Homiletic/May97/gospel
   s.html***

3. *The Birth of the Synoptic Gospels*; Fr. Jean Carmignac; ©
   1987 por Franciscan Herald Press, Chicago, (Franciscan
   Press, Quincy, IL), ISBN 0-8199-0887-8

4. *The Hebrew Christ*; Claude Tresmontant ©1989 por Franciscan Herald Press, Chicago, (Franciscan Press, Quincy, IL),
   ISBN 0-8.8199-0876-2

Carsten P. Thiede concluyó que durante los años 60 los
Evangelios de Maeo y Marcos ya habiansido copiados de rollos
a códices. [Eyewitnes to Jesus, pág. 16; © 1996, Thiede /
d'Ancona; Doubleday (Random House, Inc.).

www.catholicpages.com/dir/link.aspref=21191 *(Duggan);*
www.newadvent.org/fathers

El Cardenal Ratzinger, en su Conferencia Erasmus de 1988,
criticó igualmente a los eruditos bíblicos católicos y protestantes.
El Cardenl dijo que, además de sus grandes logros, ellos "han
producido grandes errores." Luego declaró que los textos deben
verse "a la luz del movmiento total de la história y a la luz del
evento central de la história, Jesucristo." (Orígenes)

Énfasis sobre la auténtica história bíblica y extrabíblica es esencial en la educación católica en todos los niveles así como en los seinaros católicos. (Ver *Goodbye, Good Men;* © 2002, Michael S. Rose; Regnery.)

En respuesta a la crítica a los Primero Padres de la Iglesia, El Venerable John Henry Newman, mientras era sacerdote angicano, escribió lo siguiente *en Un ensayo sobre el Dearrollo de la Doctrina Cristiana* (1845): "La historia no es un credo ni un catecismo. Da lecciones más bien que reglas; pero nadie puede engañarse de su enseñanza general en esta materia, ya sea que la acepte o tropiece en ella. Amplios resúmenes y amplias masas de color se levantan de los records del pasado. Puden ser tenues, pueden ser incompletos, pero son definitivos. Y esto es por lo menos cierto, cualquier cosa que la historia enseña, cualquier cosa que omite, cualquier cosa que exagere o atenue, cualquier cosa que diga o no diga, por lo menos la Crisitanad de la historia no es el Protestantismo ... y el Protestantismo así lo ha sentido .... Sumirse en la historia es cesar de ser Protestante.") (Image Books © 1960)
www.newmanreader.org/works/development/introduction.html
(Portal de Bob Elder: Newman se convirtió al catolicismo – y llegó a ser un estimado Cardenal de la Iglesia.

4. Jesucristo fundó, y proteje de error, una Iglesia petrina

Dios ama a todos sus hijos, incluyendo a nuestros hermanos separados (CCC, par. 822), muchos de los cuales rezan y practican su fe cristiana con gran fervor. Pero, ¿Jesús no rezó "que todos sean uno." (Jn 17:17-23)? ¿Jesús no dijo: "habrá un solo rebaño y un solo pastor." (Jn 10:16)?

Claramente la Biblia indica que Jesús fundó Una Iglesia, y Jesús: (a) fundó su Iglesia solamente sobre Pedro (Mt 16:18; Lc 6:46-49); (b) dió las llaves del Reino de los Cielos solamente a Pedro (Mt 16:19); (c) dijo "apacienta mis corderos ... cuida de mis ovejas ... apacienta mis ovejas" sólo a Pedro (Jn 21:l5-17) (d) proveyó por la sucesión papal y apostólica (Is 22:22, donde las llaves indican la autoridad transferible a un sucesor) y (e) proteje la Iglesia que fundó contra errores doctrinales. (CCC par. 888-892).
www.ewtn.com/libraryscriptur/POPE.TXT (Scott Hahn)

Cuando Jesús dijo "Tú eres Pedro y sobre esta piedra edificaré mi Iglesia (Mt 16:18), él debió habler hablado en arameo, su lengua nativa, en arameo el único sentido de estas palabras es el que le da la interpretación católica. Sobre esto los eruditos en lingüistica de todas las creencias están virtualmente unánimamente de acuerdo.

En vista de esto y otras razones está claro bajo la luz de la historia,que ser un verdadero cristiano bíblico es ser católico.

5. Después de dar la primacía a Pedro, Jesús comisionó a sus apóstoles para hacer discípulos de todas las naciones

Habiendo dado la primacía a Pedro, el Jesús crucificado y resucitado comisionó a los restantes once apóstoles (todos excepto Judas Iscariote): "Id, pues, enseñad a todas las gentes, bautizándolas en el nombre del Padre, y del Hijo, y del Espíritu Santo, enseñándoles a observar cuanto yo os he mandado." (Mt 28:18-20)

¿Las importantes diferencias entre católicos y no católicos hoy día significa que se predican "diferentes evangelios"? Tomar nota de las palabras de Pablo sobre este punto. (Gal 1:6-9)

6. El Papa y los obispos católicos hoy día – los verdaderos sucesores de Pedro y de los apóstoles – continúan haciendo discípulos de todas las naciones

Esos apóstoles y, con la aprobación de Pedro, Matías y Pablo siguieron las directivas de Jesús resucitado. Con la ceremonia de la solemne "imposición de manos" a través de los tiempo, sus sucesores – el Papa y los obispos hoy día – continúan poniendo en práctica este mandato de Jesús. "la sola Iglesia de Cristo ... subsiste en la Iglesia Católica, la cual es gobernada por el sucesor de Pedro y por los obispos en comunión con él." (CCC par. 816)

7. No hay una "excepción" bíblica para rechazar la única Iglesia fundada por Jesús.

El ministro protestante Marcus Grodi estaba obsesionado por este dilema: "Cada domingo me paro en el púlpito e interpreto la escritura para mi grey, sabiendo que en un radio de 20 kilómetros de mi iglesia hay docenas de otros pastores protestantes – todos los cuales creen que la Biblia es la única autoridad para la doctrina y la práctica – pero cada uno está enseñando algo diferente de lo que yo estoy enseñando."

Igualmente molesto para él era el conocimiento de que "Cada ministro protestante que yo conocía tenía diferentes criterios de lo que era ´necesario´ para la salvación." Después de leer mucho, especialmente los Primeros Padres de la Iglesia y *Catolicismo y Fundamentalismo* de Karl Keating, Grodi se dió cuenta de que "... la respuesta del protestantismo a la renovación de la Iglesia realmente no está basada en las Escrituras," y que la cuestión más importante era la de la autoridad." (Surprised by Truth; págs. 38-51; Basilica Press). Grodi y su esposa se convirtieron al catolicismo. El fundó el portal Coming Home Network *www.chnetwork.org* (800-664-5110) y puede verse en su programa semanal en vivo *The Journey Home* en EWTN.

Jesús dijo que habría un rebaño bajo un sólo pastor (Jn 10:16) y rezó "que todos sean unos como él (Jesús) y el Padre son uno" (Jn 17:20). Con el conocimiento previo de que Pedro lo iba a negar tres veces y abandonarlo en el Calvario, Jesús dió a Pedro primacía entre los apóstoles como se dijo arriba en el número 4 abc. Jesús prometió estar con la Unica Iglesia que él fundó hasta el fin de los tiempos y que las puertas del infierno no iban a prevalecer contra ella.

Ciertamente, por medio de la Biblia, Jesús debería habernos dado a conocer que la Cristiandad de estos tiempos iba a estar dividida en más de 33,000 denominaciones, como notó Grodi, de sus *numerosas enseñanzas contradictorias en asuntos de los cuales depende nuestra salvación.* Y una investgación cuidadosa de la Biblia revela nada más que esto:

Excepto a los que estában bajo la autoridad de Pedro, a nadie más autoriza Cristo a "hacer discípulos de todas las naciones ..." (Mt 28:18-20) y la Biblia no incluye una "excepción" por medio de la cual Jesús autoriza a alguien a rechazar a Pedro o a sus sucesores o a unirse a otra Iglesia diferente; una Iglesia diferente a la cual Jesús prometió estar siempre con ella. El exorcista en Mc 9:38 no predicó un "evangelio diferente." Tampoco "dos o tres" abrazan tal evangelio si realmente se reunen en su nombre. (Ver también Mt 7:21-23). Pablo tiene palabras ominosas para los que predican una versión contraria al evangelio de Cristo (Gal 1:6-9) como se notó arriba.

En Proverbios se nos dice que no debemos confiar en nuestra propia agudeza (entendimiento). (Prov 3:5). Y en la misma vena, Pedro amonesta contra la *interpretación privada* de la Escritura. (2 Pe 3:16) lo que ha causado la proliferación de denominaciones no cristianas que vemos hoy día.

Para cada uno de nosotros nuestra vida sobre la tierra va a

terminar un día. Excepto por la de Jesucristo, la tumba de todos y cada uno de los otros fundadores de religiones está ocupada o va a ser ocupada. ¿Vamos a cerrar los ojos más bien que buscar la Iglesia a la cual nos llama Jesús?

¿No es más razonable pertenecer a la Unica Iglesia fundada por Jesucristo, el único que cumplió las profecías mesiánicas y probó de muchas maneras que hablaba con la autoridad del Creador Omnipotente? No es sabio y prudente, sabiendo que Jesús mismo nos va a juzgar después de nuestra muerte, confirmando nuestra última decisión de escoger el cielo o el infierno basada no en las decisiones que podríamos hacer en ese instante, sino en las decisones que hicimos durante nuestra vida? (CCC par. 1033; 1020-1050).

La falsa idea de que el amor eterno de Dios por nosotros (e. g., Is 54:8) garantiza nuestra salvación es muy popular hoy día. Pero la clara enseñanza de la Iglesia sobre el amor eterno o "incondicional" puede sintetizarse de la manera siguiente: Dios nos ama incondicionalmente y lo hará eternamente ya sea que estemos en el cielo o en el infierno. El amor incondicional de Dios no quiere decir salvación incondicional. (e. g., CCC par. 1035).

La plenitud de los medios de salvación, i. e., los Siete Sacramentos incluyendo la Eucaristía, "sin la cual no tendrás vida (Jn 6:53-59)," así como la primacía espiritual del sucesor de Pedro – se encuentra solamente en la Iglesia Católica.

Considere qué puede significar hoy día algo menos que esta "plenitud": Dependiendo en quién uno escogepara seguir como cristiano, puede significar por ejemplo aprobar las relaciones sexuales fuera de un matrimonio válido, la eutansia, y un aborto inducido, asuntos que pueden resultar en la pérdida de la eterna salvación.

La gran importancia de hacernos y permanecer católicos se explica en el *Catecismo de la Iglesia Católica*, 2a ed. (par. 846-848) y en el *Compañero del Catecismo de la Iglesia Católica* (Párrafo 847).

"Observad todo lo que nos dicen, pero no lo que hacen," dijo Jesus sobre los que se sientann "en la Silla de Moisés." (Mt 23:2-3). Seguro que esto se aplica a cualquiera en la Iglesia que con su conducta escandalosa hace burla de su predicación. No todos los Papas se mostraron personalmente dignos de su oficio. Pero, como con Judas, Jesús no suprimió la libre voluntad de Pedro, los otros Apóstoles, ni sus sucesores los Papas y obispos. Pero ninngún papa ha destruido la fábrica de la doctrina de la Unica Iglesia a la cual el Padre, en nombre de Jesús, envió el Espíritu Santo (Jn 14:26; Hechos 2:1-4).

En *Cruzado el umbral de la esperanza*, el Papa Juan Pablo II declara que los documentos del Concilio Vaticano II deben interpretarse autoritativamente usando el Catecismo de la Iglesia Católica; "El Catecismo fue indispensable para que todas las riquezas de la enseñanza de la Iglesia después del Concilio Vaticano II puedan ser preservadas en una nueva síntesis y reciban una nueva dirección. Sin el Catecismo de la Iglesia universal esto no sería posible hacerlo." (p. 164; Knopf; © 1994) CCC Search Engine. ***www.scborromeo.org/ccc.htm***

Cuando te pregunten ¿por qué no consideras otra religión .... ?

La primera pregunta que hay que hacer es: "¿Quién es el fundador de tu religión, o el primero en promoverla o en reformarla?" **Si esa persona no es Jesucristo,** pregunta:

(a) "¿Qué señales manifestó para mostrar que tenía autoridad del Creador, y cómo esas señales se comparan con las de Jesús?" Excepto "YO SOY" en el Antiguo Testamento y las profecías mesiánicas que Cristo cumplió, ningún apologista de otra religión puede probar que su fundador manifestó señales comparables con las de Jesús. Ver Paso 2, (a) al (g) arriba y "Otras Religiones." En el Antiguo Testamento en hebreo Dios es llamado Elohim (plural masculino) varias veces insinuando pluralidad. Del mismo modo en el Génesis 1:26: "Hagamos al hombre a nuestra imagen ...."

(b)"¿Tu fundador o reformador indicó o afirmó que él era Dios, como lo hizo Jesús?" (Jn 20:28-29). Aún en el caso de que otros hayan afirmado esto, sus tumbas están todas ocupadas. La historia no puede guardar silencio sobre otra persona con el poder de Jesús.

(c) Finalmente pregunta: "¿Tiene sentido realmente seguir a alguien que no sea Jesus, el UNICO que mostró el poder de cumplir, en el otro mundo, las promesas que nos hizo?

Si el fundador fué Jesucristo, considere las razones en los números del 3 al 7 mencionadas arriba. Luego pregunte:

(a) ¿Cuál es el pilar y el baluarte de la verdad? La respuesta de Pablo no es "la Escritura," como generalmente se cree, sino "la Iglesia del Dios vivo." (1 Tim 3:15).

(b) "¿Sobre quién fundó Jesús su Iglesia? Solamente sobre Pedro (Número 4). Jesús hizo la diferencia entre "el fundamento" (El mismo), y la "Roca" sobre la cual ese fundamento debe descansar. (Lc 6:48-49, y Mt 7:24-27) Refiérase al Paso 3 para afirmar la autenticidad histórica de los Evangelios.

(c) "¿A quién dió Jesús las llaves del Cielo?" Unicamente a Pedro. (Mt 16:19. Lutero afirmó esta posición católica por largo tiempo después de su excomunicación. Calvino citó erroneamente a Jesús en Lucas. Muestra como la sucesión apostólica – papal está indicada en Isaías 22:22 y en Mateo 28:20.

(d) Ignacio, obispo de Antioquía, mártir y oyente de Juan el Apóstol – describe la *Eucaristía* como "la carne de Cristo" ... "la medicina de la inmortalidad.

(e) Nota que no hay "Cláusa Legal" para rechazar la UNICA IGLESIA que fundó Jesús y a la cual prometió estar siempre con ella. Contra ella, ni los poderes del Infierno podrán prevalecer. El animar a un Católico a que deje su iglesia, esa persona ¿no está tratando de "prevalecer en contrade ella?" (Mt 16:18)

Luego, sugiero que tú y tu bien intencionado amigo exploren juntos el Catecismo de la Iglesia Católica, 2a. ed. Usando el índice puedes contestar virtualmente cualquier pregunta sobre lo que enseña la Iglesia. Las extensas notas al pié de la página proveen la base bíblica de esas enseñanzas.

http://bible.gospelcom.net/languages

¿Antiguo Testamento y Nuevo Testamento, o el Corán?

Dios hizo una alianza con Abrán (como con Adán, Noé, Moisés y David – precediendo la Nueva Alianza de Jesús (Mt 26:26-28)) y prometío establecerla con Isaac. (Gen 17:21) Pero Dios no hizo una alianza con Ismaél (Gen 16:11), lo bendijo (Gen 17:20) y prometió hacerlo una gran nación (Gen 17:2). Isaac e Ismaél se separaron, pero su lazo de unión como hijos de Abrán perduró. Cuando Abrán murió, estos dos hermanos juntos lo enterraron a un lado de su esposa Sara (Gen 25:7-10). Los verdaderos descendientes de Abrán, Isaac e Ismaél trataron de vivir juntos en paz como hijos e hijas de un padre común.

Cerca de 2,400 años después, alrededor de 610 A. D., Mahoma comenzó a dictar El Corán – mensajes que él creía eran de Dios por medio de un ángel. Se dice que la ascendencia de Mahoma puede trazarse a Ismaél por medio de Kedar, su segundo hijo (Gen 25:13). Hoy hay más de 70 denominaciones islámicas separadas.

Varias suras (capítulos) del Corán parecen referirse favorablemente a la Biblia, a los judíos y a los cristianos, e.g.: Alá envió a Jesús y le dio el Evangelio en el cual hay luz y dirección (5:46); Los musulmanes deben perdonar al Pueblo del Libro (cristianos y judíos) que tratan de convertirlos (2:109); Jesús fue un profeta (2:86:136) con el cual Dios hizo una alianza (33:7). Los musulmanes honran a Jesús como un profeta.

Sin embargo, en contraste con el Corán, seguimos las palabras y las acciones bíblicas de Jesús: (a) cambió el agua en vino (prohibido; sura 5:90) en la fiesta de bodas de Caná (Jn 2:1-11); (b) dijo a una copa de vino "Bebed de él, todos ustedes, porque esto es la sangre (prohibido; 5:3) de mi alianza (Mt 26:27); (c) advirtió a sus seguidores que no siguieran a falsos profetas en el desierto (¿una velada referencia a Mahoma?) (Mt 24:24-26); (d) dijo "Yo y el Padre somos uno" (Jn 10:30) y "Antes que Abrán fuera, YO SOY" (Jn 8:58) implicando igualdad con el Padre / Alá; (e) contestando a Tomás, Jesús reconoció que era Dios (Jn 20:28-29) y (f) único en la historia, Jesús maifestó el poder y la autoridad del Creador (Paso 2).

Las siguientes suras causan a los católicos y a otros cristianos rechazar el Corán como revelación divina: (a) Jesús no es Dios ni hijo de Dios (4:171); (b) Jesús es sólo uno de varios profetas que precedieron a Mahoma, El Profeta (4:163; 2:136); y Jesús no fue crucificado (4:157-159).

Ciertamente uno debe escoger: ¿la Biblia o el Corán? ¿Jesús o Mahoma? La salvación eterna de uno puede depender de escoger correctamente y vivir de acuerdo. ¿Por qué? Porque Jesús dijo sin equívocos que El será nuestro último juez y dijo que nadie va al Padre si no es por El (Ver Bautismo; CCC 1213-1284). ¿Pero por cuál norma nos va a juzgar Jesús? Para ganar la vida eterna, Jesús dijo que debemos observar sus mandamientos (Mt 19:16-17; 22:36-39). Debemos amar a nuestros enemigos. Dios nos perdonará sólo si perdonamos a otros (Mt 5:43-44; 6:15); y debemos "perdonar de corazón" (Mt 18.35).

¿Cómo va a juzgar Jesús a los que hacen violencia a personas inocentes, judíos, cristianos, musulmanes y otros? Dentro del Islam mismo, estos actos están condednados. La Organización de Conferencias Islámicas declaró: "Nosotros condenamos claramente los actos de terrorismo internacional en todas sus formas y manifestaciones" (#7; Kuala Lampur, 1-3 de abril de 2002). *www.oic-oci.org*. "The Theological Basis of Inter-Religious Brotherhood," Budhy Munawar-Rachman, Liberal Islam Network (Indonesia), *www.islamlib.com*

¿Copias antiguas del Corán apoyan el Christianismo?

En 1972 se encontraron en el Yemen copias antiguas del Corán. **Un cuidadoso estudio fililógico de esos manuscritos han convencido a algunos investigadores que el Corán, como fue recitado por Mahoma, apoya el Cristianismo, y aun anima la participación en "la conmemoración eucarística." También concluyen que, en lugar de "jóvenes morenas de grandes ojos" Mahoma dijo que las "uvas blancas" o "pasas blancas" eran parte de las frutas del cielo.**

Entre los hallazgos documentados en el libro *Die syro-aramaeische Lesart des Koran* (La lectura siro-aramea del Corán) por "Cristóbal Luxenberg" (un seudónimo). Fue publicado en alemán en el año 2000 por Das Arabische Buch (El libro árabe) y pronto va a ser publicado en inglés. Una reseña erudita en inglés alaba este libro, y se encuentra en el sitio web "Hugo-ye" mencionado abajo. La edición de *Newsweek* del 28 de julio de 2003, la cual incluye un artículo sobre este libro, fue prohibida en Pakistán.

En vez de sembrar dudas sobre el Corán, Luxenburg y otros filólogos confían que sus estudios lo clarifican, dando una traducción más fiel del Corán tal como fue redactado por primera vez por Mahoma. Hecho con buena fe, parece que todos los musulmanes que sinceramente buscan la verdad podrán considerar tal esfuerzo como agradable a Alá ya que el Corán muchas veces exhorta a los creyentes a buscar la verdad.

Un investigador observó que una nueva traducción del Corán basada en estos allazgos (aprobada y dada a conocer a todo el mundo por personas musulmanas de autoridad) puede resultar en una mayor tolerancia musulmana para el Cristianismo y el Judaísmo basada en un nuevo conocimiento de los lazos del

Islam con ambas religiones. ¿Podemos imaginarnos lo que esto significaría en términos de libertad religiosa, prosperidad y paz mundial?

Más información sobre esto se puede encontar en los siguientes sitios web:

http://bethmardutho.cua.edu/hugoye > Volume Index > Volume 6 Number 1 > Book Reviews; Christoph Luxenberg.
www.theaatlantic.com/issues/99jan/koran.htm
www.corkscrew-balloon.com/02/03/1bkk/04b.htm
http://answering-islam.org.uk/Gilchrist/Jam/chap2. htm

¿Preguntas? Centro de Evangelización Católica:
www.corazones.org; Buenas Nuevas al Servicio del Evangelio:
http://buenasnuevas.com; Esglesia: *www.esglesia.org*;
Aciprensa: *www.aciprensa.com*; Encuentra:
www.encuentra.com; EWTN,
www.ewtn.com/vexperts/search.asp. *Catholic* Answers:
www.catholic.com (619 387-7200). Jimmy Akin, CA apologista, tiene su propio excelente portal: Nazareth Resources Library,
www.cin.org/users/james. O llama gratis a Catholics United for the Faith: **1 800 – MY FAITH** or *www.cuf.org*. O Patrick Madrid, *www.surprisedbytruth.com*; Steve Ray,
www.catholic-convert.com; John Martignoni,
www.biblechristiansociety.com; Pope John Paul II Society of Evangelists, *www.pjpiisoe.org/index.htm*;
The National Catholic Bioethics Center, *www.ncbcenter.org*;
Dave Armstrong, *www.biblicalcatholic.com*;
The Bible Gateway: *http://bible.gospelcom.net*;
http://bible.gospelcom.net/languages.

Appendix D – Wallet Outline – Spanish

La razón en siete pasos para ser católico

Resumen para guardar en la cartera.[1]

1. Fuerte evidencia científica apunta a un diseño inteligente para el universo.[1]

2. En toda la historia, sólo Jesucristo manifestó el poder del Creador y Diseñador Inteligente, incluyendo el poder sobre la muerte, y el cumplimiento de las profecías mesiánicas.[2]

3. La evidencia de un origen muy temprano y la autenticidad de los Evangélios incluyen los escritos de los Primeros Padres de la Iglesia, fragmentos antiguos de papiros y los muchos *semitismos* lo cual se indica en la rudeza de algunas traducciones de los evangélios al griego.[3]

4. Jesucristo fundó sólo una Iglesia, dijo que sería un sólo rebaño, un sólo pastor, y rezó por la unidad de todos los creyentes.[4]

5. Habiendo instituido la Eucaristía y dado la primacía de la Iglesia a Pedro, Jesucristo resucitado comisionó a los apóstoles para hacer discípulos a todas las naciones.[5]

6. El Papa y los obispos católicos de hoy son los sucesores espirituales e históricos de Pedro y los otros apóstoles.[6]

7. Aunque fue negado por Pedro, tracionado por Judas Iscariote, abandonado por todos los apóstoles excepto Juan y escandalizado por algunos sacerdotes y obispos, incluyendo unos pocos Papas en la historia, Jesucristo no nos dio una excusa para rechazar la única Iglesia que El fundó y a la cual prometió estar con ella por siempre.[7]

[1] Ver 21 web sitios relacionados en un resumen de 9 páginas en *http://7step.catholic.org*

[2] En los Evangélios, Jesucristo nos dice lo que debemos hacer para entrar al cielo y que El nos jusgará después de nuestra muerte (Jn 5:22).

[3] www.catholic.net/rcc/Periodicals/Homiletic/May97/gospels. html (Padre G. Duggan); *www.ewtn.com/library/SCRIPTUR/CERTHYPO.TXT* (Mons. M. J. Wrenn); **The Birth of the Synoptic Gospels;** Padre J. Carmignac; © 1987; ISBN 0-8199-0887-8

[4] Mt 16:18; Jn 10:6; Jn 17:17-23. Hoy día más de 33,000 denominaciones cristianas no están de acuerdo en lo que se necesita para la salvación.

[5] Mt 16:18-19; Lc 6:46-49; Jn 21:15-17; Mt 28:18-20.

[6] Is 22:22; Los Primeros Padres de la Iglesia; el Catecismo de la Iglesia Católica, 816.

[7] Prov. 3:5; Gál 1:6-9; Pe 3:16; Mt 23:2-3; Mt 7:21-23.

Tomado del libro Razón en siete pasos para ser católico, 2nd ed.; Revitalizando la fe en vista al escándalo y la disensión,

© 2008 por Jerome D. Gilmartin, jdgilmartin@hotmail.com.

Obenga un resumen en inglés, español, francés, ruso, chino, indonesio, árabe, portugués, hindi, bengalí, tamil y telugu: *http://7step.catholic.org*

Ser un verdadero "cristiano bíblico" es ser católico.

http://bible.gospelcom.net/languages

Appendix E – Wallet Outline – French

Raison d'être Catholique en 7 étapes
Résumé de poche

La copie de ce résumé est autorisée sans limites

1. De fortes preuves *scientifiques* démontrent un dessein intelligent dans l'univers. 1

2. Dans toute l'histoire, seul Jésus a manifesté le pouvoir de L'Inventeur/Créateur intelligent, possédant aussi tout pouvoir sur la mort et lui seul a rempli les prophéties Messianiques. 2

3. Les preuves de l'origine très ancienne des Evangiles et de leur authenticité comprennent: les Ecrits des plus anciens Pères de l'Eglise et d'autres, des fragments de papyrus de l'antiquité et les nombreux *Sémitismes* sous-jacents qu'ils contiennent, ce qui explique le grec bizarre des Evangiles. 3

4. Jésus n'a fondé qu'une seule Eglise, a dit qu'il y aurait un seul troupeau, un seul pasteur et a prié pour l'unité de tous les croyants. 4

5. Après avoir institué l'*Eucharistie* et donné la primauté dans son Eglise à Pierre, Jésus ressuscité a chargé les apôtres de faire des disciples de toutes les nations. 5

6. Le Pape et les évêques Catholiques aujourd'hui sont les successeurs spirituels et historiques de Pierre et des autres apôtres.6

7. Bien qu'il ait été renié par Pierre, trahi par Judas Iscariote, abandonné par tous les apôtres sauf Jean et que certains prêtres et religieux - y compris quelques papes dans l'histoire - aient été causes de scandale, *Jésus ne nous a donné aucune « clause échappatoire » dans la Bible pour rejeter la seule Eglise qu'il ait fondée et avec laquelle il a promis d'être toujours, par l'intermédiaire des apôtres.* 7

1 Trouvez 21 importants Dessein Intelligent - sur des sites Internet associés dans le sommaire gratuit de 9 pages à http://7step.catholic.org

2 Dans les Evangiles, Jésus nous dit ce que nous devons faire pour entrer au ciel et qu'il nous jugera après notre mort (Jn 5:22).

3. www.catholic.net/rcc/Periodicals/Homiletic/May97gospels.html (Fr. G. Duggan); www.ewtn.com/library SCRIPTUR/CERTHYPO.TXT (Msgr. M.J.Wrenn); La Naissance des Evangiles Synoptiques; Fr. J. Carmignac; © 1987; Editions F.X. de Guibert, Paris.

4 Mt 16:18; Jn 10:6; Jn 17:17-23. Aujourd'hui au moins 33 000 sectes ou églises chrétiennes ne s'accordent pas sur les conditions requises pour être sauvé.

5 Mt 16:18-19; Lk 6:46-49; Jn 21:15-17; Mt 28:18-20.

6 Is 22:22; Premiers Pères de l'Eglise; Catéchisme de l'Eglise catholique, Par. 816.

7 Prov 3:5; Gal 1:6-9; 2 Pet 3:16: Mt 23:2-3; Mt 7:21-23 Extrait du livre Raison d'être Catholique en 7 étapes, 2nd ed. (The 7-step reason to be Catholic, 2nd ed.

© 2008 par Jerome D. Gilmartin, jdgilmartin@hotmail.com.

Déchargez le Sommaire gratuit, d'environ 9 pages, en français, anglais, espagnol, russe, chinois, indonésien, arabe, portugais, hindi, bengali et tamoul: http://7step.catholic.org

Voyez en exemple du livre sur http://7step.catholic.org

Etre un vrai "Chrétien de la Bible"c'est être Catholique.

http://bible.gospelcom.net/languages

Appendix F – Wallet Outline – Russian

Семь причин быть католиком
План для бумажника

Неограниченное копирование разрешено

1. Убедительные научные свидетельства указывают на разумный проект Вселенной. 1

2 Во всей истории только Иисус явил власть Разумного Проектировщика/Творца, включая власть над смертью и исполнение мессианских пророчеств. 2

3. Свидетельства об очень раннем происхождении и подлинности евангелий включают в себя труды Отцов Ранней Церкви и других писателей, фрагменты древних папирусов и большое количество скрытых семитизмов, объясняющих «трудный для слуха» греческий язык евангелий.3

4. Иисус основал только одну Церковь, сказал, что «будет одно стадо и один Пастырь», и молился о единстве всех верующих. 4

5. Установив Евхаристию и дав первенство в Своей Церкви Петру, воскресший Иисус послал апостолов научить все народы. 5

6. Сейчас Папа и католические епископы являются духовными и историческими преемниками Петра и других апостолов. 6

7. Хотя от Него отрекся Петр, хотя Его предал Иуда, хотя Его оставили все апостолы, кроме Иоанна, хотя Он был возмущен некоторыми рукоположенными и посвящёнными верующими, но Иисус не дал нам никакой библейской «лазейки», чтобы отвергнуть Церковь, которую Он основал и с которой обещал всегда пребывать. 7

1 См. адреса 21-ого важного веб-сайта, относящегося к Разумному Проекту, в бесплатном девятистраничном резюме на http://7step.catholic.org

2 В Евангелиях Иисус говорит нам, что мы должны делать, чтобы попасть на Небеса, и что Он будет судить нас, когда мы умрем. (Ин 5,22).

3 www.catholic.net/rcc/Periodicals/Homiletic/May97/ gospels.html (о. Д. Дугтэн); www.ewtn.com/library/ SCRIPTUR/CERTHYPO.TXT (Монсиньор М. Д. Вренц); «Рождение синоптических Евангелий», о. Ж. Карминьяк; © 1987; ISBN 0-8199-0887-8.

4 Мф 16,18; Ин 10,6; Ин 17,17-23. Сегодня более 33-х тысяч христианских деноминаций не могут договориться об условиях спасения.

5 Мф 16,18-19; Лк 6,46-49; Ин 21,15-17; Мф 28,18-20.

6 Ис. 22,22; Отцы Ранней Церкви; Катехизис Католической Церкви, пар. 816.

7 Притчи 3,5; Гал 1,6-9; 2 Петр 3,16; Мф 23,2-3; Мф 7:21-23 Быть настоящим «библейским христианином»значит - быть католиком. http://bible.gospelcom.net/languages

книги «Семь причин быть католиком; обновление веры после скандала и раскола»

© 2008 by Джером Д. Гилмартин, jdgilmartin@hotmail.com.

Скачать бесплатное резюме, примерно на 9 страниц, на английском, испанском, французском, русском, китайском, индонезийском, арабском, Португалка, Hindi, бенгалси и Tamil: http://7step.catholic.org
Посмотреть тридцатитрёхстраничный отрывок из книги:
http://7step.catholic.org

http://bible.gospelcom.net/languages

Appendix G – Wallet Outline – Arabic, Part 1

السبب السباعي لأنّ عن الكتابة

تصميم النشرة

يسمح بنسخ هذا التصميم بلا قيد ولا شرط

1. البرهان العلمي الدامغ يشير إلى القصد الفطن بشأن الكون. (1) على امتداد التاريخ؛ أيان يسوع وحده عن قدرة الخلاق/المصمّم، بما في ذلك قدرته على الموت وأنتم النبوءات.

2. البرهان على مصدر المسيحانيّة. (2)

3. البرهان على أن يسوع وحده عن قدرة الخلاق/المصمّم، بما في ذلك قدرته على الموت وأنتم النبوءات. قطع البردياّت القديمة وما يختفي فيها من أساليب سامية تجيز تفسير لغة الأناجيل اليونانيّة المنقولة سماعًا لأجل وحدة المؤمنين (3)

4. أستَن يسوع كنيسة واحدة لا غير، وقال إنه ليس سوى قطيع واحد وراع واحد كما صلى لأجل وحدة المؤمنين. (4)

5. وبعد أن أستَن الإخوان مشتّى ومنح بطرس الأولويّة في كنيسته أوكل يسوع القائم من بين الأموات إلى الرسل أن يبشّروا أيم تلامذة من جميع الأمم. (5)

6. بالرغم من إنكار بطرس والرسل الروحيّون والتاريخيّون. بحض المكرّسين والمرسلين، من فيهم عدد قليل من البابوات وردهما أن يكون معا من خلال رسله. (6)

7. نهرِّب في الكتاب الذي نبذ الكنيسة الواحدة التي أقامها عدد قليل من البابوات وحدها أن يكون معا من خلال رسله. (7) المسيحي الحقيقي بحسب الكتاب هو المسيحي الكاثوليكي

353

Appendix G – Wallet Outline – Arabic, Part 2

1 نظر 21 موقعاً مجّاناً في المرجز المجّاني على الموقع
http://7-step.catholic.org Summary at
(22 :5 بو) وأنه سوف يقاضينا بعد الممات، وأنه سوف يقاضينا بعد الممات.

2 يخبرنا يسوع في الإنجيل ما يجب علينا فعله للدخول السماء
www.catholic.net/rcc/Periodicals/Homiletic/May97/

3 SCRIPTUR/CERTHYPO.TXT (Msgr. www.ewtn.com/library/gospels.html (Fr. G. Duggan);
M. J. Wrenn); The
Birth of the Synoptic Gospels; Fr. J. Carmignac © 1987;
ISBN 0-8199-0887-8.

4 متى 16: 18؛ بو 6: 10؛ اليوم ما يقرب 33000 فريقاً مسجّلاً يتقررون فيما بينهم
على مقتضيات الخلاص

5 متى 16: 18-19؛ لو 6: 49-46؛ بو 21: 15-17؛ متى 28: 18-20.
تعليم الكنيسة الكاثوليكية، الفقرة 816.

6 اش 22: 22؛ أبناء الكنيسة الأولين تعليم الكنيسة الكاثوليكية؛ الفقرة 816.

7 أمثال 5:3؛ غلاطية 1:6-9؛ بطرس 2: 23-2؛ متى 16: 3؛ متى 7: 21-23.
http://bible.gospelcom.net/languages
انشقاق الإيمان في وسط المسيحية والخلاف

من كتاب "السبب السباعي لاعتناق الكاثوليكية"، الجزء الثاني
لمؤلفه جيروم د. جيلمارتن في اللغات الإنكليزية والإسبانية والفرنسية والروسية والصينية
jdgilmartin@hotmail.com
http://7-step.catholic.org انظر نموذجاً عن الكتاب من على الموقع
http://bible.gospelcom.net/languages

أسقط مختصر أمجاناً مجّاناً سعته 9 صفحات في اللغات البريدي
والإنكليزية والإسبانية والعربية على الموقع
http://7-step.catholic.org
http://bible.gospelcom.net/languages

Appendix H – Wallet Outline – Chinese

成為天主教徒的七大原因
袖珍摘要
此摘要得到梵諦岡准許廣印流傳。(註1)

1. 宇宙背後能設計的有力科學證據。
2. 整個歷史中，只有那穌明瞭顯示出祂擁有智能設計者/創造者的能力。祂征服了死亡。應驗了數西亞的預言。(註2)
3. 福音記載的真實性的證據包含，由初期教會教父們的著作，原始古老的手寫本，遠古的草蒲紙的碎片，由列族的基礎語言到希臘文的聖經。(註3)
4. 耶穌只創立一個教會，並說只有一個羊棧。(註4)
5. 耶穌建立了聖體聖事，制定了伯鐸為宗徒的首席地位，祂復活後派遣宗徒們使萬民成為門徒。(註5)
6. 天主教會的教宗和其他宗徒們成是伯鐸和其他宗徒們的屬靈的和歷史的繼承者。(註6)
7. 耶穌雖然被伯譯背棄，被猶達斯出賣，被宗徒們護棄除丁若望），被祂的神職人員中傷，包括歷史上的幾位教宗。聖經上沒有留下條文，人們可以拒絕祂創立的教會，祂許諾宗徒們祂將永遠在教會內。(註7)

根據聖經，真正的基督信徒是天主教徒。
請於此網址可閱覽本書三十五頁的樣本
網址: http://7step.catholic.org

註：
1. 請於此網址 *http://7-step.catholic.org* 閱覽二十一項有關 ID.的摘要，共約九頁。
2. 在福音中，耶穌教導我們要進入天國必須做的事，祂將來在我們死時審判我們。(若五:22)
3. www.catholic.net/rcc/Periodicals/Homiletic/May97/gospels.html (Fr. G. Duggan); www.ewtn.com/library/SCRIPTUR/CERTHYPO.TXT (Msgr. Michael J. Wrenn). *The Birth of the Synoptic Gospels*, Fr. Jean Carmignac, ©1987; ISBN 0-8199-0887-8.
4. 時至今日，基督信徒數術已超三萬三千個，他們都不同意 "教意必備 的條件"。參考: 瑪十六: 18; 若十六: 6; 若十七:17-23。
5. 瑪十六: 18-19; 路六: 46-49; 若十一:-15-17; 瑪卅八:18-20。
6. 依廿二:22; 早期教會教父; 天主教教理: 816條。
7. 箴三:5; 迦一:6-9; 伯鐸三:16; 瑪 廾十三:2-3; 瑪七:21-23。

本書『成為天主教徒的七大原因』第二部分『便信仰在連串異議反駁間中傾覆』
版權: 2008 / 作者: Jerome D. Gilmartin
網址: jdgilmartin@hotmail.com
網址: http://7step.catholic.org

以下網址可免費下載約九頁不同語文的摘要
有英文、西班牙文、法文、俄文、中文、印度尼西亞文及阿拉伯文

網址: http://bible.gospelcom.org

http://bible.gospelcom.net/languages

Appendix I – Wallet Outline – Indonesian

7 LANGKAH MENGAPA MENJADI KATOLIK GARIS BESAR

DIPERKENANKAN MENGKOPI TANPA BATAS GARIS BESAR INI

1. Ada kejelasan *ilmiah* yang kuat bahwa alam semesta ini dirancang secara cerdas[Isaiah 42:6-7][1]

2. Dalam seluruh sejarah hanya Yesus menunjukkan kuasa Perancang/Pencipta cerdas, termasuk kuasa atas kematian, dan memenuhi Nubuat-nubuat Al Masih.[2]

3. Kejelasan bagi asal-usul dan otentisitas Injil meliputi tulisan para Bapa Gereja Purba dan lain-lainnya, fragmen-fragmen papirus kuno dan banyak *Semitisme* yang mendasarinya, yang berlaku bagi bahasa Yunani dari Injil.[3]

4. Yesus mendirikan hanya satu Gereja, mengatakan bahwa hanya ada satu kawanan, satu gembala dan berdoa bagi kesatuan semua orang beriman.[4]

5. Setelah mengadakan *Ekaristi* dan menyerahkan primat dalam Gereja-Nya kepada Petrus, Yesus Jaya menugaskan para Rasul untuk membuat murid-murid dari segala bangsa.[5]

6. Paus dan para uskup katolik dewasa ini adalah pengganti spiritual dan historis Petrus dan para rasul lain.[6]

7. Meskipun disangkal oleh Petrus, dikhianati oleh Yudas Iskariot, ditinggalkan oleh semua rasul selain Yohanes dan mendapat sandungan dati beberapa orang yang ditahbiskan dan dibaktikan, termasuk beberapa Paus dalam sejarah, *Yesus tidak memberi kepada kita "klausula biblis lolos" untuk menolak Gereja yang tunggal yang telah didirikan-Nya dan, melalui para rasul, berjanji akan selalu besertamnya.*[7]

[1] Lihatlah 21 situs pada ringkasan 9 halaman yang cuma-cuma pada **http://7step.catholic.org**

[2] Dalam Injil Yesus mengatakan kepada kita apa yang harus kita lakukan untuk masuk surga dan bahwa Ia akan menghakimi kita setelah kita meninggal dunia (Yoh 5: 22).

[3] www.catholic.net/rcc/Periodicals/Homiletic/May97/gospels.html (Fr. G. Duggan); www.ewtn.com/library/SCRIPTUR/CERTHYPO.TXT (Msgr. M. J. Wrenn); The Birth of the Synoptic Gospels; Fr. J. Carmignac; © 1987; ISBN 0-8199-0887-8.

[4] Mt 16: 18; Yoh 10:6; Yoh 17: 17-23. Dewasa ini 33.000 lebih denominasi kristiani tak sepakat mengenai *persyaratan untuk keselamatan.*

[5] Mt 16: 18-19; Lk 6: 46-49; Yoh 21: 15-17; Mt 28: 18-20.

[6] Yes 22: 22; Para Bapa Gereja Purba; *Katekismus Gereja Katolik*, Par. 816

[7] Ams 3-5; Gal 1: 6-9; 2 Ptr 3: 16; Mt 23: 2-3; Mt 7: 21-23

Menjadi orang kristiani biblis sejati berarti menjadi katolik

Dari buku *The 7-Step Reason to be Catholic, 2nd ed.; Science, the Bible and History point to Catholicism.* © 2008 by Jerome D.Gilmartin; jdgilmartin@hotmail.com

Silahkan dengan cuma-cuma mengambil Summary, kira-kira 9 halaman, dalam bahasa Inggris, Spanyol, Perancis, Rusia, China, Indonesia, Arab, Bahasa Hindi, Telugu, Bengali dan orang Tamil: http://7step.catholic.org
Lihatlah contoh buku: http://7step.catholic.org

http://bible.gospelcom.net/languages

Appendix J – Wallet Outline – Portuguese

Ser Católico em sete degraus
Resumo de bolso

É permitido fazer número ilimitado de cópias deste resumo

1. Sólida evidência científica realça a tese de que o universo é fruto de um desígnio de um ser inteligente.[1]

2. Em toda a História, somente Jesus manifestou o poder do Autor Inteligente/Criador, inclusive o poder sobre a morte, e cumpriu as profecias messiânicas.[2]

3. A evidência da origem inicial e a autenticidade dos Evangelhos inclui os escritos dos primeiros padres da Igreja e outros, fragments de papiros antigos e os muitos semitismos subjacentes, que explicam os aspectos inusitados da lengua grega usada nos Evangelhos.[3]

4. Jesus fundou somente uma Igreja, disse que haveria um rebanho e um pastor, e rezou pela unidade dos crentes.[4]

5. Tendo instituído a Eucaristia e dado o primado de sua Igreja a Pedro, depois da ressurreição Jesus ordenou aos Apóstolos de fazer discípulos em todas as nações.[5]

6. O Papa e os Bispos Católicos de hoje são os sucessores espirituais e históricos de Pedro e dos outros Apóstolos.[6]

7. Embora tivesse sido negado por Pedro, traído por Judas, abandonado por todos os Apóstolos (exceto João) e escandalizado por cristãos entre os ordenados e consagrados, inclusive alguns papas na história, Jesus não nos deu nenhuma "cláusula de escape" para rejeitar a única Igreja que Ele fundou, e, através dos Apóstolos, prometeu estar sempre com Ela.[7]

1 Veja 21 websites importantes relacionadoscom o conceito de "desígnio inteligente" no resumo gratuito de 9 páginas (http://7-step.catholic.org)

2 Nos Evangelhos, Jesus nos ensina o que devemos fazer para entrar no céu e que Ele nos julgará depois da morte (João 5:22).

3 www.catholic.net/rcc/Periodicals/Homiletic/May97/gospels.html (Pe. G. Duggan); www.ewtn.com/library/SCRIPTUR/CERTHYPO.TXT [Msgr. M. J. Wrenn]: The Birth of the Synoptic Gospels; Fr. J. Carmignac; © 1987; ISBN 0-8199-0887-8.

4 Mt 16:18; Jn 10:6; Jn 17:17-23. Hoje em dia as mais de 33 mil denominações cristãs não estão de acôrdo sobre os requerimentos para a salvação.

5 Mt 16:18-19; Lk 6:46-49; Jn 21:15-17; Mt 28:18-20.

6 Is 22:22; Primeiros Padres da Igreja; Catecismo da Igreja Católica, par. 816.

7 Prov 3:5; Gal 1:6-9; 2 Pet 3:16; Mt 23:2-3; Mt 7:21-23

Do livro, *The 7-Step Reason to be Catholic, 2nd ed.: Science, the Bible and History point to Catholicism.* © 2008 por Jerome D. Gilmartin, jdgilmartin@hotmail.com.

Baixe o sumário gratuito de 9 páginas em **Inglês, Espanhol, Francês, Russo, Chinês, Indonésio, Árabe, Hindu, Bengali, Tamil, Telugu e Português:** *http://7step.catholic.org*

Veja exemplos das páginas do livro (Inglês) no site *http://7step.catholic.org*

Ser "Cristão" verdadeiro é ser Católico
http://bible.gospelcom.net/languages

Appendix K – Wallet Outline – Hindi, Part 1

कैथोलिक रहने के लिए 7 कारण एक एक बिन्दु – संक्षिप्त रूपरेखा

रूपरेखा की नकल हेतु असीम अधिकार

1. विश्व की कुशल अभिकल्पना के आधारभूत एवं सशक्त वैज्ञानिक सबूत। 1

2. संपूर्ण इतिहास में, केवल जीसस में मृत्यु को पराजित करने तथा मसीहा के रूप में आकर भविष्यवाणी बताने के साथ साथ एक सक्षम कुशल रचनाकार/सृष्टिकर्ता की क्षमता पाई जाती है। 2

3. आदिकाल के गिरजाघर के पादरी एवं अन्य लोगों द्वारा लिखित साहित्य के साथ धर्म-शिक्षा के प्रारंभिक एवं प्राधिकृत सबूत, आदिकाल के भोजपत्र के खंड तथा कई अंतर्निहित सामग्रियों के सबूत, यूनानियों की ड्यूपर-ग्रेटिंग का लेखा-जोखा प्रस्तुत करते हैं। 3

4. जीसस ने केवल एक ही गिरजाघर की स्थापना की थी; उन्होंने कहा कि एक ही झुण्ड होना चाहिए और एक ही गड़रिया होना चाहिए। उन्होंने विश्वास करने वालों में एकता के लिए प्रार्थना की थी। 4

5. यूखेरिस्ट की स्थापना करने तथा अपने गिरजाघर में पीटर को महत्व देने के बाद, पुनः उदित जीसस ने ईश्वर दूती को सभी राष्ट्रों में शिष्य बनाने का निर्देश दिया। 5

6. वर्तमान पोप एवं कैथोलिक बिशप पीटर एवं अन्य ईश्वर दूत के आध्यात्मिक एवं ऐतिहासिक उत्तराधिकारी है। 6

7. यद्यपि पीटर ने साफ इन्कार किया और जुड़ास इस्कारियट ने धोखा दिया, सभी ईश्वर दूती द्वारा अलक्षित होने के बावजूद भी, जॉन तथा अन्य दीक्षित एवं प्रतिष्ठित लोगों के कारण बदनाम होने के बावजूद भी, जीसस ने बाहुबल में कहीं भी घृटि की 'छूट' का उल्लेख नहीं किया ताकि हम उनके द्वारा स्थापित गिरजाघर को अस्वीकार न कर सकें तथा उन्होंने ईश्वर दूती के माध्यम से हमेशा साथ साथ रहने का वादा किया था। 7

Appendix K – Wallet Outline – Hindi, Part 2

1. मुफ्त 9-पृष्ठ में उद्धृत 21 महत्त्वपूर्ण आइंद्वी संबंधित वेबसाइट देखें। http://7-step.catholic.org में इसके संक्षिप्त विवरण देखें।

2. धर्म-शिक्षा में जीसस स्वर्ग में प्रवेश करने के लिए हमें मार्गदर्शन प्रदान करते हैं तथा मृत्यु के पश्चात् ही अपना न्याय देंगे। (Jn.5:22)

3. www.catholic.net/rcc/Periodicals/Homiletic/May97/gospels.html (Fr. G. Duggan);
www.ewtn.com/library/SCRIPTUR/CERTHYPO.TXT (Msgr. M. J. Wrenn); दि बर्थ आफ दी सिनाॅटिक गॉस्पल्स;
एफ.आर. जे. कार्मिनेक © 1987; ISBN 0-8199-0887-8

4. Mt 16:18; Jn 10:6; Jn 17:17-23. आज 33,000 व्यक्ति और ईसाई, धर्म के विभिन्न वर्गों में उद्धृत मोक्ष की आवश्यकताओं पर विश्वास नहीं करते।

5. Mt 16:18-19; Lk 6:46-49; Jn 21:15-17; Mt 28:18-20.

6. Is 22:22; आदिकाल के गिरजाघर के पादरी, कैथोलिक गिरजाघर के कैटेचिजम, par. 816.

7. Prov 3:5; Gal 1:6-9; 2 Pet 3:16; Mt 23:2-3; Mt 7:21-23

दी सेवेन स्टेप रीज़न टॅ बी कैथोलिक, द्वितीय संस्करण : साइंस, द बाइबल रैण्ड हिस्ट्री वाइण्ट टॅ कैथोलिसिज्म © 2007 जेरेम जी गिल्मार्टिन द्वारा
लिखित jdgilmartin@hotmail.com.

मुफ्त में अंग्रेजी, स्पेनिश, फ्रेंच, क्रूसी, चीनी भाषा, इण्डोनेशिया की भाषा, अरबी, पुर्तगाली, हिन्दी, बंगाली तथा तमिल में लगभग 9 पृष्ठों के संक्षिप्त प्रस्तुतिकरण को ऑनलाइन करें।

पुस्तक (अंग्रेजी) के कुछ पृष्ठों को यहां देखें http://7step.catholic.org

एक सच्चे 'बाइबल क्रिस्चन' होने के लिए कैथोलिक होना जरूरी है। ... **http://bible.gospelcom.net/languages**

Appendix L – Wallet Outline – Bengali, Part 1

ক্যাথলিক হবার সাত-পদক্ষেপ বিশিষ্ট কারন

ওয়ালেট আউটলাইন

এই আউটলাইনের বা খসড়ার অবাধ অনুকরণ অনুমোদিত

১. বর্ণিষ্ঠ বিজ্ঞান ভিত্তিক প্রামাণিক তথ্যাবলী এই বিশ্বের সৃকর্মের পরিকল্পনার ইঙ্গিত করে।

২. সম্পূর্ণ ইতিহাসে, কেবলমাত্র প্রভু যীশুই এই বুদ্ধিমান এবং সৃকৌশল পরিকল্পনাকারীর বা সৃষ্টিকর্তার ক্ষমতার সাথে সাথে মৃত্যুকে অতিক্রম করার ক্ষমতাকেও শক্তিশালী প্রতিষ্ঠিত করেছেন এবং মানব জাতির জ্ঞাপকরূপে দিব প্রেরণাধীনভূমিকা প্রতিপালন করেছেন।

৩. গসপেলস্ (খ্রিষ্টের উপদেশাবলী ও বাইবেলে বর্ণিত খ্রিষ্টের জীবনকাহিনী) -এর বহু প্রাচীন উৎপত্তির সাক্ষ এবং তার বিশ্বাসযোগ্যতা পূর্বতন চার্চের বিশ্ব এবং অনাস্থাদের রচনা, প্রাচীন শিল্পির নিদর্শন যথাংশ এবং অনেক মৌলিক (ইহুদিস) সেমিটিজম্ -এর অন্তর্ভুক্ত, যেগুলি "কালেন-স্কীড়া প্রদানকারী" বা বিরক্তিকর হিসাবে শ্রীকের সংশ্লেষণ-এ গণ্য করা হয়।

৪. যীশু কেবলমাত্র একটিই চার্চ প্রতিষ্ঠা করেছিলেন, সেই সঙ্গে বলেছিলেন যে এখানে একটিই দল থাকবে এবং একজনই দলপতি থাকবে এবং তিনি সকল আস্থাবান বিশ্বাসী বাড়ির ঐক্যবদ্ধতার জন্য আস্থাবকতার জন্য প্রার্থনা করেছিলেন।

৫. নৈন্তোতের উৎসবের প্রবর্তন করে এবং সিটারকে তার চাচের সর্বোচ্চ যাজকের পদমর্যাদা দিয়ে, পুণ্যজীবন লাভ করে যীশু সমগ্র জাতির মধ্যে লিস্ট তৈরী করার জন্য ভলকরাক প্রচারক জন প্রধান শিষ্যদের দূত বা প্রচারক হিসাবে নিযুক্ত করেছিলেন।

৬. আজাজ্ঞের দিনে গোপন ও ক্যাথলিক বিশপরা হলেন সিটার এবং যীশুর ছামা জন প্রধান শিষ্যদের মধ্যে অনন্তম ধর্মপ্রচারক শিষ্যদের আগ্নাত্মিক ও ঐতিহাসিক উত্তরাধিকারী।

৭. যদিও সিটার অধিকার করেছিলেন, জুডেন ইসকারিয়টকে বিশ্বাসঘাতকতা করেছিল, জন ছাড়া বাকী ছাদশ জন প্রধান শিষ্যসবে পরিত্যাগ করেছিল এবং কিছু যাজকতের দ্বারা কলঙ্কিত হয়েছিলেন এবং উৎসর্গীকৃত হয়েছিলেন, যে একমাত্র চার্চটি তিনি প্রতিষ্ঠা করেছিলেন সেটিকে বাতিল করে দেবার জন্য ইতিহাসের কতিপয় শোক সমেত, যীশু আমাদের বাইবেলে উল্লিখিত কোনো "এসেকুশ ক্লুজ" (পরিত্রাতাদের বা এড়াবেলের চুক্তি) দেন নি এবং জন ছাদশ জন প্রধান শিষ্যদের মাধ্যমে সদা সর্বদা থাকতে সঙ্গে থাকবার প্রতিজ্ঞা করেছিলেন।

360

Appendix L – Wallet Outline – Bengali, part 2

১. ২২টি উল্লেখযোগ্য আইহুডি-সম্পর্কিত উত্তর সাইট্টি ক্লি ৯-পৃষ্ঠায় দেখুন সংক্ষেপে দেওয়া আছে http://7-step.catholic.org

২. গসপেল্-৭, খ্রীষ্ট আমাদের বলেন স্বর্গ প্রবেশ করার জন্য আমরা কি কি কাজ অবশ্যই করবো এবং আমাদের মৃত্যুর পরে তিনি আমাদের সেই কাজের বিচার করবেন (Jn 5:22 / জে ফন ৫ : ২২)

৩. www.catholic.net/rcc/Periodicals/Homiletic/May97/gosples.html (Fr. G. Duggan/ ফ্রা. জি. ডুগ্গান);
www.ewtn.com/library/SCRIPTUR/CERTHYPO.TXT (Msgr. M. J. Wrenn / ম্যাসেঞ্জার এম. জে. রেইন); The Birth of the Synoptic Gospels; Fr. J. Carmignac; © 1987; ISBN 0-8199-0887-8. দি বার্থ অফ দি সিনপটিক গসপেলস্, ফ্রা.জে. কার্মিগ্নাক, © ১৯৮৭, আই্.এস. বি. এন. ত্রিজো ০-৮১৯৯-০৮৮৭-৮.

৪. Mt 16:18; Jn 10:6; Jn 17:17-23. এম.টি. ১৬ : ১৮; জে.ফন ১০ : ৬ ; জে.ফন ১৭:১৭:২৩. আজ্ঞেক ০৭,০০০ + খ্রিষ্টান বিভাজনকরা মুক্তির লাভের প্রয়োজনীয়তার বিষয়ে সম্মত নয় ।

৫.Mt 16:18-19; Lk 6:46-49; Jn 21:15-17; Mt 28:18-20. এম.টি.১৬ : ১৮-১৯; এল.কে. ৬ : ৪৪-৪৯জে এল.ফন. ২১: ১৫-১৭; এম.টি. ২৮ : ১৮-২০.

৬. Is 22:22; আই্.এস. ২২: ২২; আর্লি চার্চ কানারুম ; ক্যাথলিক চার্চের প্রসোঙ্গর, পিথৃজার.২২৯.

৭. Prov 3:5; Gal 1:6-9; 2 Pet 3:16: Mt 23:2-3; Mt 7:21-23 প্রোভ ৩ : ৫; গিলিথল ১: ৬ -৯ ; ২ পাইটি ৩ :১৬ ; এম.টি ২৩: ২-৩; এম.টি ৭: ২১-২৩

বই থেকে, দি ৭-স্টেপ মিজন টু দি ক্যাথলিক , হয় বটোল্গিন... সাফেন্স, দি বাইবেল ল্যাগ হিস্ট্রি শহরেন্ট টু ক্যাথলিক ইংরাম. © ২০০৬ জেরোস ডি. গিল্মার্টিন দ্বারা , jdgilmartin@hotmail.com ইংলিশ, স্প্যানিশ, ক্রেঞ্চ, রাশিয়ান, চাইনিজ, ইন্দনিসিয়ান, আরবিক, পর্তুগীজ, হিন্দী, বাংলা এবং তামিল ভাষায় : http://7step.catholic.org

অটেনলোড করুন ফ্রি সামারি , ৯ পাতার মত , ইংরাজী, স্প্যানিশ, হিন্দী হ্যান্দ বাংলা ল্যাগ : http://7step.catholic.org উয়েবসাইটে

বইয়ের নমুনা পৃষ্ঠা দেখুন (ইংরাজীতে) http://7step.catholic.org উয়েবসাইটে পকাজন প্রাক্ত "বাইবেল গ্রীফিন" হ্বার জন্য একজন ক্যাথলিক হওয়া.

http://bible.gospelcom.net/languages

Appendix M – Wallet Outline – Tamil, Part 1

கத்தோலிக்கராக இருக்க வேண்டியதற்கான 7 காரணங்கள் சுருக்கமான கைபேசி (?)

இந்த சுருக்கத்தினை எவ்வித வரையறையையுமின்றி நகலெடுப்பினது அங்கீகரிக்கப்பட்டுள்ளது அல்லது அங்கீகரிக்கப்படாத / படைப்பினை குறிப்பிடுகிறது.

1. வலுவான அறிவியல் ஆதாரங்கள் பரம்பொருளின் / பிரபஞ்சத்தின் விகேவகமுள்ள வடிவமைப்பினை / படைப்பினை வடிவமைப்பாளரின் / படைப்பாளரின் சக்தியினை தெளிவாக வெளியிடுகிறது மற்றும் திடப்படுத்துகிறது.

2. மரணத்தினை விஞ்சும் சக்தி உடைய அனைத்துலக வரலாறுகளிலும், கர்த்தர் மட்டுமே விவேகமுள்ள வடிவமைப்பாளரின் தீர்க்கதரிசனம் தந்து வருதுவரைத்திருகிறார்.

3. தொடர்ச்சிக்க கால தேவாலய பாதிரியார்கள் மேலும் மற்றவர்களின் இலக்கிய படைப்புகள், கிரேக்க நற்செய்தி போதனைகள்(கு) காரணமாகவுள்ள தொல்லைமைக்கால கைபிடியுடியவகளின் எஞ்சிய பகுதிகள் மற்றும் பல மூது அறிய இதனெஞ்சுக்கு ஆதாரமாக அனைத்திலுள்ள கோளமாய் தேடப்பாடிலான நற்செய்தி போதனைகளின் தொடர்க்க மூலாதாரமாக மற்றும் மந்பல்லக்கத்தியவையுள்ள ஆதாரங்களாக விளங்குகின்றன.

4. கர்த்தர் ஒரே ஒரு தேவாலயத்தை மட்டுமே நிர்மாணித்துள்ளார் அந்திக்கே ஒரே சமயத்திலும், ஒரே சமய (ஒரு இருக்க வேண்டிய)மென்றும் மற்றும் நம்பிக்கையுள்ள அனைவரின் ஒற்றுமைக்காகவும் பிராந்தியை மேற்கொண்டுள்ளார். அவரனுப்பும் பெறியும் கொண்டனர்.

5. இறுதி விடுந்திருகங்களை நிரூபி அவலம்மத்து தனது தேவாலயத்துக்கு பெறுக்கு தேவைகளுக்கு(ரு பட படவியளித்து உயிரிக்தெழுக்க கர்த்தர் அவரைத்தி மக்கள் சமுதாயத்தின் தீடங்களாக திருத்துதங்களுக்கு பொறுப்பளித்தார்.

6. பெருகும் மற்றும் இதுர திருத்துதங்களின் சமயத்துடுறை சாந்த புனிதமான மற்றும் வரலாற்றுக்குரிய வாசிக்களாக. இன்று பொப்பாவையினவர் மற்றும் மற்றும் பாதிரியார்கள் விளங்குகின்றனர்.

7. பெருகினௌம் உண்மையை ஏற்க மறுக்கப்பாட்டாலும், ஞானால் இறக்கியப்பாடாண நம்பிக்கை நம்பிக்கைக்கை தரேக்கம் செய்யப்பட்டாலும்மிகும், அனைத்துது திருத்துதங்களாளும் கைகம்பிடப்பாட்ட நம்பும் கூட, கர்த்தர் நிறுவியியவமாக்கு ஒரு தேவாலயத்திருனையாம் மற்றும் எப்போதும் உடனிருப்பேன் என தகத்திருத்துதர்கள் மூலம் தரப்பாட்ட உறுதிமொழியினையும் எற்கமுறுக்க, கர்த்தர் எமக்கு கிலியியிலில் குறிப்பிட்டுள்ள தண்ட லைகளின்(ந்திரும்)குந்துப்பதன்ப உள்நிளி சைங்கப்பப வரந்தங்களைவகிவலை என ஜானன் மற்றும் நம்பிக்கையில்லை. அவழமிழ்டியுள்ள பொப்பாப்பைண சில சமபாப்ணவயிலி உட்பட சைங்கப்பப மற்றும் புளிகப்பாப்டுக்காது சிவரால் வரலாற்றிலிருந்து பரிந்துளைக்கப்பப்பாடுந்திருகிறார்.

Appendix M – Wallet Outline – Tamil, Part 2

1 http://7-step.catholic.org எனும் வலைத்தளத்தில் இவைச 9 பக்கங்களுள்ள காருத்தக்கியல் 21 முக்கிய ஜஷ தொடர்புள்ள வெப கைட்களை பார்க்கவும்.

2 தமிழகத்தி போதகைனகளில், தொளிக்கத்திற்குள் நூலழுய நாம் எனே செய்ய வேண்டும் எனபதையும் மற்றும் நாம் மரணித்த பின் அவர் தீர்மானிப்பர்ர் எனவேரம் எமக்கிந்த காந்திக் கான்டிக்றார்.(Jn 5:22).

3 www.catholic.net/rcc/Periodicals/Homiletic/May97/gospels.html (பாதிரியார் ஜி.டுக்கன்);
www.ewtn.com/library/SCRIPTUR/CERTHYPO.TXT (துதுர் எம்.ஜே.ரேன்); *The Birth of the Synoptic
Gospels*; பாதிரியார் ஜே.கார்மிக்நாய்; © 1987; ISBN 0-8199-0887-8.

4 Mt 16:18; Jn 10:6; Jn 17:17-23. இன்று 33,000க்கு மேற்பட்ட கிறித்துவ சமயப்பிரிவுகள் பாலமைவனிபர்பிருக்கான இன்றியமையாத தேவலைகளை ஓப்பிடுக்கொள்வதில்லை.

5 Mt 16:18-19; Lk 6:46-49; Jn 21:15-17; Mt 28:18-20.

6 Is 22:22; Early Church Fathers; *Catechism of the Catholic Church*, par. 816.

7 Prov 3:5; Gal 1:6-9; 2 Pet 3:16; Mt 23:2-3; Mt 7:21-23

கத்தோலிக்கராக இருக்க வேண்டியதற்கான 7 காரணங்கள், 2ம் பதிப்பு புத்தகத்திலிருந்து : கத்தோலிக்க சமய போதகைனகளை குறிப்பிடும் அறிவியல், விகிலியைம் மற்றும் வரலாறு © 2008 by Jerome D. Gilmartin,
jdgilmartin@hotmail.com

http://7step.catholic.org

http://7step.catholic.org எனும் இணையதளத்தில் ஆங்கில பல்வேறு புத்தகத்தின் மாதிரி பக்கங்களை பார்க்கவும். கத்தோலிக்க கிறித்துவமாக இருக்க வேண்டிபடுட்கு உண்மையயான விகிலிய கிறித்துவமாக இருப்பதற்கான வழி.

http://bible.gospelcom.net/languages

Appendix N – Wallet Outline – Telugu, Part 1

కాథలిక్‌గా మారడానికి 7 మెట్ల కారణం

గోడపై రూపురేఖలు

ఈ రూపురేఖలను మీరే దేనితో పనిని చేసుకునేందుకు అంగీకరించుకోండి.

1. మొదైన రూపంలో ఈ విశ్వాన్ని రూపొందించబట్టి ఇప్పుడైన స్వేచ్ఛగా సిద్ధాంతాన్ని ఉన్నాయి. 1

2. పరిశీ మొత్తంలో , మొదైన రూపంలో ఈ విశ్వాన్ని రూపొందించినస్థితిలో ఇక్ జీవన ఎక్కడ ఉండాల స్వేచ్ఛ ఉంది. ఇదిగో సూడియాను నియంత్రేత ఇట్లు అధ్యాపై ఉంది. మొదియా అక్కున్న నియం నొకారు. 2

3. కొండా ఎర్పడిన పోస్టున, గౌర్నెస్ మొదియా అభ్యాసంగా హీన్రీయుంటడాన బళ్తిల సిహిర్తాల మొదియా ఇకారులు, మొదియా
ఈమహన రూక్తాలిగా మొదియా నిర్ధి నిస్టున్న రావుడడు దారవునుడుకు అనుపికురకున్నివసు' (గికరు గాన్సి
ఉన్నాయి.3

4. దేవుడ్డి నమ్మడం ఉన్నసారంగం జ్ఞత్రాల కోసం ఒక గొరైల మంద కదిలిన ఒక గొరైల మంద కదిలిన ప్రాకీనేసుయుంరంలో ఒక
ఒక ఎర్ప్యం జ్ఞనక గర్తించారు. 4

5. మొత్తర స్థిర్కాల్లో, మేర్తున చేసిన ఫోజన కాటుత్వాల మేకరుల నం సురహాలగా నియంమినారు. మ్యాస్ట్లి శేర్త నుంది
సూర్తిస్తం హారరిన పురందాల గర్లి నంద్ల మొక పరసా కాట్వంటికే, ప్రమాదంత ఫోక్తు కారా చేసుకస్నార.5

6. నేమ మనమ మాక్స్న్ని పోక మొదియా కాట్వంటిల బొత్తిలాందిరకా పీకల్ మొదియా ఇకల నక్ గురహుగా ఇథ్యాత్తిగ మొదియా నారుత్రావన్ని
వారింటాం. 6

7. పీకల్ అంగీకరించినప్పటికీ, జంరాల ఇక్తర్మన అయంఊదతా ఊందంత ప్రాకీలం జ్ఞక మొదియా హీకరల ప్రాకీలం
దేసిన కాందరం మనపేకి మనర ప్రమాదంలోందిం మొదియా పరోక్తంని ప్రాకీలం కాందరం ప్రమాదం ఊరికేక నింబంధించిన
అంతావును, "వ్ర్లియంనేందిండన యంవన" జ్ఞనక మనక ఇందిలంమోదరన కారను. దిన్ని తరలిస్నామో అధ్యేను గురిర్ం
ప్రకర్తవీంది నొ ప్రకేంద్ర నొకల్ని యంంయు అందారం నొకరు. 7

Appendix N – Wallet Outline – Telugu, Part 2

1. ఉపరిగా లభించే 9 షీట్లో సమాచారమైన 21 ఐ.డి. సంబంధిత నేషి నేషల నాషనలను http://7-step.catholic.org లో చూడండి

2. కథనాలకూ ప్రకారం మనం మంత్రించిన వరియాళ మునక స్వర్గం (ప్రతి శ్రద కత్రియాళా పద్ధి ఇనేరి జేను మాచుకొంటారు. (జాగ-5:22)

3. www.catholic.net/rcc/periodicals/Homiletic/May97/gospels.html (హించి.ఐ.చుర్చి)

www.ewtn.com/library/SCRIPTUR/CERTHYPO.TXT (Msgr. M. J. Wrenn)
The Birth of the Synoptic Gospels; Fr. J. Carmignac © 1987 ISBN 0-8199-0887-8

4. Mt 16:18, Jn 10:16, Jn 17:17-23

నేడు 33,000+ (క్రైస్తవ ఉపశాఖల పాఠ ముక్క కాలపైన అనుసరాలను ఇళ్ళ పరిశీలిస్తా అంగీకరించం లేదు.

5. Mt 16:18-19, Lk 6:46-49 Jn 21:15-17, Mt 28:18-20

6. Is 22:22, Early Church Fathers; Catechism of the Catholic Church, par, 816

7. Prov 3:5; Gal 1:6-9; Pet 3:16: Mt 23:2-3; Mt 7:21-23

కార్తికేనా ఉందేంటను 7 మ్యూష్ కారణాలు, రెండు ఎమెన్న, నెల్, ఓ బైబిల అంక మ్యాప్ పొందిండి ఈ కాథోలిన్, కనుమాత్ - జార్జ్ డి.గిల మా
ర్టి స్టెప్లాక్ నుండి *idgilmartin@hotmail.com*

ఇంగ్లిష, స్పానిష, ఫ్రెంచ, రష్యన, చైనిస, ఇంగ్లేషమెంట, మరియం అరబిక జాపొ ఉపరిగా జాపొల సమాచారం కోసం
http://7step.catholic.org ఇతర జాపలు జార్జ అందుబాటులో రానున్నాయి.

స్టెప్లక్ని సమాచారా జాపల కోసం (ఇంగ్లిష) http://7step.catholic.org

నిజమైన "బైబిల (క్రైస్తన)" అంటే కాథోలిక చూడండి.

http://bible.Gospelcom.net/languages

Appendix O

For those who teach CCD, RCIA and other Catholic religious education programs

A few years ago I asked a Catholic catechetics instructor how his students might respond to this question: ***"Why should anyone be a Catholic rather than practice some other religion or none?"*** *"Not only can our students not answer this question,"* he replied; *"most adult Catholics can't either."*

The prevailing view among Catholics today, it seems, is this:

> ***"It is probably important to be Christian;***
> ***it is less important to be Catholic."***

If we doubt this we need only look around at Mass on Sunday. What proportion of those attending are young-adult Catholics? Where are the many graduates of our Catholic high schools and colleges? Many, of course, have simply stopped going to Church. Others in increasing numbers attend services elsewhere. The minister of a Protestant Church told a friend of mine that three-quarters of his congregation were ex-Catholics.

Virtually all such "ex" and otherwise missing Catholics attended Mass in their youth and understood the Faith, at least to some degree. Why, then, did they leave? They knew ***how*** to be Catholic. Could it be that they were never told, concisely, ***why*** it is important to be Catholic?

Without that knowledge many are at a loss to answer when someone knocks at their door and – unknowingly misinterpreting the Bible, Church teaching and history – explains the importance of ***not*** being Catholic.

It appears that the clear ecumenical initiatives of the Second Vatican Council (*Unitatis Redintegratio*), important as they are, have succeeded to a degree not intended by the Council. Somehow they have overshadowed the Council's equally clear statements on the importance of being Catholic (*Lumen Gentium*).

In *The Catholic School on the Threshold of the Third Millennium*, Pio Cardinal Laghi, former Prefect of the Vatican Congregation for Catholic Education, wrote:

> "Catholic schools are at once places of evangelization, of complete formation, of inculturation, of apprenticeship in a lively dialogue between young people of different religions and social backgrounds."

But without an ability to concisely and graciously explain the importance of being Catholic, what will be the likely result of a "dialogue between young people of different religions"? The NCCB (now USCCB) Committee on Evangelization noted the following in its mission statement:

> *"The Committee seeks effective and creative ways to challenge all Catholics to invite people in the United States, whatever their social background, to hear the message of salvation in Jesus Christ so they may come to join us in the fullness of the Catholic faith."*

But what happens today when the one invited by the young Catholic "to join us in the fullness of the Catholic faith" says: "Why? I'm already a Christian"; or, "Why? Surely the founder of my non-Christian faith is the equal of Christ."

The 7-Step Reason to be Catholic, 2nd edition is not an alternative to *Isaiah Ministries, Cultivation Ministries,* or any other evangelization or interfaith dialogue program sponsored by the USCCB Committee on Evangelization. Nor is it a substitute for the information provided by other fine Catholic apologetics and evangelization-oriented organizations, such as those noted under *Questions* in the Summary.

Instead, it is simply an important first step – *a foundational* step that can be expected to contribute significantly to the success of any Catholic religious education, evangelization or interfaith dialogue effort – not simply in the number who *become* Catholic, but in those who *remain* Catholic and who draw others to Catholicism.

We certainly respect all our non-Christian brethren throughout the world. All of us, regardless of faith, owe our existence to the one God. But are Catholics and others well served if we avoid asking this question:

> *"In what ways, if any, were other founders or reformers of religions comparable to Christ in manifesting the authority of the Creator?"*

The fact is that *no authoritative spokesperson for any non-Christian religion can present any evidence that its founder was / is at all comparable to Christ* (Step 2 of the summary and book), *particularly in overcoming death and having the power in the hereafter to keep his promises to us.* The same is true of the innumerable reformers of religions through the ages.

In contrast, *the Early Church Fathers, including some disciples of the apostles, have written thousands of pages testifying to the divinity and miracles of Jesus and the authenticity of the Gospels as interpreted by the Catholic Church.*

And today we can use the Internet to read for ourselves the words of those who lived so soon after Jesus, many of whom became martyrs rather than deny his divinity and his teaching.

It is equally important to make young Catholics aware that scholarly research affirms the Gospels as reliable history, as explained in Step 3. Surely the lack of that knowledge has resulted in many leaving the Church, seeing Jesus not as true God and true Man – our Savior and Redeemer – but largely as myth and legend.

The Summary (in English and Spanish in the Appendix section and additional languages at **http://7step.catholic.org**) is suitable as part of Confirmation preparation for young Catholics. It will be especially valuable to the extent students are encouraged to use the Internet to access the *Catechism of the Catholic Church*, the writings of the Early Church Fathers, *The Baltimore Catechism* and other Catholic Web sites recommended in the Summary and in the book.

In a simplified manner, *The 7-Step Reason to be Catholic,* 2nd *Ed.,* can also be explained – ideally by the parents – to younger children who begin to ask questions about the various religions practiced by their classmates and others. The Summary should also answer important questions for those in RCIA and other education and Bible study programs for Catholic adults.

And is there a Catholic parish anywhere in which many parishioners are not disheartened because their grown children no longer attend Mass or receive the sacraments? For such parents and others, Religious Education Directors may wish to offer programs that will answer the question, *"Why should anyone be a Catholic rather than practice some other religion or none?"* For such groups *The 7-Step Reason to be Catholic* Summary – followed by a prayerful study of the book – can provide that answer, and, in the process, be instrumental in bringing many back to the Church.

Appendix

Appendix P

The Catholic Apologist's Scriptural Response Guide

By Christopher Wong (cwong@world.std.com); September 25th, 2001. Available online as "Catholic apologist's scriptural cheat sheet": *http://world.std.com/~cwong/doc/chtsht.html*

Sola scriptura
Jn 21:25 ... not everything is in the Bible.
2 Thess 2:15; 2 Tim 2:2; 1 Cor 11:2; 1 Thess 2:13 ... Paul speaks of oral tradition.
Acts 2:42 ... early Christians followed apostolic tradition.
2 Pet 3:16 ... Bible hard to understand, get distorted.
2 Jn 1:12; 3 Jn 1:13-14 ... more oral tradition.
2 Pet 1:20-21 ... against personal interpretation.
Acts 8:30-31 ... guidance needed to interpret scriptures.
Heb 5:12 ... need to be taught.

Sola fide
Jas 2:14-26 ... what good is faith without works?
Heb 10:26-27, Rom 8:12-13 ... must avoid sin.
Jas 5:20 ... "earning" forgiveness.
Lk 6:46-49; Mt 7:21; Mt 19:16-21; Jn 5:28-29 ... must do will of God.
1 Cor 9:27 ... "buffet my body ..."
Phil 2:12; 2 Cor 5:10; Rom 2:6-13; Mt 25:32-46; Gal 6:6-10; Rev 20:12; 1 Pet 1:14-17... works have merit.
1 Jn 2:3-6; 1 Jn 3:24; 1 Jn 5:3 ... keep Commandments.
Intellectual Assent (1 Th 2:13), confidence in promise (Rom 4:2-3, Gen 15:5-6), Obedience (Rom 1:5) and love (Gal 5:6) implied by faith.

Salvation (once and for all?)
1 Cor 9:27 ... after preaching ... I myself disqualified.
1 Cor 10:12 ... thinks that he stands ... lest he fall.
Phil 2:12 ... work out salvation with fear and trembling.
Heb 4:1 ... fear of failing to reach salvation.
1 Jn 5:16-17 ... some sins are mortal, some not.
Rom 11:21-22 ... spare branches, continue or be cut off.
Heb 6:4-8 ... believers can apostasize, be damned.
Heb 10:26-29 ... those sanctified who sin can still be damned.
2 Pet 2:20-21; 1 Cor 8:10-13; Gal 5:4 ... righteous can fall.

Deuterocanonicals

Deuterocanonicals were used in NT: 2 Mach 6:18-7:42 ... Heb
  11:35; Wisdom 3:5-6 ... 1 Pet 1:6-7; Wisdom 13:1-9 ...
  Rom 1:18-32

Septuagint (Gk, w/ Deuterocanonicals) version of OT quoted in
  NT, noticeably different from Hebrew version: Is 7:14 ...
  Mt 1:23; Is 40:3 ... Mt 3:3; Joel 2:30-31 ... Acts 2:19-20; Ps
  95:7-9 ... Heb 3:7-9 etc.

Purgatory

Lk 12:58-59; 1 Cor 3:15; Mt 5:25-26 ... temporary agony.

Heb 12:6-11 ... God's painful discipline.

Mt 12:32 ... no forgiveness ... nor in the age to come.

1 Pet 3:18-20 ... might be purgatory (limbo?).

1 Pet 4:6 ... preached to the dead.

Rev 21:27 ... nothing unclean shall enter heaven.

Heb 12:23 ... souls in heaven are perfect.

Col 1:24; 2 Sam 12:13-14 ... "extra" suffering.

2 Mac 12:43-46 ... sacrifice for the dead.

2 Tim 1:15-18 ... prayer for Onesiphorus for "that Day."

1 Jn 5:14-17 ... mortal/venial sins

Eucharist

Mt 26:26-27; Mk 14:22,24; Lk 22:19-20; 1 Cor 11:24-25
  ... this is my body ... this is my blood.

1 Cor 11:26-30 ... sinning against the body and blood.

Jn 6:32-58 ... long discourse on Eucharist.

Gen 14:18; Ps 110:4; Heb 7:1-17 ... Melchizedek.

Acts 2:42 ... breaking of bread.

Ps 14:4; Ps 53:4; Is 9:18-20; Is 49:26; Micah 3:2-3; Rev
  17:6,16 ... symbolic interpretation of Jn 6 inappropriate.

Ex 12:8,46 ... paschal lamb has to be eaten.

Jn 1:29; 1 Cor 5:7 ... Jesus is lamb of God, paschal lamb.

Jn 4:31-34; Mt 16:5-12 ... Jesus speaks symbolically of food.

Baptism

Acts 2:38-39; Acts 16:15, 16:33, 18:8; 1 Cor 1:16 ... suggests
  baptism of all, incl. children.

Jn 3:5; Rom 6:4; Mk 16:16 ... necessity of baptism.

Col 2:11-12 ... circumcision (normally performed on infants Cf.
  Lk 2:21; Gen 17:12) replaced by baptism.

Acts 22:16 ... baptism removes sin.

1 Pet 3:21 ... baptism saves by water.

Forgiveness of sins
Jn 20:22-23 ... "if you forgive ... they are forgiven."
Mt 18:18 ... binding on earth and heaven.
2 Cor 5:18 ... ministry of reconciliation.
Jas 5:14-16 ... forgiveness of sins, anointing of the sick,
    confession.

Papacy/infallibility
Mt 16:18-19 ... Jesus gives Peter primacy: rock, keys, binding
    and loosing.
Is 22:22; ... keys as symbol of authority transferable to a
    successor.
Jn 21:17 ... "feed my sheep"
Mt 10:1-4; Mk 3:16-19; Lk 6:14-16; Acts 1:13; Lk 9:32 ... Peter
    mentioned first, as foremost apostle.
Mt 18:21; Mk 8:29; Lk 12:41; Jn 6:68-69 ... Peter speaks for
    the apostles.
Acts 2:14-40 ... Pentecost: Peter who first preached.
Acts 3:6-7 ... Peter worked first healing.
Acts 10:46-48 ... Gentiles to be baptized revealed to Peter.
Jn 1:42 ... Simon is Cephas (Aramaic: Kepha for rock).
Lk 22:31-32 ... "Simon ... strengthen your brethren."
Lk 10:1-2, 16; Jn 13:20; 2 Cor 5:20; Gal 4:14; Acts 5:1-5 ...
    "vicars" (substitutes) of Christ.

"Brothers" of Jesus
Mary wife of Clopas and "sister" of the Virgin Mary (Jn 19:25)
    is the mother of James and Joset (Mk 15:47; Mt 27:56) who
    are called the "brothers of Jesus" (Mk 6:3).
Acts 1:12-15 ... apostles, Mary, "some women" and Jesus'
    "brothers" number about 120. That is a lot of "brothers."
Gen 14:12-14 ... Lot, Abraham's nephew (Gen 11:26-28),
    described as Abraham's brother (KJV).
Gen 29:15 ... Laban, Jacob's uncle, calls Jacob his "brother"
    (KJV).
Jn 19:26-27 ... Jesus gives care of Mary to John, not one of
    his "brothers."
2 Sam 6:23, Gen 8:7, Dt 34:6 (KJV) ... "until."
Jn 20:17-18 ... "go to my brethren/brothers": Mary goes to disciples.

Mary

Gen 5:24; Heb 11:5; 2 Kings 2:1-13 ... Enoch and Elijah taken to heaven.

Lk 1:28 ... Annunciation.

Lk 1:42-48 ... blessed among women. All generations shall call her blessed.

2 Tim 4:8, Jas 1:12, 1 Pet 5:4, Rev 2:10 ... coronation awaits saints.

Jn 2:1-5 ... Mary's intercession.

Jn 19:26-27; Rev 12:17 … suggests Mary's motherhood of all Christians.

1 Kings 2:19 ... queen mother, intercessor.

Saints

Mk 12:26-27 ... "not God of the dead, but of the living."

Jn 15:1-8 ... vine and its branches.

1 Cor 12:25-27; Rom 12:4-5 ... Body of Christ.

Eph 6:18; Rom 15:30; Col 4:3; 2 Thess 1:11 ... intercessory prayer.

Jos 5:13-14; Dan 8:15-17; Tobit 12:15-16 ... veneration of angels united with God (Mt 18:10).

1 Cor 13:12; 1 John 3:2 ... saints also united with God.

Lk 20:34-38 ... those who died are like angels.

2 Mac 15:11-16 ... deceased Onias and Jeremiah interceded for Jews.

Rev 8:3-4; Jer 15:1 ... saints' intercession.

Is 14:9-10, 1 Sam 28:8-19, 1 Pet 3:19, Lk 16:19-31, Mt 17:3, Rev 5:8, Rev 7:9-10, Rev 6:9-10 ... those who have died are not in a coma.

Statues, images and relics

Ex 25:18-22, 26:1,31; Num 21:8-9 ... God commands images made.

1 Kings 6:23-29, 35, 7:29 ... Solomon's temple: statues and images.

Acts 19:11,12 ... Paul's handkerchiefs and aprons.

2 Kg 13:20-21 ... Elisha's bones.

Acts 5:15-16 ... Peter's shadow.

Mt 9:20-22 ... Jesus' garment cures woman.

Church and authority

Acts 2:42 ... doctrine, community, sacred rite (bread).

Eph 5:25-26 ... Christ loved the Church.

1 Tim 3:15 ... Church is pillar/foundation of truth.

Mt 16:18 ... Christ protects Church.

Heb 13:17 ... obey.

Mt 18:17-18 ... Church as final authority.

Mt 23:2-3 ... Pharisees succeeded Moses (seat of Moses).

1 Cor 5:5; 1 Tim 1:20 ... excommunication.

Jn 17:21 ... that they may be one.

Jn 10:16 ... one flock, one shepherd.

Priesthood

Acts 1:15-26; 2 Tim 2:2; Tit 1:5 ...unbroken succession.

Acts 15:6,23; Acts 14:23; 1 Tim 4:14, 5:22; 1 Tim 5:17; 2 Tim 1:6-7; Jas 5:13-15 ... presbyters/elders (priests) were ordained, preached and taught the flock, administered sacraments.

Jn 8:56; Lk 16:24; Rom 4:1,16-18; 1 Cor 4:14-15; Acts 7:2; 1 Thess 2:11; 1 Jn 2:13-14 ... Judges 17:9-10; Judges 18:19, "call no one father"?

1 Cor 7:7-9 ... Paul unmarried.

Mt 19:12; 1 Cor 7:32-33, 1 Tim 4:11-12 ... celibacy.

Gen 14:18; Ps 110:4; Heb 7:1-17 ... Melchizedek.

1 Cor 12 ... different roles of members of body.

Worship

1 Kg 8:54; 2 Chr 6:13; Ezra 9:5; Mt 17:14; Lk 5:8 ... kneeling.

Rev 8:3-4; Lk 1:8-9; Ex 30:7-8 ... incense.

Col 2:16 ... don't condemn concerning Sabbath.

Acts 20:7; 1 Cor 16:2 ... Eucharist, collections on Sundays

Rev 4:8, Mt 26:44 ... "vain repetition"?

Justification

1 Jn 1:7, 2 Pet 1:9 ... purified from sins.

Jn 1:29, Heb 9:26-28 ... takes away sin.

Acts 3:19; Ps 51:1-2, Ps 103:12, Is 43:25 ... blot out, clear away sin.

Tit 3:5-7 ... regeneration, renewal part of justification.

Rom 2:13, Rom 3:20 ... future justification.

Heb 11:8... Gen 12:1-4; Rom 4:2-3...Gen 15:6; Jas 2:21-23 ... Gen 22:1-18 ... justifications of Abraham.

2 Pet 1:4 ... become partakers of the divine nature.

Morality

Gen 38:9-10 ... Onanism.

Mal 2:14-16 ... God hates divorce.

1 Cor 7:10-11 ... don't divorce.

Mt 5:32-33; Mt 19:4-6,9; Mk 10:11-12; Lk 16:18 ... Jesus
    prohibits divorce.

Further information on Scriptural verses that support Catholic doctrine
can be found in *Catholic Doctrine In Scripture; A Guide To the
Verses That Are Key To affirming The Faith.* Written by Greg Oatis,
this concise, easy-to-use, 144-page book is available through Coming
Home Resources, P.O. Box 8290, Zanesville, OH 43702-8290; 877-
455-3208; **www.chresources.com**

Appendix Q

Contemporary Catholic Biblical Scholarship:
Certitudes or Hypotheses?
Msgr. Michael J. Wrenn, M.A., M.S., D.H.L. 1988

One of the axioms of contemporary Biblical scholarship is that the exegesis of a text depends on its dating. The question of dating truly conditions our understanding of the Gospels: at least insofar as what is essential to the text is concerned, witnesses were still very numerous when they were being composed and their statements could be verified. They were not transmitting their imaginings but rather their testimonies. In the words of the Prologue of the Gospel of St. Luke: "Many have undertaken to compile a narrative of the events which have been fulfilled in our midst *precisely as these events were transmitted to us* by the original eyewitnesses and servants of the word. I, too, have carefully placed [or been carefully informed by these witnesses] the whole sequence of events from the beginning and I have decided to set it in writing to you, Theophilus, so that Your Excellency may see how reliable the instruction was that you received."

Scholarly introductions to the New Testament demonstrate that a consensus has been established among most Catholic scholars regarding the dates of the composition of the Gospels. For example, the majority of scholars place the composition of the Fourth Gospel toward the end of the first century and place the Gospel of Matthew around 85. They generally place the Apocalypse [Revelations] and the Acts of the apostles at the end of the first century as well.

But in 1976 a bomb went off in scholarly circles with the publication of the late Anglican Bishop **John A. T. Robinson's** "Redating the New Testament." Robinson's book is not only scholarly, but it is extremely amusing. He tells us that for a long time, that is, up until the respectable age which he has attained, he believed everything which he had been taught in the field of historical-critical exegesis, everything which the German school propounded. And one day some years ago he asked himself a simple question, one of those which are at the heart of major scientific breakthroughs: "On what are the theses of the critical school, regardless of the dating of the composition of the Gospels 'SCIENTIFICALLY' based?" To this question, posed in the cocktail hour of his life, Robinson was unable to secure a response. Being the good English Empiricist that he was, he set about, in a scientific way, to look again at the entire matter of the dating of the books of the New Testament.

He starts with a very simple, evident, and startling fact. No text in any book of the New Testament proves that a particular author had been aware of that most startling event in the history of Judaism during the first century of the Christian era – namely, the Taking of Jerusalem and its destruction by the Emperor Titus in the year 70 A.D. In the entire New Testament, there is not one word of commentary on this catastrophic event, even when occasion would have seemed to present an opportunity for it, or even to warrant it, as for example with respect to Jesus' prophecies, which forecast the destruction of the Temple of Jerusalem. If the Greek texts which report these prophecies, which could be read in Matthew, Mark or Luke, had been written *after* the destruction of Jerusalem, they would have been followed by comments stressing that history had verified these prophecies.

The Gospel of Matthew is *constantly* concerned to show or to emphasize that a particular ancient prophecy is verified by the events. This would have been a golden opportunity to add a comment which would have validated the sayings of Our Lord. Everything, however, takes place as if the Four Gospels had been redacted as we read them today in Greek AT A TIME WHEN THE TEMPLE WAS STILL STANDING.

Claude Tresmontant, a distinguished scholar at the Sorbonne, sets forth his own views not only on the language but also the dating of the New Testament, and provides an argument from archaeology to help confirm the thesis of Robinson. He observes, in his recently published work "The Hebrew Christ," that almost all scholars tell us that the Fourth Gospel was redacted around the end of the first century. Yet we read in John 5:2 that "there IS (in Greek, 'estin') at Jerusalem, at the Sheep Gate, a pool named in Hebrew 'Bethzatha.' It has five porticoes." [Note once again the use of the *present* tense]. How do you conclude that around the end of the first century of our era an author would have written "there IS at Jerusalem a pool" when Jerusalem would have been destroyed some 25 or 30 years before, reduced to a heap of stones with a Roman encampment, at the very time, positioned on top of it? If one referred to a monument which existed at Hiroshima before the destruction of 1945 and which had not been reconstructed, one would not say there IS, but there WAS. Moreover, during this century, there were actually *found* the remains or ruins of this pool with five porticoes. The author wrote in the present indicative [mood] BECAUSE THE POOL EXISTED WHEN HE WROTE. The Gospel of Matthew was written, therefore, before 70 A.D.

Catholic exegetes generally think that the author of the Fourth Gospel is John, the son of Zebedee, the Galilean. If he is the author of the

"Fourth Gospel" and if he committed it to writing around the year 95, then that would make him about 95 years of age. How psychologically improbable that John would have waited 65 years to commit to writing the account of the events of which he had been an eyewitness. We have only to re-read the account of the cure of the man born blind from birth, in Chapter 9, with the dialogues which are found there. We see quite well that these scenes have been set down immediately, fresh, warm in his memory with amusing details of tremendous precision. These are not the recollections of a man 95 years of age. These are notes which were set down as they happened.

Robinson concludes his scholarly work with analysis regarding the datings which are quite different from those which have commonly been taught up until now. He believes the Fourth Gospel was composed before 70 – in the main, between 40 and 60. He also places the Apocalypse before 70.

Claude Tresmontant, in his pioneering work, "The Hebrew Christ" which [now] appear[s] in English, basing himself on arguments distinct from those of Robinson, situates the GREEK translation of the original Hebrew of the Fourth Gospel around the years 36-40 and therefore prior to the dates proposed by Robinson. He situates the original Hebrew of the Fourth Gospel before its translation into Greek and proposes reasons for believing that in its present form, in GREEK, the Gospel of Matthew had been composed before the end of the 40s. But the original Hebrew or Aramaic is of course before this time. Now, hold on to your seats! What Tresmontant is in effect saying is that the Gospels as we have them are really translations – which are actually not that late – of much earlier original compositions in Hebrew or Aramaic and therefore much closer to the 'ipsissima verba Christi.'

Tresmontant is not alone. Until his unexpected death in October of last year, the noted scholar of the Dead Sea scrolls and the world's most renowned expert on the "Our Father," **Fr. Jean Carmignac** of Paris, whose warmth, kindness and priestly friendship I will cherish until the day I die, had for the last 20 years been working on the question of the language and dating of the Gospels. Fortunately a number of his friends had prevailed upon him to write a popular description of his theories, which he did three years ago. I was privileged to translate this work, which is entitled "The Birth of the Synoptic Gospels."

Father Carmignac was a philologist, an exceptionally competent expert in Biblical Hebrew. He knew well the ravages that a particular type of contemporary exegesis was producing among priests and faithful. For, if the Gospels were later compositions, simply witnesses of the growing faith of the earliest Christian communities, Bultmann was correct and so was Loisy. Yes, indeed, as Father Carmignac once observed to me, if the Jesus of History is practically unattainable, it is the Christ of Faith who very quickly is rejected!

One day some 20 years ago, Father Carmignac started to translate the rather inelegant and ear-grating Greek of St. Mark's Gospel into Hebrew. To his astonishment, he did not encounter any real problems in retroversing into Hebrew. As he relates, a certitude began to form within him: "I was convinced that the Greek text of Mark could not have been redacted directly in Greek and that it was in reality only the Greek translation of an original Hebrew.... The Hebrew-Greek translation had transposed word for word and had even preserved in Greek the order of the words preferred by Hebrew grammar." Carmignac continues: "As my translation gradually took shape, my conviction was reinforced: even a Semite having learned Greek later on in life would not have permitted the stamp of his mother tongue to come through; he would have, from time to time at least, made use of the expression current in Greek. But no. We have here the literal, carbon copy or transparency of a translator attempting to respect, to the greatest extent possible, the Hebrew text which he had in front of him."

In order to bolster further his position, Carmignac sifted out into nine categories the hundreds of Semitisms in the Gospels: Semitisms of borrowing, of imitation, of thought, of vocabulary, of syntax, of style, of composition, of translation, and of transmission. (An example of a Semitism of transmission would be that of a copyist's mistake as a result of a similarity in Hebrew between consonants.)

Carmignac gives a number of demonstrations of Hebrew 'play on words' in the text. What follows is a quote in which he attempts to give us an example of play on words which Hebrew had a great preference for employing, taking great pleasure in making reference to similar sounds, thereby facilitating the task of memorization.

"The Benedictus, reproduced in Luke 1:68-79, is composed of three strophes, each having seven stichs; the first begins with the Biblical and Qumrânian formula, 'Blessed (be) the Lord the God of Israel'; the third begins, as frequently is the case at Qumrân, with a personal pronoun: 'And you, child'; the second has in its first stich: 'to show mercy to our fathers,' in which the expression 'to show mercy' translated the verb 'hanan,' which is the root of 'Yohanan' (=John); then follows the second stich, 'and he remembers his holy covenant,' in which 'he remembers' translates the verb 'zakar,' which is the root of 'Zakaryah' (=Zachary); then the third stich; 'the oath which he swore to our father

Abraham,' uses, in two different forms, the root 'shaba' (to swear, or to take an oath), which is the root of 'Elishabaat' (=Elizabeth). Is it by chance that the second strophe of this poem begins by a triple allusion to the names of the three protagonists: John, Zachary, Elizabeth? But this allusion exists only in Hebrew, and the Greek or English translation does not preserve it."

Moreover, Father Carmignac maintains that the destruction of Palestine by the Romans in the year 70 prevents us from supposing that such documents as the Gospels could possibly have been produced *after* the dispersion of the community for which they were originally intended. Carmignac also discovered that since the 15th century the same 80 retroversions of the Gospels had been made into Hebrew by a number of scholars in different parts of the world.

The little treatise "The Birth of the Synoptic Gospels" which I was honoured to translate is an introduction to his discovery and the five major works of retroversion which he managed to publish before his unexpected death. He once observed to me his conviction that by the year 2000 scriptural scholarship will start with the Hebrew or Aramaic rather than the Greek. "Sooner or later, specialists will be hit right between the eyes and see themselves like me staring directly at the very backdrop of the Gospels."

What follows are the provisional results of his 20 years of research on the formation of the Synoptic Gospels:

1. It is *certain* that Mark, Matthew, and the documents used by Luke were redacted in a Semitic language.

2. It is *probable* that this Semitic language is Hebrew, rather than Aramaic.

3. It is *sufficiently probable* that our Second Gospel was composed in a Semitic language by St. Peter the apostle.

4. It is *possible* that St. Matthew, the apostle, redacted the COLLECTIONS of discourses, or that he redacted the COMMON SOURCE utilized by our First and Third Gospels.

5. Utilizing internal evidence in the Epistles of St. Paul, Father Carmignac next presents a very interesting and novel *hypothesis* regarding the dating of the Gospels. In the Second Epistle to the Corinthians, St. Paul speaks in 8:18 of a person whom he describes thus: "the brother whom all the Churches praise for his preaching of the Gospel." If it is a question of the preaching of the Gospels, this would not be a distinctive designation, for it would apply to all the collabora-

tors of St. Paul. In order that the Gospel be a motive for special recognition throughout all the Churches and characterize one brother from all of the others, isn't it because this brother, alone of all the others, is the author of a Gospel? Thus it would have been "spread throughout all the Churches." Many commentators have understood this allusion of St. Paul in this way, beginning with Origen (cited by Eusebius of Caesarea, Ecclesiastical History, Book 6, Chapter 25, #6).This text of St. Paul is unfortunately not explicit enough to warrant being considered a final argument, but it constitutes, at least, an indication which is worth not forgetting.

6. Even if the indication of the Second Epistle to the Corinthians (which would not be viewed as scientific) is taken into account, it is beyond the limit of probability to situate the redaction of Luke in Greek later than the years 58-60; it is beyond the limits of probability to place the final redaction in a Semitic language of our First Gospel much later than Luke; it is beyond the limits of probability to place the redaction in a Semitic language of our Second Gospel much later than around the year 50, and equally beyond the limits of probability if account is taken of the indication of the Second Epistle to the Corinthians (which would be viewed as more scientific), to situate the redaction of Luke in Greek later than the years 50-53; it is beyond the limits of probability to situate the definitive redaction in a Semitic language of our First Gospel much later than Luke; it is beyond the limits of probability to situate the redaction in a Semitic language of our Second Gospel much later than around the years 42-45.

7. It is *probable* that the Semitic Gospel of Peter was translated into Greek, perhaps with some adaptations, by Mark, in Rome, at the latest around the year 63. It is our Second Gospel which has preserved the name of its translator, instead of its author.

As for external evidence, Father Carmignac refers to the Witness of Papias. Toward the middle of the reign of Trajan (98-117), Papias composed a treatise of five books entitled "Exegeses (or Explanations) of the Words of the Lord." We no longer possess anything except a few fragments of this work – so valuable because of its antiquity. These fragments are preserved in the "History of the Church" written by Eusebius. What follows are two texts relative to Mark, which are taken directly from Eusebius and which, for the sake of convenience, we will call "Text A" and "Text B." The first, Text A, is taken from Book 2, which covers the earliest Christian history from the Ascension to the end of Nero's reign, from 30 to 68 A.D. In Chapter 14, Eusebius recounts how Peter came to Rome to preach the good news during the reign of Claudius (41-54) and there confronted Simon the Magician. The chapter has as its title, "The Gospel According to Mark":

"So brightly shone the light of piety in the minds of Peter's hearers that, not satisfied with a single hearing or with the real teaching of the divine message, they resorted to appeals of every kind to induce Mark, whose Gospel has come down to us, as he was a follower of Peter, to leave them in writing a summary of the teachings which Peter had transmitted to them orally, nor did they cease until they had persuaded him and thus became responsible for the writing of what is known as the Gospel according to Mark."

What follows is the second fragment of Papias contained in the History of the Church by Eusebius – what we have referred to as Text B. Papias is quoted as saying:

"And this is what [John] the Presbyter used to say: 'Mark, who had been with Peter's interpreter, wrote down *carefully, but not always in order*, all the things which he remembered to have been *said* or *done* by the Lord.'

"For [here Papias is again speaking] Mark did not hear the Lord, nor did he accompany him, but later, as I said, he accompanied Peter. Peter used to give his instructions according to needs [adapt his teaching to the occasion], but without making a systematic arrangement of the Lord's sayings, so that Mark, having written down these things as he recalled them, made no mistake; he had actually one sole concern; to omit nothing that he had heard and to falsify nothing."

That is what Papias reports regarding Mark (History of the Church," Book 3, Chapter 39, 14-50).

Moreover, Eusebius tells us:

"It is said that, on learning by revelation from the Spirit what had happened, the apostle [Peter] was delighted at their zeal and enthusiasm [referring to the fact that Peter's hearers had induced Mark to set down in writing a summary of teachings which Peter had transmitted to them orally, mentioned in Text A] and that he [Peter] authorized the reading of the book in the assemblies. Clement of Alexandria reports this information in 'Outlines,' Book 6, and the Bishop of Hieropolis, Papias, confirms this by his own testimony." [History of the Church, 11,15,1-2].

"We have, therefore, in this instance, in the witness of Papias, a testimony going back to the very beginning of the Second Century, which attests that Mark had written before Peter's death; it is known that the apostle [Peter] was martyred during the persecution of Nero which followed shortly after the burning of Rome in 64 A.D."

Father Carmignac also studied the writings of Origen, Tertullian, Irenaeus, Clement, and shows that there is no need to break with the earliest tradition, and to call into question the apostolic authenticity of the Gospels.

Thanks to the efforts of Father Carmignac, a further new indication of the antiquity of the Gospels is in the process of becoming established. Prior to the year 50, Christians from Judaic circles were only able to express the message of Jesus Christ in Aramaic or Hebrew, and it is this primitive message which constitutes the basis for the gospel documents.

Time does not allow us to go into other considerations which bear upon the dating of the gospel texts and therefore upon their historical accuracy. Suffice it to say that there is renewed interest in the study of oral tradition as this would have affected the composition of the Gospels.

Father Jousse, in 1925, published an astonishing work, "Oral Rhythmic and Memory-Building Techniques," by which even Loisy would become interested in Jousse's thesis, whereby the oral tradition of a great deal of the gospel becomes a very plausible and probably well-established fact.

Research shows that, as a pedagogical method, learning by heart plays a key role in the three Jewish institutions of popular education: the family, the synagogue, and the elementary school. Chanting or 'cantillation' and memory-building devices and drills were part of this 'culture of memory.' In his study of the oral style of the Gospels, Jousse shed light on the rhythmic processes employed by Jesus and preserved by the earliest Christian recitators!

In 1957, at the Oxford Congress on the Four Gospels, the eminent Swedish specialist in the New Testament, H. Riesenfeld, maintained that not only was the Gospel tradition prior to the Easter event – therefore going back to Jesus Himself – but that:

"In the Gospels we are shown very clearly that Jesus was a teacher, especially in His relation to His disciples. This means more than His mere preaching in their presence. He gave them instructions, and in this we are reminded of the methods of the Jewish rabbi, and that implies that Jesus made His disciples, and above all the Twelve, learn, 'and furthermore, that He made them learn by heart'" [*The Gospel Tradition*, p. 22].

In the light of a number of new hypotheses set forth in the works of Carmignac, Tresmontant and Bishop John A. T. Robinson, allow me to raise the following questions, which, even if these authors had not been cited, most people in a state of doubt would answer in the negative.

1. Is it scientifically *proven* that the Gospels were written quite late, toward the end of the first century and after the years 66-70? No!

2. Is it *proven* that a lengthy (from 40-60 years) oral transmission of the essential elements of the Gospel needed to take place before they were committed to writing? No!

3. With respect to the two previous assertions, is it *proven* that a major problem would exist regarding the accuracy of the deeds and words of the Lord Jesus Christ because of oral tradition? No!

4. Is it *proven* that, if the Gospels had been transmitted only orally, there would have been a damage to the Faith? No!

5. Is it proven that Christian communities during the years between 70 and 90 A.D. altered, in the light of their own particular problems some of the words of Christ which had been handed down in order to have Christ say things capable of justifying the practices of these communities? No!

6. Is it proven that the Gospel According to John was the last to be written because it is the most spiritual and apparently the most finely-wrought? No!

In the light of this demand for certain proofs, isn't it also wise and scientific to propose other hypotheses dependent upon a no less attentive reading and based upon the obvious Hebrew substratum of our Greek texts?

For example, why wouldn't the majority of passages in our Gospels have been written, at least in bits and pieces if not all their essential elements, a short time after – if not even during – the earthly life of Jesus?

Furthermore, since the apostles began to preach the Good News of

Jesus when the Holy Spirit came upon them on the Day of Pentecost, why would they be prohibited from committing to writing the essential elements of their preaching over a period of several decades?

Why would their hearers have formally abstained from taking notes during these years? And why, all of a sudden, would this activity of committing to writing have been set in motion simultaneously in very different places, but according to very similar styles?

Why would there not have been a simultaneity between the oral transmission (especially preaching) and the writing down of a certain number of accounts, and words, as well as the major narratives such as the Passion and Resurrection – and this being done in very Jewish categories in the cultural presence of the Sacred Books of the Old Testament, in the everyday language of Hebrew and Aramaic?

Thus, we can also say that between the years 30 and 65, there was already a certain form of sporadic persecution coming from Jewish circles, though this does not mean that there was already a complete break between the synagogue and the "New Way." This is more in line with the position of the Gospels having been written *before* the year 60 – the Roman persecution beginning in full force in the year 64. The writings of the New Testament rarely point the finger at the Romans, but always do so against the adherents of the Mosaic religion.

Given the hypothesis of a lengthy, purely oral, transmission before finally being written down after the seventies, we are still permitted to present the hypothesis of an oral transmission running alongside the redaction in Hebrew of partial texts during the thirties. Gradually, these texts would be employed as the basic ingredients at the very center of the redaction of each Gospel, essentially completed before the years 60 to 65. The entire corpus would have been translated into Greek in order to respond to the needs of new Christians coming from the Greek and Roman worlds.

In the light of these various hypotheses, the scientific test or control must examine which functions the best and which avoids the greatest number of objections.

It is not anti-scientific to think that the hypothesis of the lengthy oral transmission lacks genuine proofs and is fraught with many difficulties. It is not anti-scientific to claim that the hypotheses of a short oral transmission and a rapid writing down of the accounts or words of Jesus, shortly after the events, find solid foundations through an examination of the Greek text and its retroversion into Hebrew.

In a recently published work entitled "Un Homme Nomme Salut," **Madame Jacqueline Genot-Bismuth**, who occupies the Chair of

Ancient and Medieval Judaism at the Sorbonne, ably demonstrates that in the scientific discipline which is critical exegesis, certain major errors have been taught for generations, and have totally falsified our understanding of Christian origins. Since the beginning of the 19th century, for example, it was commonly taught that the Gospel of John was a later composition under Hellenistic, Gnostic or Iranian influence. Madame Genot-Bismuth, through her exceptional knowledge of the most ancient rabbinic literature, makes a solid case for the Gospel of John's being a *script*, the translation into Greek of notes taken in Hebrew of John who was a Kohen (a priest).

Utilizing a wealth of details, she demonstrates that the Gospel of John is a contemporary collection of the words and deeds of Rabbi Yeshua. Where the German exegetes of the nineteenth century saw only fiction and mythology, she re-discovers history!

A profound disregard for the Judean ethnic milieu or environment explains the length of time that these errors have been in vogue. This disregard is due to an ingrained attitude of despisal and detestation of Judaism, which are constants in German philosophy, the mistress of German critical exegesis accepted by the majority of exegetes since Renan and Loisy. The book of Madame Genot-Bismuth will constitute a revolution regarding our knowledge of Christian beginnings.

There is a new Apologetic making its appearance in Catholic Biblical circles. Apologetics used to be a defense of Church doctrine against the Protestants, who used historical-critical exegesis as a weapon against the Church. That's the "old" apologetics. The new apologetics is the defense of Catholic historical-critical exegetes, who learn their methodology from Protestants, against attacks by Catholics.

In France, this apologetics is reflected in the work of **Fr. Pierre Grelot** entitled "The Gospels in Apostolic Tradition: Reflections on a Certain Hebrew Christ."

Besides being an apologetical defense against Tresmontant's thesis, it also seeks to respond to Father Carmignac and to **Fr. Rene Laurentin's** "The Truth of Christmas Beyond the Myths: The Gospels of the Infancy of Christ." English-language examples of this new apologetics are **Jerome Murphy-O'Connor's** "Again Under Attack." "The Bible Today," March 1984; "Danger Also From the Left," **Fr. Joseph A. Fitzmyer, S.J**. and **Fr. Raymond E. Brown, S.S.** "The Bible Today," May 1985; and "Biblical Exegesis and Church Doctrine" by Raymond E. Brown, Paulist Press, 1985. In this last-named work, Brown continues the fiercely polemical attack on Father Laurentin which he launched on September 29, 1984, at the Catholic University of America. The rapidity with which this body of apologetic writing was formed and the eminence of the historical-critical exegetes called upon to make the defense indicates that defense is a matter of considerable urgency in the historical-critical exegetical camp.

Some sort of crisis seems to be at hand for historical-critical exegesis as this methodology is being practiced in the Catholic Church. Might some of the apologetic defenses by the Catholic historical-critical exegetes just mentioned be motivated, not by purely scientific motives, but rather by that feeling of dread and worry that must come into the minds of theoreticians when they see their own theories and hypotheses *seriously* and *scientifically* threatened?

But there are signs of hope. Recently, a mutually vituperative and polemical exchange between Fr. Grelot and Mr. **Pierre Debray** in a French Catholic weekly has given way to a reconciliation of views between these two gentlemen who were in agreement that, yes, this Catholic layman's concern about the hypotheses being set forth as scientific facts were indeed something that could cause – and had caused – tremendous difficulty in France and elsewhere. In short, both of these men agreed that hypotheses should not be presented as certitudes.

(Reprinted with permission)

Appendix R

The Dates of the Gospels
Rev. George H. Duggan, S.M.

Scripture scholars were challenged to find one passage in the four Gospels giving clear evidence of a date later than 50 A.D.

When were the Gospels written? Or, to frame the question more precisely, when had the Gospels arrived at the state in which we now have them? The present text, we have reason to believe, was preceded by earlier drafts. If that is so, we could not say that the Gospel of St. Mark was written in 45, as we can say, for example, that Second Corinthians was written in 55 or 56.

If we accept the Gospels as the inspired word of God, does it really matter, one might ask, when they were written? In the days when everyone accepted the traditional dating,[1] one could perhaps have dismissed the question as unimportant. But those days are long gone. Ever since **Reimarus** (1694-1768) sought to convict the evangelists of conscious fraud and innumerable contradictions, his rationalist followers have put the writing of the Gospels late, in order to lessen their value as sources of reliable information about the life of Christ and his teaching.

D. F. Strauss (1808-1874), in his *Life of Jesus,* (published in 1835-6), anticipated **Rudolf Bultmann** (1884-1976) in holding that the Gospels, although they contain some historical facts, were mainly mythology and were written late in the 2nd century. Similarly **F. C. Baur** (1792-1860), an Hegelian rationalist, held that the Gospels were written between 130 and 170. But Strauss, in the words of **Giuseppe Ricciotti**, "honestly confessed that his theory would collapse if the Gospels were composed during the first century."[2] If they were so early, there would not be enough time for the myths to develop. Moreover, it is plain that, the nearer a document is to the facts it narrates, the more likely it is that it will be factually accurate, just as an entry in a diary is more likely to be accurate than memoirs written forty or fifty years afterwards. **John A. T. Robinson** was therefore justified when he ended his book *Redating the New Testament* with the words: "Dates remain disturbingly fundamental data."[3]

The current dating of the four Gospels, accepted by the biblical establishment, which includes scholars of every persuasion, is: Mark 65-70; Matthew and Luke in the 80s; John in the 90s. These dates are repeated by the columnists who write in our Catholic newspapers and the experts who draw up the curricula for religious education in our Catholic schools.[4]

For much of this late dating there is little real evidence. This point was made by **C. H. Dodd,** arguably the greatest English-speaking biblical scholar of the century. In a letter that serves as an appendix to Robinson's book *Redating the New Testament,* Dodd wrote: "I should agree with you that much of the late dating is quite arbitrary, even wanton, the offspring not of any argument that can be presented, but rather of the critic's prejudice that, if he appears to assent to the traditional position of the early church, he will be thought no better than a stick-in-the-mud."[5]

Many years earlier the same point was made by **C. C. Torrey**, professor of Semitic Languages at Yale from 1900 to 1932. He wrote: "I challenged my NT colleagues to designate one passage from any one of the four Gospels giving clear evidence of a date later than 50 A.D .... The challenge was not met, nor will it be, for there is no such passage."[6]

In 1976, the eminent New Testament scholar, John A. T. Robinson, "put a cat among the pigeons" with his book *Redating the New Testament,* published by SCM Press. He maintained that there are no real grounds for putting any of the NT books later than 70 A.D. His main argument is that there is no clear reference in any of them to the fall of Jerusalem and the destruction of the Temple which occurred on September 26th of that year. This cataclysmic event brought to an end the sacrificial worship that was the center of the Jewish religion and it should have merited a mention in the NT books if they were written afterwards. In particular, one would have expected to find a reference to the event in the Epistle to the Hebrews, for it would have greatly strengthened the author's argument that the Temple worship was now obsolete.

Robinson dated the composition of Matthew from 40 to 60, using dots to indicate the traditions behind the text, dashes to indicate a first draft, and a continuous line to indicate writing and rewriting. Similarly, he dated Mark from 45 to 60, Luke from 55 to 62, and John from 40 to 65.

Robinson's book was the first comprehensive treatment of the dating of the NT books since **Harnack's** *Chronologie des altchristlichen Litteratur*, published in 1897. It is a genuine work of scholarship by a man thoroughly versed in the NT text and the literature bearing on it. But it was not welcomed by the biblical establishment, and it was not refuted, but ignored. "German New Testament scholars,"

Carsten Thiede has written, "all but ignored *Redating the New Testament*, and not until 1986, ten years later, did Robinson's work appear in Germany, when a Catholic and an Evangelical publishing house joined forces to have it translated and put into print."[7]

In 1987, the Franciscan Herald Press [now Franciscan Press, Quincy, IL] published *The Birth of the Synoptics [The Birth of the Synoptic Gospels]* by **Jean Carmignac**, a scholar who for some years was a member of the team working on the Dead Sea Scrolls. He tells us he would have preferred "Twenty Years of Work on the Formation of the Synoptic Gospels" as a title for the book, but the publishers ruled this out as too long.

Carmignac is sure that Matthew and Mark were originally written in Hebrew. This would not have been the classical Hebrew of the Old Testament, nor that of the Mishnah (c. 200 A.D.) but an intermediate form of the language, such as the Qumrân sectaries were using in the 1st century A.D.

Papias, the Bishop of Hierapolis in Asia Minor, who died about 130 A.D., tells us that Matthew wrote his Gospel in Hebrew, and Carmignac has made a good case for holding that the same is true of Mark. He found that this compelled him to put the composition of these Gospels much earlier than the dates proposed by the biblical establishment. He writes: "I increasingly came to realize the consequences of my work .... The latest dates that can be admitted for Mark (and the Collection of Discourses) is 50, and around 55 for the Completed Mark; around 55-60 for Matthew; between 58 and 60 for Luke. But the earliest dates are clearly more probable: Mark around 42; Completed Mark around 45; (Hebrew) Matthew around 50; (Greek) Luke a little after 50."[8]

On page 87 he sets out the provisional results (some certain, some probable, others possible) of his twenty years' research and remarks that his conclusions almost square with those of **J. W. Wenham**.[9]

In 1992, Hodder and Stoughton published *Redating Matthew, Mark and Luke* by John Wenham, the author of a well-known grammar of New Testament Greek. Born in 1913, he is an Anglican scholar who has spent his life in academic and pastoral work. He tells us that his attention was drawn to the Synoptic Problem in 1937, when he read **Dom John Chapman**'s book *Matthew, Mark and Luke*. He has been grappling with the problem ever since and in this book he offers his solution of the problem; but his main concern is the dates of the Synoptics.

Wenham's book received high praise from **Michael Green**, the editor of the series *I Believe*, which includes works by such well-known scholars as I. Howard Marsall and the late George Eldon Ladd. The book, Green writes, "is full of careful research, respect for evidence, brilliant inspiration and fearless judgement. It is a book no New Testament scholar will be able to neglect."

Green may be too optimistic. Wenham will probably get the same treatment as Robinson: not a detailed refutation, but dismissed as not worthy of serious consideration.

Wenham puts the first draft of Matthew before 42. For twelve years (30-42) the apostles had remained in Jerusalem, constituting, in words of the Swedish scholar **B. Gerhardsson**, a kind of Christian Sanhedrin, hoping to win over the Jewish people to faith in Christ. Matthew's Gospel, written in Hebrew, would have had an apologetic purpose, endeavoring to convince the Jews, by citing various Old Testament texts, that Jesus of Nazareth was the Son of David and the long-awaited Messiah.

The persecution of the Church in 42 by Herod Agrippa I, in which the apostle James suffered martyrdom, put an end to those hopes. Peter, miraculously freed from prison, went, we are told "to another place" (Acts 12:17). There are grounds for thinking that this "other place" was Rome, where there was a big Jewish community and where he would be out of the reach of Herod Agrippa. There, using Matthew's text, and amplifying it with personal reminiscences, he preached the gospel. When Agrippa died in 44, Peter was able to return to Palestine. After his departure from Rome, Mark produced the first draft of his Gospel, based on Peter's preaching.

Luke was in Philippi from 49 to 55, and it was during this time that he produced the first draft of his Gospel, beginning with our present chapter 3, which records the preaching of John the Baptist.[10] It was to this Gospel, Origen explained, that St. Paul was referring when, writing to the Corinthians in 56, he described Luke as "the brother whose fame in the gospel has gone through all the churches" (2 Cor. 8:18).

We know that Luke was in Palestine when Paul was in custody in Caesarea (58-59). He would have been able to move round Galilee, interviewing people who had known the Holy Family, and probably making the acquaintance of a draft in the Hebrew of the Infancy Narrative, and so gathering material for the first two chapters of the present Gospel. In the finished text he introduced this and the rest of the Gospel with the prologue in which he assures Theophilus that he intends to write history.

There are no grounds for putting Luke's Gospel in the early 80s as

R. [J.] Karris does,[11] or, with **Fr. Joseph Fitzmyer**, placing it as "not earlier than 80-85."[12]

The date of Luke's Gospel is closely connected with that of Acts, its companion volume, for if Acts is early, then Luke will be earlier still. In 1896, Harnack put Acts between 79 and 93, but by 1911 he had come to the conclusion that "it is the highest degree probable" that Acts is to be dated before 62. If Luke does not mention the outcome of the trial of Paul, it is, Harnack argued, because he did not know, for when Luke wrote, the trial had not yet taken place.

C. J. Hemer, in his magisterial work, The Book of Acts in the Setting of Hellenistic History, which was published posthumously in 1989, gives fifteen general indications, of varying weight but cumulative in their force, which point to a date before 70. Indeed, many of these point to a date before 65, the year in which the Neroian persecution of the Church began.[13]

In 1996, Weidenfeld and Nicholson published *The Jesus Papyrus* by **Carsten Peter Thiede** and **Matthew d'Ancona**. Thiede is Director of the Institute for Basic Epistemological Research in Paderborn, Germany, and a member of the International Papyrological Association. Matthew d'Ancona is a journalist and Deputy Editor of the Daily Telegraph, a London newspaper.

The book is about several papyrus fragments, and in particular three found in Luxor, Egypt, which contain passages from the Gospel of St. Matthew, and one found in Qumrân, which contains twenty letters from the Gospel of St. Mark.

The three Luxor fragments—the Jesus papyrus—came into the possession of the Reverend Charles Huleatt, the Anglican chaplain in that city, who sent them in 1901 to Magdalen College, Oxford, where he had graduated in 1888. They did not attract scholarly attention until 1953, when **Colin H. Roberts** examined them. He dated them as belonging to the late 2nd century. Then in 1994, they came to the notice of C. P. Thiede, who suspected that they might be much older than Roberts thought. Examining them with a confocal laser scanning microscope, and comparing them with the script in a document dated July 24, 66, he came to the conclusion that the fragments should be dated as belonging to the middle of the first century.

The Qumrân fragment is small—3.3 cm x 2.3 cm—an area that is slightly larger than a postage stamp. It contains twenty letters, on five lines, ten of the letters being damaged. It is fragment no. 5 from Cave 7 and it is designated 7Q5. A similar fragment from the same Cave— 7Q2—has one more letter—twenty-one as against twenty, on five lines.

The identification of this fragment as Baruch (or the Letter of Jeremiah) 6:43-44 has never been disputed.

In 1972 **Fr. José O'Callaghan, S.J.**, a Spanish papyrologist, declared that the words on 7Q5 were from the Gospel of St. Mark: 6:52-53. This identification was widely questioned, but many papyrologists rallied to his support, and there are good reasons for thinking that O'Callaghan was right. Thiede writes: "In 1994, the last word on this particular identification seemed to have been uttered by one of the great papyrologists of our time, **Orsolina Montevecchi**, Honorary President of the International Papyrological Association. She summarized the results in a single unequivocal sentence: 'I do not think there can be any doubt about the identification of 7Q5.'"[14] This implies that St. Marks' Gospel was in being some time before the monastery at Qumrân was destroyed by the Romans in 68. [Editorial note: Subsequent to the publication of this article in 1997 Thiede's early dating of 7Q5 was disputed by Robert H. Gundry in, "No *Nu* in line 2 of 7Q5: A final Disidentification of 7Q5 with Mark 6:52-53," *Journal of Biblical Literature*, V. 118, No 4, Winter, 1999, pp. 698-707].

Those who object that texts of the Gospels could not have reached such out of the way places as Luxor or Qumrân as early as the 60s of the first century do not realize how efficient the means of communication were in the Empire at that time. Luxor was even then a famous tourist attraction, and, with favorable winds a letter from Rome could reach Alexandria in three days—at least as quickly as an airmail letter in 1996. Nor was Qumrân far from Jerusalem, and we know that the monks took a lively interest in the religious and intellectual movements of the time.

New Testament scholars dealing with the Synoptic Gospels will obviously have to take more notice of the findings of the papyrologists than they have so far been prepared to do, however painful it may be to discard received opinions.

When was St. John's Gospel written?

That John, the son of Zebedee, and one of the apostles, wrote the Gospel that bears his name, was established long ago, on the basis of external and internal evidence, by **B. F. Westcott** and **M. J. Lagrange, O.P.**, and their view, though not universally accepted, has not really been shaken.

St. Irenaeus, writing in 180, tells us that John lived until the reign of the Emperor Trajan, which began in 98. From this some have inferred that John wrote his Gospel in the 90s. But this inference is obviously fallacious. The majority of modern scholars do indeed date

Appendix

the Gospel in the 90s, but a growing number put it earlier, and Robinson mentions seventeen, including **P. Gardner-Smith, R. M. Grant** and **Leon Morris**, who favor a date before 70. To them we could add **Klaus Berger**, of Heidelberg, who puts it in 66. Robinson decisively refutes the arguments brought forward by **Raymond Brown** and others to establish a later date, viz. the manner of referring to "the Jews," and the reference to excommunication in chapter 9.[15] He adds: "There is nothing in the Gospel that suggests or presupposes that the Temple is already destroyed or that Jerusalem is in ruins—signs of which calamity are inescapably present in any Jewish or Christian literature that can with any certainty be dated to the period 70-100." [16] [emphasis added]

Robinson also points out that John, when describing the cure of the paralytic at the pool of Bethesda, tells us that this pool "is surrounded by five porticos, or covered colonnades" (5:2). Since these porticos were destroyed in 70, John's use of the present tense—"is"—seems to imply that the porticos were still in being when he wrote. "Too much weight," he admits, "must not be put on this—though it is the only present tense in the context; and elsewhere (4:6; 11:18; 18:1; 19:41), John assimilates his topographical descriptions to the tense of the narrative." [17]

This article will have served its purpose if it has encouraged the reader to consider seriously the evidence for an early date for the Gospels, refusing to be overawed by such statements as that "the majority of modern biblical scholars hold" or that "there is now a consensus among modern biblical scholars" that the Gospels are to be dated from 65 to 90 A.D.

The account I have given of the writing of the Synoptic Gospels is categorical in style, but it is presented only as a likely scenario. However, it would seem to be more likely than one based on the assumption that among the Jews, a literate people, it was thirty years or more before anyone wrote a connected account of the life and teaching of Jesus of Nazareth.

"I do not wish," **C. S. Lewis** once said to a group of divinity students, "to reduce the skeptical element in your minds. I am only suggesting that it need not be reserved exclusively for the New Testament and the Creeds. Try doubting something else."[18] This something else, I suggest could include the widely accepted view that the Gospels were written late.

It will be easier to do this if the reader is acquainted with the judgment of the eminent jurist, **Sir Norman Anderson**, who describes himself as "an academic from another discipline who has browsed widely in the writings of contemporary theologians and biblical scholars." At times, he is, he tells us, "astonished by the way in which they handle their evidence, by the presuppositions and a priori convictions with which some of them clearly (and even, on occasion, on their own admission) approach the documents concerned, and by the positively staggering assurance with which they make categorical pronouncements on points which are, on any showing, open to question, and on which equally competent colleagues take a diametrically opposite view."[19]

---

1   The traditional dating is given in the Douay-Rheims-Challoner version in its introductions to the Gospels: Matthew about 36; Mark about 40; Luke about 54; John about 93.

2   Ricciotti, *The Life of Christ* (E.T. Alba I. Zizzamia), Bruce, Milwaukee, 1944, p. 186.

3   *Redating the New Testament,* SCM Press, London, 1976, p. 358.

4   Thus in *The New Jerome Biblical Commentary*, Geoffrey Chapman, London, 1989, D. J. Harrington puts Mark before 70; B. T. Viviani, O.P., puts Matthew between 80 and 90; R. J. Karris, O.F.M., puts Luke 80-85; Pheme Perkins puts John in the 90s.

5   *Redating the New Testament*, p. 360.

6   Quoted in J. Wenham, *Redating Matthew, Mark, and Luke*, Hodder and Stoughton, London, p. 299, note 2.

7   C. P. Thiede and M. d'Ancona, *The Jesus Papyrus*, Weidenfeld and Nicholson, London, 1996, p. 45.

8   J. Carmignac, *The Birth of the Synoptics*, [*The Birth of the Synoptic Gospels*] (E. T. Michael J. Wrenn) Franciscan Herald Press, Chicago, 1987, pp. 6, 61.

9   Ibid., p. 99, note 29.

10 Robinson suggests that this may be the case, op. cit. p. 282, note 142.

11 R. J. Karris, in *The New Jerome Biblical Commentary*, p. 670.

12 Richard Dillon and Joseph A. Fitzmyer, S.J., in *The Jerome Biblical Commentary*, Prentice-Hall International, London, 1968, Vol. 2, p. 165.

13 J. Wenham, op. cit., pp. 225-226.

14 C. P. Thiede and M. d'Ancona, op. cit., p. 56.

15 Robinson, op. cit., pp. 272-285.

16 Ibid., p. 275.

17 Ibid., p. 278.

18 "Modern Theology and Biblical Criticism" in *Christian Reflections*, Geoffrey Bles, London, 1967, p. 164.

19 *A Lawyer Among Theologians*, Hodder and Stoughton, London, 1973, p. 15.

Rev. George H. Duggan, S.M., is a New Zealander. After earning his S.T.D. at the Angelicum in Rome, he taught philosophy for fifteen years at the Marist seminary, Greenmeadows, and then was rector in turn of a university hall of residence and the Marist tertianship. He is now living in retirement at St. Patrick's College, Silverstream. He is the author of *Evolution and Philosophy* (1949), *Hans Kung and Reunion* (1964), *Teilhardism and the Faith* (1968), and *Beyond Reasonable Doubt* (1987). His last article in HPR appeared in October 1992.

This article appeared in Homiletic and Pastoral Review, May, 1997.
Reprinted with permission.

Index

Index

Index

Index

About the Author

Jerome D. Gilmartin received a B.S. Degree, with majors in psychology and philosophy, from the University of Scranton in 1959. For the next two years he studied psychology at Fordham Graduate School, Bronx, N.Y., followed by two years of military service. He later began what would become a 20-year career in human resources with an international telecommunications corporation; an opportunity that brought him, his wife Marie and daughters Ann and Joan to Towanda, Pennsylvania; Stamford, Connecticut; and Syracuse, New York. After a subsequent seven years as a psychological services associate at a state center for the mentally retarded in Hamburg, Pennsylvania, he retired in 2001. A lifelong Catholic, he served as a member of the Apologetics Committee of the Diocese of Scranton, PA, as well as in RCIA, an ecumenical organization, Cursillo, Marriage Encounter and as an Extraordinary Minister of Holy Communion. At present he is active in the Scranton Chapter of the Men of the Sacred Heart, as a member of the local Catholic Radio Advisory Committee, as a member of the Catholic Outreach / RCIA team at a local state prison, and as a catechetics teacher and lector in his Roman Catholic parish, St. Pius X, in Royal, PA.